D1414077

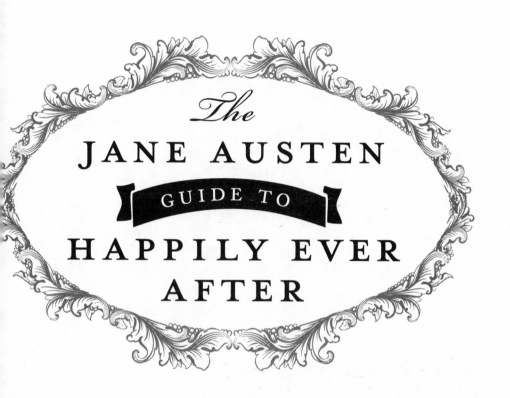

The

JANE AUSTEN

GUIDE TO

HAPPILY EVER AFTER

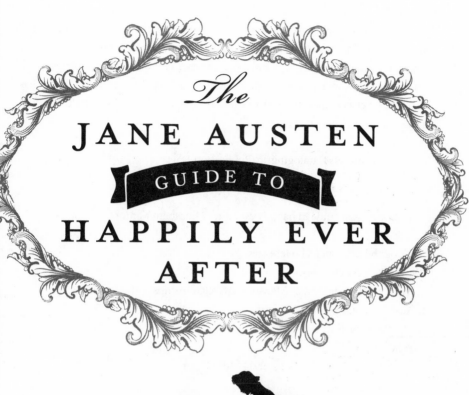

The
JANE AUSTEN
GUIDE TO
HAPPILY EVER AFTER

ELIZABETH KANTOR

Since 1947
REGNERY
PUBLISHING, INC.
An Eagle Publishing Company • Washington, DC

Library of Congress Cataloging-in-Publication Data

Kantor, Elizabeth.
  The Jane Austen guide to happily ever after / Elizabeth Kantor.
    p. cm.
  Includes bibliographical references.
  ISBN 978-1-59698-784-5
  1. Women--Psychology. 2. Man-woman relationships. 3. Mate selection.
  4. Austen, Jane, 1775-1817 I. Title.
  HQ1206.K364 2012
  306.82--dc23
                      2011040124

Published in the United States by
Regnery Publishing, Inc.
One Massachusetts Avenue NW
Washington, DC 20001
www.Regnery.com

Manufactured in the United States of America
10 9 8 7 6 5 4 3 2 1

Books are available in quantity for promotional or premium use. Write to Director of Special Sales, Regnery Publishing, Inc., One Massachusetts Avenue NW, Washington, DC 20001, for information on discounts and terms or call (202) 216-0600.

Distributed to the trade by
Perseus Distribution
387 Park Avenue South
New York, NY 10016

To Jeff,
who makes me happy

CONTENTS

$\mathcal{W}$HAT DO WOMEN REALLY WANT FROM JANE AUSTEN?

WHY DO WOMEN LOVE JANE AUSTEN SO MUCH?

There's no doubt we do. Women made Jane Austen a bestselling novelist in the nineteenth century and a blockbuster screenwriter in the twentieth. And today there's a whole industry of Jane Austen knockoffs—*Bridget Jones's Diary*, *The Jane Austen Book Club*, *Pride and Prejudice and Zombies*. They're great fun. But do they get at what really fascinates us about Jane Austen?

Jane Austen is a great novelist, of course. She's a genius on the subject of female psychology—and male psychology, for that matter. But those aren't the only reasons women love her. We go to Jane Austen for a good read, but there's more to it than that. Jane Austen shows modern women a world that we're aching to be part of. And it's not just about the clothes (though they *are* gorgeous). Let's be honest: we wish we could be Jane Austen heroines in our own lives, dealing with everything—especially men—with the sophistication and competence we admire in characters like Elizabeth Bennet. Women see something in Jane Austen that's missing from modern relationships, and we can't help wondering if there might be some way to have what we see there—without going back to Empire waistlines, horse-drawn carriages, and the bad old days before the Married Women's Property Act.

Can we learn from Elizabeth Bennet and Anne Elliot about men, sex, marriage, and living happily ever after? Can Jane Austen teach modern women to make our way through the minefields of love and courtship—to find the "permanent happiness" that Jane Austen heroines aim for? Is it possible to unlock the insights, habits of mind, intelligence about men, and choices that make Jane Austen heroines so different from us? That's what *The Jane Austen Guide to Happily Ever After* aims to do.

What Jane Austen Has, That We're Missing

The original inspiration for this book was an article that appeared in the *Washington Post* "Style" section at an earlier high-water mark for Jane Austen's popularity—after the movies and the "chick lit," but before the zombies and sea monsters. In "Jane Austen: A Love Story," Jennifer Frey asked, "Where did all this come from? What suddenly, unexpectedly, made Jane Austen so unbearably hip?"[1]

Frey quoted Bridget Jones in swoony appreciation of Colin Firth's torso in the 1995 British TV version of *Pride and Prejudice*, "emerging from the lake dripping wet, in the see-through white shirt. Mmm. Mmmm." But she also interviewed an impressive stable of experts. Besides the wet shirt angle, Austen enthusiasts were supposed to be fascinated by "her sharp rendering of class and class distinctions" for the same reasons they read *The Devil Wears Prada* and *The Nanny Diaries*, "two novels that expose the excesses and obnoxiousness of America's reigning class through the gaze of what is, essentially, a servant." Or, perhaps, Frey considered, twenty-first-century women look back two hundred years to find models for our liberated selves: "Austen, it's been suggested, is the great-great-grandmother of "chick lit"— that exploding genre about upwardly mobile young women and their wayward travails through the world of modern courtship." A Yahoo! movie critic told the *Post* that Jane Austen "has a stunningly modern sensibility. And it took the world a couple centuries to catch up with her." A chick lit author chimed in with the cliché that Jane Austen is "such a subversive writer."

Really? I thought, reviewing all this expert opinion. *Aren't they getting the Jane Austen phenomenon exactly, perfectly, 180 degrees wrong?* If women in the twenty-first century want to gawk at men's chests, get vicarious thrills from the adventures of the upwardly mobile (or, in the alternative, from the indignities suffered by the employees of the rich and famous), or cheer on the oppressed sisterhood, we don't need to resort to Jane Austen. Opportunities to drool over some hot guy's torso are not exactly in short supply at this moment in world history. Neither are tell-all memoirs or "Go for it, girl!" pep talks. And anyway, aren't people's desires and aspirations generally about what we *don't* have, not what we're suffocating in already? Jane Austen, I found myself thinking, fascinates us *not* because we recognize our lives in her books. It's just the opposite. Sure, Elizabeth Bennet and Elinor Dashwood are women whose desires and problems we can identify with. But they're not exactly like us. What we see in *Pride and Prejudice* and *Sense and Sensibility* isn't just our same old lives, only dressed up in scrumptious Regency costumes and witty dialogue.

At least that's what I thought. So I set out to analyze what's missing from modern women's lives, but all over Jane Austen. And I discovered something astonishing. Of course it's no secret that modern mating rituals have gone badly wrong. But reading Jane Austen makes it crystal clear *where* we've gone off track. The crucial question: What is it that Jane Austen heroines do (that we're *not* doing) that makes really satisfying happy endings possible for them, and not so likely for us? The great hope: Could reexamining love from the perspective of Jane Austen's heroines mean getting results that are more like theirs? Maybe Jane Austen can help us rethink from scratch what we really want out of love and sex—and figure out what we would be doing differently if we were pursuing those things the way Elinor Dashwood and Anne Elliot do.

What is it that's hard to find in the world we live in, but available in spades in Jane Austen?

"True Elegance"

First off, right at front and center, is what Jane Austen calls *elegance.* Women in Jane Austen aren't "hot" or "sexy." I mean, maybe they are, actually, hot. But Jane Austen makes sure that's not what we notice about them. The judges of female attractiveness in Jane Austen novels are interested in "elegance," not "hotness."

Jane Austen is famous for saying almost nothing about what her characters look like. She's the original Regency author.[2] But she *never* introduces a character the way the writer of a modern "Regency" romance might:

> Lady Rushworth was a striking beauty, with masses of golden hair piled atop a flawless visage emerging from a neck that would put a swan to shame, and midnight-hued eyes whose depths betrayed a fiery passion kept in check, but never extinguished. Her gown, a blue taffeta that perfectly matched the pools of her eyes, was cinched tight just under the swelling of her bosom; her neckline was cut low to reveal a splendid décolletage.

Jane Austen's one-sentence description of Marianne Dashwood is about as much physical detail as we get about any of her heroines:

> Her skin was very brown, but, from its transparency, her complexion was uncommonly brilliant; her features were all good; her smile was sweet and attractive; and in her eyes, which were very dark, there was a life, a spirit, an eagerness, which could hardly be seen without delight.

Even in this physical description, Jane Austen is painting a picture of Marianne as a person, not just a man-magnet. She glosses over the physical details—"her features were all good"—to cut to the things that show what Marianne is really like. And in the process she gives us something very different from the raw sexuality we see every day on our television and computer screens or the magazine covers at the checkout counter. Marianne is a flesh-and-blood young woman, but we see more than just her flesh. It's almost as if Jane Austen sees women the way a woman naturally sees other women, not in the *how-sexy-would-a-man-find-that-body?* way we have come to judge ourselves and each other in the age of *Maxim* and *Cosmo*.

But it's all without a hint of prudery. After all, Jane Austen is no repressed Victorian. There's no "anxious parade" about the modesty of female dress in her novels. Jane Austen heroines aren't aiming for the shock of raw sexuality, but they're not swathing the piano legs in drapery lest the gentlemen be reminded of female curves, either. They expect men to notice their bodies—their figures, their eyes, the coloring and quality of their skin. And they take notice of the men's physicality, too. But somehow in Jane Austen there's a dignity about the whole subject of physical attraction that we're missing.

Love without Humiliation

And the dignity of Jane Austen's heroines is about more than elegance versus hotness. It's hard not to think that if we could live like Jane Austen heroines, we'd be spared some of the ugliness and humiliation modern life can deal out to us. Around the time I read Jennifer Frey's *Washington Post* article, I also read *Bridget Jones's Diary*.[3] And it occurred to me, there's no better way to explain what Jane Austen heroines have, that we're missing, than to compare Elizabeth Bennet to Bridget Jones, her hapless modern alter ego. Just like Elizabeth Bennet, Bridget Jones meets a Mr. Darcy who's out of her league, class-, looks-, and money-wise. And like Elizabeth, Bridget is first repelled by her Mr. Darcy and then falls for him, hard. But the perfect parallels between their situations only show up how sadly substandard Bridget's life is, compared to Elizabeth Bennet's.

Thank heavens, we're not quite as pitiful as Bridget Jones. But her *Diary* is a bit close for comfort. The comedy wouldn't work if we didn't recognize ourselves in Bridget's life. There's her obsession with her weight, her chocolate intake, and how much she drinks—a world of things that seem to be completely beneath Elizabeth Bennet's notice. But worse, Bridget Jones regularly gets into humiliating situations that Elizabeth Bennet would never, ever find herself in.

Jane Austen heroines do embarrass themselves, of course. Elizabeth is ashamed when she reads Darcy's letter and sees how completely unfair she has been to him, and how she was taken in by Wickham: "And yet I meant to be uncommonly clever...."[4] But there's a dignity even to her embarrassment. Bridget Jones's humiliations are in an entirely different class. Think of her interview with Colin Firth, which ends in a fiasco when she dives for his torso. Or the disastrous tryst with the twenty-something hunk in her building who's weirded out by her squooshy thirty-something belly.

Helen Fielding pushes it to the point of absurdity. But there's a ring of truth to it all. The modern dating scene imposes similar indignities on real women every day. Thus Hephzibah Anderson, the real-life author of *Chastened: The Unexpected Story of My Year without Sex*, explains how the *Sex and the City* lifestyle she adopted after breaking up with her college boyfriend left her with not much more than an endless supply of absurd stories to tell her girlfriends. And then she started to notice the "pity in their eyes as they listened to me."[5] Finally, desperate to make *some* change that would break the pattern, she resorted to the no-sex-for-a-year experiment that's the premise of her book.

Competence about Men

It's not just that Elizabeth never looks as foolish as Bridget Jones, or as we sometimes do. If we had the kind of lives we really wanted, we wouldn't care so much how other people see us. The difference between us and Jane Austen's heroines isn't just about elegance and dignity. There's also a competence gap. This is where Bridget Jones's life is a really perfect picture of what we're missing. Bridget is simply incompetent when it comes to men, and love, and even understanding what she really wants. Jane Austen's heroines seem to *know what they're doing*. At the beginning of *The Edge of Reason*,[6] the sequel to *Bridget Jones's Diary*, Bridget breaks things off with Mark Darcy in an ill-timed fit of solidarity with the sisterhood. She's used to getting together with her girlfriends to grouse about the awful men in their lives—to swap those "good stories" the real-life Hephzibah Anderson talks about.[7] Emboldened by her girlfriends' *don't-let-yourself-be-pushed-around-by-those-jerks* solidarity, Bridget loses sight of everything else—that she adores Mark Darcy, that he makes her blissfully happy, that her behavior will only hurt and mystify him—and breaks up with him for no real reason. Then, of course, she immediately regrets it. Elizabeth Bennet may make some mistakes, but Bridget is totally clueless.[8]

Jane Austen heroines have a "seniority of mind" that's very attractive. They actually have a clue about male psychology. Anne Elliot can advise a guy about recovering from his broken heart, or explain how men and women differ when it comes to love, in a way that's completely convincing—without anger, defensiveness, or special pleading. Elizabeth Bennet can make allowances for a lack of emotional flexibility in the man she loves—not out of low expectations, but with genuine respect for him and confidence in her own emotional competence.[9] Their competence means Jane Austen heroines can work their way through the minefields of love and courtship without making themselves totally ridiculous. They're equipped to figure out how to live happily ever.

It's funny. Bridget has a job and Elizabeth doesn't, of course. You'd guess a grown woman living with her parents with nothing much to do but think about her love life would be a basket case. But she's not. It's the modern free-and-independent Bridget Jones who's driven to "the edge of reason." And not just the fictional Bridget Jones—real-life romance seems to be in something of a crisis at the moment. There are the women giving up on sex altogether.[10] There are the perennial complaints about "the hookup culture."[11] Books of advice for the lovelorn sound increasingly less romantic and more like advice for getting through boot camp: *The Rules*; *He's Just Not That Into You*; *Act Like a Lady, Think Like a Man*. Or else they advise giving up on romantic love altogether: *Marry Him: The Case for Settling for Mr. Good Enough*. And then there's a truly bizarre phenomenon: centuries after we gave it up for the love match, decades after feminism, *arranged marriage* is getting a second look.[12]

These signs of desperation suggest something has gone badly wrong with modern romance. Women find looking for love increasingly difficult, painful, or even pointless. The solid prospect of a happily-ever-after ending recedes to the vanishing point; counsels of despair multiply. In contrast, Jane Austen heroines don't find men a hopeless puzzle. They seem to know how to make marriage and love go together. And they understand what they themselves want—maybe not instantly, but they figure it out, applying all the intelligence and honesty they can muster to that vital question.

Taking Relationships Seriously

Maybe Jane Austen's heroines can make it all work out precisely because they take love more seriously than we do. Here's yet another thing we find in Jane Austen that's missing in our world: she takes completely seriously what has always mattered most to women—relationships.

In Jane Austen, even a foolish seventeen-year-old girl's heartbreak is taken seriously, even by the grownups. A Marianne Dashwood isn't left to struggle through her affairs of the heart alone, while the adults in her life pretend they aren't really happening, or they aren't really important. The Jane Austen heroine hasn't been taught that love is just a messy distraction from the serious business of her life (to do well in school so she can succeed in a career). She doesn't get the message that if she cares more about a boy than about anything else in the world at the moment, she's weak. She doesn't assume that planning your future around a relationship is a sign of failure. The Jane Austen heroine doesn't try to run her love life like an occasional extracurricular activity, somewhere down the list between chorus and lacrosse practice.

Okay, but it was a different world back then. In Jane Austen's day, seventeen-year-old girls got married. And back then marriage *was* a career—practically the *only* career—for women.[13] To take love seriously enough to get it right, would we have to give up education and having a profession and aim straight for barefoot and pregnant? To become Jane Austen heroines, do we have to fall off the career track and get in line for our MRS degrees?

Here's what I imagine you may be thinking at the moment:

Well, everything you say we can find in Jane Austen is lovely. It would be dreamy to live like that. But it's pointless for women today to pine after things we can't have. Pemberley is not the world we're living in. We can't have romances like that now, so there's no point wishing for them; you can't turn back the clock. And even if you could, the cost is too high. Back then, women were like children all their lives. We've gotten beyond the virginity fetish, "ruined women," "good girls," and "bad girls." We're not going back.

This is really the question at the heart of Jane Austen's fascination for modern women: Can we have Jane Austen-style elegance, dignity, and happy love only at the cost of modern freedom and equality? To take the relationships that have always mattered most to women seriously (seriously enough to get them right), do we have to give up everything else we've gained since Jane Austen's day?

No! There's no reason living like a Jane Austen heroine has to mean going back to a life of pre-feminist misery and oppression. Let me remind you that our favorite novelist was no repressed Victorian. As a matter of fact, Jane Austen's last, unfinished novel is a brilliant parody of the incipient Victorian era.[14] She understood very well the dangers of an unhealthy kind of femininity. In Jane Austen's world there are better and worse ways of making relationships central to your life. If you survey the novels looking at the matches Jane Austen makes, you'll notice that she doesn't, as a matter of fact, consider marriage at seventeen to be ideal. Her heroines are grownups.

Plenty of Jane Austen characters' lives revolve around relationships... marriage and family... men and love... but in the *wrong* way. Jane Austen could give some very good reasons why it can be a very bad idea to plan your life around a particular man, to pursue relationships in a certain way, or to let your interest in men and marriage become a stupid obsession.[15]

But her reasons are not the same reasons women today hear from our mothers, and our culture. Just because love can end badly—or can be pursued with pathetic desperation—doesn't mean that the best course is to refocus all our energy and careful attention on other areas of our lives where we think we have control. Trying to make love an afterthought, or confining it to a recreation, is not Jane Austen's solution. The things most crucial to our happiness are never a hundred percent under our control. They depend on other people. And so it's reasonable for us to spend significant intellectual and emotional capital on our relationships—but in the right way, not the wrong way.

Neither Romantic Illusions *Nor* Victorian Repression *Nor* Modern Cynicism

One of the most appealing things about Jane Austen is her eighteenth-century mindset.[16] The Age of Reason was all about balance and perspective.[17] We're used to thinking about everything, and especially about women's lives, in stark either-or terms. *Either* women can be equal and independent, *or* we'll be the downtrodden dependents of men. *Either* we make education and careers our top priorities, *or* we'll end up barefoot and pregnant. *Either* we let other people make us unhappy, *or* we take complete responsibility for our own happiness. *Either* we celebrate sexual experimentation, *or* we end up repressed and frustrated. Jane Austen didn't think that way. Her ideals are all about rational balance, not about running screaming from one extreme only to fall off the edge on the other side. If you've escaped from a fire, it's still not a good idea to jump off a bridge and drown yourself.

Since the beginning of the nineteenth century, we've been whipsawing back and forth between two unsatisfactory attitudes toward love. On the one hand, we've been swept away on successive waves of Romantic promises—of certain, total bliss if we'll just throw off all constraints and follow our hearts. On the other, we've undergone repeated waves of reaction against the inevitable fallout from that Romantic philosophy of love. The Victorians clean up after the Romantics, and then a revolt against Victorian repression breaks out at the turn of the twentieth century. Skirts get so short in the Roaring Twenties that women rouge their knees.[18] Everybody wakes up with a hangover, and hemlines come down again. The relaxed gender roles, chaos, and risk-taking of the World War II years give way to the conformity and plastic domesticity of the 1950s, which in turn yield to the Sexual Revolution, which sets us up for modern cynicism about love. At this point, the whole thing is pretty much played out.

After two centuries trapped in the same vicious circle, aren't we ready to hear something completely different? That's just what Jane Austen has to offer. Her eighteenth century was the era of reason and balance—but also of hope and ambition for every kind of human endeavor. Despite the impression you might get from the dreamy dresses, Jane Austen was a complete realist about human nature, never shocked (though often amused) by folly and vice. Because of her realism, she was a clear-eyed critic of Romanticism at its very beginning. Jane Austen saw through the Romantic obsession with liberation, authenticity, and intensity to the neglect of every other value. She was never taken in by Romantic wishful thinking. She was a complete realist about men and women. But she was *never* cynical about love. She's 180 degrees from our jaundiced modern view of relationships. The "delicacy of mind" her heroines cultivate makes a refreshing contrast with modern bitterness about men. The "rational happiness" Elizabeth Bennet aims for is a beautiful prospect to women exhausted from alternating between Romantic intensity and modern despair on the whole subject of men, love, and marriage.

Jane Austen makes you think maybe it's time for us to quit ricocheting back and forth between extremes and see what a balanced approach to love and sex might look like. The case for Jane Austen's approach to love is *not* an argument that we can "have it all"—be neurosurgeons who work eighty-hour weeks and at the same time have the kind of family where we never miss a baby's first step. (Jane Austen is all about the clear-eyed recognition of limits we can't get around; she doesn't do illusion.)[19] It's an argument that we've got the balance wrong—partly because we insist on treating love, which is really central to our happiness, as an afterthought, or a recreation, or something we can afford as a luxury once we've got the essentials of our life in order. It's not working. You may have noticed.

Respect for Female Psychology

Maybe because Jane Austen takes love seriously, she also shows us something else that's deeply attractive. Her men have a particular kind of respect for women that's nearly forgotten today. They take into account the things that women typically want, instead of always expecting women to accommodate female desires to male interests and limitations. In Jane Austen novels, men are compelled by their consciences—or, if they should happen not to have any, by society—to consider what effect their romantic attentions are having on women. Not to manipulate the woman more effectively, but out of respect for her vulnerabilities and her ultimate happiness. It's the same kind of respect you'd be demonstrating for male psychology by deciding not to walk slowly past the windows of a boys' school in your bikini while the boys were taking their exams.

You know the famous *Sex and the City* question: *Can a woman have sex like a man?* Jane Austen was interested in a totally different question: *Can a man be in love like a woman?* She was fascinated by many of the same issues that preoccupy us. She gave us at least eight case studies (that's 1.3 per novel!) of men who are, as we say, "afraid of commitment." But she was more ambitious than we are. She didn't just wonder how a commitment-shy man can be cajoled or pressured into accommodating a woman's desire for commitment. Jane Austen identified circumstances in which a man can come to passionately desire the very kind of commitment that the woman is longing to be asked for. Wouldn't it be lovely to live in her world?

Jane Austen: A Genius for Happiness

Jane Austen was undoubtedly a genius about happy love. That doesn't just mean she was born with an innate talent for understanding relationships. Like Michelangelo at the height of the Renaissance…like Beethoven at just the right point in the development of classical music…like Einstein at the dawn of modern physics…Jane Austen flourished at the precise time in history perfectly suited to her special talents. Her inborn genius met a key cultural moment and produced a masterpiece. In Jane Austen's case, that masterpiece is a body of work on a subject of even greater importance to human happiness than physics or art: love. Jane Austen lived at the precise point when Western culture was giving up on traditional arranged marriage and people were feeling their way toward a completely new way of managing sex, passion, and family life.[20] Jane Austen was in the ideal position, historically, to see all the issues involved, and to show us a way of making matches that respects women's freedom and the imperatives of romantic love, without totally abandoning the prudent concern for future happiness that had gone into arranged marriage.

In Jane Austen novels, it's the heroines themselves who make their own matches, not their parents or guardians. She shows us the most pleasant way of arranging marriages ever invented—by falling in love with the right man, at the right time, in the right way. Now that, for too many unhappy women, love and marriage seem to have come unglued again, it's time to reconsider Jane Austen's wisdom.

When we do look at Jane Austen's novels with an eye to what they can teach us about managing our love lives, her insights are surprisingly fresh. Because her view of love is unclouded by Romantic illusions, she's as realistic as the "he's just not that into you," "sex and the city" crowd—but not as brutal. She's got "rules" for women to live by, but they're not manipulative and hypocritical; she respects men as well as women. And her understanding of the psychology of love is receiving remarkable confirmation from recent discoveries in biology and sociology. ("Attachment," for example, is crucial to Jane Austen's understanding of love. But it wasn't until the discovery of oxytocin that we began to understand its physiological basis. Twenty-first-century sociologists puzzle over the fact that cohabitation before marriage raises the divorce rate. Jane Austen could have told you why.) And finally, she's the perfect model for how women can achieve the kinds of things that only men have had the opportunities for in most of history—get a first-class education, become an artist or have a profession, be anyone's intellectual equal—*without* having to pretend that the things that have always mattered most to women are not important.

Women today are settling for less than we really want. We have sex—but too often on men's terms, not our own. We have love, and we have marriage—but we have trouble fitting them together. We have careers, and we have relationships—but we can't get them into the right balance. We feel like we have to crimp and pinch ourselves into shapes that aren't comfortable or dignified for us, to accommodate ourselves to the men we don't want to live without. Jane Austen's novels remind us that there are other possibilities.

They're fiction, of course. They're only models, not true history. But then so are the other models, the ones we're living by now—whether it's the women's magazines telling us how to get a man's attention or how to hold it; the movies spinning us a line about what happily ever after looks like (or, in the alternative, how deeply cool it is to be unhappy in love); or the advice columnists reminding us once again to cut our expectations back to the bare minimum that we've negotiated for in our relationships.

If we take Jane Austen for our model instead, can she teach us how to find what we really want better than those other voices, the ones already echoing in our heads? I think she can.

CHAPTER ONE

*I*N LOVE, LOOK FOR HAPPINESS

ALL SUCCESSFUL JANE AUSTEN HEROINES SHARE one goal. In love, they look for happiness. It's what they aim for where men are concerned, and it's what they worry about for their friends.

It seems way too simple, doesn't it? Doesn't that go without saying? Everybody wants to be happy. Right?

The short answer is *No.*

Or rather, *of course* we all *want* to be happy. If life asked us the question that way—pick up or down, choose happiness or misery—we'd have no trouble getting the answer right. But Jane Austen is at pains to let us know that important questions in real life don't come to us that way. You don't get offered happiness on a plate with parsley on the side.

The Pursuit of Happiness

It's no good thinking, *Of course* I want to be happy. The difference between the *of course* sort of wanting to be happy and the serious pursuit of happiness is a tricky distinction. But understanding it is absolutely crucial. The vague *of course* kind of wanting to be happy is something we all share. *The pursuit of rational and permanent happiness* is what sets Jane Austen heroines apart.

For help seeing the difference, look at this conversation in *Pride and Prejudice*. "They can only wish his happiness, and if he is attached to me, no other woman can secure it," says Jane Bennet, about Bingley's sisters. But Elizabeth points out the flaw in Jane's argument: "Your first premise is false. They may wish many things besides his happiness; they may wish his increase in wealth and consequence; they may wish him to marry a girl who has all the importance of money, great connections, and pride." If you asked Bingley's sisters whether they want their brother to be happy, they'd say yes. *Of course* they do. They wouldn't set out to make him unhappy just for the sake of ruining his life. But life doesn't pose this kind of question in the abstract. You don't get to choose up or down, for or against everything you *of course* want.

To get to happy love, you have to make your way through a wilderness of competing desires. In the process, it's easy for an *of course I want that* kind of goal to get shunted aside by entirely different aims that you're actually pouring your time and energy into. It's only in retrospect that you see you've given up something you really wanted.

How many of us want to lose weight? *Of course* we do. But we don't get to choose thin versus fat in the abstract. We have to aim for skinny and stick to that aim, in a world full of twenty-ounce sodas and half gallons of ice cream.

In just the same way, if you ask any woman, "Do you want to be happy?" she'll say yes. But that answer is to the question in isolation, which is *never* how it comes up in the complexities of real life (or the closest thing to it, a Jane Austen novel). The real question isn't "Do you want to be happy?" It's "What do you want?" In other words, which goal—of the many competing aims you'd say yes to if any one of them was offered to you on a platter with water cress around it—are you actually pursuing? (With your limited time and energy and all the smarts you've got.) When you envision what you want from love, what's the picture in front of you? Are you really looking forward to happily ever after?

To inspire us, Jane Austen shows us heroines who win through to happiness. But to warn us, she also gives us women who don't. They fail not so much because they're looking for love in all the wrong places as because they're looking for other things where they ought to be looking for happiness in love.

"Rage for Admiration"

Take Lydia Bennet, for example, Elizabeth's flighty sister. Like a lot of us at age sixteen, Lydia is intoxicated with male attention. She has a Scarlett O'Hara fantasy of herself "tenderly flirting with at least six officers at once" on a proposed visit to the military camp at Brighton.[1] Elizabeth worries about Lydia's "rage for admiration" and tries hard to get her father to forbid the visit to Brighton. In vain.

The Brighton visit ends in disaster. It would have been complete disaster for Lydia if she hadn't been rescued by more level-headed people. Lydia runs away with George Wickham, leaving a note to say she's off to Gretna Green[2] with the "one man in the world I love, and he is an angel." But what Lydia thinks is a romantic elopement is really something much uglier. Actually, Wickham has left Brighton to escape his gambling debts. He's taken her along—taken her virginity, changed her life forever, ruined her chances of marrying anyone else—only as an afterthought, just because "he was not the young man to resist an opportunity of having a companion," no matter the cost to her. Lydia is nothing more than a temporary pleasure to him, a distraction from his money problems. He tells Darcy straight out that he never had any intention of marrying her. Even while living with Lydia, Wickham is still planning to make his fortune by marrying a rich girl as soon as he can.

Meanwhile, Lydia is completely oblivious to the reality of the situation. She's "sure" that they'll get married "some time or other, and it did not much signify when." In other words, while Lydia has been actively pursuing male attention (and excitement, and sexual pleasure), she's left long-term happiness to take care of itself. *Of course* she plans to be happy with Wickham in the long run. But she's taking happiness for granted, not pursuing it.

Lucky for Lydia, her family and friends are able to bribe Wickham to marry her after all. But it's sad, too.[3] Even after the wedding, Jane Austen shows us that Lydia is still tone deaf to the essentials of her relationship with her husband. She doesn't give a thought to what it might take to turn this "patched-up business" into a happy marriage. Instead, she's busy showing off her new status as a wife. She makes sure everyone sees her wedding ring. She offers to play the married chaperone to her sisters—to take them to balls and "get husbands for them"—and tells her oldest sister, "Ah! Jane, I take your place now, and you must go lower, because I am a married woman."

Of course Lydia assumes that whatever she's pursuing at the moment will make her happy—going to Brighton to enjoy all that male attention; running off with Wickham; showing off how important it makes her to be a married woman. But she never looks beyond the short-term pleasure she's actually pursuing to ask herself what makes for lasting happiness.

"A Comfortable Home"

At the opposite end of the spectrum from careless Lydia is Charlotte Lucas, Elizabeth Bennet's *too*-practical friend. Charlotte shocks Elizabeth by marrying a man who is unattractive in every possible way—except as a source of financial security. Mr. Collins[4] takes pompous nit-wittery to the point that it's painfully embarrassing to be in the same room with him. Charlotte is repelled by him, as any normal woman would be.[5]

Once they're married, Charlotte arranges her life so that she can avoid her husband as much as possible: she picks a small room at the back of the house to spend her days in because if she chose a more "lively" one, Mr. Collins would be with her more often throughout the day. The female reader shudders to imagine Charlotte's nights.

Charlotte's prudent planning is as different as possible from Lydia's thoughtless foolishness. But they've both missed happiness,[6] and both through aiming at something else instead. In Charlotte's case, it's "a comfortable home."[7]

"No One Loved Better to Lead Than Maria"

Maria Bertram in *Mansfield Park* seems to have everything a girl could ask for. She's an attractive blonde.[8] She's well-educated and accomplished, too, full of self-confidence, and popular. But under the surface, something is not right. Maria agrees to marry a young man who's very rich—even richer than her father—tall and handsome, but unimpressive in every other way. Her brother can't help thinking, "If this man had not twelve thousand a year, he would be a very stupid fellow."

Maria is not exactly mercenary. She's not making Charlotte Lucas's mistake.[9] For Maria, the money is more about pride—"vanity" and "self-consequence"—than security: "No one loved better to lead than Maria." It's flattering to be courted by a man of such enormous wealth, to imagine herself the mistress of so splendid an estate. Whenever we see Maria with her fiancé, she's engaged in "shewing her power over him." Not in a sadistic way, and not to make a scene (Maria doesn't enjoy drama). It's just that her sense of her own importance is flattered by her power over a man with so much power himself.

Maria also urgently wants to escape her father's house, and Mr. Rushworth is a way out. Maria has been spoiled; she's too used to having her way. Her mother is so lazy she never interferes in her children's lives at all, and her aunt spoils and flatters all the Bertram children, but especially Maria. Her rather forbidding father's authority has been the only real check on her freedom. And then, just when Maria reaches that "most interesting age" at which she's ready to think about men and marriage, her father is called away to the West Indies on business—*for two years.* By the time Sir Thomas gets back to Mansfield, Maria is too used to her freedom to be able to stand living under his roof.[10]

And after getting herself engaged to Mr. Rushworth on the strength of nothing better than vanity, Maria has fallen deeply in love with Henry Crawford. When it becomes clear that Henry has only been playing with her emotions for his own entertainment, she decides she'd better go ahead and marry Rushworth: "Henry Crawford had destroyed her happiness, but he should not know that he had done it; he should not destroy her credit, her appearance, her prosperity too. He should not have to think of her as pining in the retirement of Mansfield for *him,* rejecting Southerton and London, independence and splendour for *his* sake."

Maria Bertram is an intelligent woman, but she ends up doing an incredibly stupid thing out of vanity, injured pride, and frustration with her life at home. She marries a man she doesn't love to spite the one who doesn't love her. She sells herself for an "escape from Mansfield" and a "house in town." But in that grand house she finds that "fortune and consequence, bustle and the world" are poor substitutes for happiness.

Different Century, Same Mistakes

So what's the relevance of these nineteenth-century mistakes to our twenty-first-century lives? We don't have autocratic baronets with grave, forbidding personalities for fathers. We don't, like Maria, have to marry to shake off parental control and escape to life in the big city—much less to be assured of three square meals a day, like Charlotte. And even if we should choose to run off with a scoundrel who's skipping town to escape his gambling debts, like Lydia, it's not quite the life-changing experience it was in the eighteen-teens. Surely women today don't miss happiness for the quaint reasons in Jane Austen novels?

Oh yes we do.

Let's start with Lydia Bennet's "rage for admiration." You don't have to look far to see exactly the same impulse today. It's being catered to at the checkout in every grocery store, where *Cosmo* advises us on "10 Things Guys Crave in Bed: The Surprising Trait 80% of Men Find Sexy," "78 Ways to Turn Him On," "First, Pull Down His Pants," or "Secrets of Male Arousal: A Surprising Trigger to His Deepest Sex Cravings."[11] Are these articles selling us on the pursuit of what Jane Austen calls "permanent" and "rational" happiness? I don't think so. They're pointing straight toward the same blind alley that made poor Lydia Bennet miss her happy ending. *Cosmo* expects its readers to try some things that even Lydia Bennet might not have been up for. But the basic goal the *Cosmo* reader is being advised to pursue is exactly the same kind of male attention Lydia was craving.

And what's wrong with male attention? Nothing.[12] But here's the crucial thing. If you pursue male attention single-mindedly, you're not keeping your mind on what's going to make you happy. You've taken your eye off the ball, you may miss your chance.

Jane Austen's "rational happiness" doesn't in the end exclude any of the things women want—both from men and from life.[13] We all want to be passionately admired, courted, and cherished, which is what Lydia Bennet is obsessed with. We want to have a comfortable, well-ordered life, like Charlotte Lucas. And we all want to feel good about ourselves, and to feel free—the same things Maria Bertram wants. But just the same way these Jane Austen characters miss their happy endings, plenty of modern women miss happiness by putting it on the back burner and snatching at those other things first. Every day women go for the shiny thing right here and now, putting their ultimate dreams of real happy love on hold. They end up with sex, or money, or status—but not happiness.

In twenty-first-century America, scatter-brained boy-crazy sixteen-year-olds don't run off with cads and enter foolish marriages because they want the higher status of a wife, like Lydia. But a lot of them do have disappointing sex with the first guy who shows any interest in them, for pretty much the same reason: they're intoxicated by male attention, and they want to seem more mature to themselves or their friends…to shed virgin status for experience…not to feel left out of things.

And even in these enlightened times, a man's status or his money can still distract us, like Charlotte Lucas and Maria Bertram, from the pursuit of real happiness. The glamour of dating someone who's got money, or is older, more established, or more sophisticated than we are turns quite a lot of our heads. How many women sleep with their professors, or their bosses? (And how many of those relationships turn out well?)

Does Jane Austen suggest that our desires—to feel good about ourselves, to be wanted, to have great sex, to live comfortably—are incompatible with happiness in love? Of course not—at least not in the abstract and in the long run. But remember, life doesn't offer you happiness in the abstract. And to get everything you want in the long run, you have to get your priorities straight in the short run. Like a Jane Austen heroine, you have to fight your way to happiness through a maze of competing calls on your energy and attention.

If anything, the weeds we have to struggle through to our happy endings have only grown taller and more tangled since Jane Austen's day. Take a look around you. Everywhere you look—in films, in music, on reality shows, in your friends' lives, maybe in your own—you see women losing out on happiness in love. And a lot of the time, you can see (at least if you know your Jane Austen) that they lose the race because they've lost their focus on happy love...or they've scaled back their ambitions from it...or they never believed happiness was a realistic goal for them in the first place.

Here's what failing to aim for happiness in love looks like in modern times: Bridget Jones, madly happy with Mark Darcy, nevertheless sticking it to him on the phone because it makes her look good in front of her friends.

Here's what else it looks like: the barista played by Marisa Tomei in *What Women Want*, thinking to herself as Mel Gibson makes love to her that she'd better go through with a pretty obviously pointless one-night stand because she hasn't had sex in so long. If you're having sex to prove to yourself (or your friends) that you're still in the game—then the game you're playing is for a different prize from the one Jane Austen heroines win.

Or, to turn to real-life examples, not aiming for happiness in love looks like the adventures of Jessica Cutler, the notorious "Washingtonienne" who worked in a Republican senator's office, all the while supplementing her $25,000-a-year government salary with generous presents of cash from the older men she was having sex with, and blogging about it. Or, lower down on the same food chain, there's the story of Ashley Alexandra Dupré, the wanna-be singer, real-life prostitute at the center of the Eliot Spitzer scandal.

These women achieved a certain measure of success. Cutler got a book deal. Dupré at least had her fifteen minutes of fame, sold some downloads of her song, and saw her music all over the internet. But from the point of view of finding happiness in love, they were failures. Because, apparently, they weren't even looking for it. "Love is not enough," the Washingtonienne's fictional alter ego tells a girlfriend in Jessica Cutler's novel. "It just doesn't cut it anymore."[14]

Your wrong turn doesn't have to be quite as—how shall we put it?—sordid? public? flamboyant? as these examples to be, nevertheless, just as dead an end, compared to what Jane Austen's heroines end up with. All your mistake has to be is a distraction from the "permanent happiness" Jane Austen heroines aim for.

In chapter 6 we're going to be taking a closer look at exactly what Jane Austen means by happiness that's "rational" and "permanent." But even before we get there, it's obvious enough that some things you can pursue can't possibly be rational or permanent happiness by *anybody's* definition. Jackie (Jessica Cutler's alter ego in her novel) is pretty far down her blind alley before she hits the bumps in the road that tell her she's in a place she may not want to be. It's not until the guy who's been handing her envelopes full of cash wants sex after they've had a fight, and pays for it, that she feels demeaned: "Fred had given me approximately $20,000 in cash since our arrangement started, but this was the first time I ever really felt like a whore." And it's not until she's sleeping with six different men that the temperature of her sex life reaches the point on her moral thermometer marked "Eeew." Imagine if she'd been measuring her choices, instead, against Jane Austen's standard. It might have become obvious—long before the six guys or the money for sex—that she wasn't on the road marked "This Way to Permanent Happiness."

Even if our lives are less lurid, there are plenty of mile markers that we're more likely to notice if we've got it in mind that we're headed either in the direction of a happy ending or else on the way to somewhere altogether different. Being on the road to permanent happiness means making happiness in love a conscious aim of our actual choices here and now, not just an *of course* sort of assumption about what's bound to happen to us in the vague, unplanned future.

But We Have Plenty of Time for Happiness Later—Don't We?

Lydia Bennet's mistake, pushing what she wants off onto "some time or other" is a trap that's so much *easier* for us to fall into today. Consider how all the changes in women's lives between *Pride and Prejudice* and today make it more tempting to postpone happily ever after. We've got so much more time than they did.[15] If it was easy for Lydia Bennet, back when marriage at sixteen still seemed reasonably normal, to postpone her plans for happy love, how much easier is it going to be for us to lose focus on our ultimate goal through all the extra years we have? We're bound to think we've got plenty of time to worry about happiness later on.

TIP JUST FOR JANEITES

Don't wait to pursue happiness in love until "some time or other" in the future.

And isn't that in fact the *right* way to look at it, under modern conditions? *Don't* we have plenty of time to just have fun, play the field, or even screw up our lives completely—and still recover and find happiness later? Can't we enjoy male "admiration" to our frivolous hearts' content…or experience the perks of dating a high-status man (who doesn't really take us seriously)…or hang onto a guy we know isn't really right for us, just for the time being, because we're lonely or scared…and still go on to find "permanent" bliss with the real love of our life later on? And anyway, aren't a lot of the mistakes that Jane Austen's unhappy women make actually errors forced by the constraints of their age—disasters that can't happen to us because we have so much more time and freedom to maneuver in? Can't we *afford* to let ourselves be distracted by other things that we want from men, sex, and love in the short term, and still end up living happily ever after?

Well, yes and no. Jane Austen certainly believes in learning from your mistakes. Almost every one of her heroines has a crucial moment when she realizes that she's been managing her love life the wrong way. They make different mistakes, but they have similar moments when they recognize the errors they've fallen into. For Elizabeth Bennet, it's Darcy's letter that shows her how she's let herself grossly underestimate his value (and exaggerate Wickham's). For Catherine Morland, it's when she sees she's in danger of losing Henry Tilney's respect by her wild imaginings about his father. For Emma, it's only when she sees that her match-making schemes have unconsciously encouraged Harriett to try for a match with Mr. Knightley that she realizes she loves Mr. Knightley herself. Fortunately, Jane Austen heroines are mostly able to recover from their mistakes and go on to find happiness in love.[16]

The very same thing happens today. Women suddenly notice the qualities of a man they've overlooked, or they see through the jerk they've already given too much of themselves to. They realize they're chasing the wrong things, they change course, they grow up. At last report, Jessica Cutler of "Washingtonienne" fame was married with a baby daughter. We can hope she's changed her mind about "Love is not enough."

But notice that Jane Austen's heroines don't find happy love by persisting in their mistakes. They get to their happy endings only by seeing that they've gone wrong somewhere, reviewing their "past conduct," and *changing direction*. And that kind of change in direction isn't by any means guaranteed. Not everybody in a Jane Austen novel who goes down the wrong road turns around and heads back in the right direction. Plenty of them just keep on going.

The force of habit is very strong. Strong enough to freeze us in the shapes we've twisted ourselves into in the pursuit of things that won't ever make us really happy. That's what Elizabeth Bennet is worried about when she tries to convince her father not to let Lydia go to the military camp at Brighton.[17] The longer Lydia goes on chasing after the attention of men who don't really care about her, the harder it's going to be for her to do anything else: "Her character will be fixed, and she will, at sixteen, be the most determined flirt that ever made herself and her family ridiculous."[18]

Unfortunately, this kind of thing also still happens today—more often than the scenario where the woman realizes her mistake and recalibrates to aim for happiness after all.[19] The very elbow room we modern women have—that extra decade between the time we're first interested in guys and the time it seems reasonable to think about a "permanent" relationship—can be a liability. Those are more years we have to become "fixed" in habits that make it harder for us to look for happiness in love. It's not so easy, when you've spent your twenties pursuing attention, clinging to a guy because he's your security blanket, or enjoying the status of the high rollers you date, to do a sudden turnaround and make happy love your aim.

For a modern example of the habit-forming pursuit of things other than happiness in love, read Hephzibah Anderson's *Chastened: The Unexpected Story of My Year without Sex.*[20] Anderson broke up with her college boyfriend because "I'd fallen for another—my heart now belonged to boundless, inconstant possibilities." She was starting out in an exciting London publishing career and let herself be carried away on a wave of "fun, giddy times." And she acquired a love life to match. "On some deep-down level, I think I regarded my singleness as part of the deal. I told myself I was looking for something more meaningful, more lasting, yet I consistently chose entanglements with men who weren't really available." She spent her twenties collecting a host of self-deprecating stories[21] from relationships that either sputtered out after "a torrid few months" or never got going in the first place. By the time Anderson happened to run into that old college boyfriend—fortuitously when he was buying another girl an engagement ring at De Beers in New York—she realized he was the only man who had ever told her, "I love you."[22] And so she set off on a year without sex hoping she could change the dynamic she'd gotten stuck in.

TIP JUST FOR JANEITES

Stop making the same old bad choices about men before those choices "fix" your character, freezing you into habits you may not be able to break out of.

And then, when her sex fast was over at the end of the year, instead of the fireworks she'd been expecting after "all those months, all those lessons supposedly learned," she found herself once again having "awful" sex with a man who "felt like a stranger." She was right back in the same old pattern. In the end she decided she *had* learned something, after all—"Getting into that situation suggested I'd made absolutely no progress, but my response showed just how much I had learned. I could tell the real thing from the fake, and from that point there was no going back."[23] So Hephzibah Anderson did manage, in the end, something like Jane Austen's "serious reflection" and "self-knowledge." But those extra years that started out with "boundless, inconstant possibilities" didn't make it any easier. That's when she dug the rut that it took her a solid year of practicing the opposite to even begin to climb out of.

Jane Austen's heroines need all their extraordinary wit, energy, and "delicacy of mind" for the pursuit of happiness. We can't afford to aim any lower.

*A*DOPT AN AUSTEN ATTITUDE:

- In love, do you want happiness?
- Do you only *of course* want to be happy? Are you just assuming happiness will happen "some time or other"—and meanwhile actively pursuing other aims where men are concerned?
- Or are you pursuing "permanent," "rational" happiness?

*W*HAT WOULD JANE DO?

- She'd review her "past conduct" and consider whether she'd been aiming for happiness in love or not. For Jane Austen's heroines, that kind of review is the starting point for transforming their lives. We've seen that they're driven to rethink the course they're on by crises in their relationships. But to Jane Austen's way of thinking, it is *not* necessary to wait until you've made a complete fool of yourself and—like Emma or Catherine Morland—find you're in serious danger of losing the man you love, before you turn to "serious reflection" to gain the "self-knowledge" that will help you make the right choices in the future.[24]
- If you want to live like a Jane Austen heroine, you can decide to make today the crucial turning point in your personal novel, the apex of your story arc, the day you take stock, get to know yourself better, and go forward armed with the

self-knowledge that's the fruit of that reflection. If you do want to pursue Jane Austen's kind of happy love, ask yourself whether—up to this point in your life—you've been sticking to the path that leads where you want to go. Are your choices about men in line with what you really want? Or have you taken a detour that leads to any of the dead ends Jane Austen shows Lydia Bennet, Charlotte Lucas, or Maria Bertram ending up at?

Take your cue from Emma and Elizabeth, instead. Ask yourself: In my life up to this point, have I been distracted from the permanent happiness I really want by other enticements? Maybe because…

- I just wanted to have a boyfriend
- I was having fun, and I didn't want to have to start thinking about what came next
- I dissed him because my friends thought he was stupid; giving him the brush-off made me look cool
- He was obviously bad news…but really hot
- I felt stupid still being a virgin
- He was more street smart than anyone I'd ever known; a whole bigger world seemed to be opening up in front of me
- I didn't really like him very much, but all that attention sure was flattering
- I put off breaking up for too long because I was avoiding having to deal with his pain
- Being with him made me feel grown up, like a real woman
- My friends and family were pressuring me to find a relationship

- I hadn't had sex in so long, and I didn't want to feel completely out of things
- I didn't want to be lonely

Okay, I'll go first. Here's a choice in my past that I can look back on and say, *There's* where I got off the road to happy love—and from that point, things just got worse until I reversed course:

It's my freshman year in college, and things aren't going well. I'm having a hard time managing life more than seven hundred miles from everybody I care about—back in the days when you paid for long distance calls by the minute. I'm not making friends. Instead, I take up with C. (not his real initial), a grad student in philosophy. Because he seems to speak my language, while with the people in my dorm I feel like a creature from outer space. Because he calls me "princess," and treats me like one. Because I feel like I can't breathe if I don't have *somebody* I'm close to. But this relationship is going nowhere; nowhere good, anyway. C. and I disagree on everything really important, and I can't imagine his fitting into my real life—with my friends from back home, and my family—or into any life I want. And I'm not falling in love with him; I know that.

So I go home for Christmas, and while I'm there I see my friends and the guy I dated in high school. And he asks me whether I'm in love with C. I tell him airily that I don't think I'm really old enough to be seriously in love with anybody; the important thing is that C.—this brilliant older man—is in love with me. Somehow this rationalization makes me feel instantly more grown up, like I'm a really serious person, and gives the relationship a kind of glamour that helps me justify spending half a year of my life with a man I know I don't love, and don't look forward to a future with. A very Maria Bertram thing to do, I see now.

IF WE *REALLY* WANT TO BRING BACK JANE AUSTEN...

We won't fool ourselves into thinking love is something we can afford to play with or regard as a distracting hobby. We won't try keeping men safely in one compartment of our lives for entertainment, security, or comfort. We won't fritter away our chances for happiness by treating men and love casually. We'll take happiness seriously—seriously enough to make it the standard by which we judge all our choices about men. We won't aim for anything less than the kind of love Elizabeth found with Darcy.

CHAPTER TWO

DON'T FALL FOR A FALSE IDEA OF LOVE

OKAY, SO YOU'RE DETERMINED TO PURSUE YOUR Jane Austen happy ending. You're set to resist every other attractive temptation that could pull you off course—everything from

short-term pleasure, to...
a quick fix for loneliness, to...
feeling mature and sophisticated, to...
financial security, to...
impressing your friends...

and set your sights on happiness.

But wait a minute. Where's *love* in all this? We're used to thinking of "love," not "happiness," as the opposite of all the foolish and mercenary things women can do in regard to men. You marry for money, or else you marry for love—right? Yes, but...what exactly *is* love, according to Jane Austen? Do our ideas of a happy ending match hers? Or are they different—maybe in some subtle way that keeps us from ever reaching what Elizabeth finds with Mr. Darcy?

When we see what Jane Austen means by "permanent happiness," we can't help agreeing with her. We see Elizabeth with Darcy, Emma with Mr. Knightley, Anne Elliott with Captain Wentworth, and we want what they have. That's love, obviously. That's the happiness we're looking for.

But would Jane Austen recognize everything that *we* typically think of as "love" as the real thing?

As a matter of fact, Jane Austen is a fierce critic of a certain set of ideas about what love is. She set out quite deliberately to warn her readers against it. Jane saw one particular concept of love as a dangerous threat to women's happiness—a distraction even more seductive than money, or status, or sex.

Jane Austen versus the Romantic Sensibility

Whether we know it or not, we've inherited a whole set of notions about love that you can call Romantic with a capital R, as in "the Romantic Era" or "the Romantic Movement." And Jane Austen would disapprove. Now, nobody can deny that Jane Austen is a fan of romantic love *without* that capital R. Or, rather, she's more than a fan: she's drawn the most perfect pictures of exactly what it's like for a woman to be deeply in love with a man; to hope with every fiber of her being that he loves her, but fear he doesn't; and to come through the ordeal to love's ineffable delights. Jane Austen somehow manages to describe the indescribable. If you've ever been deeply and happily in love, just read *Pride and Prejudice*. You will instantly recognize the experience that Jane Austen somehow manages to create between Elizabeth and Darcy. It's as if she could compound endorphins out of ink and paper.

But Jane Austen was *no* fan of specifically Romantic notions about love, as we'll see. What are these Romantic notions? Well, they're hard for us today even to recognize. Not because they're difficult to find, but because they're everywhere. Romantic ideas have woven themselves into all our music, movies, and books. They've dominated our culture[1] for about two hundred years. By this point, it's hard for any of us to step outside of Romantic assumptions to see Romantic ideas objectively. Romanticism is that voice in the back of all our heads, pushing us to go for emotional intensity at all costs (intense misery, if we can't get intense bliss), encouraging us to mistake rebellion against convention for true love, and telling us that happiness is boring.

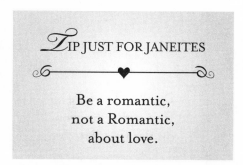

TIP JUST FOR JANEITES

Be a romantic,
not a Romantic,
about love.

But in Jane Austen's day, Romanticism and the "Cult of Sensibility" were fresh and new ideas.[2] In fact, they were so new that society hadn't yet fallen for them hook, line, and sinker. But those ideas went on to conquer the popular imagination. After they led to painful excesses in the aptly named Romantic Era, the Victorians tried to put a lid on the whole thing,[3] but Romantic ideas still weren't really seen through, or ever effectively answered. They were repressed, and they boiled away like lava under a thin crust, waiting to erupt just as soon as Victorian repression and hypocrisy should be relaxed. And in the twentieth century they broke out with a vengeance: "If it feels good, do it"…"Live fast, die young, and leave a good-looking corpse"…"Freedom's just another word for nothing left to lose"[4]….

The Cult of Sensibility

But we're getting ahead of ourselves here. Let's go back to Jane Austen's teenage years, when Romantic ideas were a raging fad—not, as they are today, a set of unquestioned axioms in the back of all our minds. She can help us disentangle the real delights of romantic love from the pseudo-thrills of Romantic sensibility—by teaching us to recognize (and laugh at) the capital-R Romanticism that's now woven into all our assumptions about love. Even before Jane Austen began writing what would become *Sense and Sensibility*, she was quite a sharp critic of the "cult of sensibility" that swept Europe in the second half of the eighteenth century. In her teens she wrote *Love and Friendship*, a spoof that makes hilarious fun of the "novel of sensibility," in which emotional intensity is set up as the be-all and end-all—to

TIP JUST FOR JANEITES

Don't fall in love
at first sight—or even
on the first date.

the extent that there's no room for honesty, responsibility, or the most basic common sense. Laura, the heroine of *Love and Friendship*, admits that her Romantic "sensibility too tremblingly alive to every affliction of my Friends and particularly to every affliction of my own," is her "only fault, if a fault it could be called." Really, Laura is proud of herself for allowing her life to be governed by intense emotions at the expense of common sense and even common decency. She falls in love in the approved Romantic manner, at first sight: "No sooner did I first behold him, than I felt that on him the happiness or Misery of my future Life must depend."

The object of this instant passion is Edward, whose "noble Manliness" is demonstrated by his spurning the girl his father wants him to marry: "No never exclaimed I. Lady Dorothea is lovely and Engaging; I prefer no woman to her; but know, Sir, that I scorn to marry her in compliance with your wishes. No! Never shall it be said that I obliged my Father." Edward's father is unimpressed with this reasoning: "Where Edward in the name of wonder (said he) did you pick up this unmeaning Gibberish? You have been studying Novels I expect."

Laura and Edward's "sensibility" makes them superior in their own eyes to unRomantic people—"that inferior order of Beings with regard to Delicate feelings, tender Sentiments, and refined Sensibility," who stupidly concern themselves with such pedestrian questions as how to have enough money to live on.[5] Their Romantic sensibilities make them keenly alive to their own refined feelings. To other people's feelings? Not so much. If other people's sensibilities don't entirely coincide with their own, why should they pretend to care? That would be hypocrisy, good manners, an inauthentic expression of something they don't really feel—everything they despise.

Laura and Edward are forced by financial difficulties to move in with Sophia and Augustus, an equally Romantic couple. The four of them are perfectly happy together, spending their time "in mutual Protestations of Friendship, and in vows of unalterable Love"—until Augustus is hauled off

Choose Your Entertainment Carefully—and Notice What It's Doing to You

ane Austen characters get themselves into
rible messes because of the books they read.
or Catherine Morland in *Northanger Abbey* is
aid she's lost Henry Tilney when he finds
t she's been speculating that his father
rdered his mother, or locked her up, just
e the villains in the Gothic novels that she's
licted to. In *Sanditon*, Sir Edward Denham
somehow managed to take the rapist in
hardson's *Clarissa* as a role model and is
nning his own future career of abduction
ordingly.[6]
And Anne Elliot, the most nearly Romantic
ane Austen's happy heroines,[7] warns against
rindulgence in certain kinds of Romantic
ding. She's been listening to the
rtbroken Captain Benwick as he quotes
on and Scott's "various lines which imaged
roken heart, or a mind destroyed by
tchedness." Worried about the young man,
ne ventures "to hope that he did not always
d only poetry; and to say, that she thought
as the misfortune of poetry, to be seldom
ly enjoyed by those who enjoyed it
npletely; and that the strong feelings which
ne could estimate it truly, were the very
ings which ought to taste it sparingly."
The idea that some kinds of entertainment
't be "safely enjoyed" doesn't jibe very well
 our modern attitudes. But notice that
e Austen is not arguing for book-banning
loing the Victorian matron act here, trying
rotect a young girl's innocent ears from
ghty stories. She's talking about the effect
.omantic poetry on a grown man, whom an
 more mature woman—"feeling in herself
right of seniority of mind"—is advising to
cise responsible judgment about his own
ntal health. If Captain Benwick, already

heartbroken and deeply discouraged, spends
his days reading poems about love and agony,
he's not taking care of himself, and he's likely
to end up dangerously depressed.

The poetry that's exacerbating Captain
Benwick's heartbreak isn't much read now; but
we absolutely do hear what Anne Elliot calls
"impassioned descriptions of hopeless agony"
every day, no matter what radio station we've
got the car stereo tuned to. Rihanna tells
Eminem, "Just gonna stand there and watch
me burn, But that's alright because I like the
way it hurts...." Adele lets the pain flow:
"Sometimes it lasts in love but sometimes it
hurts instead." Kenny Rogers sings, "This
time the hurtin' won't heal." Or k.d. lang lets
us know, "But all I've ever learned from love,
Was how to shoot somebody who outdrew ya."[8]

The songs and stories that we immerse
ourselves in *do* create expectations that we
carry with us back into our actual lives. Both
fiction and poetry or music, in their different
ways, draw us in by a certain attractiveness
that they cast over their subject matter, even
when that subject matter is in itself horribly
painful. A fantastic movie or a great novel can
make any kind of suffering—unrequited love,
grinding poverty, even child abuse, psychosis,
and suicidal depression—interesting and even
somehow more appealing than they are in real
life. Okay, so moviegoers didn't rush off to
become schizophrenic because they loved *A
Beautiful Mind*, or walk out of *Good Will Hunting*
seriously regretting their own comparatively
boring, abuse-free childhoods. But how
many of us were nudged just a notch or two
over from ordinary adolescent angst toward
actual depression by *The Bell Jar* or *Girl,
Interrupted*?

to debtors' prison. Naturally his wife's exquisite feelings make it too painful for her to visit him there.

Laura and Sophia are taken in by a cousin whose generosity they repay by persuading his daughter to reject the man her father approves of: "They said he was Sensible, well-informed, and Agreeable; we did not pretend to Judge of such trifles, but as we were convinced he had no soul, that he had never read the Sorrows of Werther, & that his hair bore not the slightest resemblance to Auburn, we were certain Janetta could feel no affection for him, or at least that she ought to feel none."

Under Laura and Sophia's influence, Janetta soon learns "a proper confidence in her own opinion, & a suitable contempt of her father's." Her new Romantic role models persuade her that she's really in love with an Army captain who's never given her a thought, but who's naturally delighted at the chance to elope with an heiress. Janetta's boringly unRomantic father points out that he's "an unprincipled Fortune-hunter."

Love and Friendship is a scream, with Laura and Sophia fainting "Alternately on a Sofa" and rapturously recognizing long-lost grandfathers and cousins at the drop of a hat. It's all very funny. But it's a bit of a shock, too. Here's Jane Austen, the creator of Elizabeth and Darcy—siding against Romantic love, making it look ridiculous and cheap.

Liberation, Authenticity, Intensity

We've seen the same plot in a hundred movies. Again and again—think *Grease, Moonstruck, Dirty Dancing, Say Anything, Titanic, How Stella Got Her Groove Back*, or the Molly Ringwald character in *The Breakfast Club*[9]— we've rooted for the girl who falls in love, if not exactly at first sight, then close to it, with someone totally unsuitable from the point of view of her parents, or the advice of too-conventional friends, or (here's a modern twist) in comparison to her current safe, boring husband or boyfriend. Our Romantic heroine gains the self-confidence to break away from the well-meaning but not-really-right-for-her plans that other people have for her and follow her own heart. At the end she's not just happy in love—she's freer, more authentically herself. She's found a life that's more intensely real than the one she broke away from. Even Disney animation uses the same plot. Sleeping Beauty disobeys her fairy godmothers' careful advice, goes out into the woods, and falls in love with a stranger. The Little Mermaid defies her father, breaks the rules, and finds true love and the kind of life she wants for herself in an alien world.

But Jane Austen portrays flouting convention "for love" as ugly and really stupid. She's not on the side of the coura-geous young people who defy everybody's advice and expec-

TIP JUST FOR JANEITES

Drama is not the same thing as love.

tations to find their own destiny. In Jane Austen's parody of the Romantic plot, the defiant young lovers are selfish and disastrously foolish. They trample other people's feelings and indulge their own in the most self-defeating way. Their kind of Romantic love is not really very loving. And it most definitely doesn't produce anything that we'd call happiness. Laura, Sophia, Augustus, and Edward seem quite satisfied to turn their lives into train wrecks—just so long as they can congratulate themselves that their Romantic feelings make them superior to the rest of us. The young Jane Austen was not impressed.

And doesn't she have a point? Forget the movies for a minute and think about real life. Say one of your friends gets involved with a man who's obvi-ously wrong for her from a conventional point of view—maybe he's much younger or much older, an obvious rich playboy or else without a real job or any prospect of one, completely outclassed by her education and accom-plishments. Are you instantly sure she's going to be happy? For long? As she raves about how he's loosening up her inhibitions, are you cheering her on 100 percent—or is there a sense of impending doom in the back of your mind? She keeps telling you, "He's so good for me." But are you sure she's right?

A woman can throw caution to the winds and "get her groove back" in a relationship with a man who, wiser heads would advise, is completely unsuitable for her. But all too often it turns out that there's some downside to the relationship that she's not able to see in the first glow of excitement.[10] Sometimes these things work out, but a lot of the time they crash and burn. As you listen to your friend in the first raptures of this kind of love, it's not unreasonable to think you may eventually be called on to help sort through the wreckage. Life isn't a movie, much less a Disney fairy tale. If you ignore all the sensible but boring advice, wander out into the forest, and meet an attractive stranger, you can't be sure he'll turn out to be a prince.

But wait a minute here. Is the creator of Elizabeth and Darcy less romantic than we are? Is Jane Austen on the side of the stodgy parents and boring husbands? Is she, disappointingly, of the it's-just-as-easy-to fall-in-love-with-a-rich-man-as-a-poor-one school of thought? Was Jane Austen a cynic about love?

Far from it! But she didn't confuse true love with rebellion against your parents, rejection of convention, or selfishness. She could tell the difference between finding the right man and "finding yourself." She knew that falling in love isn't about being struck on first sight with the irrational conviction that some random stranger is the man on whom "the happiness or Misery of my future Life must depend." She could tell the difference between the pursuit of emotional intensity at all costs and the pursuit of happiness. Jane Austen saw clearly that Romantic love in the unhealthy sense is just another blind alley—like money or the desire to be desired—leading away from happiness in love. Only it's even more seductive.

Capital-R Romantic love is way too easy to confuse with the real thing. Real love *is* truly liberating. It is full of emotional intensity. And it's natural that love will be part of a process of growing up into greater independence and your own mature identity. If those things resonate with you, don't think that Jane Austen didn't understand what you feel…or that her ideas about love are too tame for you…or that what she's offering is an anemic version of the red-blooded

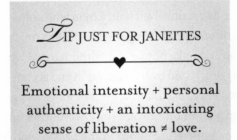

reality you're looking for. Her rejection of the Romantic template for love is *not* a rejection of the intensity of romantic love,[11] the way it makes you feel free, or the new start it gives you. It's not a rejection of personal authenticity, either. It's simply a rejection of the way the Romantic Cult of Sensibility fetishized those things, made them ends in themselves, and seduced countless numbers of real live human beings into totally unnecessary misery.

Charlotte Brontë Indicts Jane Austen

Speaking of totally unnecessary misery, let's take a minute with the Brontë sisters, authors of *Jane Eyre* and *Wuthering Heights*. Why drag them into this? Because Charlotte and Emily Brontë are a couple of nineteenth-century novelists who provide a perfect contrast with Jane Austen's attitude toward love. They're ardent practitioners and enthusiastic connoisseurs of the Romantic idea of love that Jane Austen was trying to get her readers to laugh at. If you put Emily's *Wuthering Heights* and Charlotte's snarky comments about the Jane Austen novels together, they pretty much sum up the anti-Jane Austen, capital-R Romantic position on love. The Brontë indictment of Jane Austen is the very same objection that we, unconscious heirs of Romanticism that we are, can't help feeling at least a little bit once we see how Jane Austen expected us to get a grip on our distracting Romantic impulses and reprogram our romantic GPS to aim for happiness.

Here's Charlotte Brontë on Jane Austen:

> Anything like warmth or enthusiasm, anything energetic, poignant, heartfelt, is utterly out of place.... She ruffles her reader by nothing vehement, disturbs him with nothing profound. The passions are perfectly unknown to her: she rejects even a speaking acquaintance with that stormy sisterhood.... [W]hat throbs fast and full, though hidden, what the blood rushes through, what is the unseen seat of life and the sentient target of death—this Miss Austen ignores.

In other words, Jane Austen is not intense enough for us true flesh-and-blood women. She floats on the surface above real, deep, throbbing, all-compelling passion, which she's too superficial even to understand.

And here's Jane Austen's answer to Charlotte Brontë:

> I understand you.—You do not suppose that I have ever felt much.... If you can think me capable of ever feeling—surely you must believe that I have suffered now.... The composure of mind with which I have brought myself at present to consider the matter, the consolation that I have been willing to admit, have been the effect of constant and painful exertion....

Okay, so that's not literally Jane Austen's answer to Charlotte Brontë, who hadn't yet turned two years old when Jane Austen died! I'm cheating. It's actually Elinor Dashwood in *Sense and Sensibility*, talking to her sister Marianne.[12] It is, however, Jane Austen's answer to the very accusation that Charlotte Brontë would one day hurl at her.

But how could Jane Austen anticipate Charlotte Brontë's criticism, and have Elinor answer it? How could she know that anyone would think the kind of love her heroines find is completely superficial—just a negative thing, a lack of passion? How anticipate that years after her death a Charlotte Brontë would come along and claim that she, Jane Austen, exhibited a total and embarrassing ignorance of the intense heights and depths of real love? Jane Austen knew precisely the case she had to answer because Charlotte Brontë was speaking out of the spirit of Romanticism, which was already alive and well in Jane Austen's day.

And which, unfortunately, keeps on giving two hundred years later—unfortunately, because the whole thing is a kind of bait and switch. Here's the bait: At the beginning, Romanticism is all frothy promises of certain, total bliss if you will just throw off all restraints. Love will hit you like a thunderbolt. It requires no effort on your part—certainly not the effort of asking whether you and the man you're suddenly enamored of are at all "likely to be necessary to each other's ultimate comfort." Romantic love promises instant liberation, authenticity, and emotional intensity. And then, once you have liberated yourself from convention, from the standards your parents taught you and the opinions of your friends, from every practical concern, you get the emotional intensity all right. But—surprise!—it's intense emotional pain.

"Be with me always—take any form—drive me mad! only do not leave me in this abyss, where I cannot find you! Oh God! it is unutterable!" That's the *cri de coeur* of the Romantic lover, straight from Emily Brontë's *Wuthering Heights*. Sooner or later true Romantics find out that their kind of love fails to deliver on the effortless bliss it promises. Do they, then, reconsider their premises? Does it occur to them that those unRomantic people whose advice they scorned might know something about love after all? Of course not! Here's the switch. Their agony is proof that they—and only they—are experiencing authentic love. To true Romantics, anyone who hasn't suffered as they have doesn't know what it is to love. Which, to Jane Austen, made it perfectly clear that the Romantic illusion is less about love than it is about "distinction" and "importance"—about being more "interesting" than other people.

Women in Real Love (and Real Pain)

Love as Jane Austen understood it isn't measured by the intensity of our agony. Jane Austen heroines feel all the emotions from giddy delight to terrible pain. She doesn't think the emotional roller coaster is the main point of love, but that doesn't mean she doesn't understand love's ability to put us through the ringer. Jane Austen, in fact, excels in painting realistic pictures of love's painful moments. Her true-to-life accounts aren't much like the Brontës' stormy dramas. But for all their *sturm und drang*, the Brontës never come so close as Jane Austen to what it's really like for most of us (who aren't gypsies reared on windblown heaths, or governesses wooed by men with insane wives locked in their attics) to be unhappy in love.

Jane Austen gives us women whose unhappiness in love is too close to real life for comfort. There's Fanny Price in *Mansfield Park*, hopelessly in love with a man to whom she's romantically invisible. She's Edmund's timid little cousin, sharing all his tastes, interests, and beliefs. For Fanny, growing up means realizing she's always loved Edmund. But for Edmund, Fanny is just part of the background: his cherished friend and confidante, to be sure, but not really a woman to him.

It's not until Edmund meets Mary Crawford that he begins to think of love and marriage. Mary is sparkling, fashionable, "fearless," and exciting to talk to; she's everything that Fanny isn't—and everything that Edmund isn't, either. Fanny shares Edmund's steady temperament, his quiet but deep enjoyment of natural beauty, his ramrod-straight principles. Things between Edmund and Mary Crawford never go smoothly, even from the beginning. He's continually shocked to learn how lightly she takes the things he's serious about; she's forever frustrated by his stick-in-the-mud attitudes. But until Edmund is forced to see how very little Mary cares about the things that matter most to him, it never, ever occurs to him to think of Fanny as a woman he could love.

If Fanny were a twenty-first-century teenager, she'd go through the first forty-six chapters of *Mansfield Park* humming along to Taylor Swift: "Why can't you see / You belong with me?"[13]

Fanny is ecstatic when Edmund gives her a gold chain to wear to her first ball. It's just a cousinly gesture on his part, and she does her best to hide her rapture, but still he finds her emotions a bit much.[14] This is the excruciating nature of unrequited love. Feelings that would be welcome, delightful, fascinating to a man who felt the same as we do are at best embarrassing to one who doesn't. Fanny's pain is of a distinctly unglamorous sort, and it may be trite[15] compared with the drama the Brontës cook up. But it's a very real kind of heartbreak that women are actually suffering all the time—thousands at this very moment, I have no doubt, in hundreds of high school classrooms, college dorms, and offices—even if that pain isn't dignified by perfectly timed thunderclaps and picturesque decaying architecture.

Anne Elliot's situation is no less realistic, and no less painful, than Fanny Price's. While Fanny is a teenage girl in love for the first time, Anne is a mature woman. In fact, Anne is almost past the age when a woman can (well, could then) reasonably hope to find happiness in love. She's long since come to realize that one fatal decision she made at the age of nineteen lost her the man she loved and ruined her happiness, very likely forever. When Anne first met him, Frederick Wentworth brought into her life all the things that she was missing at home. Anne's mother had died, and her father and older sister were cold fish with no affection or respect for Anne; their vanity and selfishness made it impossible for them to see any value in a person so different from themselves.

Wentworth was full of energy and warmth, with an open and generous temper, the determination to make his way in the world, and the sterling qualities to make all his ambitions realities. But her father was appalled that a penurious young naval officer should aspire to the hand of a baronet's daughter. And Anne's only real friend, Lady Russell, was against the match, too. She was sure that a long engagement to a man with no solid prospects wasn't a good idea for her young friend. Since Lady Russell was the one person Anne had to trust and look up to, she allowed herself to be persuaded that breaking her engagement to Captain Wentworth was the right thing to do. And that decision blighted Anne's life. She broke the engagement only out of a sense of duty, against the dear-

TIP JUST FOR JANEITES

The balance of power between the sexes shifts with the passage of time.

est wish of her heart—and only because she was persuaded that it would be a drag on Wentworth's prospects, that ending it would be "for his advantage." But Wentworth couldn't see it that way, and he parted from Anne in bitterness.

Anne's "what I did for love"-style choice was painful at the time. But it was only over the next seven years that she truly came to understand what she had done. She never met another man she could love. Anne seemed to be forever trapped in the old prison cell that she'd retreated back into, after that brief interval of warmth and sunshine with Wentworth.

And then he comes back into her life. All his ambitions have been realized. His courage, resourcefulness, and hard work have gained him advancement and wealth. But he's no longer interested in Anne. They're thrown together by accident, and he meets her almost as a stranger—as less than a stranger, in fact, "for they could never become acquainted."

While Wentworth meets her with cold indifference, Anne loves him more intensely than ever. "No: the years which had destroyed her youth and bloom had only given him a more glowing, manly, open look, in no respect lessening his personal advantages. She had seen the same Frederick Wentworth." Like any woman deeply in love, Anne suffers a hyper-awareness of the man's physical presence. The narration of the first scene in which Wentworth comes close enough to touch her after eight years apart is a masterpiece of psychological realism.[16]

Gradually Anne gets used to the new footing she's on with Wentworth. The painful embarrassment of the first few meetings subsides, along with the last precious hopes that he might care for her still, or ever again. He is cold and distant to Anne, but open, enthusiastic, and engaging with everyone else. Wentworth's behavior soon creates speculation about his possible interest in two young women in Anne's circle. For the Musgrove girls, the world is full of new enjoyments and possibilities opening up. And Anne's world seems to be contracting. She's more clearly than ever the quietly fading not-so-young woman whom love has passed by.

Anne's situation, like Fanny's, is all too realistic. It's "the fate," as they said in Jane Austen's day, of countless thousands of real live women—some significant multiple of however many of us have ever wrought ourselves up to Brontë-scale Romantic agony—to wake up too late to the realization that the balance of power between the sexes has shifted over time. A man can easily seem even more attractive as he ages into his thirties and forties and beyond. His "personal advantages" can be increased by the passage of the same years that sap a woman's "youth and bloom." Pace Harold and Maude (and the real-life Demi Moore), not very many women find themselves courted by men decades younger than they are.

But Anne's heartbreak isn't just about how her chance for happy love has faded with her youth. Everything she sees in Wentworth now and learns about the life he's made for himself makes it much worse. Not only does she still love him as much as ever, now she understands so much better what marrying him would have meant for her. It would have been a real liberation.

Not just from a humdrum existence into passion, or from the constraints of life in her father's house to adult independence. But from the prospect of spending the rest of her life with people so consumed by their own snobbery and selfishness that they barely acknowledge her existence—into real love, and life as a valued member of a circle of warm and generous friends. Anne's pain, like Fanny's, is real, and worthy of our respect.

Love Is a Happy Thing

If we can't help asking: "But is their suffering as *intense* as what a Brontë heroine feels?" well, that's just evidence that Romantic sensibility clings to the insides of our minds like cobwebs to the corners of an unswept attic. After all, we think, Anne's broken heart makes her suffer nothing worse than a bit of depression.[17] And even more damning, from the Romantic point of view, she can still "struggle against" it. If Anne were really in love, wouldn't she be forced to surrender to hopeless agony? In our more Romantic moments, we can't help thinking that, after all, love is real love only to the degree that, as Nicolas Cage says in *Moonstruck*, "it ruins everything. It breaks your heart. It makes things a mess."[18] The more we hurt, the more we know we're really in love. Right?

Wrong. Jane Austen's answer to these questions is *No*. Her heroines in pursuit of happiness admittedly don't suffer as much as the Brontës and their ilk. When Jane Austen describes Elinor Dashwood as "suffering almost as much, certainly with less self-provocation and greater fortitude" than her equally heartbroken (but much more Romantic) sister Marianne, she's conceding that Elinor's pain *is* a degree less.

> ### 𝒯IP JUST FOR JANEITES
>
> Despite what we learned from Cher and Nicolas Cage in *Moonstruck*, you can't tell whether it's love or not by how much it hurts.

Elinor hurts less than Marianne, but it's not because she loves less. It's because of that "greater fortitude" in the face of suffering. UnRomantic Jane

Austen heroines don't wallow in heartbreak. Their struggle to get a firm grip on themselves, and on reality, gives them extraordinary dignity. It makes them less miserable—but not any less in love.

For Jane Austen, love is a happy thing. If it makes you miserable, something's gone badly wrong. Possibly just with your circumstances: accident and chance, not to mention the lack of enough money to live on, are bound to cause plenty of misery in this imperfect world. But quite often what makes women unhappy in love in Jane Austen novels is something wrong with the man they love—or with themselves. When her heroines have to bear up with "fortitude" through heartbreak, they're sometimes coming to terms with the fact that the man they love has failed them. If only Edmund weren't dazzled by Mary Crawford…if only Captain Wentworth had come back to Anne once he could afford to marry…if only Edward hadn't persuaded Elinor to love him when he was already secretly engaged to Lucy Steele. But sometimes Jane Austen's heroines realize that *they're* the ones who've made a terrible mistake.

And they're never more admirable than when they're seeing their own mistakes clearly and undertaking the painful process of setting them right. They're also never more likely to be headed in the direction of their happy endings. There's nothing less like the hopeless agony of the Brontë heroine than the fortitude that an Emma Woodhouse, say, shows under the realization that she's put her own happiness at risk.[19] And there's nothing more classically Jane Austen.

If we want to emulate Jane Austen's heroines, we're going to have to learn to admire their ability to "struggle and endure" just as much as Brontë fans admire their heroines' Romantic self-flagellation. This is real growing up—not the Romantic counterfeit, where breaking away from your parents'

Tip Just for Janeites

Romantic heroines get their self-esteem from the intensity of their misery. Jane Austen heroines earn their dignity by exercising heroism in the face of heartbreak.

rules or your friends' standards feels like instant maturity. It's assuming responsibility for the kind of person you're going to become.

Jane Austen isn't trying to talk you out of real adventures. It's just that she believes in adventures in love, not in drama and narcissism. We have to decide whether those Romantic experiences are worth having—not to mention, worth having if, in pursuit of them, we end up missing the kind of happy love that Elizabeth finds with Darcy. Because remember, *of course* everybody wants to be happy. But only a few of us will pursue happy love as our real goal, ignoring all the shiny distractions.

Before Happiness Was Boring

We twenty-first-century women are in a better position to give up Romantic illusions and learn from Jane Austen than women have been in any generation since her own. We're more primed to see through this cult of selfishness masquerading as passion than at any time in the past two hundred years. For one thing, we know so much more about where Romanticism in love actually leads.

On the broader cultural front, we can look back on successive waves of Romantic illusion that ended in real pain. There was the original Romanticism, the Byrons and Shelleys breaking all the rules and leaving a trail of wrecked lives behind them. The Victorians cleaned up after the Romantics, and then successive waves of Romantic revolt broke out and were squelched by successive waves of reaction, all the way up to the mid-twentieth century.[20] The liberating 1960s and '70s were the definitive eruption of that volcano the Victorians were sitting on. After that party, an awful lot of people woke up in a trashed house with a splitting headache. If we're tired of ping-ponging back and forth between those two extremes, Jane Austen offers something entirely different. She's an emissary from the pre-Romantic world, from a time before happiness had become boring.

Living as we do in the long wake of Romanticism, we've spent all our lives liberated from the constraints the original Romantics chafed at. We've mostly already experienced the heady delights of Romantic-style love—and the hangover that inevitably follows. We've been able to pursue intensity, authenticity, and liberation in relationships to our hearts' content. Except our hearts aren't content. And happiness doesn't seem so boring anymore.

So we're ripe for Jane Austen's pitch against Romanticism and for happy love. On the other hand, actually learning to manage love the Jane Austen way is going to be harder in our post-Romantic era than it looks. To understand love as Jane Austen heroines experience it, in all its firm realism, sparkle, exhilaration, and solid hope of happiness, we have to shake free of the Romantic trap. In aid of that goal, Jane Austen wrote a whole novel giving us a flesh-and-blood heroine[21] who misses her happy ending because she approaches love the Romantic way—paired with another heroine who does manage to find happy love à la Jane Austen. *Sense and Sensibility* is a blow-by-blow account of the serious havoc that capital-R Romantic love can wreak in a woman's life, plus a template for successful unRomantic romantic love. It's the subject of the next chapter.

𝒜DOPT AN AUSTEN ATTITUDE:

Take a minute for Jane Austen-style "serious reflection." How do you picture the kind of love you're looking for?

- Are you pursuing happy love, or are you in the market for drama?
- Are you waiting for a relationship to liberate you? (Why do you feel trapped and stifled, and what can *you* do about it?)
- Are you looking for a man to supply the authenticity that's missing from your life?
- Looking back: If you see that you've been going for drama, intensity, or instant liberation instead of happy love, what can you do differently next time?
- Looking ahead: If your picture of what you want from a man is tinged with Romantic illusion—too close to Laura and Sophia's drama for comfort—are you ready to move that

picture a little closer to Elizabeth and Darcy, or Emma and Mr. Knightley?

*W*HAT WOULD JANE DO?

🌸 She wouldn't wait for love to grow up. (Think about it: the right guy is more likely to fall for a woman who's already a grownup.)

*I*F WE *REALLY* WANT TO BRING BACK JANE AUSTEN . . .

🌸 We'll undertake a serious program for de-Romanticizing our understanding of love. Turn the page to the next chapter. *Sense and Sensibility* is the playbook.

CHAPTER THREE

DON'T BE
A TRAGIC HEROINE

LAURA, SOPHIA, AND THE OTHER NARCISSISTS IN *Love and Friendship* are cartoons. But in *Sense and Sensibility*, Jane Austen gives us a character we can actually believe in and care about who has her head turned by the very same fad for Romantic sensibility.[1] With disastrous results. *Sense and Sensibility* is a detailed case study of exactly what happens when a warm-blooded young woman lets capital-R Romantic notions distract her from the pursuit of happiness.

Jane Austen's Only Tragic Heroine?

Poor Marianne Dashwood is in a tragic class of her own: the only Jane Austen heroine who doesn't find her happy ending. Or, at least, not the happy ending she originally wanted.

Marianne is naturally enthusiastic and emotional. She can't love or hate by halves. The things Marianne loves—music, poetry about nature, Romantic landscapes—all inspire her to raptures. The things she doesn't care

37

for—card games, gossipy middle-aged women, boring conversations about married friends' children, men so obviously past the vigor of youth that they wear flannel waistcoats—Marianne can hardly stand to be polite about.

Marianne's sister Elinor is all good sense to Marianne's enthusiastic sensibility.[2] Elinor doesn't expect Marianne to pick up "beliefs" or "sentiments in serious matters" from their neighbors. But she does think her sister should engage in a little more "general civility"—in other words, back down from the Romantic cult of authenticity at least enough to treat other people with attention and respect, even people whose ideas and feelings don't come up to Marianne's high standards.[3]

The sisters differ in more than temperament. Their beliefs about life also differ.[4] And so do their imaginings about what it has in store for them. As a result, they're really, actively pursuing very different goals in the choices they make (though if you asked them, no doubt they'd both say, like all of us, that *of course* they want to be happy).

Marianne is capable of rapturously appreciating the sublime and the beautiful in nature, music, literature, and art. She knows that Elinor appreciates those things too,[5] and so she can't understand why Elinor isn't embarrassed to be in love with Edward Ferrars, a man who doesn't seem to share those intense enjoyments:

> I could not be happy with a man whose taste did not in every point coincide with my own. He must enter into all my feelings; the same books, the same music must charm us both. Oh! mama, how spiritless, how tame was Edward's manner in reading to us last night! I felt for my sister most severely. Yet she bore it with so much composure, she seemed scarcely to notice it.

Of course, Marianne thinks this way partly just because she's so young.[6] But her ideas aren't simply the kind of thing every teenage girl since the beginning of time has believed. Some of Marianne's ideas are the latest capital-R Romantic notions about nature and love and personal authenticity. On top of adolescent hormones, Marianne also has Rousseau and Romantic Sensibility running around in her bloodstream addling her judgment. Hers is one of the first generations to grow up with the same

Romantic ideas that two centuries later we're still picking up from Hollywood and the radio.

Marianne expects so much from love that at sixteen and a half she despairs of finding a man she can have real feelings for: "Mama, the more I know of the world, the more am I convinced that I shall never see

TIP JUST FOR JANEITES

Wondering if he's "The One"? This state of mind can be fatal to the happiness that successful Jane Austen heroines aim for.

a man whom I can really love. I require so much!" But very soon—in a turn of the novel's plot that will astonish no one familiar with the lives of teenage girls—Marianne meets a man she's sure is "The One."

Marianne falls in love in the approved Romantic manner—if not exactly at first sight, then the very next day. Her first meeting with John Willoughby is a dramatic one. Seeing her fall and sprain her ankle, he catches her up in his arms and carries her into her house. She's impressed that he ignores propriety in his eagerness to get her home. And when she finds out that he's been known to dance from eight at night till four in the morning, and then get up the next day at eight to hunt, she thoroughly approves: "That is what a young man ought to be. Whatever be his pursuits, his eagerness in them should know no moderation, and leave him no sense of fatigue." (Ironically, we'll see later that Willoughby's eager, immoderate pursuit of another kind of pleasure has already set Marianne up for a broken heart.)

Willoughby comes to call the next morning, and he and Marianne get on like a house on fire. His "natural ardour of mind...roused and increased by the example of her own,"[7] is what recommends "him to her affection beyond everything else." Elinor teases Marianne that the two of them will run out of subjects to discuss by the third time they meet.[8] Her real worry, though, is that Marianne is rushing into emotional intimacy with a man she's just met. But all of Elinor's hints throughout the period of "increasing intimacy" with Willoughby fall on deaf ears. Marianne inevitably justifies her behavior by the Romantic touchstones: intensity, liberty, and authenticity.[9] Again and again she appeals from prudent convention to the higher court of her feelings.[10]

With Willoughby, Marianne is intensely, deliriously happy.[11] Love is everything that she has been looking forward to in her Romantic imagination and almost despaired of finding in real life. But it can't last. Just as in any Romantic love story, there comes a time when the lovers must part. Willoughby tells Marianne that Mrs. Smith is sending him away on business; he makes it clear that he can't expect to return any time soon. Marianne is devastated.[12] (Or she thinks she is. She won't find out what real grief and misery are until later.) She has a wretched night:

> Marianne would have thought herself very inexcusable, had she been able to sleep at all the first night after parting from Willoughby.... But the feelings which made such composure a disgrace, left her in no danger of incurring it. She was awake the whole night, and she wept the greatest part of it.

Marianne is following the Romantic script.

To the mystification of Marianne's family, no letters come for her from Willoughby. He stays away, and it's not clear when Marianne expects him back. Marianne has never actually told her family that they're engaged, and Elinor can't help worrying that maybe Willoughby isn't really serious about her sister. She presses their mother to ask Marianne about the status of the relationship. But Mrs. Dashwood's "romantic delicacy"[13] keeps her from asking Marianne any awkward questions.

Tip Just for Janeites

If you're looking forward to a broken heart, you're likely to end up with one.

Marianne eventually finds that she has only been playing at having a broken heart. She and Elinor travel to London, and Marianne assumes she'll see Willoughby there, but he avoids her. Marianne makes excuses for him at first. But soon she becomes agitated, then increasingly frantic, and finally "wholly dispirited, careless of her appearance...indifferent" to where she is and what she does. The crisis comes at a party where Marianne finally runs into Willoughby by accident. He's there with another woman. He meets Marianne with cold formality, making it clear that he has moved on. Apparently he no longer loves her, if he ever did.

The morning after the party, Marianne writes Willoughby a desperate letter asking what he can possibly have heard about her to justify such a change, or whether his behavior toward her all along was "intended only to deceive." His answer is "impudently cruel," claiming that he never meant to make Marianne think he loved her, that his "affections have long been engaged elsewhere," and that he expects to be married to the other woman in a few weeks.[14]

Elinor is shocked to learn that Marianne never was engaged to Willoughby. When she hears the inside story of the relationship—or at least Marianne's side of it—she's appalled by Willoughby's "hardened villainy," but also by the fact that Marianne offered him such "unsolicited proofs of tenderness, not warranted by anything preceding." And even now, when it has all turned out so badly, Marianne can't see why it was a bad idea:

> "I felt myself," she added, "to be as solemnly engaged to him, as if the strictest legal covenant had bound us to each other."
>
> "I can believe it," said Elinor; "but unfortunately he did not feel the same."

Willoughby's betrayal devastates Marianne, and she keeps trying desperately to blame it on some third person—preferably on the other woman and whatever "blackest arts" she may have employed to make Willoughby think ill of Marianne—rather than have to conclude that the man she loves has betrayed her. But none of it's any use. In the end Marianne can't help seeing that there's really no decent excuse for him to abandon her in this way.

Meanwhile we get some not-so-decent explanations for his behavior. First of all, it turns out that he's engaged to a very wealthy young woman. Willoughby has been living well above his means, and his debts

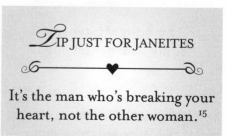

Tip JUST FOR JANEITES

It's the man who's breaking your heart, not the other woman.[15]

are now very pressing. His fiancée's money won't come to his rescue a minute too soon.

Another bit of information throws an even worse light on Willoughby's behavior toward Marianne. Colonel Brandon, the flannel waistcoat-wearing middle-aged fellow that Marianne is so sure is past real love that she can imagine his marrying only to provide a nurse for himself, tells Elinor the story of his young ward Eliza, who, it turns out, was seduced, impregnated, and abandoned by Willoughby just a few months before he met Marianne. At the very time that Willoughby was enjoying himself so intensely with Marianne,[16] he had left Eliza pregnant, "in a situation of the utmost distress, with no creditable home, no friends, ignorant of his address."

A Brontë Heroine in a Jane Austen Novel

This news about Willoughby's character makes it look like his intentions toward Marianne were predatory from the beginning. And seeing her love affair that way tips Marianne over into depression. Her mental health takes yet another blow when she finds out that Elinor has had her heart broken, too—because Elinor has handled the whole thing so much better than Marianne has.[17]

Both sisters have been treated very badly by the men they're in love with. Despite being engaged to Lucy Steele, Edward Ferrars has gotten close enough to Elinor to persuade her to fall in love with him. Elinor has as much right as Marianne to heartbreak, self-pity, and depression. But Elinor fights them, while Marianne surrenders unconditionally to "the stormy sisterhood."[18] Marianne treats it as a moral duty to feel things as intensely as she can. Meanwhile, Elinor is still stuck on those boring, old-fashioned moral duties—treating people with attention and

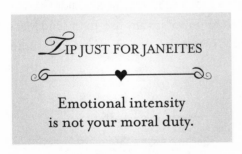

TIP JUST FOR JANEITES

Emotional intensity is not your moral duty.

kindness even if they're not her soul mates; keeping her own promises even if other people don't act honestly toward her; holding up even with a broken heart, so she can be strong enough to take care of her sister.

Even when Marianne finally has to admit that Elinor has really suffered, she's still not ready to abandon Romantic attitudes. Elinor's struggle to bear up under the same kind of pain just makes Marianne feel worse about herself. She begins to "fondly [flatter] herself" that she may fall "a sacrifice to an irresistible passion." And eventually Marianne does make herself dangerously ill. Her typical depression-induced lack of self-care (as the modern mental health professionals say) has a Romantic flavor to it.[19] Taking "delightful twilight walks" in the kind of landscape whose "wildness" is as close as Marianne—staying at a well-tended country estate—can get to the windswept heath that's the perfect setting for Romantic agony in *Wuthering Heights*, she comes home wet, fails to change, and catches a fever. At the low point of her surrender to "the stormy sisterhood," she lies in bed hallucinating and apparently "dying of a putrid fever"—a Brontë heroine in a Jane Austen novel.

Marianne follows the Romantic script for love until it almost kills her. The news that she's in serious danger gets out; John Willoughby hears about it, and he rushes to the house where she's staying, surprising Elinor in the middle of the night. Thus Elinor gets to hear the other inside story of the relationship between Marianne and Willoughby—from his point of view. It turns out to be pretty ugly. But not a case of such calculated wickedness as Marianne and her friends were guessing, once they knew how he had seduced and abandoned Eliza.

He Fooled Around and Fell in Love

Willoughby admits that he originally pursued Marianne with "no other intention, no other view in your acquaintance than to pass my time pleasantly."[20] He was in the habit of leading women on, all the while planning to marry for money.[21] At first it wasn't any different with Marianne. But despite his bad intentions, Willoughby did fall in love with Marianne. And he eventually talked himself into telling her so. But only after he had spent too long allowing himself "most improperly to put off, from day to day, the moment of doing it, from an unwillingness to enter into any engagement while my [financial] circumstances were so greatly embarrassed."

Tragedy intervened in "the very few hours" between Willoughby's resolution to finally declare his love to Marianne and his next opportunity to speak with her alone. His rich cousin Mrs. Smith, a rigidly moral old lady, found out about Eliza. Mrs. Smith threatened to disinherit him. Panicked, Willoughby decided to go back to his original plan to marry for money.

By the time he tells Elinor the whole story, Willoughby is sorry. Wealth with a bad-tempered wife he doesn't love[22] is not making him happy. He now regrets what he gave up by deserting Marianne.[23] And Elinor is glad to know that he wasn't simply using Marianne the whole time; he did come to care for her—he still does. But it's hard to imagine how Willoughby could have done more damage even if he'd been heartlessly calculating throughout.[24]

The UnRomantic Ending

Jane Austen gives Marianne's story an ending that's deliberately unRomantic. Marianne marries Colonel Brandon.

> Marianne Dashwood...was born to discover the falsehood of her own opinions, and to counteract, by her conduct, her most favourite maxims. She was born to overcome an affection formed so late in life as at seventeen, and with no sentiment superior to strong esteem and lively friendship, voluntarily to give her hand to another!—and *that* other, a man who had suffered no less than herself under the event of a former attachment, whom, two years before, she had considered too old to be married,—and who still sought the constitutional safeguard of a flannel waistcoat!

I've heard it said that "Jane Austen doesn't sell me" on the ending of *Sense and Sensibility*. That's a very common criticism of the novel. But as a matter of fact Jane Austen isn't *trying* to sell us on Marianne's marriage to Colonel Brandon in quite the way we may assume she is. She doesn't expect us to believe that Marianne will be as happy with Brandon as she would have been with Willoughby...that Brandon is really a better match for her...or that we ought to lower *our* expectations of love and marriage to the level of happiness that Marianne finds with Colonel Brandon.

How do we know Jane Austen isn't selling us that line? Because she makes sure that *that very interpretation* of Marianne's situation gets articulated in the book—by the Romantic Mrs. Dashwood, of all people. And then she has the wiser Elinor throw cold water on it. After Mrs. Dashwood knows that Willoughby has betrayed Marianne and that Colonel Brandon loves her, she talks herself into thinking that Colonel Brandon "is the very one to make your sister happy." Marianne's mother goes as far as to maintain, "I am very sure myself, that had Willoughby turned out as really amiable, as he has proved himself the contrary, Marianne would yet never have been so happy with *him,* as she will be with Colonel Brandon." If Mrs. Dashwood really believes the nonsense she's spouting here, she's delusional.

You don't have to be subject to Romantic illusions—"Is he The One?"—"finding your soul mate"—to see that some matches promise exquisite (small-r) romantic delights that others don't. Elinor's clear-eyed view of reality keeps her, unlike her Romantic mother,[25] from blinding herself to the obvious fact that Willoughby is, in Jane Austen's phrase, "exactly formed to engage Marianne's heart" in so many ways that Colonel Brandon really isn't. Whatever real happiness Marianne finds in her marriage to Colonel Brandon—and she does in the end love her husband[26]—it's not what she could have had with Willoughby.

And then, in the second-to-last paragraph of *Sense and Sensibility,* Jane Austen practically breaks *our* hearts by snatching away our only scrap of comfort about Marianne's heartbreak. Elinor has argued, pretty persuasively, that things would have gone wrong even if Willoughby had married Marianne. They would have been "always necessitous"; Willoughby's extravagance would have come into conflict with Marianne's honest impulse to economize; and he would have come to regret marrying her.[27]

There's a lot of sense in this. Willoughby is awfully spoiled. He's deeply in debt, and his only ideas for solving his money problems are of the I've-absolutely-got-to-win-the-lottery school of thought: it'll all be fixed when he inherits from Mrs. Smith; he'll marry a rich girl. He could easily become a total jerk under pressure. And marrying Marianne would bring on the pressure. He'd have large new expenses, no scheme left for acquiring any more income, and the increasing demands of his creditors to deal with. On top of all that he'd be living with a woman whose notions of how to handle money[28] are themselves a major new irritant. The picture Elinor paints is believable enough.[29]

But then Jane Austen totally explodes Elinor's reasonable argument. She lets us know that marriage to Marianne would *not* have made Willoughby "always poor" after all. Mrs. Smith eventually forgives him because of "his marriage with a woman of character." So we know that "had he behaved with honour towards Marianne, he might at once have been happy and rich."

Sometimes our hearts are broken. The man we love may not love us enough, or in the right way, or at the right time. Jane Austen didn't expect us to pretend that the love and happiness we've missed out on aren't really all that attractive, after all,[30] or that something less exciting is really more satisfying than what we wanted in the first place. If we have to give up what we want, to lose out on love—and sometimes, tragically, we do—she wanted us to do it with both eyes open, under no illusions about the real cause of our pain. In this case, she's made it crystal clear that Marianne's heartbreak has to be blamed on Willoughby's decision to desert her—and on whatever Marianne did that made Willoughby's bad choice more likely.

Hold on just a minute. Are we buying it? Isn't Marianne really a victim of her society? It's tempting for modern readers of *Sense and Sensibility* to shift the blame. We're likely to chalk the tragedy up not to Willoughby's and Marianne's choices, but to the social constraints they were living under. We can't help asking *why* exactly Marianne and Willoughby have to be permanently separated just because of a choice that's so easily reversible now. Today, we're sure, the protagonists would get it sorted out. There'd be some drama, pain, and humiliation for everyone involved,[31] but the lovers would be together in the end. At the end of the book, everybody knows that Willoughby loves Marianne and not his wife. What besides outmoded sexual taboos and an antiquated attitude toward divorce are keeping them apart? It's hard for us to relate. Probably the closest thing to this kind of unresolved triangle in modern times is the Diana–Prince Charles–Camilla Parker-Bowles debacle—which presumably resulted from the fact that the twentieth-century British royal family was still trying to live by nineteenth-century rules. These things don't happen to ordinary people any more.

How It Might Turn Out Today

But stop right there. If we're going to translate Marianne's life into modern circumstances, we have to be consistent. We can't change the rules in some places, but not in others. We have to think about what actually happens now, with *none* of those old taboos and antiquated rules in place, to young women who fall for men who set out to toy with them and then—sometimes it does happen—fall deeply in love with them after all. Do they typically end up living happily ever after together? Well, sometimes it must end that way, I guess. But I can't think of an example. I've known quite a few spoiled, Willoughby-style young men.[32] But I don't know even one who managed to settle down in his twenties, or, frankly, even to stay with one woman for more than a very few years.[33] And that's despite the fact that these guys can sometimes get really wild about a girl. It's just that the same circumstances that make it easier now for us to get *out* of a commitment that was a mistake also make it harder for us to *make* a commitment at all, in the first place. Marriage to the wrong person doesn't any more, today, necessarily separate you forever from the one you love. But then today there's a lot less reason to get married in the first place—to anybody, even a woman you're passionate about.

Too often, all the initial excitement and energy that comes with falling in love, and that in Jane Austen's day went into cementing a permanent relationship, is dissipated in the first excitement of becoming a couple, moving in together, and then the work of learning to live with another person. A man like Willoughby doesn't often stick to a woman through all that to the point of permanent commitment.

If we still lived under the social constraints Marianne and Willoughby did, there'd actually be less chance that guys like this would fritter away the energy and excitement that comes with falling in love. Men would be faced with the choice that Willoughby has to make: either man up and start taking the relationship really seriously, put it on the road to a permanent commitment, or else give the girl up. Willoughby makes the wrong decision, and Marianne's heart is broken. But at least—it has to be argued in favor of the Jane Austen-era arrangements—it's broken early rather than late, before she has wasted years on a man who's never going to commit to her.

And there's another tantalizing possibility. As Colonel Brandon says to Elinor, "Sometimes I thought your sister's influence might yet reclaim him." If Willoughby had made the *right* choice and honorably told Marianne he loved her, he would have been breaking his long habit of leading girls on without committing himself. He would have been doing something to climb out of the rut he was in, instead of digging himself in deeper. The choice for love and Marianne might have "fixed" his character in a different shape from the one it got "fixed" in by what actually happened.

We can't help thinking that Marianne's story wouldn't have to be a tragedy if she didn't have to live by the old rules and conventions. But you know what? That's just the same Romantic impulse talking, the one that messed up Marianne's life in the first place. The Romantic imperative to kick over every constraint has made big differences in courtship and marriage since Jane Austen's day. But it hasn't left women with the best possible choices.

Marianne's Mistakes

There's not much we can do about the world-historical transformation that Romanticism has made in negotiations between the sexes over the past two centuries. But we absolutely can learn from Marianne's story not to let Romantic thinking wreck our own individual lives. Romanticism leads Marianne astray in two different ways. She's got dangerous ideas about falling in love. And she's absorbed even more destructive ones about having your heart broken.

Before Marianne even meets Willoughby, she is looking to be swept away on a tide of intense emotion by, as we'd say, "The One"—the man who's a perfect emotional match for her. The only danger she can see is that she might miss that intensity. So when she meets him, all her care and prudence, such as they are, go into confirming that he's capable of rocking her world.[34]

It never occurs to Marianne to wonder whether the man she's convincing herself is "The One" is acting on the same principles as she is, or if he's bringing entirely different motives and desires to the experience. Marianne and Willoughby agree perfectly on the poetry of Scott, Cowper, and Pope. Where they don't agree, it turns out, is on what they want from each other.

Do we still act like this today? Yes, and often with even sadder results. An awful lot of our very first experiences of love in our teens are driven by Marianne's exact same mindset. Here's pediatrician Meg Meeker, writing about a teenage patient of hers:

> When Angela was sixteen, she was dating a guy she thought might be "The One" (girls often think in these terms). Tack was older than Angela and was getting ready to graduate from high school and go on to college. Since they had dated for a month, Angela felt that it was time to give Tack what he wanted.... He was thrilled, but before he got too excited, she told him there were limits.

Angela and Tack had oral sex, and she caught a painful case of herpes. "But even more painful to Angela was what Tack did. He not only told his friends that she had contracted herpes, he dubbed her 'Miss Herpes,' and she quickly became the girl no boy wanted. She was humiliated and became very depressed." Angela took a more direct route than Marianne toward "self-destruction," swallowing two bottles of Tylenol. Angela's is an extreme case, but no more extreme for our day than Marianne's is for hers.

And looking for "The One" isn't something we all grow out of after a first disastrous experiment in Romantic love—assuming we survive it.[35] A lot of grownup women are still waiting to be struck by love, like being struck by lightning.

But what's even more destructive to Marianne's happiness than her laser-like focus on finding Romantic love is her Romantic expectation of heartbreak. In a bizarre way, Marianne has been looking forward to having her heart broken just as much as she's been looking forward to being made deliriously happy by love in the first place. It's not that she ever suspects Willoughby is deceiving her—though he is. She's not afraid that he's going to desert her—though he will. Caught up in Romantic intensity, she never sees any of the danger signals that she ought to be able to pick up on in Willoughby's behavior.

When Willoughby unexpectedly tells Marianne he's leaving, gives no believable account of his reasons for going, and fails to commit himself to her before he leaves, none of this raises her suspicions. She never doubts his love. She simply turns on a dime into the *other* mode of Romantic love—self-dramatizing heartbreak. And odd as it may seem, the whole elaborate Romantic script for a broken heart[36] actually keeps her from noticing the real heartbreak she's now headed for. The Romantic ideal of a broken-hearted woman that she's living inside somehow insulates and distracts her from asking what Willoughby is really up to, why he left, and whether he really loves her the way she assumes he does.[37]

We do this, too. From that first issue of *Seventeen* magazine that pre-pares us to look forward to our "first kiss" and our "first time," we've trained ourselves to allow love a very different role in our lives from the one it plays in Elizabeth Bennet's life, or Anne Elliot's. We look forward to love as an experience, an intense but fleeting episode that will make us deliriously happy but then inevitably disappoint us. If we can tell ourselves that it's a rite of passage to have our hearts broken, then it won't be so bad. If it's normal, if it's what everybody lives through—or else they're hardly living—to be intoxicated by love's intensity and then crash to the ground, then it's all just part of the rich tapestry of human experience, and we're the better for our adventures. The more love hurts, the more we're sure we're really alive. So too many of us end up addicted to drama; we practically pursue ugliness and pain in our relationships.

Here's an example from my own days back in high school—a high water mark for Romanticism and drama for a lot of us. In the spring semester of my senior year, I was dating a guy who was then a college sophomore. I should have figured out he was seeing somebody else, but I never guessed.[38] Anyway, he eventually told me. He had broken up with the other girl and was all ready with an "it wasn't like kissing *you*" line when I, shocked and hurt, asked about what he'd done with her.

After my initial astonishment, I could feel the nature of our relationship changing, kaleidoscope-style, in the little space of time as I let him talk me around. Before he'd confessed, and despite the significant amount of drama there'd been between us (most of it my fault, I now think), I was still seeing our relationship as the kind of love story that has a happy ending. After he told me, I could have chosen to acknowledge that he'd spoiled it, and walk away—at least for the time being, long enough to see my way clear to a decision that didn't mean accepting a relationship that was diminished. But I didn't. When I let him kiss me again then, I could feel myself letting go of the happy-ending kind of story and embarking on a different kind of adventure—all about drama and intensity, and being worldly wise about getting hurt. I saw pretty clearly what I was doing, but I went ahead.

"Love" approached that way—conceptualized as an intense experience with two opposite sides, intoxicating enchantment inevitably followed by devastating pain—is just another distraction from Jane Austen's kind of happy love.

⚘ADOPT AN AUSTEN ATTITUDE:

🌹 Have you been running your relationships on Marianne's plan?

- Looking for "The One" man perfectly formed to plunge you into intoxicating Romantic love?
- Establishing instant intimacy before you understand his plans?
- When it all goes wrong, resigning yourself to "moments of precious, of invaluable misery"?

🌹 If you look back on past relationships, can you remember times when Romanticism has kept you from noticing what was really going on in your own life? Have you missed seeing his real feelings, motives, or intentions because you were so busy with your own?

🌹 The next time you meet a guy who interests you, ask yourself what you would do if you were Elinor, instead of Marianne.

- Or, even better, look around you now to see if there's anybody quite different from the men you've dated before, somebody you haven't noticed because you were really only looking to get your heart broken. If you want to be happy, you may want to give a very different kind of guy a second look.

What would Jane do?

- She'd reject Romanticism, root and branch.
- She'd tell you that the more you go through life looking for the kind of happiness at the end of *Pride and Prejudice*, the less likely you are to talk yourself into intense and painful adventures that will leave you with nothing but some more Romantic "experience."

If we *really* want to bring back Jane Austen . . .

- We'll pursue the kind of love that can make us happy, instead of letting the two-hundred-year-old Cult of Sensibility write the script for our lives.

$\mathscr{D}$ON'T LET CYNICISM STEAL YOUR HAPPY ENDING

WHAT'S THE NATURAL REACTION TO ROMANTIC illusion? Modern cynicism, of course. If you were the sixteen-year-old Angela in Dr. Meeker's story, waking up from your starry-eyed belief that your boyfriend was "The One" only to discover that he'd given you herpes and let all your friends know—wouldn't you be tempted to become a cynic? Cynicism about love, and bitterness about men, are totally understandable reactions when you find out that Romantic promises are illusions. Love gone wrong can hurt like hell. And if you've been hurt, it's natural to grow a hard shell to protect your heart.

As a matter of fact, you don't even have to wait for your heart to be broken to grow that protective shell. We're living in the wake of two hundred years of Romantic illusion—and the disillusionment that always comes with it. Cynicism is in the air. Barely teenaged girls who haven't yet *had* a boyfriend or even a hookup already have Facebook Walls full of "likes" for statuses along the lines of "My ex? Yeah, I'd still hit that. Only this time, it'd be with a baseball bat!" and "One relationship status they should have is 'getting played by _____.'" Just as we grow up expecting to be swept off our feet and have our hearts broken, we also look forward to being tough and flip and worldly wise about it all afterwards.

The Psychology of Female Disappointment

Now Jane Austen was not blind to men's shortcomings. She completely understood all the things that make women bitter about the opposite sex. And she often turned on her famous irony to expose men's faults—the typically masculine kind of selfishness, the way guys can be oblivious to other people's feelings. She could be quite severe. Just think about the happy love scene at the end of *Persuasion*. Captain Wentworth is telling Anne about the horrible suspense he suffered once he realized he still loved her—but he couldn't ask her if she still loved him because he was honor-bound to wait and see if his attentions to Louisa Musgrove had made Louisa expect to marry him. It was "dreadful," Wentworth tells Anne, "to be waiting so long in inaction." He never stops to think that he's complaining about *six weeks* of terrible suspense to a woman who waited for him for *seven years*.

Jane Austen totally got the psycho-dynamics of women's disappointment with men. Elizabeth Bennet does the same thing that Hephzibah Anderson did throughout her sex-and-the-city years; she entertains other women with witty commentary on the men who have subjected her to indignity and heartbreak. Turning her bitterness into a riff on men in general, Elizabeth tells her aunt,

> I have a very poor opinion of young men who live in Derbyshire; and their intimate friends who live in Hertfordshire are not much better. I am sick of them all. Thank Heaven! I am going to-morrow where I shall find a man who has not one agreeable quality, who has neither manner nor sense to recommend him. Stupid men are the only ones worth knowing, after all.[1]

And a little bit later, when her aunt invites her on a tour of the Lake District: "Adieu to disappointment and spleen. What are men to rocks and mountains?"

Elizabeth is speaking partly out of her disappointment with George Wickham.[2] But even more, she's wretched and angry about how Bingley has hurt her sister Jane. On that subject, Elizabeth can sound just like any of us in all-men-are-bastards mode. But Elizabeth's wise aunt, Mrs. Gardiner, who has already saved her from real heartbreak in the Wickham affair,[3] also warns her against talking about men in a way that "savours strongly of disappointment."

"Darkened, yet Fancying Itself Light"

Jane Austen sees something deeply unhealthy about the *they're-all-cads* way of talking about men. It may be justified. But as a mindset, a general attitude toward men and love, it's terribly counter-productive.

Why? How on earth can it hurt to make fun of men's flaws? They're real enough—and so is the pain they cause women. If we're on the receiving end of that misery, why should we deny ourselves the relief of turning it all into an acerbic commentary on the male sex? Why not slam men, be funny and cynical about love, amuse our friends, and make ourselves feel better?

Because, as Jane Austen shows, cynicism is a kind of blindness. When we let ourselves slip into cynicism, we think we're being clever. Maybe we used to have unrealistic hopes for love, or we stupidly trusted men. But now we know better—or so we think. But really, while we believe we're seeing through illusions that fool more naïve people, Jane Austen demonstrates that we're also seeing through some things that really *are* there. This is how she has Fanny Price describe Mary Crawford, the quintessentially cynical woman in Jane Austen's novels: "a mind led astray and bewildered, and without any suspicion of being so; darkened, yet fancying itself light." Mary loses the man she loves, and it's no accident. It's because of choices that she makes blindly, unaware that the things she sees through, and thus fails to take into account, are things of real importance to the man she's in love with.

Some of the things that we're seeing through if we're cynical about men and love are things that we have to be *able to see* in order to find happiness.

"Edward Seemed a Second Willoughby"

The most obvious way that cynicism blinds us is that if we're cynical about men in general, then we're painting with too broad a brush. We're over-generalizing from one jerk—or maybe a few we've known—to condemn all men. That's exactly what Marianne is doing when Jane Austen tells us that "Edward seemed a second Willoughby" to her. When Marianne finds out about Edward's secret engagement to Lucy, she immediately lumps him together with the perfidious Willoughby. Edward has hurt Elinor, so Marianne leaps to the conclusion that he's to blame in exactly the same way and to exactly the same degree as Willoughby is guilty for breaking her own heart. In reality, the two men could hardly be more different.

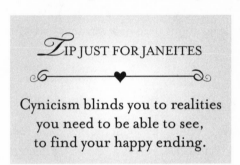

Tip JUST FOR JANEITES

Cynicism blinds you to realities you need to be able to see, to find your happy ending.

If you're going to be running your love life à la Jane Austen, it's absolutely crucial that you be able to tell the real cads from the decent guys who make understandable mistakes.[4] It's of enormous importance to our happiness for us to notice what the man we're dealing with at the moment is really like, compared to other men, and compared to what we're looking for. If you let a wholesale anti-man attitude take root in your way of thinking, then anything typically masculine that you notice about the next guy—that he's more interested in sex than talking about your relationship, or that the percentage of his weekend he wants to devote to achieving a clutter-free living room turns out to be zero—is liable to seem like evidence that here's yet another bad apple. Cynicism about men in general will only keep you from seeing the individual guys clearly enough to distinguish the good prospects from the heartbreakers.

Man-bashing diminishes *us.* That's what Hephzibah Anderson found out. Reducing the men she was sleeping with to figures of ridicule in the absurd stories she told her girl-friends ended by making her look small, too.

IP JUST FOR JANEITES

Man-bashing is beneath a Jane Austen heroine's dignity.

Jane Austen heroines inspire respect from men partly because they treat their "fellow-creatures"—Anne Elliot's gentle way of referring to the male sex—with respect, too. That's in the famous passage at the end of *Persuasion,* where Anne Elliot is arguing that women are more faithful than men. Notice that Anne is engaged in the *exact same kind* of observation of the shortcom-ings of men in general that also inspires our funny, bitter riffs on the jerks who have broken our hearts. Anne sees male deficiencies as clearly as we do. But she doesn't turn her observations into a sarcastic indictment of all men. "God forbid," she exclaims, "that I should undervalue the warm and faithful feelings of any of my fellow-creatures." She accords men respect, and the benefit of the doubt, as she herself expects to be respected.[5]

Respect for men as individuals and generous pity for their faults as a sex seems to come naturally to Jane Austen. Maybe that's because she grew up in a large family of mostly boys and, like Mary Eberstadt, another "sister outnumbered by brothers...knew unshakably that men were more to be pitied than feared."[6]

Or maybe it's because Jane Austen was consciously exercising a virtue that people in her day thought about a lot, but that has dropped off our radar screens—so much so that we no longer even have a word for it. Jane Austen and her contemporaries called it "candour." By which they meant something totally different from what the word means now. To us today, being "candid" means being frank and honest, telling the whole truth. But back then, "candid" described not the teller but the listener. That's why the Declaration of Independence says, "Let facts be submitted to a candid world." "Candour" in Jane Austen's day was the opposite of small-minded suspicion. It meant judging other people and their stories with sympathy, openness, and generosity. "The most Liberal & enlightened minds," the heroine of *The Watsons* tells us, "are always the most confiding."

Jane Austen's generous "candour" is of a piece with her eighteenth-century optimism and ambition.[7] She doesn't do illusion—about men, about women, or about love. But she's never *dis*illusioned or cynical either. Her heroines' generous "candour" keeps them from tarring all men with the same brush. That's a mistake crucial to avoid; you need to be able to see what individual guys are actually like if you want to end up with one who makes you happy.

Relationships with (and without) "Superior Affection" and "Confidence"

But cynicism is still important to avoid *after* you've picked a guy. Hostility to all things masculine can really poison a relationship once you're in it.[8] In Jane Austen's world, it's a sad marriage where there's not "superior affection" and superior "confidence" between husband and wife—where the woman loves her husband no more intensely than she does her friends, and confides in him no more freely than in them, where she continually complains about him behind his back and finds being with other people more really satisfying than being with him. Anne Elliot's sister Mary has that kind of marriage: "If there is any thing disagreeable going on, men are always sure to get out of it," she tells Anne, "and Charles is as bad as any of them. Very unfeeling!" Elizabeth Bennet's parents' marriage is another example.[9]

Modern women have raised man-bashing to an art form. If you hang out with a group of single friends, especially if they've reached the "Thought by now she'd have a man, Two car seats and a minivan"[10] stage—you've likely heard them complaining about what bastards the men they go out with are because they won't commit to a relationship. And if you hang out with a group of married friends, you've probably heard them spend their regular girls' nights out complaining about the men who *have* married them and *are* the fathers of their children.[11]

But man-bashing as an entrenched attitude is alien to the mindset of the Jane Austen heroine. You can't build up one of these grand indictments—

even just in your own head, let alone in regular gripe sessions with your girlfriends—without having it come out, sooner or later, in angry or sarcastic words aimed at the guy you've been complaining about. Harboring resentment in this way will set you up for an ugly scene that doesn't belong in a Jane Austen love story.[12] Given that Jane Austen and her heroines aren't blind to men's faults, given that they're extraordinarily intelligent and witty women, how do they steer clear of spoiling the confidence and affection they share with the men they love by making them objects of ridicule?

Their respect for men is grounded in the realization that they themselves have flaws, too. It's the generous attitude summed up by a quotation that's showing up on Facebook,[13] alongside those cynical "likes" about "my ex": "Be kind, for everyone you meet is fighting a great battle." Jane Austen's heroines nurture compassion and respect for the men in their lives as fellow-strugglers and fellow-sufferers, as people who, like themselves, are flawed human beings. The cure is what Jane Austen calls "self-knowledge."

This really works, I know from personal experience. I can make my mother, or somebody at work, or the woman who has different ideas from mine about how to run a fundraising project at my son's school—or my husband—sound like *the* most selfish, *the* most unreasonable, *the* most difficult person in the world. There's almost always some foundation of truth to my original complaint, but by the time I've got the whole case built up to perfection, there's a lot of my own creative resentment holding the structure together. And the fastest way for one of my grand mental cases for the prosecution against whomever I'm at odds with to come crumbling to the ground is for me to get a sudden glimpse of the fact that I, too, am being, selfish, unreasonable or difficult.

The quicker we are to resort to that cure—*never* blinding ourselves to men's real flaws, but meeting them with the same kind of generosity and compassion we hope other people will have for our own imperfections—the more likely we are to inspire a similar respect in the men we love. Anne Elliot, the gentlest of Jane Austen's heroines, a woman habituated to "serious reflection" on her own conduct, can hear Captain Wentworth's account of his dreadful six weeks of suspense without reminding him sarcastically of her seven years of patience. She's not doing the "women who love too much" thing, or desperately "keeping sweet" like one of Warren Jeffs' polygamous brides, taking all the blame on herself to avoid facing the fact that she's been mistreated. No, Anne judges "the right and the wrong" of her own and Wentworth's past choices "impartially" and honestly tells her lover that she believes she was in the right. But she doesn't feel the need to be nasty about it, or to build up an ugly picture of him. And, basking in her gentle love, it doesn't take Wentworth long to question—for the very first time in all those years—the self-righteous resentment that kept him from coming back to her as soon as he had begun to make the fortune that would allow them to marry.[14]

Why It's Wrong to "Settle"

Man-bashing is no part of the recipe for happy love. But letting cynicism spoil your happy ending isn't only about casting a jaundiced eye on the male sex. It's also about giving up on love.

It's no coincidence that the characters in Jane Austen's novels most subject to Romantic illusions are also the quickest to give up their hopes for real love—to be willing to "settle."[15] So it makes a strange kind of sense that after two centuries of the ebb and flow of Romanticism, modern women are reduced to the point where at least some of us are ready to give up on marriage for love. Bizarre but true, centuries after Western civilization adopted the love match and decades after the Sexual Revolution and Second Wave Feminism, arranged marriage is getting a second look. From jokes on The Simpsons,[16] to reality TV where women abdicate their choice of mate to their friends, families, or the audience,[17] to relationship advice premised on traditional matchmaking,[18] Americans seem to be taking arranged marriage more seriously today than at any time since the colonial era. And while it may be hard to see these cultural phenomena as anything but desperate cries for help, Lori Gottlieb has made a serious and widely discussed argument—in the pages of the Atlantic, no less—that women should give up on looking for true love and "settle" with a guy who will be a responsible husband and father, even if he doesn't really float their boat.[19]

Would the eminently practical and realistic Jane Austen agree? Absolutely not. She might have advised Lori Gottlieb to be less Romantic in the early stages of her dating career,[20] but Jane Austen would never get on board with cynical advice to marry a man you can't really love. Gottlieb is a classic case of "the romantic refinements of a young mind" giving way, with more experience of the world, to sad cynicism.

Jane Austen never lets her heroines settle for anything less than real love. Marianne's "strong esteem and lively friendship" for Colonel Brandon—which is at some elevation above Gottlieb's endorsement of looking in the "older, overweight, and bald category (which they all eventually become anyway)"—is the absolute bare minimum she lets any of her heroines marry on the strength of. And Jane Austen leaves us with mixed feelings about that marriage. And with entirely unmixed bad feelings about the choice of Charlotte Lucas, the Jane Austen character who settles for Mr. Collins "without thinking highly either of men or of matrimony." Jane Austen is solidly against "sacrific[ing] every better feeling to worldly advantage."

It's not that it never makes sense to marry a guy with less hair (or more waistline) than average. You can fall in love with a man who's fat or bald, but not if that's what you're mostly noticing about him. (When my cousin was worrying about whether she really wanted to marry a guy who was losing his hair, our grandmother said she shouldn't do it: "Your grandfather was bald when I married him, and I didn't even notice!" If my cousin had to ask the question, the answer was no—she obviously wasn't excited enough about the guy, or she'd have been thinking about something besides his bald spot.) Love Jane Austen-style may not hit you all at once with the force of a Romantic tidal wave. At the beginning, it can be as tentative as Elizabeth's "never had she so honestly felt that she could have loved him." But it has to be love, not calculation.[21]

We know what Jane Austen thought of marrying without love not just from the novels, but also from her own choices, and her real-life advice. She wrote to advise her niece on a marriage proposal, "I…entreat you not to commit yourself farther, & not to think of accepting him unless you really do like him. Anything is to be preferred or endured rather than marrying without Affection; and if his deficiencies of Manner &c &c strike you more than all his good qualities, if you continue to think strongly of them, give him up at once."[22] And Jane Austen herself once had thought she could marry without love, but quickly changed her mind.[23]

Austen herself wouldn't—and her heroines never do—marry without what she calls "disinterested attachment." Why? It's very simple. To "marry without affection" is "wicked." Yes, that's right. *Wicked.* As in, morally wrong. Not to mention "wretched" and "unpardonable." It's hard to think of anything else that Jane Austen has one of her heroines condemn with adjectives as strong as these—all of which Fanny Price applies to marrying without love. And it's not just Fanny, Jane Austen's most moral heroine, who sees marriage in the absence of affection as an issue of right and wrong. When Jane Bennet tries to defend Charlotte Lucas's decision to marry Mr. Collins, Elizabeth answers, "You shall not, for the sake of one individual, change the meaning of principle and integrity, nor endeavour to persuade yourself or me that selfishness is prudence, and insensibility of danger, security for happiness." Anne Elliot thinks just the same: "In marrying a man indifferent to me,[24] all risk would have been incurred, and all duty violated."[25]

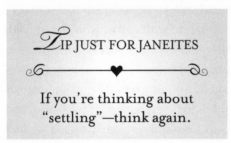

IP JUST FOR JANEITES

If you're thinking about "settling"—think again.

Why does Jane Austen condemn marrying without love in such very strong moral terms? Interestingly, for the same reason Megan McArdle, also at the *Atlantic*, called "the obvious critique" of Gottlieb's thesis: "There's, like, another human being involved in all this."[26] "Settling" isn't fair. It's a breach of integrity because it means being dishonest about the most intimate things to the person you ought to be closest to. He wouldn't want to marry you unless he honestly believed you had feelings for him. So if you're only settling for him, he's being "duped," as Jane Austen calls what Maria Bertram does to Mr. Rushworth. Settling is a kind of selling yourself—if not for money, then for security, or the chance to have a family.[27] It's a way of grabbing at happiness that's offensive to the "delicacy of mind" that Jane Austen heroines cultivate. Achieving the dignity of an Anne Elliot depends on respecting the autonomy of the man you're involved with, not cynically using him as a means to your own ends. Grabbing like that won't make you happy, anyway. What happens when a guy you *can* love comes along, after you've already committed yourself to a man you can't? As Jane Austen warned her niece, "Nothing can be compared to the misery of being bound *without* love—bound to one, and preferring another; *that* is a punishment which you do *not* deserve."[28] As Fanny and Elizabeth and Anne all know, marrying without love is as "hopeless" and "dangerous" to your happiness as it is wrong.

$\mathscr{A}$DOPT AN AUSTEN ATTITUDE:

- Have you been disappointed by Romantic illusions? Are you cynical about love, or about men?
- Do you find yourself entertaining other women with scathing observations about men?
- Has the man-bashing habit made it hard for you to see what the new men you meet are really like?
- Are you so bitter about men that it's difficult for you to maintain a relationship of mutual respect and special trust with the man you love?
- Have you been tempted to settle for somebody you can't really love?
- Are you ready, now, to approach love with Jane Austen's hope and ambition instead?

$\mathscr{W}$HAT WOULD JANE DO?

- Jane Austen would treat the men in her life with generosity and respect.
- She'd want to be able to see men clearly—and look forward to a relationship of "superior affection" and "confidence" with one of them. (If you want the same thing, then you may

want to start biting your tongue. If that's hard, try avoiding groups of women whose chief entertainment is running men down. Spend time with friends who are more like Mrs. Gardiner or Anne Elliot. And, don't forget, the most powerful antidote to the urge to marinate in self-righteous complaints is insight into our own flaws.)

- If Jane Austen were tempted to settle, she'd reconsider. (If you're tempted, ask yourself, are you being 100 percent honest with the guy? Where is a relationship based on dishonesty going to get you?)

*I*F WE *REALLY* WANT TO BRING BACK JANE AUSTEN . . .

- We'll disband the sisterhood of snark and give other women mutual support in seeing men clearly, judging them wisely, and loving them honestly. We'll expect more from men. And our respect for them will nourish their respect for us, putting us on the road to Jane Austen heroine-level dignity.

CHAPTER FIVE

*D*O TAKE LOVE SERIOUSLY

HOWEVER "COMMON" AND "DANGEROUS" IT MAY have been in Jane Austen's day,[1] the brutal practicality Lori Gottlieb recommends about marriage is really only a conversation piece in the twenty-first century. We're far more likely to fall prey to a deeper cynicism about love that doesn't have even Gottlieb's practical-seeming hopes, however misplaced they may be, to redeem it.

The ultimate cynicism is not to believe in love at all.

If there's really no such thing as Jane Austen's "true attachment" or "disinterested" love, then we're justified in settling. Or we might as well treat the illusion of love as mere entertainment. Or we'd better resign ourselves to the sad but somehow Romantically interesting fact (à la *Eternal Sunshine of the Spotless Mind* or *Being John Malkovich*) that "love" always and everywhere just makes us each other's dupes. This is the crucial question: Once you've seen through the Romantic illusions about love, is there anything real left to see? In Mary Crawford, Jane Austen gives us a woman who doubts there is.

Don't See through Real Love

Mary is the anti-heroine of *Mansfield Park*. She's Fanny Price's "rival," as they said in Jane Austen's day, for Edmund Bertram's love. Mary is a worldly wise young woman who brings her big-city London attitudes to retired and old-fashioned Mansfield, where her risqué way of talking shocks Edmund.[2] Very early on, it's clear that Mary's attitude toward love is cynical. She insists to Mrs. Grant, her married sister, that sooner or later their brother Henry, a callous heartbreaker, will be "taken in" by a woman. Mrs. Grant protests, "But I would not have him *taken in*, I would not have him duped; I would have it all fair and honorable."

But Mary insists that love is just a trick, at least 99 percent of the time: "There is not one in a hundred of either sex, who is not taken in when they marry. Look where I will, I see that it *is* so; and I feel that it *must* be so, when I consider that it is, of all transactions, the one in which people expect most from others, and are least honest themselves."

Mary is cynically determined to do well for herself in marriage; she's in the market for a guy who's going to have status and a lot of money. That's why at first she thinks she might marry Edmund's older brother Tom, heir to Mansfield Park and a baronetcy.[3] But when Tom leaves Mansfield for a while, Mary can't help being attracted by his younger brother Edmund, despite the fact that Edmund won't inherit the family estate. "There was a charm, perhaps, in his sincerity, his steadiness, his integrity, which Miss Crawford might be equal to feel, though not equal to discuss with herself."[4]

And Edmund is strongly attracted to Mary, too, despite the fact that she's continually upsetting him with her flippant way of talking about things that he takes seriously. She never really clues in to how uncomfortable she's making him, and for a while their mutual attraction smoothes over all the rough places. He excuses all her faults to himself.[5] The abortive love story between Mary and Edmund is all about blindness. Her cynicism blinds her to the things he cares about—and to the value of his love.[6] And the illusions of love blind him to the depth of her cynicism, up until the very end.

For a while, under the influence of Edmund and the other residents of Mansfield, Mary does begin to get a glimpse of the realities that cynicism has made invisible to her. She hesitates between the worldly ideas and ambitions she brought with her to Mansfield—her prejudice against the clergy (Edmund is planning to be ordained), her addiction to conspicuous consumption (Edmund is preparing for a modest life in a small country parsonage), her requirement of a house in London (Edmund can't afford one) on the one hand—and on the other hand the sterling qualities, more really valuable than money, that she's just learning to appreciate in her new Mansfield friends: "You have all so much more *heart* among you, than one finds in the world at large. You all give me a feeling of being able to trust and confide in you; which, in common intercourse, one knows nothing of."

Sex and the City

But then Mary leaves Mansfield for a visit with her old friends in London. Edmund sees her there, and doesn't think much of them. Janet Fraser, the friend Mary's staying with, is "a cold-hearted, vain woman, who has married entirely from convenience, and though evidently unhappy in her marriage, places her disappointment, not in faults of judgment or temper, or disproportion of age, but to her being after all, less affluent than many of her acquaintance, especially than her sister, Lady Stornaway."

Mrs. Fraser has learned nothing from the mistake she made in marrying for money; she's still "the determined supporter of everything mercenary and ambitious, provided it be only mercenary and ambitious enough." And Mary can't see what her friend did wrong, either.[7]

> Poor Janet has been sadly taken in, and yet there was nothing improper on her side; she did not run into the match inconsiderately, there was no want of foresight. She took three days to consider of his proposals; and during those three days asked the advice of every body connected with her, whose opinion was worth having; and especially applied to my late dear aunt, whose knowledge of the world made her judgment very generally and deservedly looked up to by all the young people of her acquaintance; and she was decidedly in favour of Mr. Fraser. This seems as if nothing were a security for matrimonial comfort! I have not so much to say for my friend Flora, who jilted a very nice young man in the Blues, for the sake of that horrid Lord Stornaway,

who has about as much sense, Fanny, as Mr. Rushworth, but much worse looking, and with a blackguard character.

You can see exactly what Fanny means by "a mind led astray and bewildered, and without any suspicion of being so; darkened, yet fancying itself light." The "knowledge of the world" that all these women—Mary's friends, Mary's aunt, Mary herself—rely on is actually ignorance of everything that's really important. They're London sophisticates, too worldly wise to marry for love. They think only naïve people believe in "disinterested attachment." To them, it seems much smarter to marry for money and status than to be "taken in." And when their mercenary, ambitious marriages don't after all make them happy, they have no clue what went wrong.

Back among this London set, Mary relapses into cynicism. She's "cooled" toward Edmund "by a return to London habits." Fanny is appalled by the letter Mary writes her, and particularly by the way Mary thinks about Edmund now that she's back in London: "The woman who could speak of him, and speak only of his appearance!—What an unworthy attachment! To be deriving support from the commendation of Mrs. Fraser! *She* who had been intimate with him half a year! Fanny was ashamed of her." Mary is thinking about Edmund's looks and how his attachment to her gives her status in the eyes of her friends, but also about how his profession will lower her status if she marries him.[8] She sees everything in terms of money, ambition, and sex appeal.

Edmund knows that proposing marriage is risky while Mary is with her London friends; they'll advise her against such an unworldly match. So he hesitates. And events intervene. Edmund is called away by his elder brother's dangerous illness—which makes Mary suddenly more interested in Edmund, who will inherit Mansfield Park and be a baronet if Tom dies.

And then Edmund's sister Maria horrifies the whole Mansfield family by leaving her husband for Mary's brother Henry. And Mary's reaction to this adulterous affair finally opens Edmund's eyes. He can hardly believe that the woman he wanted to marry thinks that Maria's only real mistake in her affair with Henry was...getting caught. Edmund is deeply upset by his sister's adultery, and he finds Mary's flippant way of talking about it painful. He tells Fanny,

I do not consider her as meaning to wound my feelings. The evil is yet deeper; in her total ignorance, unsuspiciousness of there being such feelings, in a perversion of mind which made it natural to her to treat the subject as she did. She was speaking only as she had been used to hear others speak, as she imagined every body else would speak.

Mary's cynicism kills Edmund's feelings for her, and he ends up marrying Fanny—to the reader's delight! Mary is so careful not to be "taken in" by the illusion of love that she misses the real thing.

So what application can Mary Crawford's failure with Edmund possibly have for us? We're not likely to meet many men as straitlaced as Edmund Bertram.

Still, the hard shells we grow to protect our hearts can keep out the good guys as well as the heartbreakers. The cynical way Mary judges Edmund when she's with her friends in London has a very familiar flavor. If we haven't done it ourselves, we've heard women talk about men in that calculating way—as if the dating game were some kind of competition in looks, money, and status. We don't like it when men judge women in that brutal manner, and particularly when they get together in groups and rate us like meat.[9] It doesn't improve matters if we fall into a similar habit, setting up with our girlfriends to judge men in hotness, or other competitive categories.

Dawn Eden, a veteran of the sex-and-the-city-style New York dating scene who gave it up because of a religious conversion,[10] describes how the longer she did that kind of dating, the more she saw sex and romance as a competition, ranked men in terms of how

TIP JUST FOR JANEITES

Don't judge men
by whether they have
"alpha male" characteristics.

they measured up in alpha male qualities, and consequently lost the ability to notice the kind of man with whom she might find real love.[11] She had to recover from the female version of the disease my husband calls "shopping for a sports car"—when a male friend's love life is a series of predictable disasters because he insists on picking girls for their looks and the status their hotness confers on him, instead of a woman he can imagine actually spending his life with.

A lot of our cynicism amounts to a kind of mimicry of the worst men's bad habits—on the unstated theory that if we can't beat 'em, we might as well join 'em. That's the thinking behind the famous *Sex and the City* question, "Can a woman have sex like a man?" There's a lot of evidence that most of us can't, at least not if to "have sex like a man" means to use and discard partners casually and painlessly, the way the most callous players do.[12] But why would we *want* to be like those guys?

"As Much Attached to Another Person As I Can Be to Any One"

Jane Austen did create one female character who exhibits all the callous selfishness of the deliberate male heartbreaker. *Lady Susan* is an early novelette Jane Austen wrote in a series of letters. The title character is Jane Austen's version of the Marquise de Merteuil, the scheming villainess Glenn Close played in *Dangerous Liaisons*. Lady Susan may not "have sex like a man,"[13] but she's as cold as any player.

You don't finish reading the book wanting to be like Lady Susan, the way you wish you could step into Elizabeth Bennet's shoes, or Emma's. Lady Susan's mental world is a kind of desert, void of everything that makes life worth living. She *sees through* all the things that matter, more thoroughly than even Mary Crawford. To Lady Susan, personal integrity and honorable love are nothing but weaknesses. "There is a sort of ridiculous delicacy," she complains about Reginald de Courcy, the idealistic young man she's wrapping around her little finger, "which requires the fullest explanation of whatever he may have heard to my disadvantage." Reginald loves Lady Susan only because she has cleverly managed to explain away her well-deserved reputation.

"This is *one* sort of Love," says Lady Susan, "but I confess it does not particularly recommend itself to me. I infinitely prefer the tender & liberal spirit of Manwaring, which impressed with the deepest conviction of my merit, is satisfied that whatever I do must be right." Lady's Susan's hard-bitten lover Manwaring doesn't care that Lady Susan has deliberately broken up his marriage; has simultaneously "detached" a suitor from his sister; and is cruelly insisting that her own fifteen-year-old daughter marry a man she despises. Reginald loves Lady Susan only as long as she can trick him into believing that none of these things is true. But it's nothing to Lady Susan to be loved by a man of integrity: "If I were not already as much attached to another person as I can be to any one, I should make a point of not bestowing my affection on a Man who had dared to think so meanly of me." She isn't capable of real love. Like all the cynics in Jane Austen, Lady Susan is maimed and blind.

She overestimates her control of the situation—which is the only thing that matters to *her*—gets caught in her outrageous lies in spite of her considerable powers of persuasion and charm, and fails in her schemes. All she can see in the honest people she's attempting to manipulate is a repulsive "milkiness." But by the end of the novelette, boring domesticity and naïve sentiment look suddenly fresh and attractive in comparison with Lady Susan's

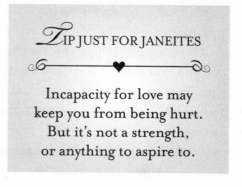

TIP JUST FOR JANEITES

Incapacity for love may
keep you from being hurt.
But it's not a strength,
or anything to aspire to.

devious mind and heart of stone. One-upping the nastier members of the male sex in callous disregard for other people is no solution for the fear we have that men can never really give us what we want from them.

Take Love Seriously

And neither is the even more common way we modern women have of answering that fear. The standard technique for protecting our hearts—one that's woven into our whole culture—is to tell ourselves that love can't hurt us too badly just as long as we're careful never to take it seriously.

You can understand where this impulse comes from. In a controversial article in the *Atlantic*,[14] Caitlin Flanagan describes how her mother, the kind of pioneering feminist who volunteered at Planned Parenthood in the '70s and helped get sex education past the eyes of the watchful dragons on the P.T.A., used to startle the teenaged Flanagan by "sneaking up on me and then delivering some report on the nature of human sexuality" at the most inopportune moments—in the middle of the dog's bath, say, in a tone of voice more appropriate to "Do you want me to get the flea dip?" Mothers like Flanagan's were trying to spare their daughters the mistakes too many women made in the repressed '50s—marrying the wrong man just because you wanted to go to bed with him, pairing up too early because marriage in your early twenties was the only way to become a grownup, or ending up stuck with somebody truly awful for life because you got pregnant. It's not hard to see why mothers wanted to spare their daughters these miserable outcomes, or why they thought that lowering the temperature around the whole subject of sex was the way to keep it from being such a high-stakes game for women.

The idea was to mitigate the pain by making love lower-risk. If less in women's lives depended on love and sex, then women could afford to experiment, make mistakes, recover, and try again. So much of what women like Caitlin Flanagan's mother were doing was in aid of *making sex and romantic love less important.*

And large societal trends were cooperating to bring about the same result. Sex education in school helped chip away at the taboos that had made the whole subject seem momentous because forbidden—and at the '50s culture's hard, bright line between "good girls" and "bad girls," so that women wouldn't end up as humiliated outcasts because they were more sexually adventurous.[15] Meanwhile, the Pill and *Roe v. Wade* made it possible to fend off the most obvious life-changing consequence of sex. And the explosion of divorce and the simultaneous entry of women into the workforce in large numbers meant that choices about love and sex were becoming less decisive for women's long-term financial security.

So girls began to think of love and sex less in terms of momentous, life-changing decisions. The new approach to love, Flanagan explains, was one, "in which sex did not cleave the girl instantly and permanently from her home and her family": "I was going to get to be a daughter living at home, studying for algebra quizzes and putting Gee, Your Hair Smells Terrific shampoo on my mother's grocery list, and also a young woman beginning a private and womanly sex life."

But another way of looking at it is that eventually women learned to treat "womanly" love and romance as merely a side issue, something apart from the main trajectory of our lives. We learned to call it "having a sex life." Now men go in a separate compartment from our serious plans, lest they upset them. Ultimately, acknowledging how much love and sex mean to us comes to seem shameful, or at best sub-standard. That's what comes out when a professor asks a class at the University of Chicago what they think will be the most important decision in their lives…and only one student—a guy—is willing to say that it's going to be picking a mate.[16]

This is one reason Jane Austen is so compelling to us. In her novels, everyone takes sex, love, and the pain they can cause seriously. Even a seventeen-year-old girl's heartbreak is a subject of serious adult concern, not eye-rolling.[17] That's a breath of fresh air to us. Taking love as seriously as the people in Jane Austen novels do certainly fits better with how we feel about love when we're actually in it. We all know that when we fall in love, it *can't* seem like a side issue to us. It's earth-shattering. Pretending not to take it seriously creates a kind of double vision. You're experiencing love as supremely important, but you feel you have to keep it under control, as if it doesn't really matter to your life. And then when you come to a fork in the road and you have to choose—say, you have to decide whether to move to the same city where your college boyfriend gets his first job—then either you give up a love that might make you happy in the long run, or else you choose to change the trajectory of your real life, and you end up feeling compromised, like you're not a serious person. Taking love seriously seems to make you weak.

Setting aside the intensity of romantic love as we experience it, we also can't help but notice that there's a level-headed, objective case to be made for the importance of love to our ultimate happiness. Granted, modern trends have stripped away many of the consequences that used to depend on women's choices about men—our reputations, our financial security, even whether or not we'll have children. But a large proportion of female happiness in the world still depends on how we manage our love lives. Everything that sex education, no-fault divorce, modern contraceptives, and anti-depressants can do has been tried. We're left with the stubborn truth that love can still break your heart and mess up your future. We know women who are happy because they've managed to get love right, and women whose lives seem to be a mess because they haven't. Even in the modern world, which guy we end up with—not to mention whether we end up with one at all—is going to make a huge difference for our ultimate happiness, no matter what other success we achieve.[18] Jane Austen would not be surprised.

Jane Austen was keenly aware of the fact that love can wreck our lives if we go about it wrong. Her novels are full of sad examples of lives blighted this way. Putting aside the Maria Bertrams and the Charlotte Lucases, Jane Austen gives us a whole other cast of characters whose lives have been ruined by botched romance. She makes it impossible for us to miss the lessons of their lives because we meet them only long after they made the mistakes that wrecked their futures. Jane Austen introduces us to these women (or tells us about them in retrospect) only in the squalor, or the hopeless reflections, or the bitter poverty and loneliness that the original false step led them into. We get just glimpses of Mrs. Tilney, who frequently had "much to bear" from the awful temper of her hypocrite of a husband, and of Lady Elliot, whose "youthful infatuation" for Sir Walter bought her a lifetime managing his stupid vanity.[19]

We see more of the original Eliza—not the girl Willoughby seduces, but her mother, who let herself be bullied by an uncle into marrying his elder son though she was in love with the younger brother, the future Colonel Brandon.[20] Eventually "provoke[d]" into "inconstancy" by her husband's nastiness, she found herself divorced, and then abandoned by the man for whom she'd broken up her awful marriage. By the time Colonel Brandon was able to return from India and look for her, Eliza was dying in debtors' prison; she'd been reduced to living off a series of lovers, or even by prostitution.[21]

And of course there's poor Mrs. Price, Fanny's mother, who married "in the common phrase, to disoblige her family, and by fixing on a Lieutenant of Marines, without education, fortune, or connections, did it very thoroughly." A decade later she's overburdened by "a large and still increasing family, an husband disabled for active service, but not the less equal to company and good liquor, and a very small income to supply their wants." Eloping with a marine seems dashing and Romantic; even a large family on a small income may sound charming to us. But Fanny's visit to Portsmouth leaves no doubt about just how squalid Mrs. Price's life really is: her once-gentle voice "worn into fretfulness" by the demands of a household she can't manage; the proud, judgmental relatives she defied and scorned at the time of her marriage now the only resource she can turn to for any kind of future for her children; her husband a coarse, hard-drinking lout who doesn't seem to contribute anything to his family, either by working or by getting a house full of rowdy boys under control; and the passion that got her into this situation now a distant memory.

You can't say Jane Austen underestimated the stakes involved in love, sex, and marriage. She saw the problem very clearly. She just wanted to solve it differently. Jane Austen didn't think we could make it all better by becoming cynics about love—by trying to isolate sex with all its complications from our serious hopes for our lives because we've given up on the bliss love promises. She wouldn't see the point of trying to limit romance to a recreation, instead of a chance for "permanent happiness." She was more ambitious than we are. Jane Austen was firmly convinced that human relationships are the solid basis for happiness.

So what exactly is Jane Austen's solution to the undeniable fact that love gone wrong causes women terrible pain and blights lives?

Get love right.

ADOPT AN AUSTEN ATTITUDE:

🌹 Are you so caught up in a competitive dating scene that you find yourself judging guys superficially—mostly by their bodies, or their status, or how much money they make? If you're living the high-octane sex-and-the-city dating life, has your heart grown a hard shell? If you want to be able to notice what's really important about guys—and not miss good prospects—consider stepping out of the fast lane.

✿ Do you talk about men with the Fanny Prices in your life, or with the Mrs. Frasers and Lady Stornaways? Think about which of your friends is more likely to help you see guys clearly, not just go for "alpha male" characteristics.

✿ Have you got sex and love confined safely to a manageable area of your life? Do you treat men as a kind of distraction? Have you given up hope that the right kind of love can deliver happiness? If you've demoted romance to a side issue in your life, think about whether you're willing to risk living like a Jane Austen heroine, and take love seriously.

*W*HAT WOULD JANE DO?

✿ Jane Austen wouldn't want you to despair of "permanent happiness" or "disinterested attachment." She believed in real love, and she didn't think it was stupid to plan your life around it.

*I*F WE *REALLY* WANT TO BRING BACK JANE AUSTEN . . .

✿ We'll see modern cynicism about love as the blind alley it is. We'll quit thinking we can protect ourselves from heartbreak by giving up our hopes.

Not a Cheat—a Good Beginning

Not long ago, I told my husband that the more I read Jane Austen's novels, the more I foresee some rough spots ahead for the Knightleys and the Darcys.

Mr. Knightley, who believes he could never love Jane Fairfax because she "has not the open temper which a man would wish for in a wife," still doesn't know the extent of Emma's deviousness at the time of their marriage.[22] By the end of the novel Emma is going around saying (in imitation of the man she loves),[23] "Oh! if you only knew how much I love every thing that is decided and open!" But she has proven to us time and again that for her, giving up scheming is like peeling an onion with your fingernails.[24] What will Mr. Knightley think when he finds out that Emma's matchmaking extended to mistakenly encouraging Harriet to believe he loved her, and that she egged Frank Churchill on to bully Jane Fairfax with suggestions that one was in love with a married man?

But the Darcys are likely to have an even tougher marital adjustment ahead of them. My husband, who's much less social than I am, found my worries about them quite compelling. Especially when after a party at our house I quoted him Darcy's confession of his social awkwardness—"I certainly have not the talent which some people possess, of conversing with those I have not seen before. I cannot catch their tone of conversation, or appear interested in their concerns, as I often see done"—and Elizabeth's retort—"'My fingers,' said Elizabeth, 'do not move over this instrument in the masterly manner which

I see so many women's do. They have not the same force or rapidity, and do not produce the same expressions. But then I have always supposed it to be my own fault—because I would not take the trouble of practicing.'"

"He is going to be miserable," was my husband's immediate reaction.

Darcy—really a shy man, more than a proud one—is a sensitive plant compared to Mr. Knightley, who will undoubtedly be able to cope with Emma. Elizabeth Bennet can be awfully sharp, and Darcy, as she notices even in the first flush of happy love, "had yet to learn to be laughed at, and it was rather too early to begin." When Elizabeth does begin laughing at him . . . is he going to like it?

Hearing my worries about the Darcys and the Knightleys, my husband said, "You'd better quit reading those novels, or you won't be able to write your book." And I said, "No, no. It's not like that. Think about us."

Jane Austen's blissful couples are going to be all right, really. When my husband and I first fell in love, we were just as caught up in each other's perfections and the prospect of total bliss as Elizabeth and Darcy. And of course we turned out not to be perfect, either as individuals or as a couple. We both have hard edges and weak spots. We've hurt each other. Happily ever after is not quite like what we pictured, looking ahead. But looking back, the initial bliss doesn't seem like something to be cynical about. It wasn't a cheat. It was a good beginning.

CHAPTER SIX

ATIONAL HAPPINESS"
What It Is,
How You Can Find It

BUT HOW ON EARTH CAN WE GET LOVE RIGHT? IF WE can't be Romantic about love, but we're not supposed to be cynics either, what are we supposed to be?

Happy Jane Austen heroines don't believe in instant intimacy with "The One" they immediately recognize by the intensity of their emotions...but they won't settle for a diminished kind of love that's less than honest or less than truly life-changing, either. So what's the third possibility? What's the happy medium that Elizabeth Bennet's thinking of when she talks about "rational happiness"?

Well, first of all, it is exactly that—a happy medium, a perfect midpoint balanced between extremes. Does the idea of a happy balance seem tepid and uninspiring to you? That's the Romantic Sensibility talking in your head. Tell it to shut up; listen to Jane Austen instead. Her eighteenth-century mind is so different from ours!

We've been trained by two centuries of Romanticism to despise the well-balanced—it's boring and conventional—and to sneer at the perfectly normal. Jane Austen thinks just the opposite way. Her idea of rational balance is dynamic and exciting. Happy love in Jane Austen isn't just a static Goldilocks "not too hot, not too cold" midpoint between two extremes. Getting things exactly right is not about dull compromise, or being insipid and lukewarm. Avoiding extremes to aim for perfection doesn't exclude passion or bliss. It's the only way you can reasonably expect to have them.

To Jane Austen, it's the extremes that look partial and defective. They're the mistakes we make when we miss what we really ought to aim for—the dead ends, the temptations always pulling us off the ideal balance. A Jane Austen heroine is a tightrope walker, disaster on either side of her, happiness dependent on maintaining the perfect balance. To Jane Austen and her heroines, normal is a rare and desirable state of perfection, from which we're always in danger of slipping back into one or another kind of partial vision or self-defeating error.

Jane Austen's Art of Perfect Balance

In Jane Austen, getting love right—getting *anything* right—has a lot to do with avoiding extremes. If you read every piece of fiction Jane Austen wrote in the order she wrote it in, you can see that she built up to the creation of her nearly perfect heroines and their nearly perfect love stories only through a long process of working her way past every possible defective extreme toward the happy normal. Jane Austen wrote Shakespeare-style love comedies, stories where the heroes and heroines are like real flesh-and-blood people, and we laugh *with* them out of sheer delight when they find happiness. But she worked her way up to them by first practicing on the other kind of comedy, stories where you laugh *at* the characters because their faults make them so ridiculous.[1]

The stories Jane Austen wrote as a girl are full of characters twisted into bizarre shapes by one or another ruling obsession that pulls them off center. There are the Miss Simpsons in *Jack and Alice*, the eldest "pleasing in her person, in her Manners & in her Disposition; an unbounded ambition was her only fault. Her second sister Sukey was Envious, Spitefull, and Malicious.... Cecilia (the youngest) was perfectly handsome but too affected to be pleasing." There are the extreme Romantics in *Love and Friendship*, despising every practical concern—and at the opposite end of the spectrum, in *Lesley Castle*, the absurdly practical Charlotte Lutterell, so obsessed with the minutiae of housekeeping that when her sister's fiancé is thrown from his horse, Charlotte's chief concern is how to dispose of the wedding feast.[2]

These absurd characters go about love in every possible wrong way. Mary in *The Three Sisters* is so status-obsessed that she "would willingly ensure herself everlasting Misery by a marriage to Mr. Watts" to prevent her younger sisters from marrying before she does. Charlotte Drummond, "whose character was a willingness to oblige every one," accomodatingly accepts proposals of marriage from two different men and, when she suddenly realizes her mistake, "the reflection of her past folly, operated so strongly on her mind, that she resolved to be guilty of a greater, & to that end threw herself into a deep stream which ran thro' her Aunt's Pleasure Grounds in Portland Place."[3]

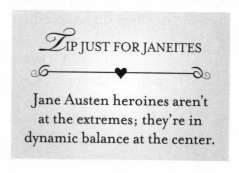

Tip Just for Janeites

Jane Austen heroines aren't at the extremes; they're in dynamic balance at the center.

In *Sense and Sensibility*, Jane Austen is still giving us ridiculous minor characters so distorted by one or another reigning preoccupation that we have to laugh at them.[4] But these absurd people have moved off center stage—Jane Austen is writing real novels now. The extreme "sense" of some minor characters[5] and the extreme "sensibility" of others[6] show off how comparatively (and delightfully) normal Elinor and Marianne are. Though Elinor has just a little more "sense" than would be ideal, and Marianne has a good deal more "sensibility" than will make her happy, both are real rounded characters we can't help loving. They point to an ideal we can aspire to, not just absurdities for us to avoid.

"The Loveliest Medium"

And in *Persuasion*, look at how Captain Wentworth comes to realize that he has made a terrible mistake in pursuing Louisa Musgrove instead of Anne. He has been operating on the idea that what he wants in a woman is "a strong mind." It's obvious why. This requirement is in reaction—in fact, in overreaction—to what happened between him and Anne Elliot all those years ago, when Anne was persuaded by Lady Russell to end their engagement. Anne's persuadability broke Captain Wentworth's heart.[7] After that miserable experience, he has concluded that all he needs in order to be sure of happiness in love is a woman who's hard-headed.[8] When Louisa, encouraged by Wentworth's enthusiastic praise of her "firmness" to think stubbornness is a virtue,[9] insists on being jumped down from the steps at Lyme and ends up giving herself a dangerous concussion, Anne wonders

> whether it ever occurred to him now, to question the justness of his own previous opinion as to the universal felicity and advantage of firmness of character; and whether it might not strike him, that, like all other qualities of mind, it should have its proportions and limits.

Anne is thinking like a Jane Austen heroine, remembering to value all things in their right proportions. She wonders if Captain Wentworth is ever going to stop thinking the other way, in extremes.

As a matter of fact, at the very moment when Anne is wondering about him, Captain Wentworth is just beginning to recover his balance. He begins to love Anne again—or to realize that he has always loved Anne—at almost precisely this point in the story. When Louisa's unconscious, her sister Henrietta's fainting, Mary Musgrove is hysterical, and Wentworth and Benwick can't think what to do, Anne is competent. She's as gentle as ever, but quite as tough as she needs to be in an emergency—the steadiest person on the spot. Seeing her then, Captain Wentworth explains later, he began to learn "to distinguish between the steadiness of principle and the obstinacy of self-will, between the darings of heedlessness and the recollections of a collected mind." On closer examination, Anne's "character was now fixed in his mind as perfection itself."[10]

And what does the "perfect excellence" that Wentworth sees in Anne consist in? She maintains "the loveliest medium of fortitude and gentleness." Louisa, in contrast, is only a "good-humoured, unaffected" enough girl.

She's ready to be persuaded by Captain Wentworth that it's admirable to be stubborn, and she acts stubborn to please him. Then later, when she's falling for Captain Benwick, she is just as ready to be a quiet, gentle lover of poetry. But Anne is a grown-up woman in perfect balance, and Captain Wentworth can see how extraordinary she is, now that he has corrected the imbalance in his own way of thinking.

"Rationally As Well As Passionately Loved"

For Captain Wentworth, loving Anne is all about appreciating what's really lovable about her. Here you find "rational" and "permanent" happiness—where men and women come together because each of them has a genuine "regard" for the other person's real value. Thus Jane Austen says that Henry Crawford—despite the flaws that doomed his courtship of Fanny—loved her "rationally as well as passionately." He didn't just passionately want her; his reason recognized her excellence. It's the exact opposite of what makes people like Lydia and Wickham so unlikely to find happiness in the long run. They're "a couple who were only brought together because their passions were stronger than their virtue."[11]

But Jane Austen's heroes and heroines don't belong to some special class of super-excellent human beings who aren't subject to folly and vice. Their ability to see clearly and judge wisely is not inbred or automatic. To arrive at the point where they can recognize the real value in the other person—the excellence that promises true "felicity"—they have to resist temptations to fall into the same extremes and absurdities that govern less balanced characters who aren't fully realized heroes and heroines. Captain Wentworth let himself be pulled off center by his angry resentment of Anne. He could easily have ended up as just another example of how to get love wrong, another character who lost his balance and fell out of the main line of the story.

We learn about Captain Wentworth's struggle only in retrospect and from the outside, as he tells the tale to Anne. But that very same struggle—to see things in their right proportions and limits, so that you can recognize true excellence and value it when you meet it—is exactly what we get to see from the inside, from the woman's perspective, in Jane Austen's most exciting love stories.

For months Emma has romantic fantasies about Frank Churchill,[12] all because she's in scheming, matchmaking mode, and he's fodder for her overactive imagination. The whole time she's toying with the idea that Frank may be in love with her, it never occurs to her to think about Mr. Knightley as a romantic prospect. When her matchmaking schemes explode in her face and she finally does get around to taking stock of Frank Churchill and Mr. Knightley as men—thinking about which one she really admires and values more—there's no contest.[13]

TIP JUST FOR JANEITES

Is there a man in your life that you've never thought of as a romantic prospect, but who's a truly admirable human being? Go ahead, compare him to the guys you actually date, and see how it comes out. Don't miss your Mr. Knightley!

And of course there's Elizabeth, who so very nearly misses her happy ending with Mr. Darcy because of her "prejudice" (not to mention his "pride"). Their love affair is the one we picture when we think of happy love in Jane Austen. It's not Jane Austen's most mature work of art; there's more delicate psychological realism in her later novels. But Elizabeth with Darcy is our ideal of what we see in a Jane Austen love story, what we want for ourselves. In *Pride and Prejudice* Jane Austen really gets inside the love story, and shows us most intimately how these two difficult people come to love each other both rationally and passionately.

How to Be "a Woman Worthy of Being Pleased"

Elizabeth and Darcy both start out with faults that keep them from seeing each other clearly. She's prejudiced against him because of his incivility. He makes little effort to please other people in general—his behavior verges on rudeness—partly because he is proud and selfish to a certain degree, and partly because he's shy, not naturally social like her. And she finds that making fun of him is "such an opening for wit." She's also naturally prejudiced in favor of Wickham, who has all the social skills Darcy lacks, and who feeds her full of lies about Darcy's past misdeeds.

Darcy's pride hits a course-correction when Elizabeth refuses his proposal. For Darcy, the process of falling in love with Elizabeth "rationally" as well as "passionately" only begins then. It means learning two separate lessons—one about himself, and one about her.

Up to the point of his first proposal, Darcy loves Elizabeth more "passionately" than "rationally." He himself says, at the time of his original declaration, that his feelings for her aren't supported by "reason" and "recollection." He's bewitched by her saucy manner and her "fine eyes." And eventually he talks himself into believing that he has to have her, even though he can't really approve of her—or of himself for choosing her. (That's why he says he's been "kinder" to Bingley "than towards myself." Darcy has extricated his friend from an embarrassing family connection that he is ashamed to be pursuing himself.) When Darcy proposes to Elizabeth the first time, he thinks he's yielding to a weakness.

But the shock of her refusal makes him reconsider all his assumptions. Only when it becomes clear that Elizabeth has good cause for not returning Darcy's feelings (she accuses him, with some reason, of "arrogance," "conceit," and "selfish disdain for the feelings of others") does he begin to think of her as "a woman worthy of being pleased"—and to realize "how insufficient were all my pretensions" of pleasing her. He begins to have a real rational regard for her (not just a passion he's half ashamed of) at the same time that he begins to realize he is not worthy of her. Elizabeth's rebuke starts a complete revolution in Darcy's ideas. He begins to question himself. And he has to conclude that he's "been a selfish being all my life." He traces his faults to his childhood, when he was taught good principles, but not expected to put them into practice. Being an only son, he was spoiled by his parents, and he grew up "to be selfish and overbearing, to care for none beyond my own family circle, to think meanly of all the rest of the world."

The realization that Elizabeth is someone he doesn't automatically deserve jogs Darcy out of this complacent pride. He sees that he'd actually have to stretch to live up to her. And the rebalancing that follows on that realization makes him able to see her and all things connected with her more clearly, in terms of their real worth.[14] The next time Darcy sees Elizabeth,[15] he's determined to show her that he has been improved by the lesson she gave him: "I hoped," he explains to her later, "to obtain your forgiveness, to lessen your ill opinion, by letting you see that your reproofs had been attended to."

Meanwhile, Elizabeth too has been forced into self-examination and reexamination of Darcy's real value. Disliking Darcy has been as irrational for Elizabeth as liking Elizabeth was for Darcy. Beginning with his proposal and accelerating with his letter, her visit to Pemberley, and the generous part he plays in arranging for Wickham to marry Lydia, Elizabeth also has to learn that she has completely undervalued Darcy. Her own character flaws have blinded her to his real worth. She started out by indulging her dislike of Darcy and let Wickham flatter her into believing lies about him. She never bothered to think clearly about which man was actually more likely to be trustworthy. Darcy's letter forces her to reevaluate both men— and also herself. Her humiliating discovery: the evidence of Wickham's dishonesty was obvious all along. But her vanity kept her from noticing the contradictions between what he said and how he acted.

After Darcy's letter, Elizabeth recalibrates her balance and begins to see more clearly. She's in a much better position to judge Darcy rationally by the time she gets to Pemberley. Mr. Darcy may have disdained people outside his own family circle. But in that circle, he's an exemplary guardian to his orphaned and vulnerable teenage sister; a responsible and benevolent landlord; and a kind and gracious master to the large number of people whose very livelihoods depend on him. Darcy has got the enormous power and wealth that tend to make people tyrannical to their dependents. (Think about how Hollywood stars treat their domestic staffs.) The testimony of his servants is extraordinary: "I never heard a cross word from him in my life, and I have known him ever since he was four years old."

But it's his role in the Lydia-Wickham affair that really proves his worth to Elizabeth. Before, Darcy was too proud even to speak to Wickham. Under Elizabeth's influence he becomes willing to negotiate with him, to save her family from disgrace.[16] "Oh! how heartily did she grieve over every ungracious sensation she had ever encouraged, every saucy speech she had ever directed towards him. For herself she was humbled; but she was proud of him. Proud that in a cause of compassion and honour, he had been able to get the better of himself." And Darcy is thinking almost exactly same way about Elizabeth: "Such I was, from eight to eight and twenty; and such I might still have been but for you, dearest, loveliest Elizabeth! What do I not owe you! You taught me a lesson, hard indeed at first, but most advantageous. By you, I was properly humbled."

This is what it's like to be plunged deeply into real rational love—not the inferior emotion that Jane Austen calls "infatuation" or being "bewitched." On both sides it's grounded in a humble, generous estimation of the value of the other person, but an estimation based in reality. Elizabeth and Darcy are now in perfect balance, each seeing the other person for who that person really is. But that perfect balance is not some static state, or a lukewarm average of opposites. It's a kind of dynamic balance, which they've achieved by their struggles—each inspired by the other—to cast off their partial views and the absurdities that made them less than fully rounded, really admirable characters. It's that struggle that gives real weight and importance to their love. Darcy and Elizabeth are feeling the

> ## 𝒯IP JUST FOR JANEITES
>
> ◖———❤———◗
>
> Finding the right kind of love will help you transcend your own limitations (not just your parents' expectations, your friends' assumptions, and society's conventions).

delightful frothiness that belongs to the beginning of any love affair. But while you can fall in love over poetry, like Benwick and Louisa—or over a shared passion for collecting matchboxes, for that matter—the theme of Darcy and Elizabeth's love affair is their mutual inspiration to each other to become better human beings.[17]

This love is life-changing, all right. But it's nothing like Romanticism's false promise of instant liberation and authenticity. For one thing, love hasn't changed Elizabeth and Darcy's lives instantly and painlessly. There's been quite a lot of embarrassment and pain involved in the changes they've both been through. They've been humiliated by having to face their own flaws. And they've both had to stretch to understand the value of a person so different from themselves.

The Genuine Article, and the Cheap Knock-Offs

In fact, there's so much language about pain and humiliation in Darcy and Elizabeth's love story that it's easy for us to get the wrong impression about why the story's so exciting. Especially if Regency "erotica" is anywhere on your radar screen, it's hard to read Darcy's "your reproofs had been attended to" or "by you, I was properly humbled" without snickering. (And I can't write that Elizabeth "has to learn" humiliating lessons from Darcy without expecting guffaws from the peanut gallery.) To our cynical modern minds, language like that has a cheap sexual charge. We're likely to suspect that all the talk about being reproved and humbled is just a smokescreen for a certain kind of sexual tension.

But if we come to that conclusion, we've got the whole thing exactly backwards. The delight that Elizabeth and Darcy feel in being humbled by and in awe of each other can't be reduced to the kind of excitement you can get from dabbling in sadomasochism. It's the other way around. Sexual playacting[18] of that sort is a pitiful substitute for the real life-changing transformation Jane Austen's characters experience. Her kind of domination and submission involves her characters' whole personalities, not just their sexual hobbies.

Everything that happens between Darcy and Elizabeth is sexual, but it can't be reduced to the *merely* sexual. If Darcy hadn't felt a sexual passion for Elizabeth, her disdain for him would never have spurred him to re-think his self-image and his attitude toward people outside his circle. It's only because she's a *woman* "worthy of being pleased" that he's inspired to think what kind of *man* he'd have to be to please her. And from Elizabeth's point of view, it's because Darcy is an attractive man that the self-conquest he achieves moves her in the way it does. If you think about it, it makes a lot of sense that S&M is the most common sexual interest, beyond the basics.[19] It's a poor shadow of the actually creative and life-changing humiliations that Darcy and Elizabeth suffer on their way to deserving a noble love, and the pride they feel in each other once they've found their happy ending. After all, *Pride and Prejudice* is the real thing. *A Rake's Pleasure*, *Between Linen Sheets*, and *Passion at Pemberley* are the cheap knock-offs.

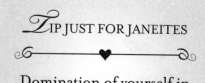

TIP JUST FOR JANEITES

Domination of yourself in submission to the life-changing power of real love beats the cheap imitations all hollow.

Jane Austen would tell you that *every* other kind of submission that love can involve is a cheap substitute for the real thing, the life-changing rebalancing of her whole world that Elizabeth finds with Darcy. Remember, Darcy's original proposal also involved a kind of submission, but of an inferior sort. He was all set to submit to the force of his irrational passion for Elizabeth and give up what he thought were rational and principled objections to a connection with her family.[20] At that time he saw his declaration to her as lowering himself, stooping to a love that was beneath him. That kind of love submits, too. But it's a submission that makes the lover less than he was before, not more.

Who wants to be loved *that* way? Well, unfortunately, *we* sometimes do. It's possible to take pride in having that sort of power over a man. That's the very kind of submission that Mary Crawford wants from Edmund. It's why she tells Fanny that if she could relive one week of her life, it would be the week of their rehearsals, when Edmund gave up his principled objections to the play out of love for her: "His sturdy spirit to bend as it did! Oh! it was sweet beyond expression." It's a boost to your ego for a man to be willing to give up even things he thinks it's wrong to give up, for you. Not to mention that it's a great convenience, especially if you really like having things your own way. If your guy is so bewitched by you that he's willing to abandon his principles to please you, there's not much he won't give way on. You can run right over him to your heart's content. Only, will it really content your heart to lead a man around by the nose like a prize bull? Will a guy who's made himself less than he was to be with you make you happy? Not the way Elizabeth is happy with Darcy.

Adopt an Austen Attitude:

- If you're in the market for love, think about what you're looking for. Does the next guy really have to be the exact opposite of your last awful boyfriend? Or are you able to evaluate guys by a standard that makes some kind of rational, objective sense?

- If you're in a relationship, have you noticed how it's changing the two of you as individuals? Is it for better, or for worse?

What Would Jane Do?

- She'd look for the kind of man that she could esteem and admire. And for the kind of relationship that promises "rational happiness" because it's built on a foundation of mutual regard for each other's real value.

- She'd do her best to outgrow the extremes, obsessions, and other kinks and absurdities that make it hard to choose well in love.

If We *Really* Want to Bring Back Jane Austen . . .

- We'll reject both Romanticism and cynicism for Jane Austen's ambitious realism. We'll be on the lookout for a love that will demand a lot of us, but end up making us and the man we love better people in the end—and that will be deeply exciting for that very reason. Love done wrong can be a source of life-long misery; there's no reason love done right shouldn't make us happy.

CHAPTER SEVEN

ORK ON *ALL* YOUR RELATIONSHIPS

OKAY, HAVE YOU GOT THAT DOWN?

Elizabeth Bennet, Anne Elliot, and Emma Woodhouse get love exactly right by finding the perfect balance, defining the happy medium, realizing in just the nick of time which man they really value, and being willing to humble themselves for the right kind of noble love—but never for the wrong kind of selfish passion. It's that simple.

But it doesn't sound so easy, does it? It's quite a tightrope act. No wonder getting love right is obviously touch and go even for Jane Austen heroines—who seem to have a head start on us, somehow. They arrive at the critical moments in their love stories already equipped with a whole toolbox of useful concepts and mental habits that we don't have. How do they manage to show up at the starting gate so ready for the race?

Well, for one thing, they're used to approaching their relationships— *all* their relationships, including their friendships and their family life— with the kind of deliberation that we usually apply only to our important career goals, our artistic ambitions, or, just possibly, that one significant relationship with a member of the opposite sex. The problem is, by the time we're putting that much effort into a romantic relationship, it's usually because something has gone badly wrong. We're wondering what happened to the initial excitement, or why we're ready to commit so much sooner than he is—or even why this relationship is making us miserable in the very same way as every disappointing relationship we've had in the past. We don't try to master the subject until our love affair (or our love life in general) requires emergency attention. Ransacking the self-help aisle of the local book store in a desperate attempt to fix something that's already broken is no substitute for the expertise Jane Austen heroines bring to all their relationships from the beginning.

For reasons that will become clear later, Jane Austen was no fan of "working on your relationship" in our modern sense. But her heroines do put an enormous amount of energy and care into working on their relationships in general. They approach ordinary friendship and family life with deliberate attention. And the principles and skills they apply to those relationships are different from anything you can learn from our whole advice industry—though there are some interesting parallels to insights from modern psychology.

Think about it. You can't just wake up one morning and say that from now on you'll always judge men by their real worth. The clear head and keen sight that Jane Austen heroines bring to their romantic adventures can't be ginned up on the spot, just as soon as you decide you want to improve your love life. Internal balance and good judgment about other people aren't available on demand. You have to be already practicing having them. Elizabeth and Darcy help each other to find a more nearly perfect balance, but they don't start from zero. Long before they ever notice each other, or even meet, they're both already used to thinking—and talking—quite a lot about how to be the kind of people they want to be, and how to judge other people accurately. You can't wait to become a Jane Austen heroine until after you've met your Mr. Darcy. If you're not already on that trajectory when he comes along, you won't be ready.

Jane Austen on Relationships and "Independence"

One reason Jane Austen heroines are so much better at managing love and romance than we are is the simple fact that they have more practice. Not practice specifically at love and romance—we're definitely ahead of them in false romantic starts—but practice at managing close relationships with other people, in general. Practice really does make perfect, even in knowing how to get along with people. And living in the eighteen-teens, you pretty much *had* to learn how to live with other people in a way that twenty-first-century people can mostly avoid.

Houses were mostly smaller, and families were quite a lot bigger. They didn't have dishwashers and washing machines; instead, they had servants, often living in the house.[1] Single women shared bedrooms, and quite frequently beds, with their sisters (and, on long visits, their female friends and cousins) all their adult lives. They didn't go off to college, get jobs, and rent apartments; they never left home, or else they came back after a few years at a boarding school and lived with their families.[2] All the trends that are giving us ever more independence and elbow room (think McMansions for one- and two-child families; colleges building new dorms with only "singles" to accommodate freshman classes full of kids who've never shared a room in their lives; and cell phones so ubiquitous that it's becoming awkward even to ask a stranger the time) were either non-existent or in their infancy in Jane Austen's day. Almost any

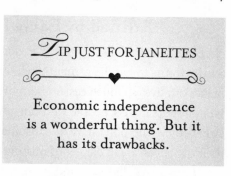

TIP JUST FOR JANEITES

Economic independence is a wonderful thing. But it has its drawbacks.

kind of entertainment required a cooperative effort. To hear music, you had to actually collect live musicians in one place. Games were with fellow guests around a card table, not at your solitary screen.[3] And getting to a ball often meant having to be grateful to more well-to-do neighbors for a place in their carriage.[4]

Jane Austen would not begrudge us our independence. Far from it. "Independence" is something her characters value very highly. Then, as now, it required money. Being able to pay your own way means not always having to please, compromise with, and be grateful to the people you depend on for the bare necessities of life. It means freedom from the temptation to do really shabby things to avoid offending them.[5] Jane Austen was proud to be earning cash from her novels. And she invested her earnings exactly as a person who valued independence would—so that her small nest egg would provide her with a steady stream of income to make her a little less dependent on her family for every comfort and convenience. We don't think of ourselves as rich. But most of us take it for granted that we can afford to live apart from our parents as single women. That kind of independence was beyond the wildest dreams of Jane Austen and her heroines. "Independence" was something they aspired to; for us, it's a non-negotiable minimum of adult life. Jane Austen would be delighted at the prosperity of our modern lives, which—even in the midst of the worst recession since the 1930s—are still replete with comforts and freedom unimaginable in her day.

"Ruined by Early Independence"

But she would also notice that our prosperity has actually made it harder for us to handle romantic relationships well—precisely *because* it makes our lives so much easier and more independent of other people. In Jane Austen's novels, people who can afford "independence," and particularly people who don't have to consult anyone else in the arrangement of their own lives, are in danger of missing happy love.

"Emma Woodhouse, handsome, clever, and rich," Jane Austen tells us, suffers from two "disadvantages" that Emma, strange as it may seem, doesn't class as "misfortunes" at all—"the power of having rather too much her own way, and a disposition to think a little too well of herself." Though Emma herself can't see it, her independence, and the fact that she's rather spoiled as a result, actually are disadvantages when it comes to finding happy love. Women who aren't used to having to accommodate other people (Emma, Maria Bertram, Mary Crawford) don't have the chance to exercise some capacities that are crucial for success in love. Jane Austen makes the down side of "independence" even more explicit in the case of some of her male characters—men, after all, were much more likely than women to be financially independent in her day. Willoughby is a victim of "the irreparable injury which too early an independence, and its consequent habits of idleness, dissipation, and luxury, had made in the mind, the character, the happiness, of a man who, to every advantage of person and talents, united a disposition naturally open and honest, and a feeling, affectionate temper." And Henry Crawford, who "indulged in the freaks of a cold-blooded vanity a little too long," lost the woman he loved because he was "ruined by early independence and bad domestic example."

Financial independence doesn't automatically give us big egos, make us lazy and selfish, or turn us into cold fish who are callous about other people's feelings. But it does make it dangerously easy for us to fall out of the habit of getting along with other people at close quarters—something we'd have more practice at if we were forced to live as close to other people as Jane Austen heroines do. A teacher at my son's school once pointed out to me that virtually all our really close, important, and lasting relationships are formed during the few periods of our lives when we are forced to live with other people—our siblings, the friends we make in our freshman dorm at college, the other guys in boot camp or in the unit in Afghanistan.[6] We find those relationships uniquely satisfying. And yet, ironically, we also find independence so compelling that we avoid putting ourselves in situations where we're likely to form those kinds of friendships.

Of course we're "independent" in a different way from rich people in Jane Austen novels. We've achieved financial independence from our families by working for a living. Granted, we do have to please our bosses and our customers, but the fact that we're modern employees—instead of governesses, companions, or teachers in residence at boarding schools—means that it's only in the limited hours when we're at work that we have to be "professional" in our dealings with other people. And once we leave work, we feel that we should be able to relax.[7] Which too often means we don't think of putting any actual work into the interactions we have with people in our private lives. When we're with our friends, or with a guy, we're expecting what we want from those relationships to happen naturally, without much deliberate effort on our part. Until, that is, we get into a bad patch with a boyfriend and find ourselves inspired to "work on our relationship." Whereas Jane Austen believed every kind of relationship—friendship, marriage, family life—requires "forbearance" on the part of both parties. It's just hard for two people to fit into the same space; it takes work.

Why Are "Relationships" Harder for Us?

Paradoxically, Jane Austen thought it was *easiest* to manage the very kind of relationship that seems *hardest* to us. She counts it as achieving "independence" when a woman leaves her parents' house—or her job as a governess-companion, as Mrs. Weston does at the beginning of *Emma*—to marry. To Jane Austen, a man and woman in love with each other are the two people on earth who come closest to being able to comfortably fill the exact same space at the same time. Men and women are so different from each other that they naturally complement as well as compete with each other. And of course the division of labor between the sexes was more rigid then.[8] Those differences—the complementarity and the possibility of some kind of natural harmony between men and women—make sense of the idea that while it's "dependence" to share a house and an income with your parents or your employers, it's "independence" to share them with your husband. Plus, in that case, there's the excitement of new love (not to mention the sex) to help smooth over the rough spots.

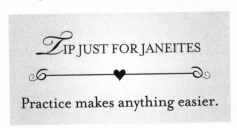

TIP JUST FOR JANEITES

Practice makes anything easier.

So why do "relationships" seem so much harder for us today than relationships in general—friendships and so forth—do? I don't think it's only because instead of relying on traditional gender-based assignments we have to negotiate who does the dishes and who balances the checkbook. It's that, these days, a romantic relationship is almost the *only* really close relationship a lot of us even try to have as adults—"close" in the practical sense that we're sharing living space, money, and decision-making about anything more important than where to have lunch.

We turn to our friends for sympathy about the parts of our lives we're actually having to "work on"—our jobs and our relationships with men. Friends are there when we step out of the hurly-burly of life onto the sidelines, when we do the post-game analysis. We share our thoughts and feelings with them, or maybe with our mother or our sister; but after we leave college and those tiny shared apartments where we moved when we got our first jobs, we don't often share our *lives* with anybody but a guy. Which means that we're trying to manage our "relationships" without the kind of practice at relationships in general that Jane Austen heroines have.

Arbiters of Manners and Morals in Their Own Right

But Jane Austen heroines don't just have more practice at relationships than we do. They also have a lot more *theory*. Jane Austen's characters continually think and talk about the right way to act in relationships with other people.

They theorize about romantic relationships, of course. Elizabeth Bennet and Charlotte talk over Bingley's courtship of Jane; they disagree about whether she should let him see that she's beginning to fall in love with him. Mrs. Gardiner advises Elizabeth on what to do when you realize you're interested in a man who can't afford to marry you.

But Jane Austen gives us similar conversations about every kind of situation between people, not only about their love lives. And these discussions don't take place just between the people whose choices are being canvassed. Jane Austen's characters consider it their right—even their duty—to take a position on other people's choices, and to hold up their own and their neighbors' behavior to certain principles by which relationships ought to be managed.

Elizabeth and Colonel Fitzwilliam discuss whether Darcy had a right to use his influence with Bingley to persuade him to give Jane up. Fitzwilliam doesn't think it at all odd for Elizabeth to have a strong opinion on the subject—even though he has no clue that they're actually talking about her sister! He's heard the story from Darcy and retailed it to Elizabeth, not realizing it has anything to do with her family, just because it sheds an interesting light on his friend's character. Colonel Fitzwilliam finds it quite natural that Elizabeth should take a keen interest in the abstract question of how much influence Darcy should presume to exercise over a friend's choices.

Applying their reason and principles to interesting questions about people's "conduct" and their "character" is simply something ladies and gentlemen do. They talk about whether writing letters quickly is something to be proud of. They disagree on whether walking three miles to visit your sick sister at a neighbor's house—and arriving there with your petticoat "six inches deep in mud"—is justified by your affection for your sister, or shows a "conceited…indifference to decorum." They discuss what qualifications entitle you to call yourself a "really accomplished" woman. They debate whether it's admirable, or weak, for a man to be willing to change his plans at a moment's notice to accommodate his friends. They consider it their right—and even their responsibility—to take a position on the correct way to conduct yourself in any conceivable set of circumstances.

By the time a Jane Austen heroine finds herself in what we'd call a "relationship" with a man, she's better practiced at relationships in general than we are. And she's also armed with more theory about how to deal with other people. We, in contrast, are starting out with a huge relationship-expertise deficit.

"Her Attention Was All for Men and Women"

So how can we close the gap? Well, we can start by taking questions of "conduct" and "character" more seriously—instead of expecting that the natural course of things is for us to be able to get along effortlessly with the people we're close to. We can remind ourselves that our relationships would benefit from some of the same deliberate attention we put into work or school, and that no Jane Austen heroine would be ashamed to take relationships more seriously than she takes anything else in her life.

After all, Jane Austen expected *other human beings*—not money, not accomplishments, not "independence," as much as she valued those things—to be the most reliable source of happiness in this life. Caring about people as she did (and understanding romantic love in all its glory), she must have been devastated never to marry and have children.[9] But she still treated relationships as the most important thing in her life. She was the kind of aunt her nephews adored, the one her niece turned to for advice on whether to marry a man she was dubious about. Jane Austen wasn't impatient with them if they interrupted her work, or prickly about her reputation as a novelist. She was not just kind about but deeply interested in their (vastly inferior) literary creations. She arranged to do her own writing under conditions that allowed her to put it away quickly to attend to visitors.[10]

And yet, all the time that she was living the life of a traditional woman—a typical English spinster, in fact—putting relationships first, Jane Austen managed to make herself the most accomplished female writer in the history of the English language. How did she do it? Not by shunting family aside

TIP JUST FOR JANEITES

Don't be afraid to put relationships first in your life. (You can get them right and still succeed in a demanding career.)

for her art. And not by trying to "have it all," either. At least not all at once. She did it, first, by picking an artistic project that played to her deepest interest—other human beings. And then she exercised almost superhuman patience. She wrote and revised and wrote some more. For decades. Her first novel wasn't published until she was thirty-five years old—about twenty-five years after she began writing fiction, and more than fifteen years after she began writing *that particular novel*.

A lot of us could have a lot more of what we want if we were willing to go about it the same way: Don't be ashamed to admit to ourselves that the people in our lives matter more to us than any accomplishment of our own.[11] Don't be embarrassed to choose a career that's compatible with taking a big chunk of time off to tend to family, or feel like we're selling ourselves short if we pick a profession that's associated with traditionally feminine interests. And then keep at our ambitions, when we can and as steadily as we can, in the interstices of paying attention to the people we love, until we've achieved something great.

If we want to bridge the chasm between Jane Austen heroines' consummate relationship expertise and our own sad deficit in these matters, we can treat the rough spots in our friendships and relations with family members as opportunities for developing skills we may have to call on at any time, to get love right. And we can take an interest in the rights and wrongs of our behavior, and that of other people. Instead of idly or even maliciously gossiping about our co-workers, friends, and neighbors,[12] we can seriously discuss what kind of behavior is substandard, what kind we admire, and why. The point isn't to build yourself up by cutting other people down, the way Bingley's awful sisters do whenever they talk about Elizabeth. It's to think yourself into a state of mind where you're used to asking what kind of "conduct" will make you an admirable human being—a person of "character." It's a sophisticated way of evaluating behavior that we're not really used to. Emma and Mr. Knightley demonstrate; turn to the next chapter, and you'll see how it's done.

ꞇ𝒜DOPT AN AUSTEN ATTITUDE:

- Notice that getting along with other people is a skill that improves with practice. Are you out of practice?
- Ask yourself how much time and deliberate attention you spend on your relationships in general—compared to your job, your hobbies, your TV, the internet.
- Jane Austen heroines take relationships seriously enough to think and talk quite a lot about how people should behave toward each other. Could you ramp up the attention you pay to this subject?

*Wh*AT WOULD JANE DO?

🌺 Even if she could afford to live on her own, she might actually choose to share with housemates, or even with family. Jane Austen complained about certain indignities and unfairnesses of her "dependent" situation.[13] But she derived enormous satisfaction from living, all her life, with people she really loved.[14] (Don't neglect the possibility that living with family may provide Jane Austen heroines with at least some minimal protection against the disastrous glom-onto-a-guy-just-because-you're-lonely mistake.)

🌺 Jane Austen would have no hesitation about being an arbiter of "conduct" and "character" in any set of circumstances.

🌺 She'd value relationships—all kinds of relationships—over any other possible source of happiness in this life.

*I*F WE *REALLY* WANT TO BRING BACK JANE AUSTEN . . .

🌺 Maybe colleges will stop building new dorms full of "singles" and expect freshmen to learn to live with another human being again!

🌺 Seriously, we'll remember that loving and sharing our lives with other people (or not) is what makes us happy (or not) in the end.

🌺 We'll learn again to pay deliberate attention to all our relationships, not just our "relationships."

🌺 We'll work to close the relationship-expertise gap between us and Jane Austen's heroines. When your Jane Austen hero appears on the scene, you want to be ready.

"RIGHT CONDUCT," "SELF-KNOWLEDGE," AND "DELICACY TOWARDS THE FEELINGS OF OTHER PEOPLE"

IF WE REALLY WANT TO IMPROVE THE LEVEL OF OUR relationship-expertise, we're going to have to go in for some theory, as well as a lot of practice. And there's no better model for theorizing about how to treat other people than Jane Austen's heroes and heroines. Let's take a close look at one particular conversation between two of them. If we watch Emma and Mr. Knightley in action, we can uncover where Jane Austen's principles for good relationships come from. (Remember, that's relationships *in general*, not just "relationships.")

Here's the issue. Emma and Mr. Knightley are discussing why Frank Churchill hasn't yet paid his respects to his father and new stepmother on the occasion of their marriage. Frank has sent a handsome letter, he continually talks of paying the visit, but he never actually shows up.

This is not a trivial matter. Frank's neglect is hurting his stepmother's feelings. The slight is a reflection on the fact that she was a social nobody before her marriage.[1] Emma and Mr. Knightley debate to what degree Frank's financial dependence on his rich aunt and uncle excuses Frank

Churchill's neglect of this duty, and what effect it would have on his relationship with them if he paid the visit against their wishes. Emma—who admits to herself that she's "taking the other side of the question from her real opinion"—defends the "amiable young man," maintaining that it's absurd to expect him to defy the relatives he's totally dependent on. After all, he would risk being disinherited.

But Mr. Knightley is disgusted.[2] And he argues that if Frank did the right thing by his stepmother, then his aunt and uncle would actually respect and trust him more than ever before. It would "fix his interests stronger with the people he depended on." They'd be sure he'd always treat *them* with the gratitude and attention he owed them, too:

> Respect would be added to affection. They would feel that they could trust him; that the nephew, who had done rightly by his father, would do rightly by them; for they know, as well as he does, as well as all the world must know, that he ought to pay this visit to his father; and while meanly exerting their power to delay it, are in their hearts not thinking the better of him for submitting to their whims. Respect for right conduct is felt by everybody. If he would act in this sort of manner, on principle, consistently, regularly, their little minds would bend to his.

"Right conduct" on the basis of "principle"—that's the bedrock on which Jane Austen's heroes and heroines base their judgments of other people's behavior, and their own. Of course there's a superstructure of manners and conventions built up from that basic foundation; nobody in Jane Austen claims that things like "the forms of introduction" or the rules about who gets to be "the principal lady in company" are laws of morality. But Jane Austen's characters follow even those conventional rules because it's part of their "duty"—in the

*❧*IP JUST FOR JANEITES

You can take "right conduct" seriously without going in for sickly sentimental Victorian morality.

sense of what's "due" to other people. There's a strong element of morality in the judgments that Jane Austen characters make about how to manage your relationships with other people.

But Mr. Knightley's "right conduct" and "principle" are *very* different from the icky Victorian morality that can still make us shudder, more than a century after that pudgy queen's reign ended. Jane Austen's characters don't wax lyrical about a saccharine angelic goodness that's the special preserve of innocent virgins, dying children, and downtrodden poor relations. (Yes, Charles Dickens, I'm looking at you.) In Jane Austen's vigorous eighteenth-century mind, morality hasn't been made the exclusive preserve of women and children, much less reduced to a hypocritical concern about women's sexual "virtue"—and an unhealthy interest in that subject. The men in Jane Austen novels are as eager as the women to work out standards of "right conduct"; to judge other people's choices by those standards; and to run their own lives in accordance with them. And none of her characters are looking anxiously over their shoulders all the time to see whether Mrs. Grundy approves. They consider *themselves* to be independent and competent judges of the best way to behave. But on what basis do they judge? Where do Jane Austen's characters find the rules that they go by to manage their lives so elegantly?

Well, they mostly do take their religion pretty seriously. But it's nothing like as simple as that. You don't see Jane Austen heroines sitting down to look up what the Ten Commandments have to say about whether or not to let your family and friends know that you've learned a charming officer in the militia is really a scoundrel who schemed to elope with an heiress for money and revenge. You don't catch them asking themselves what insight the Sermon on the Mount can offer a woman on how to answer the impertinent questions of the busybody aunt of the man she loves.

"Respect for Right Conduct Is Felt by Everybody"

Jane Austen heroes and heroines, like Jane Austen herself, have a very eighteenth-century way of thinking about the connection between 1) the right principles to live by, 2) religion, and 3) how to be happy in this life—all three go together. Jane Austen and her contemporaries believed that rules of "right conduct" aren't *just* written in the Bible. They're also, as a famous eighteenth-century American put it, "self-evident" truths. They're "the laws of Nature and of Nature's God," in other words, principles written into the very nature of things—especially into *human* nature[3]—by the Author of the universe. And those self-evident laws of human nature show us the right way to behave if we want to succeed at "the pursuit of happiness."

As Thomas Jefferson wrote in another context, "We are firmly convinced, and we act on that conviction, that with nations as with individuals, our interests soundly calculated will ever be found inseparable from our moral duties...."[4] Jefferson here sounds a lot like Jane Austen, who writes that the same virtue that "prepares us for the spiritual happiness of the life to come" will also "secure to us the best enjoyment of what this world can give."

Mr. Knightley is thinking along these very same lines when he says that Frank Churchill would "fix his interests stronger" with his aunt and uncle by following his conscience and treating his father with respect. Acting on the self-evident principles of right and wrong is always ultimately in your best interests, because the right way to conduct yourself is written into the very nature of things. "Right conduct" is respected by us all—deep down, even if we don't admit it—and we're disgusted with people who act without principle. We can't help it; it's written into our nature. And if you conform your behavior to the laws inherent in human nature, you'll be pursuing happiness in the most effective way possible.[5]

TIP JUST FOR JANEITES

Doing the right thing
is in your best interests.

So why should we take this two-hundred-year-old way of looking at human nature, morality, and relationships seriously? Could it possibly be applicable to us? Well, the proof of the pudding is in the eating. If you can read Jane Austen and not be impressed—if you're sure you're running your life better than Elizabeth Bennet and Anne Elliot run theirs—then by all means forget about it. If the way they think about their relationships and make their choices doesn't appeal to you, put down this book. But if you think there's something compelling in Elizabeth Bennet's struggle to give up her prejudices and see Darcy for who he really is...in Emma's belated recognition that she wants to quit manipulating other people and embrace "every thing that is decided and open"...in Anne Elliot's gentle but unbending determination always to value the things that are really important even though she has to live in a world ruled by selfish vanity, then it's worth asking how we can discover the principles they run their lives by. The respect that most of us will admit to feeling for *them* is one bit of evidence for Mr. Knightley's claim that everyone respects "right conduct."

Its principles are self-evident. But "self-evident" doesn't mean "obvious to people who've never bothered to think about it and don't give a hoot." Two plus two equals four, and parallel lines can never cross—those axioms are also "self-evident" in the sense that once you understand what they mean, you can't think the opposite. But you have to "get" the basic ideas of arithmetic or geometry in order to "get" that they're self-evident. The same thing is true about the principles of right conduct. In some sense you "can't not know"[6] what you owe other people, in terms of fairness and respect— if you actually think about. But a lot of people do their best not to think about it. And the longer they go on ignoring the whole issue, the less motivated they are to focus on it, as they'd have to realize their own conduct doesn't merit respect. Plus, there's the fact that the more sophisticated principles that Jane Austen heroines debate—about the right conduct in particular complicated social circumstances—are more like the complexities of Newtonian physics than like two plus two equals four. Her ladies and gentlemen start with obvious principles of right conduct and build up from there to a more complex structure of sophisticated ideas about how men and women should behave, the way Newton depended on mathematical and geometric axioms to create an elegant explanation of how physical objects act.

Look again at how Mr. Knightley talks about Frank Churchill's choices. When Emma argues that Frank can't be expected to resist pressure to slight his father and stepmother because he has all the "habits of early obedience" to his aunt and uncle "to break through," Mr. Knightley answers, "I can allow for the fears of the child, but not of the man. As he became rational, he ought to have roused himself and shaken off all that was unworthy in their authority." Being "rational"—being a grownup—means you're capable of understanding what you owe the people you have any kind of relationship with. But you can make your grasp of it clearer or fuzzier, depending on whether you're in the habit of putting it into practice. When Emma maintains that Frank Churchill "may have as strong a sense of what would be right, as you can have, without being so equal under particular circumstances to act upon it," Mr. Knightley counters, "Then, it would not be so strong a sense."

There's a great example from *Mansfield Park* of how a principle about the right way to treat other people can be completely self-evident, and at the same time really hard to see—if you're not used to making yourself pay attention. It's Fanny's first dance, and she's enjoyed the first four dances immensely. She's very eager to dance again, but has to sit out the next two because, though there's an even number of men and women, her cousin Tom has gone out to the stable to look in on his sick horse. She expects that he'll ask her to dance when he gets back. But instead he sits down by her, tells her all about the sick horse, picks up a newspaper, and says "in a languid way, 'If you want to dance, Fanny, I will stand up with you.'" Tom makes it very obvious that he doesn't want her to say yes, and so she can't. And yet a few minutes later, when his annoying Aunt Norris tries to draft him to play cards with the chaperones, he leaps up, tells Mrs. Norris he was just going to dance with Fanny, and "indignantly" exclaims, "A pretty modest request upon my word! ... To want to nail me to a card table for the next two hours.... And to ask me in such a way too! without ceremony, before them all, so as to leave me no possibility for refusing! *That* is what I dislike most particularly. It raises my spleen more than any thing, to have the pretence of being asked, of being given a choice, and at the same time addressed in such a way as to oblige one to do the very thing—whatever it be!"

Fanny is happy to be dancing again, but she can't be grateful to Tom "or distinguish, as he certainly did, between the selfishness of another person and his own."

You don't think of "Never ask a girl to dance in a way that makes it impossible for her to say yes" as a moral principle. It's not anywhere in the Bible. But Tom's clearly done a shoddy thing here, and Jane Austen shows that he ought to be able to see that he's being selfish. The abstract principle of "right conduct" in this situation is self-evident to him; Tom himself does an impressive job of articulating exactly what he's done wrong. But he doesn't apply the lesson to judge his own behavior, only his aunt's. The basic underlying moral principle is obvious to anybody who cares about "right conduct": Treat other people the way you would want to be treated. (That one *is* in the Bible.) It's just that seeing exactly how the basic principle applies in all the sophisticated complexities of social life is a lot easier when you're the victim of other people's selfishness than when you're the one being selfish.

All the complicated questions that Jane Austen's ladies and gentlemen debate with each other have to be decided, ultimately, by reasoning from basic principles that are self-evident to everyone. But it's not just a question of seeing these principles. You also have to be in the practice of acting on them. If you never act on them, after a while you won't even be able to see them clearly. The longer you let yourself go *on* being selfish, the harder it is to see the right conduct in your particular circumstances.

The Personal Is Personal (and Never Mind the Political)

This is another reason that the keen interest Jane Austen characters take in "principle" and "right conduct" feels so different from Victorian morality. In Jane Austen, the right way to conduct yourself in the tangled realities of life with other people isn't about conforming to authority. In fact, it's often about *resisting* the authority of parents and guardians. In Jane Austen it's the older generation who have let their long habits of selfishness make "self-evident" principles obscure to themselves. And it's Jane Austen's young people who come to these questions with energy and high ideals.

The fourteen-year-old Susan Price, "acting only on her own unassisted reason,"[7] is a real force for good in her parents' mismanaged household, dominated by chaos and favoritism. And when Sir Thomas Bertram puts the force of his formidable character behind his advice that Fanny accept Henry Crawford's offer of marriage, his young niece stands firm on the principle that it would be wrong to marry a man she can't love and respect.

General Tilney cynically eggs his son Henry on to court Catherine Morland because the General thinks she's an heiress; when he hears she's actually poor, he expects Henry to drop her like a hot potato. But the son, knowing himself now "bound as much in honour as in affection to Miss Morland," proposes to Catherine in defiance of his father because he's "sustained in his purpose by a conviction of its justice."

Again and again, Jane Austen's twenty-something heroes and heroines insist on doing the right thing against the unreflecting selfishness of the older generation. Where Jane Austen's fictional parents and guardians have too often learned from their experience only to be short-sightedly selfish, or simply not to care any more, her heroes and heroines strive for clear and impartial judgment about how people ought to behave.[8]

Jane Austen heroines are utterly uninterested in all things political. In the novels, "politics" is practically a synonym for "the most boring thing you can possibly talk about."[9] But Jane Austen does mention "justice" very frequently, in all the novels. Only the kind of justice she's interested in isn't about the poor, or conflict between classes, or improving social conditions.[10] What Jane Austen was really interested in was whether men and women "do justice" to the people in their personal lives: whether they judge the people they actually know fairly, and whether they're loyal or untrustworthy friends, grateful or ungrateful children, impartial parents or the kind who play favorites. The kind of "justice" Jane Austen finds inspiring is Catherine Morland's "innate principle of general integrity."[11] Jane Austen heroines bring all their youthful idealism—the very same moral fervor that college students over the past half century have poured into political action on Civil Rights, the Vietnam War, divestment from South Africa, and Occupy Wall Street—to conducting their personal lives with scrupulous justice to everyone they're close to and compassion for other people's flaws and struggles.

Just Plain Good Manners

There's a paradox about Jane Austen's stress on "principles." On the one hand, she's got very high standards about the right way to behave. But on the other hand, she's totally against bossing, bullying, arguing with, and generally interfering in the lives of other people on the excuse they're not living up to those standards. *Not* because she doesn't think the same "principles" apply to everybody. The self-evident principles that her heroines live by have universal application; they're the same standards that they apply to other people's conduct when they exercise their judgments about how those other people should behave. They freely judge other people by those principles, in the sense of debating and deciding on what's right and wrong about their conduct. But they *don't* judge other people in the sense of 'standing in judgment over them' from a position of moral superiority. They're not judgmental.

"Self-knowledge" inoculates them against self-righteousness and ugly Victorian hypocrisy. They're always on the look-out to be sure that they're not making the too-common error Tom Bertram falls into at Fanny's first dance: seeing other people's flaws as clear as day, all the while being utterly blind to your own. On one of the very rare occasions when a Jane Austen heroine gives unsolicited advice—when Anne Elliot advises Captain Benwick on more cheerful and edifying reading—she immediately fears "that like many other great moralists and preachers, she had been eloquent on a point in which her own conduct could ill bear examination." Jane Austen heroines are sparing even of *solicited* advice.[12]

That's because Jane Austen heroines know something we tend to forget. It is almost impossible for people to hear any advice about their own behavior. If you tell them that they're going about something the wrong way, or that the thing they're pursuing isn't worth having, they'll almost never listen to you. What they *will* do, quite frequently, is get angry about it. That's why it's "a wonderful instance" of advice-giving "without being resented" when Elizabeth actually listens to Mrs. Gardiner's advice that she should discourage Wickham. It's "injudicious" to attempt to control things you don't have any power over—as when Susan Price tries to make her brothers keep their noise down at home though she doesn't really have the authority to make them behave. Failing attempts to influence other people's choices are inevitably conducive to quarrelsomeness, discord, and the kind of too-frank exchange of views in which you end up flinging accusations and ugly characterizations at the people closest to you, without any kindness or even respect—all things that Jane Austen's heroes and heroines recoil from with horror. They make efforts to "keep the peace" because they don't want to live in chaos and hostility. And they particularly don't want their closest relationships to spiral downward into undignified spats.[13]

Jane Austen's heroines know that if you want to get other people to take your insight into how they ought to live seriously, you can't use the direct attack method—though that's always most tempting to try. Instead, you have to 1) set them a really good example by actually living up to the principles you want them to see, and 2) treat other people with respect, approaching anything remotely like telling them what to do *very* carefully and gently. That's why Fanny Price would be more likely than anyone to influence Henry Crawford for the better. She's "firm as a rock in her own principles" but with "a gentleness of character so well adapted to recommend them." A lot of our modern therapeutic culture, from "the serenity to accept the things I cannot change" to any good therapist's insistence that you focus on your own issues instead of trying to fix other people, does the work that good manners did in Jane Austen's world. Well, make that good manners *and* self-knowledge.

As Jane Austen points out, real self-knowledge supplies a "higher species of self-command" than mere "politeness." The honest realization that in your own mind you'll almost always overstate other people's flaws and underestimate your own is what saves Jane Austen's good manners from turning into Victorian hypocrisy. Real Jane Austen-style "forbearance" with other people's faults doesn't mean pretending that you think everyone's better than you, meanwhile storing up all your secret criticisms and resentments of them for an eventual explosion.[14] When Jane Austen heroines are running their lives the right way, they're tougher on themselves than on other people—honestly, because they actually see how much harder it is to judge yourself by your principles than anybody else. Things that you could easily see are mistakes, if only someone *else* were doing them—like how

TIP JUST FOR JANEITES

The very highest standards for yourself are perfectly compatible with the highest degree of respect and compassion for other people—in fact, they tend to go together.

stupid and dangerous it is for you to keep pinning your hopes on a man who's obviously pursuing your already-engaged sister and only pretending to pay attention to you when the chaperones are watching—are the very things that never take a clear shape in your mind if you're lacking in "knowledge of [your] own heart" (as Jane Austen says about Julia Bertram). Really holding yourself up to your own principles is a stretch, but it's necessary if you're going to be fair to other people, get along with them, and have any chance of influencing them for the better.

That's how Elizabeth begins to do justice to Darcy. When she remembers the arrogant way he proposed to her, she's "full of indignation." But when she thinks about "how unjustly she had condemned and upraided him, her anger was turned against herself; and his disappointed feelings became the object of compassion." She gets to Mr. Knightley's "delicacy towards the feelings of other people" by seeing that the way she hurt him wasn't fair. Jane Austen's ideal was "to be severe only in the examination of our own conduct, to consider our fellow-creatures with kindness, and to judge of all they say and do with that charity which we would desire from them ourselves."

ADOPT AN AUSTEN ATTITUDE:

- Mr. Knightley claims, "Respect for right conduct is felt by everybody." Can you think of an example—some time when you did the right thing, or you saw somebody else do something fair but hard and thus earn respect even from people who might not have the intestinal fortitude to do the right thing themselves?

- Jane Austen heroines think about what's due to the people they're close to. If you were thinking about "justice" and "right conduct" as the way to manage your close relationships, might there be something—respect, gratitude, some particular act of attention, maybe "delicacy" toward another person's feelings—that you would realize you owe someone?

- Do you care about justice? Jane Austen would say that it's in your power to "do justice" to the people you're close to.
- Is there someone you're blaming? Imagine applying Jane Austen's prescription to your relationship. If a Jane Austen heroine felt the urge to condemn, she'd ask herself whether her own conduct could "bear examination."
- Is there someone you want to change? Have you tried gentleness?

*W*HAT WOULD JANE DO?

- She'd consider herself an arbiter of manners and morals, fully capable of applying self-evident principles to complex social situations.
- She'd treat other people the way she'd want to be treated. She wouldn't judge them more severely than she'd judge herself.
- She'd relate to her parents, siblings, co-workers, and friends with justice and "delicacy towards the feelings of other people."

*I*F WE *REALLY* WANT TO BRING BACK JANE AUSTEN . . .

- We'll find our way back to an approach to relationships that means applying our intelligence to discover principles (not mindlessly obeying authority), doing justice to people we actually know (not just taking political stances), and treating other people and their feelings with genuine respect (not judgmental self-righteousness).

CHAPTER NINE

RIENDSHIP, THE SCHOOL OF LOVE

YOU CAN PRACTICE "JUSTICE," SELF-CONTROL, "delicacy towards the feelings of other people," and "forbearance" toward their faults in any personal relationship you have—by trying to get along better with your parents or your siblings, for instance, or with your co-workers. Every extra bit of Jane Austen heroine-style effort you put into those relationships is so much exercise that will get you into better shape to manage your relationship with your hero when you meet him.

But there's one particular kind of relationship that prepares you for romantic love in a unique way. Sure, getting along with your family will help you know how to get along with the man you love one day. But you can't learn how to *pick* the right guy from your relationships with your family members—or with anyone else who's a "given" in your life. Your family, you don't get to choose. Your friends, you pick for yourself. And picking the right guy is obviously crucial to happiness in love. It's only in your friendships that you get any practice at this vital skill. True, we're almost always closest to people we were thrown together with at some point by circumstances beyond our control. But of everybody we meet on that first day in high school or in the dorm freshman year, there are one or two we pick out—and they pick us—because we seem to belong together.

Better People Make Better Friends

There are interesting lessons about friendship in Jane Austen's novels. The most obvious one is simply that better human beings make better friends. The whole Isabella Thorpe subplot in *Northanger Abbey* is a hilarious send-up of the friendship from hell. Isabella makes professions of undying friendship.[1] She continually tells Catherine that she would do anything for her friends.[2] But in fact she won't inconvenience herself in the smallest way for Catherine.[3] Isabella takes no interest in Catherine's concerns; she doesn't mind hurting or embarrassing Catherine in any scheme in her own interest that she happens to have in hand at the moment.[4] Isabella's "shallow artifice" eventually becomes so obvious that even Catherine, naïve as she is, sees through it. And Catherine finds a much better friend in Eleanor Tilney. Eleanor never gushes about undying friendship, but she does really love Catherine.[5] While Eleanor is much smarter and more sophisticated than Catherine is, they're alike in the fair and honest way they treat other people, in contrast to a scheming manipulator like Isabella.

Something similar but more subtle happens in *Pride and Prejudice*. When Charlotte Lucas accepts Mr. Collins's proposal, Elizabeth realizes that

TIP JUST FOR JANEITES

For lasting friendship, pick people you can respect and trust.

she has a lot less in common with her best friend than she thought: "She had always felt that Charlotte's opinion of matrimony was not exactly like her own, but she could not have supposed it possible that when called into action, she would have sacrificed every better feeling to worldly advantage." From now on it's going to be impossible for Elizabeth and Charlotte to share the same "unreserve" they've always enjoyed in the past.[6]

Elizabeth stays friends, of a sort, with Charlotte. Though "persuaded that no real confidence could ever subsist between them again," she still loves Charlotte and cares that Charlotte will be miserable with Mr. Collins—even though that misery is of her own choosing. So though Elizabeth feels "all the comfort of intimacy" is "over," she keeps up a correspondence "as regular and frequent as it had ever been" with Charlotte, and agrees to visit her (and her awful husband) in their new home. Elizabeth's letters and visit are bright spots in Charlotte's bleak existence, and Elizabeth is willing to make that kind of contribution to cheer her friend up "for the sake of what had been" between them, though she expects "little pleasure" from it.

But because her relationship with Charlotte is no longer an intimate, "unreserved" friendship, Elizabeth comes to appreciate and rely on her sister Jane more than ever before: "Her disappointment in Charlotte made her turn with fonder regard to her sister, of whose rectitude and delicacy she was sure her opinion could never be shaken." Elizabeth can respect and trust Jane, and share her secrets with her. She can go to her for advice— when she learns the truth about Wickham's character and needs to decide whether to let other people know, and when she realizes how unfair she has been to Darcy and needs a sympathetic friend to talk the whole thing through with. Jane is a better friend to Elizabeth because she's a better person.

"They Will Neither of Them Do the Other Any Good"

But in Jane Austen novels the wrong kind of friend isn't always somebody with defective principles, like Charlotte Lucas.[7] Sometimes the wrong friend for you is a perfectly nice person, but you've picked her for the wrong reasons. Not every man who's a decent human being would necessarily be a good match for you, and not every woman who's a person of character is the right friend for you, either. Sometimes the problem isn't either one of the friends—it's the kind of friendship they have.

The case of the wrong kind of friendship in Jane Austen is the relationship between Emma and Harriet Smith. What Mr. Knightley guesses at the very beginning of it turns out to be true: "They will neither of them do the other any good." The problem with their friendship isn't so much one or the other of the young women, as why they become friends in the first place, and how the friendship affects each of them.

Emma picks Harriet because she's "a pretty girl, and her beauty happened to be of a sort which Emma particularly admired. She was short, plump, and fair, with a fine bloom, blue eyes, and a look of great sweetness." Note the "short" and the "sweetness." Emma likes Harriet's manners, too: "so pleasantly grateful for being admitted to Hartfield, and so artlessly impressed by the appearance of everything in so superior a style to what she had been used to, that she must have good sense and deserve encouragement."

> ### ◿IP JUST FOR JANEITES
>
> ◦⟋⎯⎯⎯⎯❤⎯⎯⎯⎯⟍◦
>
> Don't pick your friends for their "delightful inferiority" to yourself—and don't let anybody pick you for that reason either.

Emma has plans for Harriet: "*She* would notice her; she would improve her; she would detach her from her bad acquaintance, and introduce her into good society; she would form her opinions and her manners." Harriet's "not clever" like Emma, or like the equal companion Emma has just lost—Mrs. Weston, her former governess who's just gotten married.[8]

We've all seen friendships like this, where the personality of one of the friends is much stronger than the other's. It's a staple of young adult fiction.[9] And like a lot of those relationships, the friendship between Emma and Harriet ends badly. It's embarrassing to watch Emma put her plan for Harriet's improvement into effect—especially the part of the plan where she "detach[es] her from her bad acquaintance."

Undue Influence

Harriet has been staying with the family of a Miss Martin, a school friend. When Emma realizes that the girl's brother, a young farmer, likes Harriet, and Harriet seems to like him, too, Emma immediately decides that if Harriet "were not taken care of, she might be required to sink herself for ever"—to sink, that is, below the higher social position that Emma has decided to get Harriet into by arranging a better match for her, one with some gentleman of independent means. So Emma starts advising Harriet about her friendship with the Martins. She insinuates that Harriet is out of their class: "I wish you may not get into a scrape, Harriet, whenever he does marry;—I mean, as to being acquainted with his wife—for though his sisters, from a superior education, are not to be altogether objected to, it does not follow that he might marry anybody at all fit for you to notice.... I want to see you permanently well connected—and to that end it will be advisable to have as few odd acquaintance as may be."

When Robert Martin sends Harriet a letter declaring his love, she naturally shows it to her great friend Miss Woodhouse, hoping for help making up her mind how to answer his proposal. Emma makes a parade of refusing to advise Harriet one way or the other, all the while pulling out every stop to make sure that Harriet refuses Mr. Martin. First Emma reads the letter, and when it's better than she expected—"as a composition it would not have disgraced a gentleman; the language, though plain, was strong and unaffected, and the sentiments it conveyed very much to the credit of the writer"—she tries to think that Mr. Martin's sister must have helped him write it. Next she pretends that Harriet wants advice only on *how* to write her letter of refusal, not on *whether* she should refuse or accept—because she wants Harriet to think accepting Mr. Martin is out of the question.

Then, when Emma begins to be afraid Harriet will give in to "the bewitching flattery of that letter," she begins to give her *general* advice on how to evaluate a proposal of marriage: "I lay it down as a general rule, Harriet, that if a woman *doubts* as to whether she should accept a man or not, she certainly ought to refuse him." The whole time, Emma pretends she's not really putting her finger on the scale: "'Not for the world,' said Emma, smiling graciously, 'would I advise you either way. You must be the best judge of your own happiness."

Finally Harriet hits on the answer that Emma has been hinting at so broadly: "Miss Woodhouse, as you will not give me your opinion, I must do as well as I can by myself; and I have now quite determined, and really almost made up my mind—to refuse Mr. Martin. Do you think I am right?" To which Emma quickly answers, "Perfectly, perfectly right my dear Harriet. You are doing just what you ought. While you were at all in suspense I kept my feelings to myself, but now that you are so completely decided I have no hesitation in approving."[10]

Okay, so we can see why Jane Austen called Emma "a heroine whom no-one but myself will much like." Her manipulations are almost too painful to watch. Emma talking Harriet into refusing the "warm attachment" of this worthy young man—he's really *too* good for her—and, almost worse, persuading Harriet to drop her friendship with his sister, is even more appalling than Emma busily (and vainly) scheming to make Harriet a great match with Mr. Elton or Frank Churchill. True, Harriet will suffer painful disappointments as a result of Emma's having talked her into daydreaming about men who never give her a second thought. But in giving up Robert Martin and his family, she's losing love and happiness that are actually within her grasp.

Emma is "no friend to Harriet Smith," as Emma herself eventually comes to see. But Emma is not an Isabella Thorpe or a Lucy Steele. She's not scheming to use Harriet for her own ends. Far from it! It's all in aid of Harriet's own betterment. Eventually, Emma will see how stupid and wrong it was for her to stop Harriet from marrying Robert Martin. But how did Emma's good intentions get her into so much trouble in the first place?

"Her Ignorance Is Hourly Flattery"

Before Emma has even begun to interfere in Harriet Smith's life, Mr. Knightley guesses that their friendship is a very bad idea. In another one of those conversations between Jane Austen's ladies and gentlemen, he and Mrs. Weston discuss the budding friendship between Emma and Harriet. Mr. Knightley explains why he's concerned, and Mrs. Weston defends Emma. How can he guess so early that the friendship will be disastrous? As usual with Jane Austen's heroes and heroines, he's applying universal principles about relationships to observations of his own friends and acquaintances.

Mr. Knightley is afraid that Harriet will end up like Eliza Doolittle at the end of *My Fair Lady*, too much the lady to be happy as a flower girl any longer, but not able to find a place for herself in the more sophisticated world she's been taught to pine for.[11] That's easy for us to understand, I think. What may be harder for us to grasp is how the friendship is so obviously[12] bad for *Emma*: "I think [Harriet] the very worst sort of companion that Emma could possibly have. She knows nothing herself, and she looks on Emma as knowing every thing. She is a flatterer in all her ways; and so much the worse, because undesigned. Her ignorance is hourly flattery. How can Emma imagine she has any thing to learn herself, while Harriet is presenting such delightful inferiority?"

When he calls Harriet's ignorance "hourly flattery," Mr. Knightley is pointing to the dangers of inequality in friendship. Jane Austen gives us several pictures of unequal friendships—relationships that are about mutual manipulation, instead of mutual respect. We sometimes fall into the mistake of thinking that Jane Austen is all about money and class.[13] But when Jane Austen says about the Elliots' disappointment when Mrs. Clay runs off with Mr. Elliot, "They still had their great cousins, to be sure, to resort to for comfort; but they must long feel that to flatter and follow others, without being flattered and followed in turn, is but a state of half enjoyment," she's putting her finger on a feature of human nature that doesn't depend on money or titles of nobility. It can just as easily be about other things, like intelligence or looks or strength of personality. Basically it's a preference for mutual manipulation over mutual respect. It's the same reason Lady Susan, world-champion devious manipulator of other people, prefers the flattery of her married lover to the honest love of Reginald de Courcy.[14]

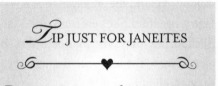

TIP JUST FOR JANEITES

Do not give in to the temptation to roll up your sleeves and take charge of your friends' lives.

Relationships that involve flattery are always about manipulation. Sometimes it starts with good intentions, like Emma's toward Harriet. And sometimes the whole point from the beginning is to use other people for your own profit and convenience, as the Mrs. Clays, Lucy Steeles, and Lady Susans of this world do. Equal relationships, on the other hand, are about respect and what Jane Austen calls "delicacy" toward the other person. In a real friendship you have enough respect for your friend not to just roll up your sleeves and start reorganizing her life.

Harriet calls Emma "Miss Woodhouse"; Emma calls her "Harriet." All the things that made Emma want to pick Harriet for a friend in the first place are ways that Harriet is inferior to herself.[15] Emma is excited about Harriet as a grand improvement project, with herself as the impresario. The tell-tale sign that Emma likes Harriet mostly because the friendship makes Emma look good to herself is that Emma carefully avoids getting close to the one other person she *would* be friends with if she weren't running away from a real friendship of equals.

That person is Jane Fairfax, "so very accomplished and superior!—and exactly Emma's age." Both their friends and family have been expecting Emma and Jane to make friends all their lives,[16] but Jane Fairfax bores Emma stiff.[17] Jane is an orphan who has been raised by a Colonel Campbell, a superior officer of her father, who died in combat. Throughout her adolescence Jane comes to visit her grandmother and aunt in Highbury, where she's to a degree forced on Emma's society. But for reasons that Emma can't exactly explain, the acquaintance has never progressed into a friendship. Jane is beautiful. She's even tall. She's had a superior education. She's accomplished. She plays the piano, in fact, much better than Emma. In other words, she's "the really accomplished young woman, that [Emma] wanted to be thought herself."[18]

Flattery versus "Equal Society"

So what's wrong with flattery (whether it's designed or undesigned)? It spoils people. It makes them more self-satisfied, and increasingly impatient of any kind of challenge to that self-satisfaction. That includes even the mild challenge that comes from the company of people who are in any sense better than yourself—people smarter or more together than you are, people whose standards are higher than yours. If you're used to flattery, you won't want to get close to those people. Flattery unfits you for "equal society"—it's the very opposite of what friendship ought to be. But it's a very tempting substitute for a real friendship, when we're not up for the challenge of being close to another person on an equal basis.

And think of the implications for your love life. Do you want to be training yourself to avoid people who challenge you in any way? Will you be happy if you get yourself into a state of mind in which you expect everyone closest to you—including your boyfriend—to cater to your ego, instead of sharing an equal relationship? That's what Emma is doing to herself. It's no accident: the longer she's friends with Harriet, the less Emma pays attention to anything Mr. Knightley has to say. And notice that her one experiment in romantic love during this period is a flirtation with Frank Churchill, who encourages Emma in all her worst habits. Frank listens to Emma's nasty gossip about Jane Fairfax being in love with a friend's husband.[19] He even eggs Emma on by teasing Jane about it. He flatters Emma's ego with the most outrageous public gallantry—"Ladies and gentlemen, I am ordered by Miss Woodhouse (who, wherever she is, presides)...."

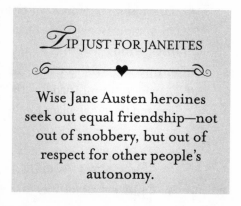

TIP JUST FOR JANEITES

Wise Jane Austen heroines seek out equal friendship—not out of snobbery, but out of respect for other people's autonomy.

Ask yourself. What kind of man is likely to treat you this way? Possibly a guy who isn't living up to very high standards *himself.* Or else a man who doesn't have much respect for—or any serious interest in—*you.* Both things are true about Frank Churchill. He's a pretty weak character. And he's flirting with Emma, it turns out, only to hide the fact that he's secretly engaged to Jane Fairfax. All the time Emma has spent with Harriet Smith is time she has been practicing screwing up her love life in advance—*not* being ready to take the man who really loves her seriously, and setting herself up to be used by the man who doesn't, instead.

$\mathscr{A}$DOPT AN AUSTEN ATTITUDE:

🌹 If friendships have gone wrong for you in the past, was it for any of the reasons in Jane Austen's novels? Was there something wrong with the friend...something wrong with you...or something wrong with the reason you picked her?

🌹 Do you treat your friends with "delicacy" toward their feelings and their own plans for themselves?

$\mathscr{W}$HAT WOULD JANE DO?

🌹 She'd pick equals for friends, and treat them with respect, not try to run their lives for them—or let them run hers.

🌹 She'd pay attention to how she was relating to her friends, and steer clear of flattery and manipulation.

$\mathscr{I}$F WE *REALLY* WANT TO BRING BACK JANE AUSTEN...

🌹 We'll value friends who share our high standards and respect our autonomy.

🌹 We'll realize that in choosing our friends we're practicing for choosing the love that will make us happy, or not.

$\mathscr{D}$ON'T FIND YOUR SOUL MATE

What Jane Austen Heroines Aren't Looking for in a Man (and What They *Are*)

"FULLY TWO-THIRDS OF AMERICANS BELIEVE IN THE concept of soul mates, where 'two people are destined to be together,'" reported the *Washington Times* in September 2010. Even more women than men, researchers found, accept that theory of love. An impressive 69 percent of us, versus 63 percent of men, are on board with the soul mate concept. The down side? People who believe in soul mates are 150 percent more likely to end up divorced than people who don't.[1]

What does Jane Austen have to say on this subject? Are her heroines looking for their soul mates? Do they marry the men they're destined for? She sure doesn't sound like it. Here's Elinor Dashwood, doing her best to talk her Romantic sister out of the soul mate theory of love: "And, after all, Marianne, after all that is bewitching in the idea of a single and constant attachment, and all that can be said of one's happiness depending entirely on any particular person, it is not meant—it is not fit—it is not possible that it should be so."

By the time you've read this far, it's not going to shock you to find Jane Austen on the realistic rather than the Romantic side of any question. But if Jane Austen heroines aren't looking for their soul mates, what are they looking for? And if they don't end up with "The One" perfect match that it's their destiny to be with, how come the matches they've found at the end of their novels seems so...perfect?

A Guy Who's Really Great, Not Just "Great for Me"

A Jane Austen heroine thinks a lot less than we do about finding a guy who's "great for her," and a lot more about finding a guy who's just plain old, flat out great. It's not that compatibility doesn't come into the equation at all—Jane Austen is no proponent of the "don't be so picky, you can be happy with any decent man if you put your mind to it" school of thought.[2] But her heroines think and talk about guys in terms of objective qualities that make them impressive men, not just in terms of how well they suit the heroines' own subjective preferences and needs. Jane Austen has a whole sophisticated vocabulary for talking about every aspect of a man's personality. Because we've forgotten that language, our thinking about any guy—at least when it goes any deeper than looks and status, into questions about what kind of a person he is—tends to collapse almost immediately into a subjective evaluation of what appeals to us personally. A Jane Austen heroine has better criteria for evaluating men. Not with exact scientific accuracy, of course, but by measuring them against standards that have some kind of universal application. She thinks about how "perfect" a guy is in the abstract before she asks if he's "perfect for me."

It's funny. We've forgotten how to think about people's personalities in the objective categories that Jane Austen heroines use. But we can still do that very thing when it comes to people's looks. We talk about whether guys are good-looking not just "for us," but in reality. Of course there's no scientific standard of hotness. The objectivity of our judgments on guys' physical appeal is only a rough and ready sort of objectivity. But it is a more universal measure than the sheer subjectivity of our own personal "type." Think of Tiger Woods and his international harem of cut-rate Elin look-alikes. Elin

Woods is good-looking, but there are plenty of beautiful women who look nothing like her; Tiger was obviously going for a particular physical type.[3] Despite our individual preferences, we can still see that a man is handsome even if he's not our type—just as we know a woman can be beautiful, whether or not she happens to float a particular guy's particular boat.

That ability to see attractive qualities apart from who's your type is something that Jane Austen heroines *also* apply to characteristics that are even more important than looks—to everything, in fact, that makes up a man's personality, mental outlook, and approach to life. A Jane Austen heroine judges a man's "manner," his "address," his "understanding" and "information," his "temper," his "principles," and so forth—before she starts thinking about whether he's the perfect fit for her. Or at least that's the order she does her thinking in, if she's going about picking her hero the right way.

Jane Austen doesn't pretend that looks don't matter. She tells us about Mr. Darcy's "fine, tall person, handsome features, noble mien." Her heroines notice men's looks right away and can discuss the finer points of their social skills and attitudes at least as readily. But then—if they're serious about finding happy endings—they look deeper, at the qualities that make up a man's essential "character."

Mr. Bingley, for instance, is not only "good looking," with "a pleasant countenance." He also has "easy, unaffected manners." Colonel Fitzwilliam is "not handsome," but he's "in person and address most truly the gentleman." Jane Austen's heroines measure guys' manners—whether the men they meet are comfortable with other people, whether they take the trouble to be "generally pleasing"—against an objective standard.[4]

And they're on the lookout for tip-offs about even more important qualities as well. Or they ought to be. Thus Elinor undertakes the due diligence that her sister has so dangerously neglected, taking the trouble to make inquiries of anyone who "might be able to give some more particular account of Willoughby's character" in pursuit of "a confirmation of his merits."

If they skip that step, Jane Austen's heroines are sorry. Elizabeth Bennet, like Marianne Dashwood, foolishly lets herself start to fall for a man before she has thought much about the most important qualities that Jane Austen expects her heroines to notice in men. Elizabeth and Wickham get along beautifully from their first conversation with each other. He's naturally social and comfortable with people, with a "happy readiness for conversation," just like her own. They're both a lot of fun to listen to.[5] Even after Elizabeth realizes that she and Wickham can't afford to be serious about each other, and he defects to become "the admirer of someone else," she's still sure "that whether married or single, he must always be her model of the amiable and pleasing." In their very last conversation before Darcy's letter opens her eyes to Wickham's real character, Elizabeth is still on board with what Wickham says about their natural affinity for each other, believing that "their opinion of every body—would always coincide."

It's not until the letter from Darcy clues her in to what Wickham is really like that Elizabeth tries frantically to figure out if she has ever heard anything about his being a decent human being—"some instance of real goodness, some distinguished trait of integrity or benevolence, that might rescue him from the attack of Mr. Darcy." She suddenly realizes that she has completely neglected her job (and *our* job, if we want to find happy endings) of looking into the actual character of the man she's interested in: "Of his former way of life, nothing had been known in Hertfordshire but what he told himself. As to his real character, had information been in her power, she had never felt a wish of enquiring. His countenance, voice, and manner, had established him at once in the possession of every virtue…. She could see him instantly before her in every charm of air and address; but she could remember no more substantial good than the general approbation of the neighborhood, and the regard which his social powers had gained him in the mess."

> ## 𝒯IP JUST FOR JANEITES
>
> ❦
>
> Don't neglect the job every happy Jane Austen heroine undertakes: discerning the "real character" of the man you're interested in.

He's Just Her Type

Elizabeth's "prejudice" toward Wickham is a classic case of going for your "type"—of thinking *way too much* about whether a man suits you to a T, and *not nearly enough* about whether he's a person of any quality. There's a problem with going for your type. Your individual preferences— whether in looks or in personality traits—are very likely going to arise from quirks on your own part that at worst are dysfunctional, and that even at best unnecessarily limit your choices. If you notice, à la Lori Gottlieb, that you keep picking the same "spontaneous and grounded" type of man with a "sense of wonderment about the world" over and over again, and yet those guys never make you happy, it's definitely time to widen your horizons.

I was well into adulthood before I figured out that I'd always felt comfortable with dark-haired men and been nervous about blond guys, all on the basis of an unexamined assumption that blond men were untrustworthy. Which, I belatedly realized, was probably because my father was brilliant and charming but tragically addicted to alcohol, gambling, and women—and the only blond male in my large extended family. (It didn't help, either, that I watched way too many episodes of *Starsky and Hutch* as a kid.)

Lots of Jane Austen characters pick their partners because of something defective about that person's character that matches up very nicely with some similar defect of their own. John and Fanny Dashwood are *perfect* for each other!

> *𝒯IP JUST FOR JANEITES*
>
> Don't confine yourself to "your type" when you're looking for love.
> (Either the physical type that tends to attract you or the personality type you gravitate toward.)

John is Marianne and Elinor's cold fish of a brother. He has married a woman even more cold-hearted and selfish than himself. And Fanny eggs John on, making all his bad tendencies worse.[6] After John promises his father on his deathbed to provide for his sisters, his wife cleverly talks him out of his promise by appealing to the selfish impulses the two of them share. She knows he won't be able to bear the thought of letting go of even a tiny percentage of the huge fortune they're accumulating to pass down to their spoiled son.[7]

The Eltons are made for each other, too: "'Happy couple!' said Frank Churchill, as soon as they were out of hearing:—'How well they suit one another!—Very lucky—marrying as they did, upon an acquaintance formed only in a public place!'" But what they have in common is "a sort of sneering consciousness" with which they meet any challenge to their vanity and self-importance.[8]

Lucy Steele and Robert Ferrars are exactly suited, as well. They're perfect matches in vulgar, unscrupulous self-promotion. The two of them are equally adept at getting their hands on whatever they want, mostly because no amount of trampling other people's rights is beneath them.[9] Here's how Jane Austen describes the end of Robert and Lucy's story: "They settled in town, received very liberal assistance from Mrs. Ferrars, were on the best terms imaginable with the Dashwoods [John and Fanny, that is]; and setting aside the jealousies and ill-will continually subsisting between Fanny and Lucy, in which their husbands of course took a part, as well as the frequent domestic disagreements between Robert and Lucy themselves, nothing could exceed the harmony in which they all lived together." It is a happy ending, of a certain sort. But not of a sort Jane Austen would recommend.

Opposites Attract

So finding "your type" is obviously not a fail-safe recipe for the kind of happiness Jane Austen holds up for our admiration. But neither is acting on the "opposites attract" principle, and going for someone who seems perfect for you because he balances all your deficiences and you fill in all his gaps. There are lots of Jane Austen characters in relationships of *that* kind, too. And those partnerships aren't necessarily any more attractive than the "just my type" relationships that John and Fanny, the Eltons, or Lucy and Robert have.

Take the absurd Charlotte Palmer in *Sense and Sensibility*, whose unfailing good humour is the perfect complement to the ostentatious rudeness of her husband. "Mr. Palmer is just the kind of man I like," says Charlotte. And in a strange way the Palmers *are* ideally suited to each other: "Charlotte laughed heartily to think that her husband could not get rid of her; and exultingly said, she did not care how cross he was, as they must live together."[10] As Elinor observes, Mr. Palmer's "contemptuous treatment of every body, and his general abuse of every thing before him...were not likely to attach any one to him except his wife."

TIP JUST FOR JANEITES

Opposites may attract, but just because you're smitten with a guy who's really different from you, he's not necessarily Mr. Darcy to your Elizabeth.

And Jane Austen shows us the same phenomenon in the case of less absurd characters as well. It's quite realistic that a couple can seem perfect for each other precisely because their differences provide more scope for both of them to relax into their own faults. John Knightley, Mr. Knightley's younger brother, is a basically decent human being. But he doesn't have the best temper in the world.[11] And it isn't at all improved by the fact that he has married Isabella Woodhouse, a nervous and compliant person who assumes that her husband is right about everything and sympathizes with all his bursts of impatience, however unreasonable.[12] Think of the Bertrams, too. Could Lady Bertram be quite as appallingly lazy as she is[13] if Sir Thomas weren't such a take-charge kind of man?

"Hopes of Happiness from Dissimilarity of Temper"

The author of *Pride and Prejudice* clearly grasped the appeal of the opposites-attract kind of match. But she didn't think it was a sure recipe for happiness. Look at the romantic double plot of *Mansfield Park*. The book's happy ending—the marriage between Edmund Bertram and Fanny Price—is definitely *not* that kind of match. Edmund and Fanny are as alike as two peas in a pod.[14] And the match between them comes about only because two different classic opposites-attract matches fall apart, 1) between the stolid Edmund and the sparkling Mary Crawford, and 2) between mousy Fanny and Mary's brilliant brother Henry. When Edmund finally falls in love with Fanny at the end of the book (she has been in love with him the whole time), Jane Austen tells us, "Having once set out, and felt that he had done so, on the road to happiness, there was nothing on the side of prudence to stop him or make his progress slow; no doubts of her deserving, no fears from opposition of taste, no need of drawing new hopes of happiness from dissimilarity of temper." Of course that reference to "drawing new hopes of happiness from dissimilarlity of temper" describes exactly what Edmund was doing when, infatuated by Mary Crawford, he tried to talk himself into believing that their completely opposite personalities made them ideally suited to each other.[15]

Jane Austen actually makes a good case for the possibilities inherent in these opposites-attract matches that never come to pass. She goes out of her way to tell us that Fanny is wrong to be sure Mary Crawford would always be unworthy of Edmund.[16] And then she paints a really enticing picture of what might have happened between Fanny and Henry Crawford if Edmund had married Mary. Jane Austen points out that Fanny's principles would have made her do her best to stifle her love for Edmund once he was married. And further, that she'd naturally have been thrown together more with Henry, whose character and whose love for her—while both are far from perfect—do hold out some intriguing possibilities.[17]

Henry once claims that he deserves Fanny not because he's perfect like her (or like he, being in love with her, thinks she is), but because he appreciates her perfection better than anyone else does.[18] There's truth in his claim. We're happy at the end when Edmund finally notices Fanny and gives her her heart's desire. But there's something disappointing about the foreclosed possibilities of Henry's love for Fanny. Edmund will be the star of *their* marriage; it'll be more about her adoration of him than his of her. We know Edmund comes to love Fanny. But does Edmund ever appreciate her in the way the brilliant Henry Crawford does?[19] You can't see Edmund bringing Fanny out of her shell the way Henry plans to.[20] Edmund will let her stay a mouse. A blissfully happy mouse, and a mouse who will grow in confidence over time, but still a mouse.

But with Henry, Fanny might have suddenly blossomed; she might have been transformed. As might Henry with Fanny. We actually get to see Fanny beginning to change Henry's life for the better. Because of her, he's taken a new interest in managing his estate. He has actually begun to assume some responsibility for the many human beings who depend on him. Henry hasn't overnight become a model landlord like Mr. Darcy, but he has taken a first crucial step toward applying his impressive intellect and energy to the benefit of his fellow man—something it has never occurred to him to try before. We can imagine that a marriage between Fanny and Henry might have been a more really transformative, Darcy-and-Elizabeth kind of match than the marriage that actually takes place, between Fanny and Edmund.

That's why some readers have always wished *Mansfield Park* would end differently. Critics like Lionel Trilling have pointed out that dinner with Mr. and Mrs. Edmund Bertram would not be the most entertaining evening imaginable. And Jane Austen's sister (and best friend) Cassandra begged her to let Henry marry Fanny.[21] Jane wouldn't do it. In Jane Austen, the real characters of the individual people involved always weigh more heavily than the chemistry between them—whether it's the "just my type" or the "opposites attract" kind of chemistry. Whatever may be true about investments, past performance really *is* the best indicator of future results when it comes to human beings. Henry destroys his chances (and Fanny's) for an especially exciting and transfor-

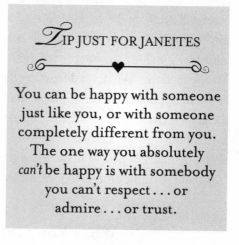

Tip just for Janeites

You can be happy with someone just like you, or with someone completely different from you. The one way you absolutely *can't* be happy is with somebody you can't respect . . . or admire . . . or trust.

mative marriage by slipping back into the womanizing habits that made Fanny think returning his love would be unwise.[22] Jane Austen shows us the potential that Henry and Mary Crawford hold out for Fanny and Edmund, but also the risk. Later—in contrast to his earlier hopes built on the shaky foundation of "dissimilarity of temper" between Mary and himself—Edmund is sure he's on "the road to happiness" because he knows that Fanny's "mind, disposition, opinions, and habits wanted no half concealment, no self deception on the present, no reliance on future improvement. Even in the midst of his late infatuation, he had acknowledged Fanny's mental superiority [to Mary Crawford]. What must be his sense of it now, therefore?" Edmund's prospects for happiness are solidly grounded in Fanny's real excellence as a person,[23] not just in the fact that the two of them share so much.

So what does Jane Austen's take on romantic suitability boil down to? Well, you can be happy with someone very different from you, as Elizabeth is with Mr. Darcy. Or you can be happy with someone almost exactly like you, like Fanny with Edmund. There may be more room for personal growth and transformation from stretching to meet the other person in the Elizabeth-Darcy kind of match—and thus more sparkle and excitement, at least at first.

But don't forget, life is full of other challenges, and so is love. If personality differences between you and your man don't provide enough challenge to make you stretch and grow, then life as you live it together will throw up hurdles. No need to fear that you're missing out. The obstacles that you meet will heighten the value of your relationship, provide ample opportunity for both of you to push yourselves, and add drama and excitement to your love—as long as both of you are the kind of people capable of rising to the occasion.[24] Whatever differences there are between the "just my type" and the "opposites attract" kinds of matches are completely swamped by the gaping chasm between the happy matches grounded in the real excellence of both people's characters (however like or unlike they are) and the unhappy matches people make when they're so caught up in who's good "for them" that they forget to look for somebody who's really good.

What You Get in Love
Is *the Other Person*

Before we get into the nitty gritty of how to evaluate men if we want to avoid that Romantic dead end, let's consider one last reason that Jane Austen puts less stock than we do in how especially suitable the guy is to you, and more in evaluating the guy you're interested in as an independent individual. Somehow, Jane Austen's genius showed her something that we can easily observe from our greater experience.[25] When you fall for a guy and you're "perfect for each other," then all the things you share—the music you listen to together, the places you spend time, the way you kiss—seem like they belong uniquely to your unique relationship. The things you're discovering together are the very essence of what's between the two of you; you wouldn't have found them otherwise. Or so it seems. But we all know somebody whose boyfriend (or, worse, husband) has turned out to be taking another girl to a place she thought was their special place, or doing with the other girl the exact something she thought had unique meaning to their relationship—and been hurt by it, the way in *Spider-Man 3*, MJ is upset when Peter kisses another girl from hanging upside down: "That was *our* kiss."[26]

That's exactly the way Marianne Dashwood feels—only it's much worse, because it's so much more than a kiss—when she finds out that before he even met her, Willoughby seduced, impregnated, and abandoned Eliza, apparently employing all the charming warmth and energy that made Marianne fall in love with him too. Confessing his past to Elinor, Willoughby himself actually compares the two relationships in a very revealing way:

> If the violence of [Eliza's] passions, the weakness of her under-standing—I do not mean, however, to defend myself. Her affec-tion for me deserved better treatment, and I often, with great self-reproach, recall the tenderness which, for a very short time, had the power of creating any return.... I have injured one [Marianne], whose affection for me—(may I say it?) was scarcely less warm than hers; and whose mind—Oh! How infinitely superior!

The difference between Willoughy with Eliza and Willoughby with Mari-anne isn't some special magic unique to his love affair with Marianne. Both relationships seem like love at the time—to the women, and even to Wil-loughby himself, though in Eliza's case only "for a very short time." The real difference turns out to be no more and no less than the difference between Eliza (with her violent passions and weak understanding) and Marianne (with her "infinitely superior" mind).

The fact is, so much of what *seems* like the unique spell between the two of you really boils down to just him, and just you. What really matters is what kind of human beings you are, which determines what each of you is going to be like with any person you love. Which makes it *really* important to look at what any guy is actually like, rather than to be hypnotized by the magic between the two of you.

To us recovering Romantics, it feels a little flat at first to think that the apparently unique spark between you and a man is mostly just what he'd bring to any relationship, plus what you'd bring to a relationship with any man. But really it means that Jane Austen's kind of love is about *love*. It's more about *actually knowing and valuing the other person*—appreciating him for what he uniquely is, and being really seen, celebrated, and treasured by him for what you are—than it is about a chemical reaction that's quite common even between people who aren't destined for permanent happiness.[27]

Or to put it another way, you could say the chemical reaction[28] is an even more thrilling one precisely when the ingredients being mixed—the two people involved—are of a more powerful quality. If you want the most truly exciting adventure in love, you don't short circuit the process by going straight for the cheap, easy reaction. You hold out for the kind of fireworks you can get when really potent explosive material is involved: Mr. Darcy-grade TNT, not just cheap Wickham-style sparks.

How Elizabeth Gets It Right
the Second Time Around

That's the lesson Elizabeth Bennet learns from her mistakes. She discovers that "gratitude and esteem" for Darcy's real superiority as a human being are "good foundations of affection." Better, in fact, than the instant affinity she felt for Wickham. Jane Austen editorializes, "If the regard springing from such sources is unreasonable or unnatural, in comparison of what is so often described as arising on a first interview with its object, and even before two words have been exchanged—nothing can be said in [Elizabeth's] defence, except that she had given somewhat of a trial to the latter method in her partiality for Wickham, and that its ill success might, perhaps, authorise her to seek the other less interesting mode of attachment."

With Wickham, Elizabeth fell right into easy intimacy with a guy who was "her type" without thinking first about whether he was really a man worth her time. They clicked immediately: she noticed right away how entertaining he was, and how good he made her feel. She never thought, *Is he somebody I can admire, respect, and trust?*—at least, not until long after she should have been raising those questions in her mind.

But Elizabeth recovers from her mistake, does her evaluation of her next serious romantic prospect in the right order, and ends up with a man who's most definitely not "her type"—but who's nevertheless perfect for her. With Darcy, she *first* notices that he's a trustworthy human being (when she has to acknowledge the truth of the claims in his letter); that she can respect him (at Pemberley, when she learns how his self-control, his liberality to the poor, and his care for his sister have impressed the people closest to him); and that he's a man truly worth admiring (when she observes that he's been inspired by her rejection to overcome his pride). Only *then* does she start to ask herself whether she can love him.[29]

Well, we all know how it ends. Elizabeth decides that she wants to make Darcy happy—and that being with him will be bliss for her. And her hopes for "rational" and "permanent" happiness with him are grounded firmly in her knowledge of his character. She has chosen real quality over cheap chemistry.

$\mathcal{A}$DOPT AN AUSTEN ATTITUDE:

- Notice that neither a "just my type" nor an "opposites attract" match is any guarantee of happiness—at least, not of the kind of happiness we see and admire in Jane Austen's novels.
- Ask yourself what you're looking for in a man. Your soul mate? Or a guy of such quality that his character is a solid foundation for permanent happiness?

*W*HAT WOULD JANE DO?

🐝 She'd look through cheap romantic chemistry to guys' actual objective qualities. She'd think it was her job to notice the real character—as much as the looks and status—of the men she met.

*I*F WE *REALLY* WANT TO BRING BACK JANE AUSTEN . . .

🐝 We'll forget about finding our soul mates. We'll start looking for a man who's not just "great for me," but really great.

CHAPTER ELEVEN

*J*ANE AUSTEN'S SKELETON KEYS TO A MAN'S POTENTIAL

(They're More Useful Than Any Compatibility Test)

SO HOW DO YOU RECOGNIZE A GUY WHO'S REALLY great? What exactly are you looking for? Jane Austen heroines have a well-stocked toolbox of categories for analyzing men—a kind of informal checklist of discrete qualities, starting with height and hair color and going all the way to the most important features of a guy's "real character."

"First impressions"[1] naturally start with looks and what Jane Austen calls "manner." Just as naturally, the qualities that matter most are harder to see. But Jane Austen makes it a lot easier. She's got a whole vocabulary—concepts long ago lost to us in the waves of Romanticism and Victorian reaction that swept away her clear-eyed eighteenth-century approach to love, sex, and marriage—for analyzing a man's temperament and mental qualities: his "address"; his "feeling" or "sensibility"; his "education," "information," and "understanding"; his "principles"; his "temper"; and so forth. Jane Austen heroines are just as likely to sit around discussing whether some man has a "calm, decided temper" or one "open to dangerous impressions" as they are to talk about his appearance. More so, in fact.

139

Seeing Men As They Really Are

Not that Jane Austen ever pretended looks and sex appeal don't matter. She wanted us to see those things clearly, too. It can't be emphasized enough how much stock Jane Austen put in *seeing men as they really are*. That means not deceiving ourselves in any way—whether it's about a guy's appearance, his manners, or his innermost beliefs.

Jane Austen was deeply suspicious of anything that makes us forget what's in front of our eyes. She knew all about jaundiced views and rose-colored glasses. And she expected her heroines to correct for them—to realize when their perceptions were being skewed or their judgment about anything, even something as superficial as a guy's looks, was being bought off. Thus it's evidence of Elinor Dashwood's self-awareness and competence to manage her own love life that she realizes Edward is looking more physically attractive to her as she gets to know and like him better.[2] Seeing things in perspective doesn't mean ceasing to see them at all.[3]

"Principles" and "Temper"— the Non-Negotiables

But what precisely *are* the more important qualities we need to be able to recognize in a man? Of all Jane Austen's skeleton keys for unlocking a man's real potential, the two most important are "temper" and "principles."[4] Those are the qualities it's most important to look for when you're considering a guy as a potential mate. If he doesn't qualify in either of those two categories, scratch him off your list. For Jane Austen, temper and principles are not negotiable. Why? Because they're what make a man ultimately admirable, worthy of respect, and possible to trust with your happiness. Temper and principles are what divide the Mr. Darcys and the Captain Wentworths from the Wickhams and Mr. Elliots of this world. They're the most important qualities that ensure you you're getting a man of real quality.

What Jane Austen means by "principles" are those self-evident (though often ignored) rules of right conduct written into human nature. A man with good principles understands that you're obligated to be honest, treat other people the way you'd like to be treated, not take more than your fair share, respect other people's rights and feelings, and so forth. A man with bad principles—or no principles at all—is the kind of person who doesn't pay attention to those self-evident rules. He's a sure bet to make any woman who loves him very unhappy.

So how can you tell if a guy doesn't have good principles? Well, some people will come right out and admit to their bad principles, or even to not having any at all. But most unprincipled guys aren't going to say

Tip just for Janeites

Avoid unprincipled men like the plague.

straight out that that's what they are. They don't sing that they're "gonna break, break, your, break, break, your heart."[5] You have to discern that fact from their behavior, and from the indirect hints they drop in their conversation. If they brag about things they ought to be ashamed of—getting ahead at work by screwing colleagues or customers, making fools of their friends or stiffing them, treating women in a callous way, blowing off the people who depend on them—then you know what you're dealing with. But lack of principles isn't always so easy to discern.

Keep Your Eyes Open

The best evidence, of course—much better than anything he says about himself—is direct observation of a man's behavior. That's where Fanny is lucky; it happens that she was a bystander when Henry Crawford callously charmed her two cousins, deliberately gave Maria reason to believe that he was in love with her, and then abruptly said good-bye just when she expected him to propose. Through the whole affair, Henry showed no sign of having any principle that might make him hesitate for a second to break a woman's heart for his own entertainment. So Fanny happens to know[6] that Henry has no principles when it comes to women. There are points in the novels when Jane Austen holds out hope that people of bad character will reform. But there aren't any real successes at a complete turnaround—such as Henry's case would have been, if Jane Austen had listened to Cassandra and let him marry Fanny.[7] True to past form, Henry gets entangled with Maria again and screws up everything with Fanny—ironically, even after his appreciation of Fanny has taught him the importance of principles. Because of Fanny, Henry Crawford is coming to understand that being a person with principles means you can be trusted.[8] Unfortunately, he's not that kind of person.

The No. 1 Regency Ladies' Detective Agency

It's rare that you get a bird's-eye view of your current romantic prospect's past, as Fanny does.[9] That's why the rest of Jane Austen's careful heroines are detectives when it comes to men's principles. In *Sense and Sensibility*, Elinor plays Sherlock Holmes for her sister Marianne's sake, trying to dig up any clues to Willoughby's character wherever she might be able to find them, asking Mrs. Palmer about his reputation in his own neighborhood in Somersetshire. In *Persuasion*, Anne pursues the same kind of curiosity about Mr. Elliot's true character. Even before she realizes that her friend Mrs. Smith has information to fill in the gaps in what she knows about his past, Anne has worked out—by very careful attention to any hint he gives in conversation with her about how he spent his youth—that there's a conflict between the principles Mr. Elliot now professes and the way he must have actually behaved in the past.[10]

IP JUST FOR JANEITES

When it comes to discovering a man's real principles, Jane Austen heroines are polite detectives.

Anne's detective work keeps her well clear of danger. When Mrs. Smith's revelations about Mr. Elliot—that he married for money, was unkind to his wife until she died, treated old friends with callous cruelty, and got close to the Elliot family only to stop Sir Walter from remarrying so he could inherit a baronetcy one day—confirm him to be a "disingenuous, artificial, worldly man, who has never had any better principle to guide him than selfishness," Anne isn't really shocked.[11]

From Elizabeth Bennet's Hertfordshire to Our Global Village

In my old job as a book club editor, I read quite a lot about how technology is changing our lives. Social critics worry that the internet shortens our attention spans and teaches us to read differently; that email and cell phones exhaust our energy by forcing us to be "on" all the time, maintaining too many too shallow connections; that young kids are under relentless pressure to perform socially—to answer every text immediately and to maintain a Facebook presence that attracts and impresses—and that adult lives will be blighted by youthful indiscretions.[12] But if you think about how social life has changed since Jane Austen's day, you notice that in some ways computers, cell phones, and social media are actually changing our lives *back* toward the way they were *then*. (Not in every way, obviously. Sexting is *not* advisable if you want to live like a Jane Austen heroine.)

One thing that makes social media really retro is the pressure to put a lot of effort into the image of yourself that you show the world. Up until the last ten or fifteen years, virtually every change in social relations for decades had been in the direction of less formal, more casual.[13] The great relaxation of dress and manners[14] continued apace until email, then blogs, then Facebook and Twitter began to change things back in the direction of putting more effort into shaping the appearance you showed in public.

At first email seemed like the next extension of the same relaxing trend.[15] But then something interesting began to happen. Electronic communication—beginning with email, but accelerating with blogs and social media—began to actually reverse what the telephone had done to make long-distance communication ephemeral. When you communicate by computer rather than phone, you're not just expressing yourself, you're also creating a lasting record that represents you. You know you may be judged by it after the passing moment. The opportunity for turning electronic interactions into a lasting representation, a kind of performance, became clearer to many people with blogging—and to almost everyone with the advent of MySpace and Facebook. Because a little extra thought and effort make you look so much more interesting, and because it's so

A Jane Austen Heroine in the Twenty-first Century

Michelle Oddis is a twenty-something communications director for a non-profit in Washington, D.C. I got to know her when she was an editor for a weekly newspaper owned by the company I work for. Among friends and colleagues at the paper, Michelle was known and respected for her savvy vetting of guys by their electronic profiles. So I asked her to tell me how a twenty-first-century woman can exercise the kind of prudence that Elizabeth Bennet demonstrates by inquiring about Mr. Darcy's character.

Social media, Michelle explained, are really much more useful than internet search engines for finding out about men's personal lives, as opposed to their professional accomplishments. "There are two red flags," Michelle told me, "if he doesn't have a Facebook page, or if there's no Wall or a very limited Facebook." Those are warning signs that the man you think you're getting to know doesn't really want you to know about his life. Which in turn could very well mean he's dating multiple girls and not being straight with you about it—and that you're not the one he's serious about.

But, I asked Michelle, what about guys who simply aren't into social media, or who are just naturally shy, private, or technophobic? I give a male friend and colleague as an example. He's a thirty-something single guy with a serious girlfriend, and he uses Facebook pretty much exclusively to renew contact with old friends; his Facebook page isn't a contemporary record of his social life, the way it is for Michelle and her set. He doesn't have much of a Wall, but he's not hiding anything; he just hasn't made the leap into social media—he's slightly older (not running his social life on Facebook, still using email instead of messaging).

It *can* be a generational thing, Michel concedes. Older men (from her perspectiv that can mean men in their thirties) might ha no or a very limited Facebook for innoce reasons. But among guys her age, pretty mu everybody uses it, no matter how shy or priva they are. (Michelle has even dated a CIA age who had a Facebook page!) But in any case, s points out, with a little prudent investigati you ought to be able to tell the differen between a guy who just doesn't use Facebo much and a man who's deliberately hidi something from you. Even if he doesn't spe a lot of time on Facebook, he's going to ha friends who do. And even if he limits what y can see about his life there in order to keep y from knowing what he's really like, you may s be able to put the pieces together.

"I met a guy through Match.com Michelle tells me. "His photo there was ki of blurry, so right up front I asked to see Facebook page. There were a few pho there, including one that looked like h with an old girlfriend, but his Facebook really limited. When I'd been dating him about a month and he was out of town business,' I looked on her page (she tagged in the photo). The girl's prof picture turned out to be another photo of with the guy; it looked like they were vacation together. I called him and asked i had a girlfriend." The guy told Michelle t the girl in the picture was an ex-girlfrie they were just friends now. But she found story hard to believe, and she beca increasingly skeptical about whether he being honest with her. Michelle decided didn't want to be in a relationship that— evidence indicated—was "supplemental what the man had going with a seri girlfriend. Elinor Dashwood would appr easy for friends and family to play appreciative audience with their comments and "likes," everybody gets to cut a figure of sorts, to have a public persona. It does put us under some pressure—pressure that has a lot in common with the responsibility Jane Austen's ladies and gentlemen feel to create and maintain a "character."[16]

We're all leaving a trail behind us, a really permanent record. So all this twenty-first-century technology makes it much harder to be an entirely anonymous stranger whenever you meet new people. The virtual "global village" that the internet is creating has something in common with the real English country villages that Jane Austen's heroines all lived in.

In Jane Austen's day, women didn't socialize with men who hadn't been formally introduced by somebody who at least knew somebody who knew somebody who … knew enough about their pasts to vouch for them. Men's reputations—their "characters"—were expected to precede them, or at least not to lag too far behind. Elizabeth Bennet is frantic when she suddenly realizes that she doesn't really know anything about Wickham's past.[17]

But then, over the course of the nineteenth and twentieth centuries, it became easier to leave your past behind—*without* having to run away and join the army.[18] It became normal to accept a strange man at face value. The internet takes that trend further—so far, in fact, that it starts to collapse in on itself and work in reverse. Sure, computers make it even easier to get together with a total stranger. On the other hand, social media shrink the world so much that even total strangers are getting easier to find out about. Facebook, MySpace, Twitter, blogs, and so forth have created a kind of virtual society in which our pasts all leave traces that can't be so easily erased.[19] A man's past has likely created a cyber-trail, a rough equivalent to the reputation a man had built for himself in Jane Austen's day.

Those cyber-trails certainly make Jane Austen heroine-style detective work about the men we meet easier.[20] It's as natural for you to look around the Facebook page of a guy you're getting to know as it was for Elizabeth Bennet to ask Darcy's housekeeper about her master's character—and it can be just as revealing.

Men of Real Quality

Jane Austen's women don't take an interest in men's principles *only* to avoid unprincipled men—and the unhappiness they inevitably create[21]—like the plague. Her heroines are also on a positive quest for principled men.

Elinor Dashwood, Elizabeth Bennet, Fanny Price, Anne Elliot, Catherine Morland (in her own naïve way), and even Emma (when she isn't tripping herself up in manipulative schemes) are all keen discoverers and honest judges of real quality in human beings. Catherine, plain and honest herself, is as naturally attracted to Henry Tilney's

> **𝒯IP JUST FOR JANEITES**
>
> ⎯❤⎯
>
> Jane Austen's heroines are discerning judges of real quality in human beings.

integrity as she is repelled by John Thorpe's braggadoccio; she feels the difference even though she's not sophisticated enough to be able to explain it. Elinor loves Edward because he cares about the things that really matter. Coming from a family impressed by nothing but money and making a splash in the world, he's somehow managed to acquire simple tastes, honest principles, and a natural bent for domestic happiness.[22] Fanny Price, even as a little girl, admires the good principles that make Edmund consider her feelings when the rest of the family are too selfish to notice or care that she's miserable. Anne is originally smitten with Wentworth's honest, energetic masculinity. Seven and a half years later she's bewitched again by the easy, generous, really genuine friendships he enjoys with his brother officers, who share a "hospitality so uncommon, so unlike the usual style of give-and-take invitations, and dinners of formality and display."

Here's where else practicing "right conduct," self-knowledge, and "delicacy toward the feelings of other people" pays off. Those self-evident rules for living are the very best "principles" a man can have. The Jane Austen heroine who has made them a habit naturally recognizes other principled people as kindred spirits.[23] This is a big part of what makes Jane Austen heroines seem so dignified to us. They, their real friends, and the principled men they love are walking on more solid ground; they're breathing a freer air.

"There Goes a Temper Which Would Never Cause Pain!"

But "principle" is only the first skeleton key Jane Austen heroines make use of to unlock a man's potential. "Temper" comes next. It's the more *practical* as opposed to the *theoretical* part of what makes a man worthy of admiration, trust, and respect. Having high standards isn't enough; a guy also has to have enough "self-command" to be able to live up to those standards.

Jane Austen's men with bad tempers aren't monsters who murder, lock up, or beat their wives. Lack of self-control on that scale, it should go without saying, absolutely disqualifies a man from consideration as a possible Jane Austen hero. John Knightley, Dr. Grant, and General Tilney aren't violent.[24] They just offload the unavoidable frustrations of ordinary life onto other people. They speak sharply; they complain freely. Essentially, they make a lot of fuss about whatever inconveniences and frustrations come *their* way, while overlooking the fact that other people have their own difficulties. In fact, they *create* unpleasantness for other people, by outsourcing their own share of the discomforts that plague everybody in this life onto the people closest to them.[25] Think of Dr. Grant in *Mansfield Park*, who can't "get the better of" his "disappoint-

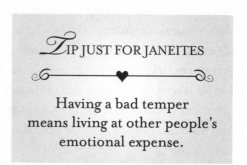

ℒIP JUST FOR JANEITES

Having a bad temper means living at other people's emotional expense.

ment about a green goose." Whenever Mrs. Grant serves a dinner that falls below his high expectations for epicurean enjoyment, Dr. Grant makes life miserable for everybody else. So miserable that the rest of the family is "driven out" of the house—leaving poor Mrs. Grant behind to apply her patience to soothing him down again. If you don't want to end up in her position, avoid bad-tempered men.

Jane Austen had *very* high standards where temper is concerned. You don't have to be even rude (not to mention violent) for her to make it clear that you are, as it were, living at other people's emotional expense. There are all kinds of different ways to take your frustrations out on other people—imposing discomfort on them to make yourself more comfortable—ranging from loud and incessant complaining to habitual sulking.[26] Jane Austen expected her heroes and heroines to undertake a positive effort to make life pleasant for other people. That can consist of simply taking the trouble to keep the conversation going. (That's where Colonel Fitzwilliam's civility is superior to Darcy's pre-Elizabeth's-refusal manners.) Or it can mean stepping in to smooth things over when someone else has said an angry or insulting thing, as Mary Crawford does when Mrs. Norris publicly reminds Fanny of her dependent position. "There," thinks Edmund of Mary, "goes a temper which would never give pain!"

Of course Mary Crawford's temper isn't quite as perfect as Edmund thinks it is. Fanny's impressions of Miss Crawford's temper are quite different from Edmund's.[27] When the two girls are alone together, Mary isn't shy about letting Fanny know her displeasure at Fanny's choices—particularly, Fanny's refusal of her brother—in terms that seem quite strong to a person as shy as Fanny is. Like many of us, both men and women, Mary is on her best behavior in the presence of the person of the opposite sex that she's romantically interested in—which is why it can be very instructive to see a man in the company of his friends, his family, his co-workers, waiters, and store clerks. And even more interesting to learn how he treats those people when you're not around. Because if you get close to him, there will inevitably come a time when he's no longer on his best behavior with you. You want to know in advance what his ordinary or habitual standard of self-control is.

You have to judge carefully here. As with principles, you're going to be a much better judge of temper if you've got a good one yourself—though for a different reason. We're all in competition with the people close to us for the same emotional space. For those of us who don't have very good tempers ourselves,[28] it's all too easy to mistake a failure—on the part of your friends, or your roommate, or your boyfriend—to cater to your own bad temper for a bad temper, if you see what I mean. In fact, expecting other people to kowtow to our psychological comfort all the time is the essence of bad temper as Jane Austen saw it. Her concern that a heroine steer clear of men with bad tempers does not authorize us to expect that the men in our lives will never frustrate or annoy us in any way—much less to hector them on the subject of their insufficient attention to our emotional needs.

Those of us with less than perfect tempers ourselves are hardly in a position to demand a perfect temper in a man. (Though, as Jane Austen points out, "nobody minds having what is too good for him.") But we can learn from Jane Austen to understand the value of the kind of self-command that allows us to live in harmony with someone we love, and to be honest with ourselves about the disadvantages, for our happiness, of loving a man with an "uncertain temper."

Beyond "the Sterling Good of Principle and Temper": "Open" vs. "Reserved" Temperaments

Jane Austen uses "temper" in two different but related senses.[29] Sometimes she means the command of ourselves that's absolutely necessary to other people's comfort. That's what we've been discussing up to this point. "Temper" in that sense is an open-and-shut proposition, something you get right or wrong. "Uncertain" is simply the wrong kind of temper to have; your self-command should be dependable.

But at other times Jane Austen uses "temper" to mean something less absolute, about which it's possible to have legitimately different preferences. "Temper" in the second sense is more or less equivalent to what we might call *temperament*; Jane Austen sometimes calls it "disposition."[30] Her heroes and heroines talk about people who have a temper that's "open," versus one that's "reserved."[31] We've already seen that Anne found the "clever, cautious" Mr. Elliot hard to trust. But it's not only villains who have reserved tempers in Jane Austen novels. Think of Edward Ferrars, Edmund Bertram, and Mr. Darcy. Think of Jane Fairfax, whom the discerning Mr. Knightley talks about with enormous respect and admiration.[32] He essentially says that Jane is perfect in every way, except one. She lacks "the open temper which a man would wish for in a wife."[33]

Beyond Jane Austen's really non-negotiable, one-size-fits-all skeleton keys—beyond "the sterling good of principle and temper"—there are a whole range of valuable qualities that are still quite useful for evaluating your romantic prospects, even if those qualities don't give you a 100 percent clear Yes or No about a man. "Temper" in the sense of temperament is one of those qualities. Honest forthrightness is of real value, and so are prudence and self-control. Thus there's value in both "open" and "reserved" tempers. Under the right circumstances, most of us could probably get really excited about either kind of temperament. We could be wowed by the manly openness of a Captain Wentworth, or thrilled by the impressive self-command and moral force of an Edmund Bertram.

But individual preferences can play a legitimate role here, in contrast to the realm of principles and temper (in that first, absolute sense). *Nobody* is going to end up happier picking an unprincipled man, or one with a really bad temper. But some of us might possibly be happier with a guy with an "open" or "firm" temper rather than a "reserved" or "yielding" temperament—or vice versa. Noticing what kind of temperament a man has won't in itself tell you whether to cross him off your list, but it will give you some very useful information about him. It can be a more valuable insight into whether you could be happy with him than the usual data points we gather: his taste in music, the style he dresses in, his politics, the causes he's passionate about.

Besides "principles" and "temper" in its two different senses, what are the rest of Jane Austen's criteria for value in human beings? I count "feeling," "affections," or "warmth of heart" (a.k.a. "sensibility"), which is related to the question of whether a man is "amiable" or not. There's also "fancy" (or "imagination"). "Taste" and "talent" play a role in her character evaluations, too. Then there's the whole constellation of qualities that Jane Austen's heroes and heroines discuss under the labels "sense," "understanding," "information," "education," and "judgment." And finally there are the qualities that she calls "manners" and "address."

"She Knew His Heart to Be Warm and His Temper Affectionate"

"Feeling," unlike "principle," is something you can have either too much or too little of. Emotional intensity pretty obviously fits into Anne Elliot's rule that all "qualities of the mind" should have their "proportions and limits."[34] Clearly, Marianne Dashwood overdoes sensibility, while Lucy Steele's cold-hearted scheming demonstrates that it's also possible to have too *little* feeling. Looking at the question from a woman's point of view, you don't want a man who's a quivering bundle of emotions—who's going to expect you to pour all your energy into the unnecessary drama he's perpetually creating. But you don't want a cold fish like John Dashwood, either.

When it comes to romantic love, of course we want to know whether a man is acting out of real love or from some colder, more calculating motive.[35] But it's also really important to a lot of women to know whether the guy we're considering as a possible romantic prospect is capable of passion, or not. This may possibly be less important to some women than to others.[36] But judging from the number of us who resort to romance novels

TIP JUST FOR JANEITES

In Jane Austen (and in life), when it comes to human beings, past performance is an excellent predictor of future results.

to supply what we're missing in our real-life relationships, it would seem that passion is something a lot of women have a deep desire for.

So how do you know if a guy is capable of being a passionate lover? Looking at the question from a man's perspective for a minute, it's interesting to see how Henry Crawford—who has an awful lot of experience with women—thinks he can find out the capacity for passion in the woman he's in love with. He appeals to the warmth and intensity of Fanny's relationship with her brother as evidence that, however shy and reserved she is with Henry himself, she's no cold fish: "Her affections were evidently strong. To see her with her brother! What could more delightfully prove that the warmth of her heart was equal to its gentleness?—What could be more enouraging to a man who had her love in view?" Henry reasons that if Fanny truly loves her brother with such warmth and enthusiasm, then she's not really as prim as she seems to be. If Henry could only persuade her to love him, all that emotional warmth would be at his disposal; he could look forward to a marriage of real passion. And he's right.[37]

Once again, Jane Austen's characters understand something that it's all too easy for us recovering Romantics to forget: what you get, if your love is successful, is essentially *the other person*, with all her—in our case, with all *his*—inherent capacities or defects. And it's quite possible to observe those qualities from the outside, when you're first getting to know a man. In fact, as we'll see, you're actually in a better position to make these observations *before* you've really fallen for him.

"Sense" and "Understanding," "Talent" and "Taste"

Besides valuing a warm heart, Jane Austen also puts a lot of stock in a cool head. Her heroes have "sense," "understanding," and "judgment." "Education" and even general "information" are also qualities she values in men. As are "taste" and "talent."

But is this really fair? We democratic twenty-first-century Americans can't help being a little squeamish about an intelligence requirement for love. Are Jane Austen heroines intellectual snobs? Would they unfairly reject a man because of a lack of education that wasn't his fault? After all, not everybody has the same opportunities for mental development.

Well, Jane Austen's heroines *can* be snobs—but not when they're living up to Jane Austen's standards. Emma is certainly acting the snob when she manipulates Harriet into rejecting Robert Martin on the grounds that no farmer could possibly be good enough to marry her own "intimate friend."[38] In reality, Robert Martin is an intelligent young man who has made the best of every opportunity to improve his mind, as well as his farm; he's extraordinarily competent at his job, and he has managed to acquire a respectable amount of book-learning as well. He's no Mr. Knightley, but Mr. Knightley commends his intelligence: "I never hear better sense from anyone than Robert Martin."

The men Jane Austen suggests *do* deserve contempt for their ignorance are just the *opposite* of Robert Martin. They're rich fools who've managed to preserve their self-satisfied stupidity despite every opportunity for self-improvement afforded them by expensive educations and extensive leisure. The fabulously wealthy Mr. Rushworth, for example, is "an inferior young man, as ignorant in business as in books, with opinions in general unfixed, and without seeming much aware of it himself." Rushworth can hardly be blamed for not being the sharpest knife in the drawer; what Jane Austen calls "nature" (we might think "DNA" or "heredity") seems not to have blessed him with much native intelligence. But if that were his only defect, we could feel compassion for him. Unfortunately, Mr. Rushworth's vanity, laziness, and selfishness make him a lot dumber than he has to be. In the memorable phrase of Forrest Gump's mother, "Stupid is as stupid does." When Rushworth married Maria Bertram, "she had despised him, and loved another—and he had been very much aware that it was so. The indignities of stupidity, and the disappointments of selfish passion, can excite little pity."

Stupidity isn't just a low I.Q. If Jane Austen classes someone as lacking in sense, that person is likely guilty of serious mental laziness. An absence of "sense," "understanding," "talent," and even of "information" very often turn out to be the result—as well as the further cause, in a kind of vicious circle—of a narrow, selfish outlook on life. Jane Austen can seem a bit harsh with her ignorant characters. She makes Harriet look really silly for knowing no geography,[39] and Lucy Steele contemptible because of her poor grammar.[40] We're ashamed to laugh at this sort of thing, but, once again, Jane Austen is being realistic. People who haven't bothered to learn about the world beyond what immediately interests and directly benefits them are less interesting and less worthy of our respect than people who have taken that trouble.[41] And education really does broaden your mind, as Elinor Dashwood thinks when she mulls over the mismatch between Lucy and Edward Ferrars.[42] Edward has spent his early twenties expanding his horizons—growing from an unformed boy into an educated, well-informed man. Meanwhile, Lucy, who's far from unintelligent,[43] has been learning nothing but how to get ahead by "pursuing her own interest in every thought" and "courting the favour" of every wealthy acquaintance who might possibly do anything for her.[44]

As always, Jane Austen is the ultimate realist. Just as good looks inspire admiration and desire, intelligence naturally earns our respect. A woman can be "too ignorant and giddy for respect."[45] And a man can be too stupid to take seriously. Sir Thomas told himself his daughter Maria could be happy with Rushworth "if she could dispense with seeing her husband a leading, shining character." That's a really big *if*. How many women can do without admiring the mind of the man they love? He doesn't have to be in Mensa; he doesn't have to display a flashy brilliance. We don't all want "a clever man, a reading man."[46] A lot of us can respect a man of "simple taste" and "diffident feelings" like Edward Ferrars. But *not* a guy who seems to us to be stupid. If a man can't "meet" us "in conversation, rational or playful," he won't seem like a real match. A "disparity, too great a disparity, and in a point no less essential than mind" is going to be a deal-breaker for a lot of women. Or worse, a deal spoiler, after the deal is done.[47]

His "Manners" and "Address"

Jane Austen's characters also take note of the different styles of "manners," "air," or "address" with which men habitually meet the world.[48] And she shows us a range of men with very different ways of relating specifically to women, ranging from the plain, blunt Mr. Knightley, whose "manners had in general so little gallantry," to the insinuating Henry Crawford, whose habitual address tends "to make girls a little in love with him." Jane Austen heroines think a man has good manners when he can converse "pleasantly," with "readiness and ease." A man of truly good breeding doesn't make the other person do all the work. But he doesn't monopolize everyone's attention, either.

Mr. Darcy, Edward Ferrars, and (you could argue) Edmund Bertram deviate from this golden mean in one direction.[49] And Mr. Palmer, with his deliberately rude "inattention" to other people, goes even farther off course. Robert Ferrars and John Thorpe fall off the horse on the other side. They're two different examples of men whose vanity is large enough to suck all the oxygen out of any room they're in.[50] *Good* manners in a man range from gentle to blunt, but they're inevitably marked by "sense, sincerity, and good-humour." Apart from the extremes, we've all got our own mental picture of the ideal "air" and "address" in a man. Jane Austen tells us at the end of *Northanger Abbey*, when she has occasion to mention that Eleanor Tilney married "the most charming man in the world," that "any further definition of his merits must be unnecessary; the most charming young man in the world is instantly before the imagination of us all." Of course our imaginations won't all coincide. But whatever you're picturing in your dreams—and however the manners of the men you meet either measure up to those dreams, or fail to—it's worth thinking about the question in Jane Austen's terms. Which means first noticing that every man approaches social situations with a certain "address," and then analyzing what elements his "manner" consists of. How much attention does he pay other people? What kind of attention? How much vanity and affectation are there in the way he relates to people, and especially to women? How much sincerity?

"They Are All Clergymen Together"

Can Jane Austen's skeleton keys really still work for us today? We tend to think that Jane Austen characters inhabit a simpler, more unitary culture than ours. Maybe her ladies and gentlemen already had so much in common—they were all living in the same world, sharing the same beliefs and interests and entertainments—that they could afford to pay attention to these fine distinctions. Things are more complicated for us. We just *know* that a vegan in a Che Guevara T-shirt simply isn't going to connect with a Tea Partier waving one of those "Don't Tread on Me" flags, no matter how principled they both are, what great tempers they have, and how capable they both are of passion.

Well, first of all, Jane Austen's characters don't all live as much in one same world as you might assume. Anne Elliot's delight in the naval world that opens up to her when she meets Captain Wentworth's friends isn't all that different from what a lot of us have experienced when a guy we liked introduced us to what seemed like an exciting new scene—new music, new style, new politics. And think about Mary Crawford, coming from the sophistication and convenience of London to Mansfield. At first she's put off by the inconveniences and limitations of life in the country. It's a real culture shock. But in the end she's charmed by the intimacy of a country neighborhood—by a really different way of living.

Speaking of Mary Crawford, we see her doing just what we do, grouping people together by profession and social group and assuming that it's natural to find your mate among your own kind: "Sir Thomas Bertram's son is somebody; and now, he is in their own line. Their father is a clergyman and their brother is a clergyman, and they are all clergymen together. He is their lawful property, he fairly belongs to them." But that's Mary

Crawford's shallow way of looking at people. If you want to be a Jane Austen heroine, try seeing beyond the categories we too often freeze people into, to the principles, feelings, sense, temper, and other qualities that make up their "real character."[51]

Turning from Mary Crawford to her brother Henry: to state the obvious, he's not the ideal lover from Jane Austen's perspective. In fact, he's a classic failure. He doesn't get the girl, and it's entirely his own fault. But when he tells his sister Mary that he loves Fanny Price, his catalogue of her excellences is still superior to what a lot of us have heard from the men who've loved us—because Jane Austen has him talk about Fanny in the very same terms she expects us to use to evaluate our romantic prospects. First Henry raves about her physical beauty, her "face and figure." Then he expatiates on her "temper," which "he had good reason to depend on and praise. He had often seen it tried. Was there one of the family, excepting Edmund, who had not in some way or other continually exercised her patience and forbearance?" Next Henry moves on to Fanny's capacity for passion—finding evidence in her love for her brother, as we've seen, that "her affections were evidently strong." Then he gets to the subject of Fanny's "understanding," which is "beyond suspicion, quick and clear"; "and her manners"—"the mirror of her own modest and elegant mind." Finally, Henry takes a stab at praising Fanny's principles, her "high notion of honour," the "integrity" that he'll be able to depend on.

Wouldn't you love to know a man was talking about you like that? It beats "she's so great for me" all hollow. And the difference isn't just Jane Austen's fabulous language. It's that Henry *sees* Fanny (her "charms" *and* her "character") as valuable in herself. He's thinking what a glorious girl she is; his hopes for happiness are grounded in the knowledge of her excellence. If the dignity of a Jane Austen heroine requires—and our happiness depends on—treating our "fellow creatures" as we want to be treated, then it's incumbent upon us, too, to value the men in our lives according to their real worth.

ISO "The Most Charming Young Man in the World"

Sure, for each of us, some of Jane Austen's skeleton keys are going to be more important than others. Principles and temper are non-negotiable. No amount of charm, intelligence, or passion is going to make you happy with a man who is brazenly dishonest or treats you in a really ugly way. But beyond the non-negotiable categories, there's scope for our preferences and our own personal idiosyncrasies. Even there, though, it can't hurt to do our best to balance what seems overwhelmingly important to us with different qualities that Jane Austen sees are important, but that we'd naturally tend to overlook—if she weren't there to remind us.

The whole arrange-your-own-marriage project that Jane Austen's novels are the crown and culmination of is about young women's somehow being able to manage or sublimate youth's naturally extreme passions and preferences (my own nearly exclusive value for intelligence in my youth,[52] for example, or another woman's pursuit of passion without regard for principle in a man) and take responsibility for making their own matches. Note that this is the very responsibility that used to be lodged in the more mature hands of these same young women's parents. But Jane Austen didn't think you have to be older and wiser to do a good job of weighing a man's character and judging him a good or a bad match. As a matter of fact, she suspected that age often subtracted more idealistic adherence to principle than it added maturing experience.[53] Jane Austen thought it was quite possible to add balance and maturity to your decision-making without losing youthful idealism and passion. But she expected you to weigh the man's character in every interesting aspect, to measure his real quality. Don't let her down!

𝒜DOPT AN AUSTEN ATTITUDE:

🌹 Are you paying attention to the "real character"s of the men you meet? Or are you stuck at "first impressions"?

𝒲HAT WOULD JANE DO?

🌹 She'd pay more attention to men's innate qualities—first and most importantly, "the sterling good of principle and temper." She'd remember that if your love is successful, what you'll be getting is the other person, with all his qualities and defects.

*I*F WE *REALLY* WANT TO BRING BACK JANE AUSTEN . . .

We'll use her skeleton keys to unlock the secrets of a man's real potential to make us happy. We'll realize that it's a woman's job to do due diligence on her romantic prospects. We'll carry a checklist something like this one around in our heads, and apply it to any guy we might be interested in—*early on*:

- Principles: What standards does he live by? Can we discover any instances of "integrity" or "benevolence" that justify us in believing he's a decent human being?
- Temper: Is his temper "uncertain," or does he have dependable self-control? Does he routinely offload the frustrations of life onto other people (by outbursts, incessant complaining, or fits of gloom that ruin occasions for everyone else)? Or does he take the trouble to make other people comfortable?
- Temperament: Does he have an "open" temper or a "reserved" one? Is he "supine and yielding" or "firm"? Is whatever kind of personality he has one you think you could be happy with? Or would you always be secretly pining for the opposite qualities?
- Feeling and sensibility: Can you tell whether he's acting out of a genuinely warm heart, or from more calculating motives? Have you seen evidence that he's capable of passion?
- Understanding, talent, and information: Can you respect his intellect?
- Manners and address: Are his marked by "sense, sincerity, and good humour"?

CHAPTER TWELVE

"*H*E HAD NO INTENTIONS AT ALL"

How to Recognize Men Who Are "Just Not That into You"

SO JANE AUSTEN PROVIDES US WITH AN ELABORATE array of really useful criteria for choosing the right man. The obvious snag: you can pick all you want, but what if the guy you pick doesn't pick you? Henry Tilney tells Catherine Morland that marriage is just like dancing because the "man has the advantage of choice, woman only the power of refusal." That's not true about dancing any more. But it's still too close for comfort when it comes to love.

Jane Austen heroines do evaluate their romantic prospects according to her criteria, but they spend at least as much time worrying about whether the man they've chosen is going to choose them. And as with most aspects of romantic relationships, Jane Austen's characters have a useful (and long-ago-forgotten) vocabulary for discussing this question. A Jane Austen heroine knows it's her job to determine a man's "intentions"—the very same task, actually, that the authors of *He's Just Not That into You* urge women to take on to succeed at love. (The popularity of which advice is some evidence that after nearly drowning in the intervening waves of Romanticism and reaction, women are ready to try Jane Austen-style realism again.)

Discerning His Intentions— Whose Job Is It?

"What, Sir, are your intentions toward my daughter?" The question reeks of Victorian melodrama. You can envision the scene: the family patriarch—or perhaps the heroine's older brother, complete with a handsome set of mutton-chop sideburns—demands that the mustachioed villain declare his intentions, or cease annoying the innocent young girl with his poisonous attentions.

That's *not* Jane Austen's scene. Her heroines don't sit there like china dolls and let their male relatives run interference for them. The question of men's "intentions" is a live one in every Jane Austen novel. But in her world, it's a job for *the heroine herself*—not for her male guardian—to gauge the "intentions" of the men in her life. For better or for ill, no Victorian patriarch is going to come crashing through the tropical foliage in the conservatory demanding a clarification of the man's motives and plans with respect to her. She's going to have to figure them out on her own, as best she can. Jane Austen makes it clear that her heroines' happiness will often depend on how well they manage this crucial job.

Where *are* the overbearing patriarchs in the lives of Jane Austen heroines? Well, that's an interesting question. They're fading into the past.[1] Jane Austen's women are able to run their love lives quite independently, free of oppression or even guidance. Jane Austen, in fact, resorts to a variety of character choices and ingenious plot devices—hustling fathers and uncles off the stage or putting them out of action before the romantic adventures begin[2]—to maneuver her heroines into the position where they have sole responsibility for reading the signals that the men in their lives give off.

> ### 𝒯IP JUST FOR JANEITES
>
> ❤
>
> Acquire the forgotten skill Jane Austen heroines possess: the ability to discern his intentions.

Why does Jane Austen go to such lengths to arrange things so that her heroines are on their own when it comes to their love affairs? Well that's the kind of novel she was writing! The whole point of the "novel of manners," as invented by Samuel Richardson, improved by Fanny Burney,[3] and perfected by Jane Austen, is to show a young woman dealing with men *on her own*, without oversight by her parents and guardians—either their oppressive interference *or* their helpful advice. The idea is to watch the heroine pick her way through the minefield of courtship using nobody's wit and wisdom but her own. So parents, and especially overbearing patriarchs, have to be gotten out of the way.[4]

These plot devices are all in aid of fast-forwarding the changes that were happening in real-life marriage and courtship in Jane Austen's day, and putting women's new responsibility for their own romantic choices under a microscope. That way Jane Austen's readers, who really did have more power to arrange their own marriages than previous generations of women, would have a model for making use of the newly increased independence they actually had (even if their fathers hadn't died, retreated to their libraries, or sailed off to the other hemisphere). The question her whole society was trying to decide—by trial and error, but also by working out the theory in books like Jane Austen's novels of manners—was this: Can young women make better marriages for themselves than their families can arrange for them? If so, how?

Jane Austen sometimes lets slip a hint that maybe her heroines' parents *ought* to take a more active role in their children's love lives.[5] But by hook or by crook, Jane Austen heroines *are* on their own in their romantic deliberations. And that's lucky for us. Because we're living in a real world that's as free of parental interference in women's choices as Jane Austen's fictional one is. Our fathers don't have to be in the West Indies to be out of our hair; it's taken for granted by everyone that *we're* going to be fully responsible for making our own matches.

"I Do Not Suppose That He Ever Thinks of Me"

Jane Austen knew all about men who just aren't "that into you." In fact, she took it as a given that a very large proportion of male "admiration" doesn't amount to the kind of serious interest that a woman's looking for from a man—at least, the kind that she's looking for when she's seriously interested in him. If you're 100 percent sure you'll be content with a man's "having no design beyond enjoying the conversation of a clever woman for a short period," then by all means enjoy his transient admiration. But if

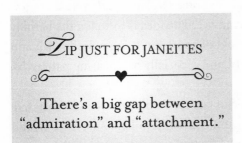

you're hoping for love, you need to ask yourself what, if anything in particular, he intends by any attention he's paying you. Ask it early and often.

ZIP JUST FOR JANEITES

There's a big gap between "admiration" and "attachment."

It's almost second nature to Jane Austen's female characters to practice this kind of discernment. In *Northanger Abbey*, Catherine's bosom friend Isabella keeps rushing her to stake emotional claims on Henry Tilney, and Catherine keeps reminding Isabella (and more important, herself) that those claims aren't yet warranted by proofs of his attachment: "I do not suppose that he ever thinks of me." Henry *is* beginning to think of her—some. But her progress in thinking of him is certainly more rapid,[6] and it's wise of her to remember that what happens between them will depend on what's going on in his head, as well as her own. When Elizabeth Bennet meets Darcy's cousin Colonel Fitzwilliam, he clearly likes her, and she enjoys his company, too. But she soon learns that he has "no intentions at all" towards her—when he tells her frankly that very few younger sons like himself "can afford to marry without some attention to money."

When Jane Austen's women don't remember to discern men's intentions, they're sorry. Elizabeth, flattered by Wickham's attention,[7] never asks herself what *Wickham* thinks *he's* doing, getting so close to a woman he obviously can't afford to marry. It's only later that she guesses, "His behaviour to herself could now have had no tolerable motive; he had either been deceived with regard to her fortune, or had been gratifying his vanity by encouraging the preference which she believed she had most incautiously shown."

Julia Betram misses even more obvious red flags. Both Julia and her sister Maria have fallen for Henry Crawford. But then Henry goes to his own country house to hunt for two weeks. "He went for a fortnight—a fortnight of such dullness to the Miss Bertrams as ought to have put them both on their guard, and made even Julia admit, in her jealousy of her sister, the absolute necessity of distrusting his attentions, and wishing him not to return." Meanwhile, we see Mary Crawford protecting her heart and pacing her relationships by paying attention to the very same tell-tale signs that Julia is ignoring—a man who has been paying her a lot of attention has left town and doesn't seem to be in any hurry to come back and enjoy more of her company. When Tom Bertram goes off to a racing meet and Mary's presence at Mansfield isn't enough of a magnet to get him back at all soon, she reasonably concludes that he's not getting serious about her.[8] Of course, it's easier for Mary to be prudent—her interest in Tom is mostly mercenary!

> ## Tip Just for Janeites
>
> Use a space of time away from the guy you're becoming smitten with to evaluate the progress of the relationship. Ask yourself, *Is the speed this is moving at justified by what his feelings and intentions probably are?*

It would be harder for Julia because she's really falling for Henry. But it's not impossible. That's the trick—the amazing trick that Jane Austen's successful heroines pull off: being prudent in real love. That's what you have to do to find your happy ending: not lose your head entirely even when you're falling head over heels in love. It's part of that tricky balance between a prudence that's too calculating and a passion that's too abandoned and Romantic.

When Jane Austen's women fail to ask themselves about a man's intentions, it can be because they are, in the true Romantic style, spending too much time thinking about their own feelings. You can be so busy asking if he's "The One" capable of fulfilling all your fantasies that you fail to realize that what you ought to be asking is whether *you're* "The One" from *his* point of view. Have you grabbed his attention just for the moment, or is he thinking about you as a woman who's going to change his life? In *Sense and*

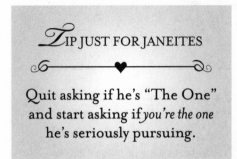

Tip Just for Janeites

Quit asking if he's "The One" and start asking if *you're the one* he's seriously pursuing.

Sensibility, we've got the classic case. What Dusty Springfield sings is quite likely to turn out to be true: "hold him and kiss him and squeeze him and love him.... And after you do, you will be his."[9] The more interesting question, though, is will *he* be *yours*? After all, Willoughby is clearly "The One" who captures Eliza's heart and alters her life forever. But she isn't "The One" from his point of view. Eliza ends up pregnant and abandoned while he pursues Marianne.

But Marianne isn't "The One" for him either—or at least he doesn't see that she is until it's too late. If Marianne had noticed that Willoughby's "intentions" were lagging behind her hopes and plans and slowed the pace of their relationship, he might possibly have come to see her that way in time. But Marianne, caught up in the throes of her Romantic love story, doesn't ask the most obvious questions about Willoughby. What are his intentions? Why hasn't he said straight out that he loves her? Why has he left the neighborhood without saying when Marianne will see him again? Even if he's not in a financial position to marry now, why is he hesitating to enter into an engagement? If he really loved Marianne, wouldn't he be eager to put their relationship on a more secure footing—both for his own sake and for hers? Marianne knows very well—or she *would* know, if she thought about it for two seconds—that if it were *her* role to propose an engagement by declaring her love to Willoughby, she wouldn't hesitate for a second. If he really feels the same way she does, what's he waiting for?

Tip Just for Janeites

Discerning his "intentions" means pacing your side of the relationship to match his level of commitment.

It's Marianne's sister Elinor who ends up asking those awkward questions.[10] Which isn't surprising. It's always easier to see these obvious, upsetting things about other people's relationships than about our own. That's the truly remarkable thing that Jane Austen gives us in her heroines who find happy endings: women who consider it their responsibility to notice the uncomfortable things—the kind of things friends or parents find it easier to notice—about their *own* relationships, and to ask the painful questions that those others would ask. (If they thought it would do any good. They usually don't, because they're sure we won't listen. And they're usually right.)

Elinor cares enough about her sister to ask those painful questions, and to take a stab at interfering, but it doesn't do much good.[11] We've all seen it in real life, too. Perhaps you've tried gently asking a good friend awkward questions about her relationship, or pointing out to your sister some obvious indicator of disengagement in the behavior of a man she was dating. What's extraordinary is that Elinor also does a pretty good job of asking these same awkward questions about her *own* relationship.

When Elinor and Edward are staying in the same house in the period of time after her father's death, he pays her a lot of attention and they get close. But he doesn't follow that attention up by telling her he loves her. So Elinor tries not to pin her hopes on him.[12] Elinor can imagine a good reason for Edward to go slow; he's financially dependent on his mother, who's not going to approve of his marrying a girl without status or a large fortune. But Elinor doesn't embrace that reason as a blanket excuse for Edward—the way her mother and sister resort to Willoughby's financial difficulties to excuse all his inconsistent behavior to Marianne. When Edward pays Elinor less particular attention as time goes on, she worries. When he's not enthusiastic about the prospect of visiting her family in their new home, she considers that she may have exaggerated his interest in her. When he does visit but acts depressed the whole time, she wonders what's going on. And especially when he can't explain why he needs to end his visit, but he decides to leave anyway, she knows there's reason to doubt him. She sees that there's no creditable explanation for his pulling back from her, his failure to declare his love, and his other odd choices—odd choices, at least, if you start from the premise that he hopes to marry her.

Elinor is biased in favor of Edward, and of the possibility that he's in love with her. Obviously she's in love with him, and she can't help giving him the benefit of the doubt at least a little more than she does Willoughby.[13]

But she manages to pull off the essential task of discerning Edward's intentions from his behavior—at least to the extent of internalizing some warning that prepares her for the truth. When Lucy reveals that Edward has been secretly engaged to *her* all along, Elinor is devastated, but she doesn't quite fall apart. Elinor's preparation for the horrible news is of a piece with her dignity as a successful Jane Austen heroine. She certainly bears up better under the shock than the totally blindsided Marianne. We'll do well to take Elinor for our model in keeping our eyes open and maintaining a realistic picture of a guy's intentions toward us.

How You Can Tell What He Intends

What signs do Jane Austen's heroines look for? What in a man's conduct betrays his intentions?

Well, sometimes a guy makes it easy. There are men like Colonel Fitzwilliam ("in person and address most truly the gentleman") who deliberately make it clear that they're not going to let their admiration of you develop into a real attachment. But failing that sort of notice, you're going to have to analyze what a man says and does for signs about his "intentions." And there are some universal indicators, applicable in almost every case.

There's the degree to which his attention and his memory are preoccupied by you, and by what you've shared. When Elizabeth finally sees Bingley again, months after he left Jane and Netherfield, she's delighted "to find his memory so exact" about the date on which he last saw Jane: "It is above eight months," he tells Elizabeth. "We have not met since the 26th of November, when we were all dancing together at Netherfield."

Then there's the indicator that Julia Bertram (like the women in *He's Just Not That into You*) ignores at her peril—if he doesn't make it a point to go out of his way to see you; if he seems to have a great time when he's with you, but he doesn't call; if he's obviously much less anxious than you are about "when will I see you again?" then you'd be wise to pace yourself, like Catherine Morland, by reminding yourself that he may not be thinking about you in the way that you're thinking about him. Anne Elliott draws exactly the right conclusion from the facts that Captain Wentworth knew perfectly well where to find her for the past seven years, and that he hasn't done anything about it.[14]

But of course there's enormous individual variation in how serious male intentions get expressed. Not to mention that there's a subset of callous jerks who will deliberately mimic all the signs of serious intentions to deceive women. In Jane Austen's day there were no self-identified "PUAs" (pickup artists) who bragged about their mastery of "the Game"—such as we lucky twenty-first-century women are blessed with—but there were jerks like Henry Crawford. That is, there were men who pretended to more serious intentions than they really had, with the avowed purpose of plunging women into love they had no intention of returning. Which is one reason that, in her six novels, Jane Austen gave us eight detailed case studies of what we might call "men who are afraid of commitment"—that is, men who confuse us by seeming unwilling to commit themselves, for reasons that we can't fathom. Some of these men who mysteriously fail to commit are real villains, while others have the potential to be Jane Austen heroes.

In chapter 14 we'll be looking at just what Jane Austen has to teach about separating the sheep from the goats when it comes to men "afraid of commitment." But in *all* cases the first and essential thing is to be aware of the chance that the man you're getting interested in has "no intentions at all." His "admiration," as Jane Austen calls it, may be just admiration and not "attachment"; maybe he's just not that into you. You need to keep that possibility clear as clear in your mind, or you're going to make excuses for even really obvious signs of lack of interest and commitment, deceiving yourself[15] and setting yourself up for totally unnecessary heartbreak.

The general rule, applicable in all cases, is to look for inconsistencies.[16] You're measuring what you can observe about a man's conduct against two different standards, as it were: 1) what you know of his character; and 2) what you're hoping about his intentions. The fundamental question that the wise Jane Austen heroine asks herself: *Knowing what I know about him, is this the way he would act if he really felt the way I hope he feels?* Or does his actual conduct betray intentions that don't match what I'm wishing and hoping? It's a tricky question, because the answer depends on all kinds of *givens* that vary from situation to situation and man to man. But it's exactly what Elinor Dashwood manages—not only when it comes to her sister's lover, but even when it comes to her own. *Given* Willoughby's open temper and habits of unreserve about everything else, is it really reasonable to believe that he would leave without declaring his love to Marianne if he had honorable intentions? *Given* Edward's quiet habits and apparent affection for the Dashwood family, is his unhappiness when he visits them—not to mention his insistence that he must leave their house after a week, without any definite plans for where he's going next—really compatible with an intention to be Elinor's suitor?

Jane Austen's eight different ways that men have of being, as we say, "afraid of commitment" supply plenty of opportunity for similar questions from her female characters—though they don't always think to ask them. But before we plunge into a really close look at the range of her male characters and of their "intentions," it's time to take a look at a question that some of you may think is long overdue in this discussion of men's intentions.

How Come *We* Have to Do This Job?

Why do *we* have to discern *their* intentions?

Okay, so maybe Jane Austen heroines have to let men take the lead and, as Emma rather pompously advises Harriet: "Consider what you are about. Perhaps it will be wisest in you to check your feelings while you can: at any rate do not let them carry you too far, unless you are persuaded of his liking you. Be observant of him. Let his behaviour be the guide of your sensations." But to the extent it's true for Jane Austen heroines that they have to keep their antennae up for evidence about how quickly and deeply a man is committing himself, isn't it a relic of their pre-feminist era when Jane Austen could say (tongue firmly in cheek) that "there certainly are not so many men of large fortune in the world, as there are pretty girls to deserve them"? What's dignified about parsing men's words, reading their conduct, putting all this elaborate effort into deliberating the signs of their intentions? Doesn't pacing our relationships by men's progress from "admiration" to "attachment" give them way too much say over our happiness? Isn't the whole exercise a concession of weakness—a weakness that we no longer need to concede in modern conditions of equality?

Well, actually, in Jane Austen, women as well as men have "intentions."[17] And sometimes Jane Austen's men do have to struggle to figure out the intentions of the women they're interested in.[18] When Mr. Knightley canvasses the match between Frank Churchill and Jane Fairfax, he's no less struck by the fact that her character "vouches for her disinterestedness" than by Frank's genuine attachment to her.[19]

But still, there *is* a difference. "Women fancy admiration means more than it does," is Jane Bennet's excuse for Bingley. Darcy says, "A lady's imagination is very rapid; it jumps from admiration to love, from love to matrimony, in a moment." Admittedly, that's from the male point of view. But notice that there's no such thing as *Modern Groom* magazine. And there's no bestselling self-help book entitled *She's Just Not That into You*. (Instead, there's *The Game: Penetrating the Secret Society of Pickup Artists*.) Women do seem to be at more risk of letting our imaginations carry us ahead of where the guy is.

When it comes to falling in love, there are some important differences between men and women. Those differences fascinated Jane Austen. Whether she saw them as weaknesses where women are concerned is the subject of the next chapter.

ADOPT AN AUSTEN ATTITUDE:

- Keep in mind that the future of your relationship depends as much on what's going on in his head as in yours.

WHAT WOULD JANE DO?

- She'd know it was her job to determine the intentions of any man toward whom she was developing serious intentions of her own.

$\mathcal{I}$F WE *REALLY* WANT TO BRING BACK JANE AUSTEN . . .

🌹 We'll pay attention to how "exact" a man's memory is for the times and events that mean something to us. We'll take advantage of time apart from him to come to a more accurate perspective on whether his intentions and ours are keeping pace. We'll take note of whether he goes out of his way to pursue us. We'll follow Elinor's example and consider it our job to compare what we think and hope about a man's intentions toward us with what we know about his character.

$\mathscr{A}$RE WE THE WEAKER SEX, AFTER ALL?

SO *ARE* WOMEN THE WEAKER SEX? WHY ARE WE THE ones who have to discern men's intentions (in the nineteenth century) and read self-help books (in the twenty-first)—while they get to stumble through life blithely unaware of the need for any tips or special skills to manage their relationships? How come they never write letters to advice columnists asking why we don't call the next day? Why do we put so much more effort into dealing with *them* than they do into dealing with *us*? Are women after all the sensitive plants, more easily hurt than men? Do we really need special protection?[1]

Did Jane Austen believe that women were weaker than men—that we're not equal? Well, she certainly believed the sexes were *different*. She writes about differences that have a powerful effect on how men and women relate to each other, and on how they ought to. Her observations on sex differences are quite instructive—if we want to run our love lives more intelligently and get more of what we want from men. But to profit from her insights, you have to be willing to see past your assumptions to what's in front of you. In this chapter I'm going to ask you, reader, to play clear-eyed eighteenth-century realist and look straight at some important differences Jane Austen noticed between men and women—before getting up on your high horse and objecting that those differences can't be real because you're afraid it all might mean we women will have to think of ourselves as second-class citizens. (And honestly, there's no need to panic. You can trust Jane Austen to maintain the dignity of our sex.)

The Fidelity Gap

Let's start with the fact that women are generally more faithful than men. In Jane Austen, as in reality, women regularly find male infidelity not only painful but astonishing. It's not simply that men are more likely to cheat, though that is the case. It's that the gap between the capacity for fidelity in men and women is so wide that women routinely fail to imagine what men are capable of. We're continually relying on men's being as committed to our relationships as we ourselves are. And we're inevitably getting nasty surprises.

Elinor worries about Edward's mysterious failure to follow through on the beginning of their love affair. But until Lucy Steele reveals his secret engagement to her, it never occurs to Elinor that the answer might be another woman. Marianne is completely blindsided when she finds out that Willoughby's going to marry somebody else: "Who is she?—Who can she be?—Whom did I ever hear him talk of as young and attractive among his female acquaintance?—Oh! no one, no one—he talked to me only of myself."[2]

Jane Austen is brutally realistic about the male capacity for inconstancy. Henry Crawford's adulterous elopement with Maria while he's actually in love with Fanny was too much for some contemporary readers to swallow.[3] Do *we* find it believable? "He was entangled by his own vanity, with as little excuse for love as possible, and without the smallest inconstancy of mind toward her cousin.... he went off with [Maria] ...regretting Fanny, even at the moment, but regretting her even more, when all the bustle of the intrigue was over." From our twenty-first-century perspective, Henry's behavior seems all too realistic. Fanny is shocked, of course—exactly the same way we've virtually all been shocked at one point or another by the discovery that we're less important than we thought to a man we were sure was in love with us.[4]

Women and "Attachment"

Fanny is shocked *despite* the fact that she knows all about the ugly side of Henry's character. She watched him entertain himself by breaking her cousins' hearts and quite rightly concluded that he wasn't to be trusted. But still, Jane Austen lets us know, Fanny's "disesteem" of Henry almost certainly wouldn't have saved her from having her heart broken by him in just the same way if she hadn't already been in love with Edmund. When Henry originally (before he fools around and falls in love with her) decides to "amuse" himself by "making a small hole in Fanny Price's heart,"[5] Jane Austen tells us that without her "love for another" Henry would very likely have succeeded[6] in his plot against her peace—he'd have been able to reduce her to a state in which, when Henry left her flat, she'd have felt "that she shall never be happy again."

And what amazing seduction technique does Jane Austen suggest would be able to accomplish this, despite Fanny's eminently justified dislike and distrust of Henry, *in just two weeks?* Paying attention to her. That's it: "his continued attentions—continued, but not obtrusive, and adapting them-selves more and more to the gentleness and delicacy of her character."

Jane Austen points out that Fanny is really not that unusual in being so highly susceptible to male attention, so ready to form an emotional attach-ment even when she knows perfectly well it's a stupid thing to do: "although there doubtless are such unconquerable ladies of eighteen (or one should not read about them) as are never to be persuaded into love against their judgment by all that talent, manner, attention, and flattery can do,[7] I have no inclination to believe Fanny one of them."

Male Attention:
The Ultimate Intoxicant

Jane Austen's novels are full of women who let male attention[8] persuade them into an "attachment" that's at least premature—if it's not flat out a bad idea. There are Maria and Julia Bertram, of course, tricked by Henry Crawford, who nearly catches Fanny, too. And Marianne and Elinor fall for Willoughby and Edward when neither man has committed himself. Catherine Morland obviously learns to like Henry Tilney faster than he does her; lucky for her, an attachment on his side eventually arises out of "gratitude" for hers. Lydia falls for Wickham, and Elizabeth almost does, too, despite the fact that he has no serious intentions. Jane is in love with Bingley before he has a chance to get attached enough to stick around. And Louisa has clearly got Captain Wentworth picked out before he definitively chooses her.

Why are we in such a hurry to attach ourselves to some guy? Why does male attention turn our heads in this appalling way? If this is what women are really like—if two weeks of concerted attention from a man she *knows* is an untrustworthy jerk could theoretically make even the hyper-cautious Fanny Price forget all her distrust and start seriously crushing on him, to the extent of adopting his opinions[9] and feeling heartbroken when he goes away—then *aren't* we the weaker sex? And *isn't* the only cure for our nearly hopeless weakness the modern solution? That is, for women to change, to become different from what women have been like in the past—to be less, not more, like Jane Austen's heroines? To build up a hard carapace of bitter cynicism about the male sex...grow out of our vulnerability...toughen ourselves up until we can compete with men in callous disregard for tender feelings—both their feelings (presuming they ever really have any) and our own?

In just a minute, let's look at how that modern solution is actually working out for women. But first I want to make one preliminary suggestion here, working from Jane Austen's attitude of mutual respect and compassion between the sexes. Seeing how vulnerable we are to falling for a guy who takes the trouble to pay us a little attention, it's easy to get angry. The strange power that a man's focus on us can have over us can make us feel like we're really pathetic. They chat us up, they flirt with us, they spend a little time, and we lose our heads. When they don't lose theirs, we look pitiful. And we find ourselves asking indignantly how they can *do* that to us—make love to us in a way that's bound to "attach"[10] us, without reciprocating the desires that they're creating.

But hold on a second. Put that way, does the complaint sound familiar at all? Where have you heard this kind of bitter frustration at the power of the opposite sex? Think about it. Don't men make a very similar complaint out of *their* frustration with the power that *we* have over *them*? At its ugliest extreme, this accusation is the infamous Australian Sheikh Taj Din al-Hilali saying that for a woman to leave home without being covered from head to toe—let alone wearing makeup and a short skirt—is like leaving meat uncovered in your yard and complaining when the neighbor's cat eats it.[11] But a man doesn't have to be a rape-justifying mufti to feel impotent rage at women's power over men. You can hear the same frustration elsewhere, and not just from unenlightened men who've somehow managed to go on living in Archie Bunker's world. Read Michael Kimmel's *Guyland: The Perilous World Where Boys Become Men* to hear from a new generation of young men whose hostility to women is clearly a function of their feeling that they're at our mercy.[12] Because if women make ourselves pathetic by thinking with our hearts instead of our heads, then men make themselves laughingstocks by—well, you've heard the jokes about what organ they really think with.[13] And half the time the guy just has to *see* us. We don't even need to pay him any attention to reduce him to the pitiful state of lust that Sophocles said was like being at the mercy of an insane and cruel slave master.

In the survival-of-the-fittest-style free-for-all that the current hookup scene can devolve to, members of the opposite sex—whom Jane Austen heroines somehow manage to see as "fellow creatures" deserving of our compassion and respect—can seem like the enemy. Men prey on our weaknesses, and we on theirs. And even when they're not deliberately playing with our hearts à la Henry Crawford (and we're not deliberately blue-balling them à la Lady Susan), women are still going to be walking through the world making guys miserable with our charms,[14] and men are still going to be chatting us up, showing their plumage, and then going away without even understanding the havoc they've caused. Jane Austen had zero interest in the solution that would preoccupy the Victorians and that still recommends itself to the Australian mufti: that women should hide our attractions beneath head-to-toe fabric to protect men from the powerful effect our bodies have on them. No one in Jane Austen's novels seems particularly agitated about modesty in female dress, or preoccupied with the special difficulties of managing the male libido. She had pity (as well as blame) for men whose "pleasures" are "not what they ought to" be. But her real interest was in the other side of the question: how to manage the mismatch between what men mean when they pay us attention, and what that attention means to us. The modern solution for *that* problem—that women should encase our hearts in a thick protective shell, now that we've given up swathing our bodies in yards of cloth—fails to solve the problem that Jane Austen saw so clearly.

"Some Zenlike Form of Nonattachment"

The "constancy" and "attachment" gaps are points on which Jane Austen's insights are borne out by the much greater experience of romantic and sexual relationships that we have as modern women. In the spring of 2008, the *New York Times* "Sunday Styles" solicited essays from college students exploring "the plain truth about what love is like for them." The winning essay[15] is an indictment of what Jane Austen would call the "instability" of the writer's own lovers, and of the other men she knows. It's also evidence that male attention is still as powerful an intoxicant as ever. The essay is Exhibit A for the case that the differences Jane Austen saw between men and women have survived the two centuries between her day and our own. It's also evidence that the grow-a-thick-skin-to-protect-your-emotions cure is not working.

Marguerite Fields, who submitted the winning essay to the *Times*, describes having tea with a male friend who actually is somebody's boyfriend (the author hasn't had a boyfriend for four years, since back when she was still living at home with her mother) only to learn that the "main thing" about the relationship in her friend's mind is that he doesn't object if his girlfriend sleeps with other people—because he doesn't want *her* expecting *him* not to. The writer also goes on a few dates with a guy she sleeps with and starts to like. She asks when she'll see him again, only to have him launch into a "long, boring, aggravatingly rehearsed, and condescending" story full of flimsy excuses for why he's not going to get serious about her. They go their separate ways, and she tries to remind herself "that when we first met I thought he was an arrogant, presumptuous little man."[16]

Despite her disappointments, Marguerite Fields doesn't indulge in sarcasm, vitriol, or man-bashing. She's committed to "actively seeking some Zenlike form of nonattachment." She's got it in her head that her heart-breaks will be easier to manage if she just remembers

> that no one is my property and neither am I theirs, and so I should just enjoy the time we spend together, because in the end it's our collected experiences that add up to a rich and fulfilling life. I tried to tell myself that I'm young, that this is the time to be casual, lighthearted and fun; don't ruin it.

And yet she can't help wishing for something quite different: "despite the fleeting nature of most of my encounters…I think what I have been seeking in some form from all of these men is permanence."[17] Her experience "never seems to diminish my underlying desire for a guy to stay, or at least to say he is going to stay, for a very long time."

Is "Love" Different Things to Men and to Women?

The Zenlike detachment that Ms. Fields is so painfully striving for seems to come quite naturally to the men in her life. The illustration[18] that accompanied her essay when it ran in the *Times* showed a woman standing against a heart-shaped target, pierced by many arrows. Next to her is a man who's walking away from his own target heart unscathed; he's leaving behind a man-shaped, arrow-free space right in the middle of it. Cupid aims the same slings and arrows at both the guy and the girl, but only the girl, apparently, is vulnerable to love. Or maybe love means different things to men and to women.

This is the mystery that Jane Austen delves into in some of the most painfully realistic bits of her novels. Elizabeth Bennet had it firmly fixed in her head that Bingley was falling in love with Jane at Netherfield until his sisters and Darcy managed to separate them. When she reads Darcy's take on the Bingley-Jane affair, revealed in his letter, it feels like being hit in the face with a bucket of ice water. Darcy doesn't deny that Bingley was in love with Jane; but he sees love very differently from the way Elizabeth does: "It was not until the evening of the dance at Netherfield that I had any apprehension of his feeling a serious attachment. I had often seen him in love before."

That's a nasty shock: to suddenly see being "in love" from a man's point of view. What Darcy is talking about is not what Elizabeth means by love. It's certainly not love as Jane has been experiencing it—something that, months after she last saw the man she's in love with, still matters to her so much that her depression is seriously affecting her health. Mrs. Gardiner (Elizabeth and Jane's aunt, a married woman with, presumably, more intimate familiarity with the male character), had tried to tell Elizabeth that "the sort of love" Bingley was in might not be the life-changing passion Elizabeth was imagining: "A young man, such as you describe Mr. Bingley, so easily falls in love with a pretty girl for a few weeks, and when accident separates them, so easily forgets her, that these sorts of inconstancies are very frequent." But it's still an ugly shock for Elizabeth[19] to read Darcy's cavalier reference to his friend's having been in love "often" before.

Marianne Dashwood suffers the same shock, only much worse—up close and personal, you might say. We've seen that after Willoughby has betrayed her, Marianne finally tells Elinor what happened between the two of them, explaining, "I felt myself...to be as solemnly engaged to him, as if the strictest legal covenant had bound us to each other." Elinor points out that it's unfortunate that Willoughby "did not feel the same way," and Marianne protests, "He *did* feel the same way, Elinor—for weeks and weeks he felt it. I know he did. Whatever may have changed him now (and nothing but the blackest arts employed against me can have done it,) I was once as dear to him as my own soul could wish."

This is that familiar kick in the gut. The shared weeks of falling in love, or moments of physical intimacy, or years of living together—in which it seems that the two of you are feeling just the same—give way to a time when he feels different. What's the truth of the matter? Were both of you really feeling the same thing, only a man can feel like that for a while, and then change more easily than you can? Or were your feelings really different the whole time—you wouldn't have been as excited about falling in love, or making love, or moving in together, if you hadn't been looking forward to a future that the man didn't need to expect in order to feel the same excitement. Can men feel just the same way as we do, and then forget? Or do men never really feel what we feel when we love them?

Can a Man Be in Love Like a Woman?

The question they famously asked on *Sex and the City*—"Can a woman have sex like a man?"—did not interest Jane Austen.[20] What she wanted to know was the exact opposite: *Can a man be in love like a woman?*

Jane Austen takes up that question in the famous passage at the end of *Persuasion*,[21] where Anne Elliot tells Captain Harville that it "would not be in the nature of any woman who truly loved" to forget her lover as soon as Captain Benwick[22] has forgotten the deceased Fanny Harville for Louisa Musgrove—as soon, in fact, as men somehow manage to forget women all the time. "We certainly do not forget you, so soon as you forget us," Anne claims.

When Anne asserts that it wouldn't be in a woman's "nature" to forget a man this way, Captain Harville isn't buying it. So Anne backpedals just a bit—not on her basic claim, but on what we might call the nature-nurture question: "It is, perhaps, our fate rather than our merit. We cannot help ourselves. We live at home, quiet, confined, and our feelings prey upon us. You are forced on exertion. You have always a profession, pursuits, business of some sort or other, to take you back into the world immediately, and continual occupation and change soon weaken impressions."

But when Harville points out that this argument doesn't apply to Benwick, who has been living quietly at home with Fanny Harville's family ever since he found out she died, Anne goes back to her original claim, that the difference is in the "nature" of men and women.[23]

What's fascinating about this issue is that we twenty-first-century women have so much more evidence on Anne's point than she had—evidence that all tells in the same direction: to prove that nature, not nurture, explains this gaping chasm between the sexes. The attachment gap between men and women has survived enormous changes in men and women's lives in modern times—beginning with women's liberation from living "at home, quiet, confined" back in the days when only men had "a profession, pursuits, business."[24] And the "nature" explanation for male-female differences when it comes to love is also backed up by a lot of recent scientific research. Our modern biologists confirm the reality of this difference between the sexes. Women experience what both Jane Austen and modern science call "attachment" more readily than men do. And in oxytocin,[25] modern scientists have discovered something about the biochemical mechanism behind that fact. Twenty-first-century physiological knowledge seems to confirm Anne Elliot's insight that the analogy "between our bodily frames and our mental" ones makes it natural that while men's feelings may be stronger, women's are more "tender" and "long-lived."

Hogamous, Higamous

So would Jane Austen advise us to give up hankering for men to ever really love us the way we love them? Would she tell Marguerite Fields that her deep desire for "permanence" with a guy is simply hopeless? If she did, she'd be in numerous (if not unreservedly good) company. The chorus of

> Hogamous, higamous
> Man is polygamous.
> Higamous, hogamous
> Woman, monogamous[26]

seems to echo from all the hills. A woman's larger "reproductive investment" in her mate[27] naturally leads her to maximize selectivity and put all her eggs in one basket, as it were, while a man can spread his genes most effectively by trying for the largest possible number of sexual partners. Or so say the evolutionary psychologists (charming fellows to a man, I'm sure). "Social and cultural analysis" out of a major research university asks whether "polygamy might not offer some potential benefits to women."[28] A large and fast-growing world religion accommodates male polygamy and female monogamy by allowing men to have up to four wives, but women only one husband. And modern literary figures, ranging from the breeziest to the most earnest and high-minded, concur.[29]

Would Jane Austen agree with this cloud of witnesses? Does she offer the same counsel of despair: Men are incapable of fidelity, and women might as well learn to live with it? There's simply a hopeless mismatch between male and female sexuality? It's no good expecting a man to love you the way you love him; it's not in his nature?

No, she doesn't. Jane Austen absolutely would not advise us to resign ourselves to male "polygamy." Her realism is ambitious; she never sank to cynicism about the male character. She never despaired that men and women can find permanent happiness with each other. She saw that the two sexes are very different in their "natures"—while equally deserving of respect—and that it's quite a tricky thing, finding the precise conditions under which both men and women can love in a way that satisfies the deepest desires of both. But she didn't despair of our picking our way through that minefield. Just the opposite! It was Jane Austen's unique genius to map the secrets of happy love.

Getting there depends on truly understanding and working with the differences between men and women. Because, as we'll see, Jane Austen believed that women's special capacities are unique strengths, not weaknesses. That includes both the especially tender and long-lived nature of the kind of love that Anne Elliot claims for us, and also the delicate insight into human psychology that

TIP JUST FOR JANEITES

Don't write off male fidelity as a lost cause.

Anne herself demonstrates. Jane Austen didn't see women's tendency to be relationship-centric as pitiful. She saw it as a valuable resource for constructing human happiness. The impulse that drives us to pore over bridal magazines, ransack the self-help aisle at the book store, and "work on our relationships" is the same impulse that inspires Anne Elliot to theorize about the limits and conditions of male fidelity. Some modern expressions of women's special flair for sticking to relationships and understanding them may be misguided and counterproductive, but that underlying bent of our nature is a valuable strength.

The final speech Jane Austen gives Anne Elliot in this debate on love with Captain Harville expresses 1) unshaken certainty that the differences between men and women are real, and have a huge impact on our happiness, and 2) absolute confidence that men can offer us real devotion worthy of the name of love:

> No, I believe you capable of every thing great and good in your married lives. I believe you equal to every important exertion, and to every domestic forbearance, so long as—if I may be allowed the expression, so long as you have an object. I mean, while the woman you love lives, and lives for you. All the privilege I claim for my own sex (it is not a very enviable one, you need not covet it) is that of loving longest, when existence or when hope is gone.

Two things are clear here. First, men are capable of real love—given the right circumstances. And second, while women are, in other circumstances, more faithful than men because our love is more "tender" and "long-lived," that's not just a vulnerability. It's also a "privilege." Anne's not making a shamefaced admission of women's weakness; she's staking a claim to female superiority.[30]

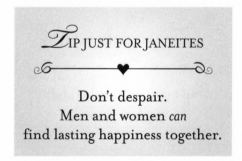

Tip just for Janeites

Don't despair. Men and women *can* find lasting happiness together.

So what exactly are the circumstances in which men are capable of offering us the kind of love we crave? Anne concedes to Captain Harville that "you, and those who resemble you" are capable of love, fidelity, and "domestic forbearance" "in your married lives," "so long as you have an object." But we all know that marriage is no guarantee of male fidelity. Anne Elliot understands that fact as well as we do. And clearly it's not enough for a woman to "live for" the man she loves either. Marianne does that for Willoughby. So does Eliza, for that matter. A woman can't just "live for him" and expect *her* love will guarantee *his* constancy. A woman's love may be a necessary condition, but it's certainly not a sufficient one. First, before a woman starts "living for him," she needs to be sure that, in Anne's words to Harville, she's "the woman you love." It's what Anne says about "so long as you have an object" that really gets to the heart of the mystery about when a man can truly love a woman, and when he can't.

Men: Living in the Moment

So what's the difference between a man like Harville, who does "have an object" in a woman he really loves, and a man like Willoughby? We may guess men like Willoughby simply aren't capable of real love—the kind of love we have for men and want from them, the kind of love that makes a man capable of fidelity—under any circumstances. There are undoubtedly some men whose principles and long-ingrained habits have made it a vanishingly small possibility that they'll ever be able to pull themselves together and truly love a woman. After all, when Anne tells Captain Harville that men are capable of real love, she says it not about men *in general* but about "you, and those who resemble you." (Which takes us back to using Jane Austen's skeleton keys to help us identify and steer clear of guys whose principles and habits make them bad bets.)

But there's much more to unpack here in Jane Austen's insights into male psychology. After all, Willoughby comes awfully close to happy love with Marianne. And even the still *less* principled Henry Crawford, with still *worse* ingrained habits where women are concerned, misses being the hero in Fanny's happy ending by just a thread. If you look really closely at the course of the affairs in which both men so nearly succeed at loving a woman—and especially at Willoughby's, because we actually get to hear him recount the whole story of how close he came—you can see exactly what would have had to be different for them to get to real love.

Look at Willoughby at the beginning of his relationship with Marianne. He confesses to Elinor that when he first got close to Marianne, he had "no other intention" "than to pass my time pleasantly while I was obliged to remain in Devonshire." This is standard operating procedure for men. And *not* just for unprincipled ones. Guys' time horizons are just different from ours. Where women are concerned—and *compared to* women—men's default setting is to live in the moment. Listen to Reginald de Courcy, a really decent young man,[31] reassuring his father that he's not considering marriage with a well-known coquette a decade older than himself: "I can have no view in remaining with Lady Susan than to enjoy for a short time (as you have yourself expressed it) the conversation of a woman of high mental powers." There is a strong tendency for any man's views to be bounded by the present—limited to what's in front of him right *now*. That's why it's so much easier for him to forget a woman, in Anne Elliot's words, "when existence or when hope is gone."[32] While it comes naturally to a woman to hold a man in her heart even after he's gone, he can be faithful only so long as he has "an object." Object *not* in the "objectification of women" sense, but in the "object of pursuit" or "object of attachment" sense: a goal, an aim, a treasure.

Anne Elliot is explaining how men and women are so different about the *end* of their love affairs. But the same principle applies at the *beginning*, too. Men aren't just quicker to forget us; they're also slower to become attached in the first place. The really interesting question is, under what circumstances can a man transcend his tendency to live in the moment—his natural ability to "just enjoy the time we spend together" with no expectations for the future (which Marguerite Fields, being female, finds it impossible to achieve) and start really loving a woman in the first place?

Because you'll notice, that's Jane Austen's plan for men and women. She doesn't expect her heroines to adapt themselves to guys' modus operandi by cultivating "Zenlike nonattachment" and vainly hoping to piece together "a rich and fulfilling life" out of random "collected experiences" of the most fleeting and unsatisfactory sort. Instead, she expects her heroes to transcend their usual present-bound style of dealing with women, actually fall in love, and commit themselves to the kind of permanent happiness that women crave.

Is Sauce for the Goose Really Sauce for the Gander?

And exactly why is that expectation fair? It does seem outrageous that women have been somehow maneuvered into the position where *we're* supposed to accommodate men's psychology by cultivating the carpe diem-style "nonattachment" that comes so naturally to *them*. In the seventeenth century, Andrew Marvell had to write world-class lyrical poetry to persuade a woman to live and love only in the passing moment.[33] In the twenty-first, women are dutifully working to inculcate the same attitude in themselves, as a kind of last-ditch effort to avoid being emotionally crushed by the male-measured speed their love lives are set at. That can't be right. But is it any more reasonable for us to expect *men* to suddenly start doing relationships *our* way?

The modern cliché is that women are always wanting men to behave like the heroes of romance novels, so why shouldn't guys expect girls to act out porn? Well, Jane Austen is not romance novels. And nobody is going to be happy catering to the other sex's lowest denominator.[34] What Jane Austen heroines expect of men is not that they'll be feminized or gelded or made to fulfill our selfish desires, but that they'll transcend their limitations and stretch themselves to accommodate our actually superior understanding of what's going to make both men and women happy in love.

We're the Experts

Because if there's one sex that has the better chance of really understanding relationships, it's us. Face it: relationships are our hobby, our fascination, our obsession. Make Facebook friends with a couple of fourteen-year-old girls, and you'll soon see that they're as preoccupied by relationships as fourteen-year-old boys are by—well, let's just say, by women's physical endowments. Park next to a construction site outside a commuter train station and watch the men and women on their way to work.[35] Every man will be watching the backhoes move dirt, and every woman will have her eyes on some human being's face. It's true about us even as infants. Baby girls respond to facial expressions; baby boys' eyes follow moving objects.[36] And women grow up to possess "emotional intelligence," verbal facility, an awareness of other people's feelings, and a head for relationship dynamics that men can't compete with.[37]

That's why Fanny sees exactly what Henry Crawford is up to with Maria and Julia, while Edmund is totally oblivious to the fact that his good friend is playing with his sisters' hearts.[38] (Mary Crawford sees it all very clearly, too, though without Fanny's compassion.)[39] And Fanny understands the progress of Edmund's love for Mary much better than he understands it himself. Anne Elliot, we've already seen, advises Captain Benwick on his heartbreak from a position of "seniority of mind"—and also, of course, very ably makes the case for her deeper understanding of men, women, and love to Captain Harville. And when Anne sees that Captain Wentworth's attention has thrown both Louisa and Henrietta Musgrove into "a little fever of admiration" for him and that their cousin Charles Hayter has become jealous on Henrietta's account, Anne sees where it's all likely to lead: "Anne longed for the power of representing to them all what they were about, and of pointing out some of the evils they were exposing themselves to. She did not attribute guile to any.... There was no triumph, no pitiful triumph in his manner. He had, probably, never heard, and never thought of any claims of Charles Hayter. He was only wrong in accepting the attentions—(for accepting must be the word) of two young women at once."

And notice that Anne is an expert on the how-to aspect of the situation as well as on the realities of the sexual psychology: "As to Captain Wentworth's views, she deemed it of more consequence that he should know his own mind, early enough not to be endangering the happiness of either sister, or impeaching his own honour, than that he should prefer Henrietta to Louisa, or Louisa, to Henrietta." Anne longs to deploy her expertise for the benefit of all concerned.[40]

We Look Before and After

But besides having a bigger skill set when it comes to understanding and maneuvering through the dynamics of relationships, women also do a better job of seeing the end game. We have a picture of where things ought to be going when it comes to sex, love, and romance. We've already heard Darcy, in pre-softened-by-love-for-Elizabeth mode, snarking, "A lady's imagination is very rapid; it jumps from admiration to love, from love to matrimony, in a moment."

True, our readiness to attach and our eagerness for the happy ending can cause us pain and embarrassment. (I'm thinking of a friend's sister who went out to dinner with a man she really liked, had a bit too much to drink, and blurted out that he was... *the man she planned to marry*. That one actually worked out all right for her in the end; the guy didn't bring what she'd said up again until much later—until, in fact, they really were well on their way to getting married.) It can seem like a weakness, and make us feel stupid, that we want more, earlier, from a man than he has yet learned to want from us.

But this feature of female psychology is a weakness only under the wrong circumstances. Think about it. Which is wiser, really, and more conducive to happiness? 1) considering how our present actions, pleasures, and choices are likely to affect our future, or 2) blithely living in the moment with no thought for long-term consequences or plans? On any other subject that's important to how our lives turn out—education, career, how we handle money—do we admire the person who lives in the present, or the one who thinks about the future? Do we trust that good results in these other areas of our lives will magically appear out of a random collection of experiences, while we put tomorrow out of our minds?

For the Common Good

And anyway, does love make *only women* happy? Finding somebody you're wild about, making a long-term commitment, living with the person you love, having children, and growing old together—quite a few men have admitted to finding excitement and lasting satisfaction in these things.[41] But it's women who are more likely to be thinking about how we want them, and whether what's happening *now* is likely to lead there, or not. In the era of "failure to launch,"[42] the indefinite extension of male adolescence,[43] the erosion of family formation,[44] and the national crisis in specifically male unemploment,[45] the value of women's preoccupation with lasting love as the basis for permanent happiness should be easier to see than ever before.

For Jane Austen heroines, women's relationship expertise is not about having everything our way. And it's not about wielding power over men for our selfish benefit. The woman who acts like that in Jane Austen is a villainess, not a heroine. Lady Susan Vernon uses her typically female verbal virtuosity to manipulate men. She understands that "consideration and esteem as surely follow command of language, as admiration waits on beauty," and she takes unfair advantage of that fact. (Language, that key skill for relationships, being another area where modern psychologists have demonstrated women's comparative advantage.)[46] But who wants to be Lady Susan? You might as well aspire to be the Wicked Witch of the West. Jane Austen heroines use their powers for good, not for evil.

They wield those powers with real respect for men. Their superior feel for the dynamics of relationships doesn't lead them to despise the other sex for being a little slower to grasp what's really going on between people.[47] Notice that Anne's insight into Wentworth's limitations—she sees that he doesn't understand the rapidity of women's imaginations when it comes to love, so that he doesn't realize the effect he's having on Henrietta and Louisa— does not make him despicable in her eyes.[48] Like Jane Austen heroines in general,[49] Anne is confident in her superior grasp of the emotional situation, and her confidence is justified. But that doesn't keep her from respecting and admiring Captain Wentworth. In the end Wentworth comes to discover, very belatedly, a number of truths that have been crystal clear to Anne for the better part of a decade: that her susceptibility to reasonable persuasion under the right circumstances is a character strength, not a weakness; that he's the one chiefly to blame for the eight years he and Anne have spent apart; that he should have written and asked her to renew their engagement as soon as he could afford to marry.[50] But however slow he has been to make these discoveries, Captain Wentworth is never reduced to bumbling sitcom male idiot status—in Anne's mind, in ours, or in Jane Austen's.

And at the end, both Anne and Wentworth get what they really want. More to the point, they've both come to want what will make them both happy. But it was Anne who held onto that desire for all the years that Wentworth forgot it. Like every Jane Austen hero, Wentworth has learned to really love a woman with a passion like her own. And Anne, like the heroine at the end of every Jane Austen novel, really is "as dear to him as [her] own soul could wish."[51] Captain Wentworth isn't feeling crowded or pestered into commitment, saddled and bridled, or cornered, trapped by incomprehensible female demands. Wentworth is happy in love in a completely masculine way. In Anne, he has taken a rich prize. He's bringing home a precious cargo. He's a conqueror, a triumphant hero.[52]

This is the side of the equation that Jane Austen was fascinated by: how a man can come to *want* to give us what we want most.

Jane Austen didn't think women are the weaker sex. As a matter of fact, some of the unique characteristics of female psychology that we fear demonstrate weakness seemed to her to be superior merits. Jane Austen didn't want us to play to our vulnerabilities, or men to play to theirs. Or, especially, for either men or women to play *on* the weaknesses of the other sex. In the worst-case scenario, both sexes prey on each other's vulnerabilities and learn to use, resent, and despise each other. But Jane Austen is the best-case scenario. She teaches women to apply our talent for relationships to figure out how both sexes can avoid the pitfalls our weaknesses expose us to. She shows how men and women can transcend our limitations to meet each other in a place where we'll both be happy.

Jane Austen's novels were written partly to help women develop our natural talent for relationship expertise. Being expert at relationships Jane Austen-style means measuring the dynamics at work between men and women by the yardstick of "permanent happiness." It means keeping your eye on that ultimate goal, which is almost always easier for women to envision—but which is equally satisfying to men. It means seeing, more clearly than men usually do, the implications of present events, choices, and patterns for the future outcome of the relationship. A happy ending is always going to involve a balance between the psychological dynamics of the heroine and her hero. It's going to require *both* the man *and* the woman to transcend their limitations. It's just that the woman can usually see more moves ahead in this game.

In aid of bulking up that capacity in us, Jane Austen supplies us with several case studies of men who are, as we say today, "afraid of commitment." In other words, of men who confuse and frustrate women by failing to want to give the women the love they want. We can learn a lot about the circumstances under which a man *can* be in love like a woman by looking at all the different ways there are for a man to fail at it. They're the subject of the next chapter.

*A*DOPT AN AUSTEN ATTITUDE:

- Don't close your eyes to the real differences between men and women out of fear that women will turn out to look weak or pathetic if you admit them. Be willing to notice that men and women both have their own special vulnerabilities and limitations, but also special strengths.
- Don't assume that whatever you share with a man—however perfectly you seem to be on the same page in the moment—means the same thing to him as it does to you. Remember when you're enjoying the delights of love with a man who seems to feel just the same way you do, that it may be easier for him to feel different later.

*W*HAT WOULD JANE DO?

- She'd regard her preoccupation with (and special insight into) relationships not as a weakness but as a valuable resource for building "permanent happiness."
- She wouldn't indulge in the soft bigotry of low expectations where men are concerned. She'd maintain her faith that men are capable of loving us in just the way we long for.

*I*F WE *REALLY* WANT
TO BRING BACK JANE AUSTEN . . .

- We'll use our natural relationship expertise to pick our way through the minefields of men and women's vulnerabilities to a place where we can both be happy.
- We won't prey on men's weaknesses, and we won't let them prey on ours.
- We won't settle for sharing anything less than the kind of faithful, committed, and truly satisfying love that Jane Austen knew men are capable of.

CHAPTER FOURTEEN

MEN WHO ARE "AFRAID OF COMMITMENT"
Jane Austen's *Eight* Case Studies

SO WHAT DOES IT TAKE FOR A MAN TO STOP LIVING in the moment? Under what circumstances will a guy transcend his present-bound views, go outside his standard operating procedure—which is to enjoy what he shares with you only "for a time"—and shift into the mode where he's ready to get serious? Ready to realize that one woman is a rich prize..."an object" worth pursuing with all that restless male energy...the only woman for him? How can he come to see that there's something about her that requires him to step up his game? To reach the place where Darcy says to Elizabeth, "You showed me how insufficient were all my pretensions to please a woman worthy of being pleased"? Is it possible to define the conditions under which a man can really be in love?

If it can be done by process of elimination, we ought to be able to figure it out from Jane Austen, all right. She gives us at least eight case studies— that's 1.3 per novel!—of men who are, in our modern catchphrase, "afraid of commitment." In other words, eight different examples of men who pay women the kind of attention that's very likely to make her fall in love with him, without ever developing the serious intentions that are necessary for "permanent happiness." Jane Austen's men who aren't ready to commit range from the deliberate heartbreaker Henry Crawford to one genuine Jane Austen hero who realizes his mistake just in time to keep from "endangering the happiness" of the woman in question or "impeaching his own honour."

There's so much in Jane Austen about men who just aren't "that into" the women they're paying attention to that you have to believe she thought it valuable for her readers to really understand the phenomenon. She gives us examples of all the various possible reasons a man might seem to be courting you, without really falling in love. At a minimum, it's certainly useful for the preservation of our "tranquillity" (something Jane Austen heroines prize very highly[1]) to be able to really understand what men are up to when they act this way.

Say a man's been paying you attention and you, carefully discerning his intentions, figure out that he's not serious. You're going to want to know why. Is he a player, or a decent guy who's just not ready to commit? Should you hope he'll get over his "fear of commitment" or should you write him off as a guy who's "just not that into" you, and never will be? Is there any point in continuing to see him, or is there "nothing to do but to keep away," if you want to preserve your peace and keep pursuing happiness in love? Is the problem hopeless, or curable?

Jane Austen gives us a whole batch of samples that we can hold up for comparison with the men in our own lives—something like those color swatches you get at the paint store, each one all of the same color but ranging from light to dark, with all the various possible shades in between. Jane Austen's case studies can save us from totally unnecessary heartbreak. But beyond that, they give us help in answering that central question: When *can* a man be in love like a woman? These unsuccessful scenarios contain key information about men who aren't—and who almost are—really falling in love. And if we use our relationship-expertise to understand the psychological dynamics at work under the surface in each different sad case, we may be able to understand how it could have turned out differently.

The Anatomy of a Villain:
Callous Cruelty

Let's start with the worst-case scenario. A guy can make love to you, obviously enjoy your company, apparently pursue you…just because he deliberately gets his kicks out of making women fall in unrequited love with him. And if you think this phenomenon is a relic of the nineteenth century, with its rakes, cads, and villains, take a look at www.seduction.com, where you can see "Speed Seduction® Student" lessons in "How to Manage Her Commitment Expectations."

"Fear of Commitment" Case Study #1:
Henry Crawford

We've already seen Henry Crawford in action, undertaking two separate campaigns to make women miserable about him. He plays both Maria and Julia Bertram, letting Julia off the hook only when his game with the already engaged Maria is becoming too absorbing for him to keep two fish on the line at once.[2] Henry says lots of things that lead Maria to believe she's his object, but he shies away from saying anything that seals a commitment to her. Eventually he's paying her enough attention that she feels it's safe to quit soothing down the jealousy of Mr. Rushworth, her stupid fiancé.[3] But then— just when she's almost sure of Henry—he leaves her flat. And when the broken-hearted Maria, in cut-off-your-nose-to-spite-your-face mode, has married Mr. Rushworth and gone off on her honeymoon, Henry's bored. So he announces to his sister that he means to "amuse" himself by the "wholesome" mental exercise of making Fanny Price fall in love with him.

"Fear of Commitment" Case Study #2:
Frederick Tilney

Captain Frederick Tilney in *Northanger Abbey* is pretty much the same sort of heartless seducer. He lets Isabella Thorpe think that he's got serious intentions, pays just enough attention to her to detach her from her fiancé— and then unceremoniously drops her. Henry Tilney puts up a half-hearted defense of his brother on the excuse that Isabella would have "to have been a very different creature" in order "to have had a heart to lose'" in the first place. And we can see that if Isabella had cared more about real love and real quality in men, and less about money, she probably wouldn't have been so susceptible to Captain Tilney's glamour. The fiancé she dumps, James Morland, is a really great guy, and he sincerely loves her.

But unfortunately players don't hurt only gold-diggers; they're a danger to the rest of us too. You don't have to become a cynic to understand that there are callous and cruel men out there. It's just Jane Austen's realism to notice the fact that the attention some men pay women is part of a game they play for their own amusement at our expense. It's no insult to the men who are decent human beings to set your intelligence to the important task of distinguishing the upstanding guys from these disgusting parasites. There's nothing to be done about them besides recognize them and avoid them like the nasty plague they are.

The Picture of a Rake: Indulging Himself, Disregarding Your Feelings

"Fear of Commitment" Case Study #3: John Willoughby

Marianne Dashwood, like Maria Bertram, finds herself in love with a man who somehow never gets around to making a commitment to her. "But he told you that he loved you?" Elinor asks. (Because in Jane Austen's day, a "declaration" of love was tantamount to a "proposal" of marriage.) Marianne's answer feels painfully familiar to any woman who has suffered from a man's "fear of commitment": "Yes—no—never absolutely. It was every day implied, but never professedly declared. Sometimes I thought it had been—but it never was."

Willoughby isn't a designing villain like Henry Crawford. He doesn't set out to make Marianne miserable; he's no deliberate connoisseur of broken female hearts. He just allows himself a lot of leeway in these matters. We've seen that when Willoughby first became emotionally "intimate" with Marianne, he intended nothing more than "to pass the time pleasantly." Pleasantly for himself, that is, with total disregard for how the experience was likely to affect her. Up to a point, Willoughby is just doing what comes naturally to any man. His very natural response to Marianne's "lovely person and interesting manners" is frank enthusiasm. And Marianne, in turn, responds very naturally to his enthusiasm about her by falling for him, hard. "But at first," Willoughby confesses when he's telling Elinor the whole story, "my vanity only was elevated by it. Careless of her happiness, thinking only of my own amusement...I endeavoured, by every means in my power, to make myself pleasing to her, without any design of returning her affection."

But Willoughby does fall for Marianne, after all: "Yes, I found myself, by insensible degrees, sincerely fond of her; and the happiest hours of my life were what I spent with her, when I felt my intentions were strictly honourable." Notice, though, that Willoughby only *felt* himself to be committed to Marianne. He never got around to actually committing himself with words or actions. Why? He was still keeping his options open.

Here's where he definitively crosses the line from just living in the present, the way even decent guys tend to do. In a strange way Willoughby *is* making a commitment. (But not to Marianne.) If he were just living in the moment, going with the flow, following his present feelings, those feelings would keep carrying him closer to Marianne. Sooner or later, he would find himself telling her he loved her. But Willoughby stops himself. He makes a commitment—to look after his own interests. He doesn't want to become engaged while he's in so much debt; he's afraid to rule out the option of solving his financial problems by marrying an heiress. As Willoughby himself comes to see later, "The event has proved, that I was a cunning fool, providing with great circumspection for a possible opportunity of making myself contemptible and wretched forever." Because Willoughby has carefully left his options open, when old Mrs. Smith suddenly finds out about how he seduced Eliza and threatens to disinherit him, he can still take advantage of his prudently preserved freedom to say good-bye to Marianne and marry a rich girl.

Does this happen today? All the time. (It's not usually about money these days, though guys will put off committing if they think being tied down might interfere with their career ambitions. It can sometimes also be about sex.)[4] There are plenty of married men who will tell you that a sudden conviction that it was time to settle down emerged in their consciousness at some definite point—usually soon after the guy had gotten his act together in regard to work and other adult responsibilities. A married male friend of mine claims it hit him just that way. He literally woke up one morning—possibly, he admits, a bit hung over—around his thirtieth birthday, after a decade of playing the field, to realize that it was time to get married.[5] That very morning, he made a mental list of women he already knew who might be good prospects, set about systematically asking them out, and was married within a few months. Sixteen years and six kids later, he still talks about his wife like she's Wonder Woman and the Platonic ideal of the California Girl rolled into one.

TIP JUST FOR JANEITES

Waiting for a guy who's ready to commit is a much better bet than waiting for a guy to be ready to commit.

There are all sorts of things in my friend's story that offend our Romantic sensibilities. We don't want there to be a list, or a plan that predates his choosing us. We want him just to see us ("a stranger / Across a crowded room"[6]) and be so struck with us that true love emerges like Venus from the ocean foam. We don't want to wait for a man already ready for commitment to come along; we want a man's love for us to be so transformative that it alone empowers him to overcome his "fear of commitment." But as we can see from what happens between Marianne and Willoughby, counting on love for you to inspire an immature man to grow up—or a selfish man to blossom into a "generous attachment"—is a very risky proposition.

Inspired by Marianne, Willoughby comes very near to pulling it off. But he doesn't quite get to real love. He himself admits, "I did not then know what it was to love. But have I ever known it? Well may it be doubted; for, had I really loved, could I have sacrificed my feelings to vanity, to avarice?—or, what is more, could I have sacrificed hers?—But I have done it." Elinor upsets Marianne by calling Willoughby "selfish." But it's true. He *just* fails to reach the point at which he could really love Marianne. Willoughby misses happiness because he never gets beyond putting himself first. Until he has to make a choice, he lives in the moment, as men usually do. And when he does have to choose, he commits not to Marianne but to leaving his own options open—so that when the crisis comes, he's still got an easy option to betray her. And he takes it.

"Fear of Commitment" Case Study #4: George Wickham

Wickham is a sort of cut-rate Willoughby. Wickham, too, has a vague plan to repair his fortunes by finding a rich girl to marry. Just as in Willoughby's case, Wickham's fortunes need repairing because he has lived a life of self-indulgence. He's been as careless with money as with women. The very unserious attentions he pays first to Elizabeth, then later to Lydia, are pure selfishness. When he finds himself in a nasty financial spot and flees his creditors, he takes Lydia along, because why not take advantage of her stupid trust? In Wickham, Jane Austen gives us a picture of the ugly dead end that a thoughtless pleasure-lover like Willoughby is headed toward. (Meeting Marianne was a last-ditch opportunity for Willoughby to raise himself out of self-indulgence and truly love a woman. He fails the test.)

Another Woman in the Picture?

"Fear of Commitment" Case Study #5: Frank Churchill

But the men who seem to be suffering from "fear of commitment" in Jane Austen aren't all callous players and self-indulgent jerks who refuse to grow up. Frank Churchill completely confuses Emma—and her friends and neighbors too—by paying her the kind of attention that leads everybody to think he's probably falling in love with her. But Frank is really using Emma to create a smokescreen for his secret engagement to Jane Fairfax. Luckily, Emma doesn't fall for Frank Churchill. He's sure Emma is not really interested in him, and he does turn out to be right. But his opinion on this point is just a lucky guess, wishful thinking rather than a real understanding of her feelings.[7]

"Fear of Commitment" Case Study #6:
Edward Ferrars

Next after Frank Churchill in the spectrum of men who seem to be afraid of commitment (ranging from villains to heroes) comes Edward Ferrars. Edward actually causes more confusion and pain than Frank Churchill, though he's harder to blame. Both things are true for the same reason. Edward is bound to Lucy Steele only by his sense of integrity. His feelings are actually disengaged—that is, free to be engaged by Elinor Dashwood. All the enthusiasm that got him into his youthful commitment to Lucy has long since worn out in the four years during which he's gotten an education and grown up, while Lucy has only grown more sharp and selfish. Edward stays engaged to Lucy only because he's convinced she sincerely loves him still.

> **TIP JUST FOR JANEITES**
>
> If a man pays you attention but seems ambivalent or afraid of commitment, ask yourself whether there may already be another woman in his life.

That's why it's so hard for even Elinor, the most prudent of Jane Austen's heroines, to guess the reason for his aggravating hot-and-cold style of courtship. Edward hesitates to tell Elinor what she guesses he feels. He takes two steps into intimacy with her and one step back. Edward obviously likes Elinor; they're clearly getting close—and then, suddenly, they aren't; they're moving apart. Edward's ambivalence is maddening. He's a classic case of apparent fear of commitment, and she can't figure him out any more than we can figure out the men who drive us crazy. And until Lucy tells her about the engagement, Elinor never guesses that there's another woman in the picture.

Secret engagements have fallen out of fashion. The revelation that the man you love is already honor-bound to a girl he no longer cares for is not going to be the major plot twist in your personal drama. So what application do these cases have for us? Well, plenty of men today will pay attention to a woman when they're already attached to some other woman, either by their feelings or else by some sense of obligation. There are plenty of men who will show up in your life "with affection and faith engaged" on the one hand, and on the other "with manners so very disengaged"—just as Emma complains about Frank Churchill. They don't necessarily worry about what right they have to behave this way. They leave us to wonder about it, as Frank left it to Emma.

So wonder about it! If the guy who seems to be interested in you hesitates or blows hot and cold, ask yourself why you're assuming that you're his only or his first object. Don't be blindsided by the late discovery that he has already has a commitment elsewhere.

And if he does? What do you do about it? Jane Austen heroines are not much into scheming to detach men from other women, in order to attach them to themselves. They tend to step back and put their energy into preparing themselves to deal with the reality that they may lose the man, rather than get out there and fight for him. That's what Elinor Dashwood does, and Fanny, and Anne Elliot. Why? Are they doing the Victorian shrinking violet thing, sitting on the sidelines while the men get to do all the fighting, working, and choosing? No. But they're aware that disentangling a man from another woman he's entangled himself with—like making the decision he's going to grow up, quit being selfish, and really love a woman—is something a guy has to do for himself, if he's going to do it right. You may be able to inspire a guy to get his act together, overcome his past mistakes, and love you. But you can never *make* it happen, however much you pour yourself into the effort. Jane Austen heroines respect men's autonomy and their own dignity, and they're willing to face up to the reality that sometimes a prior commitment is going to mean you have to let the guy go.

Falling in Love, but at Different Paces

"Fear of Commitment" Case Study #7: Charles Bingley

"We must not be so ready to fancy ourselves intentionally injured," says Jane Bennet. "We must not expect a lively young man to be always so guarded and circumspect. It is very often nothing but our own vanity that deceives us. Women fancy admiration means more than it does." "And men take care that they should," answers Elizabeth. They're discussing Mr. Bingley's character—whether he's to blame for courting Jane until she fell in love with him, and then leaving. Jane knows that Bingley isn't a villain of the Henry Crawford sort: "If it is designedly done, [men] cannot be justified; but I have no idea of there being so much design in the world as some persons imagine." Elizabeth agrees that Bingley hasn't injured Jane on purpose, but points out that he may have committed some sins of omission: "Without scheming to do wrong, or to make others unhappy, there may be error, and there may be misery. Thoughtlessness, want of attention to other people's feelings, and want of resolution, will do the business."[8]

Here, once again, we've got a case of a man's attention meaning more to the woman than it means to the man. And more than the man realizes it means to her. Bingley was falling in love with Jane. Darcy and Bingley's sisters noticed it. Darcy had "often seen him in love before," but now observed that Bingley's "partiality for Miss Bennet was beyond what I had ever witnessed in him." And Jane was falling in love with him, too. Only she was falling a little faster than he was. Or a little deeper. That's why Bingley was capable of being persuaded that marrying Jane wouldn't be prudent, and so he'd better go away—but she couldn't forget him when he was gone.

This happens today, too. You meet a guy, you really like each other, everything seems to be proceeding toward the happy ending. And then something changes. You may never know what changed his mind, or pulled him off course, or simply distracted him.[9] Maybe he gets really absorbed in a big project at work and his pursuit of you loses momentum. Maybe he has to leave town on business or goes on a trip with friends, and your relationship looks different to him when he gets back. Maybe he meets another girl. If any of these things, or a thousand other possible intervening events, happens before he's gotten to that crucial point—before real love for you has taken him out of a man's typical present-bound views—then your affair will fizzle. Until he's "all in for life,"[10] until you're the object of the kind of committed love that Captain Harville and Anne agree men are capable of, a guy is going to be susceptible to any number of distractions that may at any point derail his interest and keep him from ever getting there.

The Portrait of a Gentleman

Elizabeth Bennet, we've seen, indicts Bingley for being thoughtless, for "want of attention to other people's feelings." Jane Austen's heroines have very high expectations of men in one crucial area where we've quit expecting virtually anything from them at all. They expect that a man should take into account the effects his attention is bound to have on a woman. Jane Austen heroines are well aware that insight on this particular subject does not come naturally to men. They don't expect it in the sense of foolishly relying on all men to notice or care about leading women on. They expect it, instead, in the sense that Jane Austen heroines have little respect for men who carelessly destroy women's peace of mind, and they admire and seek out men of that rare kind who take responsibility for the effect their attention is having on women. These men are the real heroes they're looking for.

"Fear of Commitment" Case Study #8:
Frederick Wentworth

Jane Austen's Case Study No. 8 in male "fear of commitment" illustrates the value of a man who meets these high expectations. Captain Wentworth returns to England ready to meet a woman he can love and marry, goes to stay with his sister, and meets Louisa and Henrietta Musgrove. We've already seen Anne using her fine-tuned sense for relationship dynamics to discern that Wentworth ought to "know his own mind early enough not to be endangering the happiness of either sister, or impeaching his own honour." Anne sees that her own former lover is not acting in bad faith. He's "not in the least aware of the pain he [is] occasioning." Anne guesses that of the two girls, Louisa is "rather the favorite," but "as far as she might dare to judge from memory and experience," she divines "that Captain Wentworth [is] not in love with either." Henrietta eventually abandons the field to her sister—a previous attachment to her cousin having triumphed over a "little fever of admiration" for Wentworth. And Wentworth continues to pay Louisa a lot of attention.

The most intense intimacy that we see in this courtship is probably the conversation behind the hedgerow. Actually, we don't see it; we only overhear it with Anne, who listens as Wentworth tells Louisa, "Yours is the character of firmness, I see," and—comparing her "with playful solemnity" to a glossy hazelnut—"My first wish for all, whom I am interested in, is that they should be firm. If Louisa Musgrove would be beautiful and happy in her November of life, she will cherish all her present powers of mind." Soon afterwards, on the visit to Lyme, this relationship—such as it is—is at its height. Louisa is "jumped down" from all the stiles along their walk by Captain Wentworth. They're walking together; he's responding to her energy and determination with admiration and even allowing her to assume something of a proprietary air about him.

That pretty much sums up the extent of the relationship between Louisa and Wentworth when its course is suddenly suspended by her fall. Louisa is "too precipitate" in jumping down one last time, Captain Wentworth reaches out for her half a second too late, she falls and is taken up unconscious. The accident makes a break not unlike Bingley's going to London. Louisa's relationship with Wentworth is essentially frozen in place, and he can step back and take stock of the situation. What Wentworth discovers is that he doesn't love Louisa. He concludes, in fact, that his attempts to see whether he could fall in love with her were motivated by injured pride and resentment of Anne, whom he still loves.

Captain Wentworth may or may not be right to believe that he could never have loved Louisa. We can only guess what would have happened if her fall at Lyme hadn't given him the opportunity to recalibrate. But up to that moment he looked just like Bingley at Netherfield. From the point of view of the woman he was courting, he seemed to be falling in love. The fact that it took him only a few hours' break from her company (in combination with some striking reminders of Anne Elliot's value) to completely change his course may possibly indicate that their relationship would have fizzled eventually, one way or another. Or it may just be another bit of evidence that until you are a man's real object—in other words, at any time before he's made that ultimate commitment to you—there's always the possibility that something will interrupt a progress that seems inevitable to you, but isn't really. The case of Wentworth and Louisa reminds us not to assume that, even barring accidents and distractions, a guy will keep going in the direction it looks like he's headed in.

It also sheds light on an interesting difference between Jane Austen's world and ours. Once Wentworth understands his own desires, he decides he is not free to pursue them. Some of his friends, he discovers, assume that there is a "mutual attachment," even an engagement, between Louisa and himself:

> I was startled and shocked. To a degree, I could contradict this instantly, but, when I began to reflect that others might have felt the same—her own family, nay, perhaps, herself—I was no longer at my own disposal.... I had been unguarded. I had not thought seriously on this subject before. I had not thought that my excessive intimacy must have its danger of ill consequence in many ways; and that I had no right to be trying whether I could attach myself to either of the girls, at the risk of raising even an unpleasant report, were there no other ill effects. I had been grossly wrong, and must abide the consequences.

It's quite clear to Wentworth that his own feelings aren't yet engaged. But he suddenly sees that Louisa's may be. He has been living in the moment, enjoying her company and her admiration, and only "trying" to see whether it all might lead him to commit his heart. But what if she—being a woman, being more likely to freight present intimacy with future significance—has already become attached? If so, he decides he's "hers in honour if she wished it." In Jane Austen's world, a decent guy doesn't encourage a girl to jump unless he's going to be there to catch her.

To us, this seems completely over the top. We really, really don't want men to marry us out of a sense of duty when they're in love with other women. We're delighted when Jane Austen extricates Captain Wentworth from his obligations of "honour" to Louisa by arranging for her to fall in love with Captain Benwick.

On the other hand, you can't get around the fact that Captain Wentworth's acting the gentleman about Louisa makes him an even more attractive man. There is something particularly impressive about a guy who actually takes responsibility for the effect his attention is having on a woman. Captain Wentworth's readiness to act as if Louisa's understanding of what's between them is just as valid as his own makes him a sort of anti-Henry Crawford, a model for the kind of man you can respect and trust. Because when Wentworth comes to the same fork in the road as Crawford or Willoughby—when the momentum of what he's enjoying and admiring in the present propels him to a place where he has to choose whether to commit to selfishness or to care about another human being—he makes the right choice.

Honesty Is Not Good Enough

Captain Wentworth's standard of "honour" points up a deficiency in the way we manage the expectation gap between men and women. The shock that Wentworth feels on realizing that what's happened between Louisa and him may mean more to her than to him is something that men still experience daily. They're as likely to be blindsided by our readiness to attach as we are by their easy "Zenlike nonattachment." What's different is that today everybody agrees "honesty" is the solution. This cliché—that as long as all parties are honest about their expectations, then all obligations have been met and no one can complain—is so widely accepted that you can find it in such unlikely places as the www.seduction.com blog that I mentioned, where "Ross Jeffries Uncensored" advises the students of his "Speed Seduction® Student" program on "the thorny problem of having women fall for you and fall for you hard, when all you want is a little bit of fun."[11]

Okay, let's stipulate that the pitiful specimens of masculinity who subscribe to the "Speed Seduction® Student" vision may be indulging in extreme wishful thinking, and that Jeffries is just puffing his brand when he warns them, "As guys, we have to be aware that even the most bitter, cynical, hardened woman can have her heart burst wide open and her feelings of wanting to be loved really come to the surface when she is properly seduced." Still, when the universal ethic of "The key here is to be honest about your intentions" is providing cover for the bottom-dwellers at this sub-basement level of the sexual culture, you begin to suspect it's a universally acknowledged truth. And if our "honesty" standard is elastic enough that it can be worked into Speed Seduction® then there's something seriously wrong with it. Don't get me wrong. Male honesty is certainly an improvement over the typical scuzziness of cut-rate Henry Crawfords like Ross Jeffries. But it falls far short of Jane Austen's standard for heroes.

Of all Jane Austen's men who are "afraid of commitment," only Henry Crawford might be said to fall short of our honesty-about-his-intentions standard. And even Henry squeaks by all right if you add on the rather weaselly "if she asks" qualifier that Ross Jeffries is careful to append. None of Jane Austen's heartbreakers actually lie to women. The worst they do is act like they feel more than they do. And most of them don't go even that far. But as we've heard from Elizabeth Bennet, even "without scheming to do wrong, or to make others unhappy, there may be error, and there may be misery." Captain Wentworth is a remarkably admirable and attractive man precisely because he (eventually) figures out that honesty is not all that's required.

After all, Captain Wentworth was 100 percent honest about his intentions the whole time with Louisa. By the honesty standard, Wentworth hasn't done anything wrong, or even anything that should lead Louisa to form any particular expectations of him. His deeds have been as forthright as his words. The attention that he has paid her is entirely honest, in the sense that he has truly felt exactly as interested in her as he has shown himself to be, throughout. He has really enjoyed her company to the

TIP JUST FOR JANEITES

For a man to be honest about his present intentions is not good enough to make him a Jane Austen hero.

precise degree that he has expressed that enjoyment. His heartfelt expressions of admiration—the "words of interest, spoken with such serious warmth" that Louisa can't readily answer them—are true expressions of what he actually felt and believed in that moment. Captain Wentworth has made no attempt to deceive or manipulate Louisa in any way. Quite the contrary. As he confesses above, he's been blundering along with no design at all, trying to see whether he might be able to fall in love with her. Isn't that fair enough, as long as he was up front about the whole thing?

Well, no. Wentworth ultimately realizes it isn't. The problem, as Marguerite Fields of *New York Times* essay contest fame could tell you, is that a woman who welcomes this kind of attention from a man is likely to be disappointed if his enthusiasm—real at the time, and expressed honestly, with no promises about the future—turns out to be less lasting than her own. And it's not just women who keep being surprised by the inadequacy of honesty to navigate the gap between the sexes. It's apparent that men today are continually surprised by women who want more than the men are spontaneously interested in giving them, and more than they've ever promised. Modern men's surprise arises from the same source as Wentworth's shock after Louisa's accident. If the standard is only that everybody has to be honest about how they feel now, then that standard will continually trip up the person whose sexuality is oriented toward the future, instead of the passing moment. The current regime is so out of step with what women are actually like that normal female psychology ends up looking abnormal. In the immortal words of "Ross Jeffries Uncensored"—and I promise this is the very last time I will quote him: "Of course, if a girl is desperate and needy enough, she will CREATE those bonds, even though you never used any patterns[12] at all! That's when we can get into some trouble even though we proceeded with care. The problem isn't with us, but with our 'subject'; she's just too friggin' needy to deal with it."

It would totally rot to be a "ruined" woman like Eliza. But are the societal conventions we modern women have to contend with really all that big an improvement? At least nobody claimed that the aching need Eliza felt for Willoughby after he seduced and deserted her was some bizarre psychological deficit.

Just imagine living in a context where men were forced by their consciences—or, if they should happen not to have consciences, by the people around them—to take into account the effect their present attentions were likely to have on a woman's future happiness. That's the standard Captain Wentworth holds himself to.

The "Retarding Weight" of Jealousy

In all eight cases we've looked at so far, we've been dealing with men who are "just not that into" the women they seem to be courting. At least not yet. That's the best possible scenario out of all these cases: a Bingley or a Wentworth who's on the way to a point at which, if he doesn't get side-tracked or change his mind, he'll eventually commit himself to loving you. He's moving along the same path you are, if at a slower rate. In worse cases, what you seem to be sharing with him means something very different to him from what it means to you. Possibly he's simply playing you. Or maybe he's feeling pulled toward you, but he's choosing to commit to his own freedom instead. All these cases of male "fear of commitment" require generous doses of caution on a woman's part. She needs to be on the lookout for the players and the guys who are married to their own immaturity. And even if the man is a grownup who seems to be falling in love with her, she needs to remind herself that until he definitively does, it's not a sure thing. Even a Captain Wentworth is capable of leading you on unintentionally, before he clues in.

"Fear of Commitment" Bonus Case Study: George Knightley

But Jane Austen also gives us one more type of case in which men appear to be afraid of commitment. Look at Wentworth with Anne at the end of *Persuasion*, or at Mr. Knightley at the end of *Emma*. Why do they hesitate to tell the women they love that they love them? Emma is so late understanding her own heart that she doesn't have much time to suffer from Mr. Knightley's hesitation—she's still beating herself up for her own blind folly when he gets back from London and takes her out of her misery. But Anne is on tenterhooks, watching Wentworth advance and retreat. When they see each other in Bath for the first time after Louisa's accident, he's noticeably embarrassed to meet Anne; his front of "apparent indifference" has melted. But then, at the concert the next night, he seems ready to walk right by her with only a bow. Then again, when she makes it easy for him to talk to her, he's even warmer; he seems to have "a heart returning to her at last." And then *again* something seems to go wrong; after their "interesting, almost too interesting conversation," she can't catch his eye again, and she becomes anxious.[13] Finally, when he does approach her toward the end of the evening, "the difference between his present air and what it had been" makes it clear that "something must be the matter." She's "encouraging," and his mood seems to improve; he looks like he's ready to sit down next to her. But then her attention is distracted by Mr. Elliot, and Captain Wentworth retreats.

It looks like another classic case of "fear of commitment." Except in this case, it turns out that Captain Wentworth *is* just that into her. But he's jealous of Mr. Elliot; that has been "the retarding weight, the doubt, the torment" that's kept him from telling her he loves her. Mr. Knightley has exactly the same motive for keeping out of Emma's way by going to London after the Box Hill excursion: "It was jealousy of Frank Churchill that had taken him from the country."[14]

Notice that while jealousy—when it amounts to the belief that the woman he loves is actually encouraging another man's attentions, or is (as we might say) "already taken"—has a "retarding" effect on the courtship of a Captain Wentworth or a Mr. Knightley, the mere "admiration" of other men has the opposite effect. Captain Wentworth is "roused" to notice Anne's physical attractions again by the fact that Mr. Elliot is checking her out at the hotel in Lyme. And Mr. Knightley's initial jealousy of Frank Churchill, before Emma even met him, seems to have "enlightened him" to the fact that he loved Emma himself. Jealousy of this milder sort can spark men's competitive natures and make them notice us. But the genuine Jane Austen hero doesn't want to be (as we might say) the kind of creep who goes after another guy's girlfriend. That smacks of "the haphazard of selfish passion"—the sort of thing an egoist like Henry Crawford would do. In short, other men's admiration ought to help you with the kind of man who can turn out to be your Jane Austen hero, or at least it shouldn't hurt. What *won't* help you with him is if he gets it into his head that you're already attached to somebody else.

Thus Anne has to let Wentworth know that she's not committed to Mr. Elliot[15] and hint that she still loves him.[16] Notice that we've *finally* reached a species of apparent "fear of commitment" that's an exception to

A Jane Austen Heroine in the Twenty-first Century

✓lice Breyer (not her real name) dated
 man for seven and a half years. And now
's finally engaged to be married and
king forward to her happily ever after—but
vith her long-term boyfriend.

nstead, she's marrying a guy she has
wn since they were both in junior high
ool, but who never would have let her
w he wanted to go out with her if her
friend hadn't finally, after years of acting
aid of commitment," broken up with her.
e was understandably devastated at the
k-up. But three weeks later she got an
il from Tom King (not his actual name,
er), then serving in the U.S. Navy in
n. A mutual friend had told him Alice
now available. Alice had always thought
 was attractive, and it turns out he'd been
ested in her, too—except (like Mr. Knightley
Captain Wentworth) he wasn't the kind
y to horn in on another guy's girlfriend.

But when he heard Alice was free, and he happened to be traveling back home and attending a Valentine's Day wedding, he asked her to be his date. They had a great time at the wedding, and after a few months of a long distance relationship with Alice, he was out of the Navy and starting business school in Nashville, where she lived. When she returned my call asking about her story, she apologized for the delay—she was hard at work on her wedding invitations.

From her experiences, Alice is totally sold on Jane Austen's insight that while it's pretty pointless to try to persuade your typical "afraid of commitment" guy to love you the way you want to be loved, it's a very good idea to disentangle yourself from the wrong man and look available to the right one. As she told me, you may like a guy but think, "There's no way he would be interested." Until you're free, you may never know.

the general rule. Extreme caution is generally requisite in these cases. It makes sense to slow yourself down if you suspect deliberate manipulation, selfish immaturity, or even just that the guy's not falling in love as fast as you are. Jealousy is the only case I can see in Jane Austen where it actually makes sense to apply the opposite strategy—the one we're always tempted to resort to: helping him along, reassuring him that we're interested. Encouragement comes so naturally to us, but it's only in the rarest cases that it's the right move. And even in those cases, the most important thing you can do is to be sure that when your Jane Austen hero comes along you don't already look "taken" by some other, not so heroic guy.

$\mathscr{A}$DOPT AN AUSTEN ATTITUDE:

If a man is paying you attention but he's giving off signs of no serious intentions, compare him to the men in Jane Austen who seem afraid of commitment:

- Could he be a deliberate, heartless player like Henry Crawford?
- Or is he just indulging himself in the natural male tendency to live in the moment—and pushing his self-indulgence to the point of real selfishness (and disregard of you), like Willoughby?
- Is he sending mixed signals because either his integrity (Edward Ferrars) or his feelings (Frank Churchill) are already committed elsewhere? Is there another woman in the picture?
- Or is he, like Bingley (or like Captain Wentworth with Louisa), very possibly on a course to fall deeply in love with you if everything goes exactly right, but *not there yet*? If so, don't forget that he's still quite capable of being pulled off course by any number of distractions—or, at any point, of simply realizing that you're not the woman for him.
- Is he hesitating on account of jealousy, like Mr. Knightley, or like Wentworth with Anne? Might he possibly be ready to love you, if he didn't think you already loved somebody else?

$\mathscr{W}$HAT WOULD JANE DO?

She'd remember that it's usually harder for men than for us to really fall in love, and she'd proceed with caution.

She'd value that rare man who takes into account how his present actions are likely to affect a woman's future happiness.

*I*F WE *REALLY* WANT
TO BRING BACK JANE AUSTEN . . .

We'll calibrate our relationships to take into account the whole range of reasons a man may seem not to be in step with our expectations. When he's confusing us...going too slow...blowing hot and cold...we'll use our natural relationship expertise to see through his apparent "fear of commitment," diagnose the real cause, and act accordingly.

CHAPTER FIFTEEN

THE REAL, ORIGINAL "RULES"

Not for Manipulating Men—for Preserving Women's Peace of Mind, and Our Freedom to Choose

IN 1995, ELLEN FEIN AND SHERRIE SCHNEIDER PUBLISHED *The Rules: Time-Tested Secrets for Capturing the Heart of Mr. Right.* Fein and Schneider revealed what they said were the unique secrets of "rules girls," passed down from generation to generation among those special women who know the tricks of getting men to fall in love with and marry them. "The Rules" required you to keep your distance in the early stages of the relationship. You shouldn't be too eager, or too accommodating to the guy too early on. Don't agree to go out with him on Saturday unless he calls by Wednesday. Make sure you're the one who ends every phone call. Wait to have sex, and when you do, "stay emotionally cool no matter how hot the sex gets."[1] Essentially, play hard to get until you've got him hooked.

There are rules for women in Jane Austen novels, too. And some of them may seem to us even more bizarre and arbitrary than "The Rules." For example, Jane Austen heroines know that they must never write a letter to a man before they're already engaged to be married.[2] In *Sense and Sensibility* a breach of that very old-fashioned rule, which our author and her

213

heroines[3] take very seriously, turns out to be a serious mistake. But Jane Austen also has some fun with the whole subject of rules for courtship, suggesting at one point that "if it be true, as a celebrated writer has maintained, that no young lady can be justified in falling in love before the gentleman's love is declared, it must be very improper that a young lady should dream of a gentleman before the gentleman is first known to have dreamt of her."

That's obviously absurd. What we dream about is entirely beyond our control. And when we fall in love is equally out of our power—right? Well, yes and no. We've seen that Jane Austen is a critic of the Romantic love-at-first-sight, Is-he-The-One? method of proceeding in these matters. She doesn't paint love as something you should fall into in a "haphazard" manner ("randomly," as we'd say).[4] Jane Austen didn't think men *or* women should allow themselves to get attached without considering the character of the person they're attaching themselves to.

She also frowned on falling in love without at least some "encouragement" from the other person. (When men act like that, she calls it "selfish passion.") Ideally, a man and a woman will fall in love more or less simultaneously, and effortlessly get to a place where their "hearts…understand each other." But of course the plot of every Jane Austen novel, like the drama in our real-life love lives, arises from the fact that the course of true love hardly ever runs as smoothly as all that.

As we've seen from the impressive array of cases in which men give every evidence of "fearing commitment," we often outpace guys in falling in love. And it can also sometimes happen (as in the case of Elizabeth and Darcy) that men turn out to be in love with us before we even guess they're falling. Out-of-sync timing in love, with all the attendant misunderstandings and missed opportunities for happiness, is an inevitable feature of the romantic landscape.[5] When you think about all the possible variations on this theme—all the myriad ways men and women can miss each other if their progress in love isn't perfectly in sync—it's a wonder all our relationships aren't permanently stuck in Bob Dylan "you'll love me, or I'll love you" hell.[6] It seems miraculous that we ever do manage to find each other.

What's the solution? Can we slow ourselves down? Or should we speed the guy up? How can a man and a woman come to love each other—and let each other know—at just the right time? How can we prevent misfires and short circuits in love? What's Jane Austen's solution?

Not manipulating men. That much is absolutely clear. Jane Austen is almost as scornful as Mr. Darcy of the "meanness in *all* the arts which ladies sometimes condescend to employ for captivation." Plenty of characters in Jane Austen make use of such "arts" for getting a man to fall in love faster. But they aren't the characters we admire. The repellant, simpering Margaret Watson, in unrequited love with the absurd Tom Musgrave in *The Watsons*, leaves town for a month at a time "on purpose to egg him on, by her absence"—with no effect whatsoever. Tom doesn't even realize she's away. Elizabeth Bennet, on the other hand, who emphatically does not believe in "increasing" a man's love "by suspense,"[7] does attract Mr. Darcy's interest because she's so much less eager to please him than the other women he knows. Jane Austen tells us Elizabeth "roused" and "interested" Darcy by an attitude that was so unlike the "deference" and "officious attention" he was used to. Elizabeth attracted him by being different from the women "who so assiduously courted" him.[8] But she wasn't playing hard to get, like a "Rules Girl." She was *being* hard to get. The "liveliness" of Elizabeth's mind was quite natural to her, and her "impertinence" to Mr. Darcy came very naturally, too—it was her perfectly normal reaction to his rudeness. It was "simple" and natural, not "a trick"[9] on her part.

Ironically, "always speaking and looking and thinking" for a man's approval—as we see Caroline Bingley doing with Darcy—can also be "a trick." Flattery and eagerness to please can be applied just as deliberately to strengthen a man's feelings for you as can the opposite devices, the ones intended to increase his love by "suspense." That's because, depending on the circumstances, both "suspense"—if for whatever reason he's unsure of your feelings—and "gratitude"—if he *does* realize that you like him first—can be natural fuel for love.[10] And either gratitude or suspense can also be generated artificially by the kind of woman who doesn't mind manipulating men. In Jane Austen's

TIP JUST FOR JANEITES

Don't play hard to get.
Be hard to get.

novels, Lucy Steele[11] and Mrs. Clay[12] are the most notable practitioners of the art of flattering a man into love. And Charlotte Lucas explains the theory behind it.

The too-prudent Charlotte Lucas sees the precarious nature of Bingley's regard for Jane before Elizabeth Bennet can see it. But Charlotte's solution to the problem is not Jane Austen's solution. Charlotte wants to bridge the gap between how fast Jane and Bingley are falling in love by artificially speeding things up on his end. Lest Jane "lose the opportunity of fixing him," Charlotte thinks Jane should manipulate Bingley's feelings to "help him on": "There is so much of gratitude or vanity in almost every attachment, that it is not safe to leave any to itself. We can all *begin* freely— a slight preference is natural enough; but there are very few of us who have heart enough to be really in love without encouragement. Nine times out of ten, a woman had better shew *more* affection than she feels.... When she is secure of him, there will be leisure for falling in love as much as she chuses."

ZIP JUST FOR JANEITES

Keep your distance.
Not to increase his love by
suspense—but so you can
make up your mind
about a man while you can
still see him clearly.

But Elizabeth objects: Charlotte's advice is suited only to a woman who's "determined to get a rich husband, or any husband." Jane can't be sure yet of her own feelings, or of Bingley's deserts. And she's not "acting by design."[13]

What exactly is wrong with Charlotte's advice? She does see things that Elizabeth misses. Charlotte notices as it's happening that Bingley probably doesn't see how much Jane cares for him, while Elizabeth realizes only later "that Jane's feelings, though fervent, were little displayed, and that there was a constant complacency in her air and manner, not often united with great sensibility." And Charlotte understands more clearly than Elizabeth does the potential for a mismatch between the rate at which the guy's falling in love and the speed at which you are responding to him. What Charlotte doesn't have is Jane Austen heroine-style dignity and Jane Austen heroine-level respect for men as autonomous human beings. Charlotte's deliberate manipulations are not Jane Austen's preferred method for dealing with men.[14]

Jane Austen heroines are really scrupulous about doing anything even remotely manipulative vis à vis men.[15] Why are Jane Austen's heroines so reluctant to act "by design"? It's not just about fear of exposing themselves to ridicule by tipping other people off to how interested they are in a certain man.[16] Emma's quite ashamed of her scheming,[17] even though it was all for Harriet, so it doesn't carry any danger of revealing Emma's own romantic interests. It makes her blush because she sees, in retrospect, that her attempts at manipulation were "adventuring too far, assuming too much, making light of what ought to be serious, a trick of what ought to be simple." It's like Mr. Knightley warned Emma at the very beginning of her matchmaking: this kind of scheming is neither a proper nor a delicate use of a woman's time—or of a man's, for that matter; think of Henry Crawford and our pickup artists. Manipulation is indelicate because it involves manhandling other people's feelings. And it's not proper because it's not your place to decide when or with whom other people fall in love. That applies to Emma's scheming about Harriet and Mr. Elton just as much as it applies to "Rules"-style tricks we're tempted to use to "fix" or "catch" any man we're interested in.[18] However much you want him to love you, you have to respect his right to decide freely. Otherwise you're half way to Lady Susan Vernon's complete disrespect for men: "It is undoubtedly better to deceive him entirely; since he will be stubborn, he must be tricked." She gets what she wants out of guys most of the time, but what she wants isn't worth having: because she is entirely without respect for any man, Lady Susan is incapable of real love.

Jane Austen heroines take pride in being honest, and they want to "be paid the compliment of being believed sincere." But we've already seen that honesty is not enough to make things work between men and women. And somehow you can't see a Jane Austen heroine ever acting like Audrey Raines in *24*, telling Jack Bauer she thinks she's falling in love with him 1) after they're already having sex, and 2) before he's said anything about loving her. The kind of honesty that Jane Austen heroines are proud of does *not* mean being forthcoming abut their feelings to guys who haven't yet said they love them.

In fact, Jane Austen's heroines spend quite a lot of energy concealing their feelings. Because if we're totally straightforward about our intentions, and men tell us theirs up front, too, that mutual honesty is no foolproof recipe for happy love. We're still all too likely to be caught in the gap between the male and the female psychology of love. We'll outpace him in commitment, or we won't be able to keep ourselves from assuming that what we share means the same thing to him as to us. We're still going to freight what we do with him with import for the future that he won't necessarily feel. A woman with a policy of total honesty is all too likely to end up wondering, like Marguerite Fields, why she's so much more interested in permanence than any of the guys she hooks up with. So what *is* the right method for dealing with men? If manipulating guys is beneath your dignity, and honesty won't make you happy, what can you do?

Fortunately, there's a third option: The choices aren't just either manipulate his feelings or else be totally frank about your own. There's also prudent reserve, maintaining emotional distance until there's a good reason to get close, pacing yourself so you don't get ahead of the guy. You don't have to choose between letting it all hang out and scheming to catch a husband like a "Rules Girl." Jane Austen's way means applying *self*-control, rather than attempting to control the emotions of other people whose autonomy you ought to respect. You, after all, are the one person on earth whose feelings you have the right to control.

All the peculiar rules that Jane Austen heroines take seriously—never write him a letter until you're engaged, don't go riding around the countryside and dining at inns with young men,[19] never let a suitor give you big expensive presents, don't let him take you on a tour of a house he expects to inherit if you haven't been introduced to its present owner[20]—are simply particular applications, appropriate to a different time and place from ours, of the underlying principles that Jane Austen heroines apply to their love lives. Most of the little, specific rules no longer apply today. (Do *not* wait for a proposal of marriage before you're willing to text a guy.) But the bigger principles absolutely do apply, as much now as they did two centuries ago: Don't offer a guy "unsolicited proofs of tenderness" that are "not warranted" by a "preceding" commitment. Remember that what you enjoy together may mean something different to him from what it means to you.

Wait till he's all in before you dive in yourself. Pace yourself carefully until you can be sure you're not getting out ahead of him.

𝒯IP JUST FOR JANEITES

You are the only person you have a right to control.

Sometimes Jane Austen heroines do fall very thoroughly in love before the men commit themselves. *All* of them, at one point or another, find themselves to a degree in love and "in some doubt of a return" of love from the man. But they never simply tell the guy, à la Audrey Raines. And they don't set about trying to ensure he falls in love, either. If a Jane Austen heroine sees a mismatch between how fast or how deeply she and the man she's interested in are falling in love, she addresses it first where she has control and has a right to control. She thinks of managing her own expectations rather than just putting her feelings and desires out there, or manipulating the man. Instead of dreaming up schemes to speed him up, she slows herself down.

We twenty-first-century women know all about sex, a subject Jane Austen hardly mentions. It's axiomatic today that to be a gentleman instead of a jerk, a guy has to be willing to slow himself down sexually, to pace himself in the act of making love—in order to accommodate a woman's typically slower sexual response. In comparison, we're pretty clueless about love. Jane Austen, who knew all about love, understood that a woman often needs to slow down her emotions and hopes for the future, to pace the speed at which she's falling in love, in order to accommodate a man's typically slower speed of emotional attachment. In Jane Austen, self-control is empowering. It's not about being a repressed woman who has no "voice," who doesn't know she can go all out for what she wants. Jane Austen heroines understand exactly what they want. But they know that grabbing doesn't get you love.

The kind of pacing, careful distance, self-control, and self-knowledge that happy Jane Austen heroines maintain doesn't just protect you from unnecessary heartbreak—though it definitely will help there. Elinor, Elizabeth, Fanny, Emma, Catherine, and Anne all seriously contemplate the possibility that they won't get the happy ending they're aching for with every fiber of their beings. Elinor does her best to mentally prepare herself for Edward's marriage to Lucy Steele.[21] Elizabeth considers the possibility that family pride and Lady Catherine's influence may keep Darcy from proposing again and decides, "If he is satisfied with only regretting me," giving her up out of motives she can't respect, "when he might have obtained my affections and hand, I shall soon cease to regret him at all." Fanny reminds herself continually that her feelings for Edmund aren't justified by his for her.[22] Emma realizes that Mr. Knightley may never love her—that he may even marry Harriet Smith—and does her best to prepare herself for the worst. Catherine resists Isabella's attempts to persuade her to let her happiness depend on Henry Tilney before there's any reason to think that Henry is seriously interested in her. Anne, who is older and already has significant experience with heartbreak under her belt, sees that she may lose Wentworth again. Contemplating that possibility, she chooses always to love him, whether or not she ever gets to be happy with him; she'd rather live without love than ever accept another man.[23]

Each in her different way, these six ultimately happy Jane Austen heroines are to some extent prepared for all events. Following the real, original rules of courtship, they've kept some distance between themselves and the men who haven't decisively committed to them yet. If the men never make that commitment, Jane Austen heroines' mental peace and "tranquillity" stand a better chance. (Which is not to be sneezed at. Heartbreak, self-loathing, and clinical depression are still no joke, even with our chemical antidepressants, helpful therapists, and the various other advantages of modern medicine that by and large—though not always—keep even Marianne-level lack of self-care from seriously endangering our physical health.)

But the rules aren't just about avoiding misery. The real, original rules actually *set you up for a happy ending.* That's how Jane Austen heroines get there. By keeping some distance from the men they're coming to love—neither forcing early emotional intimacy by premature honesty, nor rolling up their sleeves and presuming to play puppeteer with a man's feelings—Jane Austen heroines free up more room for themselves to maneuver in. They retain a freedom of action and a liberty of choice that we've lost. Remember the grand civilizational project that Jane Austen was engaged in? (That she

A Jane Austen Heroine in the Twenty-first Century

Becky Finn (not her real name) was interested in a man she had known for a while. She put out feelers about his relationship status to a mutual friend, who told her he was already dating someone. So she steered clear, but later the guy started showing interest in her. Learning from the mutual friend that he and his girlfriend had now broken up, Becky started going out with him.

The relationship was "totally G-rated," Becky explains—not physical. "It was looking like it could go that way, but I was being kind of cautious because I knew he had been very serious with the other woman." Still, they did keep "ending up at his place, like on his couch."

Then Becky went to a party where she saw him with his old girlfriend.

The next time he called and asked her to dinner, she said yes. But as soon as she hung up, she thought to herself that she didn't want to be anybody's meantime girl. So she emailed him to ask what was up with the other woman. He told her, "We've been on a break since August," but admitted to still hoping to get back with the old

girlfriend. So Becky told him that it sounded like he was emotionally entwined with the other girl, and that she didn't want to be dating him under those circumstances. At which point he asked if they could still see each other as friends.

Becky admits, "I am interested in him"—still. But she decided to lay down some ground rules. "If you want to be friends," she told him, "we can see each other during the day—see each other for lunch—but not getting cozy on your couch." So they go out to lunch from time to time.

"I have to say it feels empowering," Becky says. "For the first time it feels like I've set some sort of parameters." Until she did make some rules, the relationship, despite being G-rated, "kept feeling like a physical romantic relationship"—with a guy who wasn't available to commit to her.

Maybe he'll get back together with his old girlfriend, or maybe they'll definitely break up and he'll get serious about Becky. Meanwhile, she's is keeping her distance (and her perspective) until and unless the guy is in a position to make a real emotional investment in her.

was in fact the zenith and acme of!) European society in her day was figuring out how women could be sufficiently emancipated to choose their own husbands—without losing their peace of mind and, worse, their freedom to the first man who asked for their love, and missing their chance at happily ever after. This is the project that Jane Austen brought to perfection by fine-tuning the way in which a woman can protect *herself*, rather than relying on her parents, or the patriarchy, or anybody else in the world to make her choices for her. The self-control Jane Austen heroines engage in is protection against more than heartbreak. Following the real, original rules for dealing with men is the way Jane Austen heroines preserve their freedom to choose (or refuse) a man who's chosen them—instead of miserably waiting around to see whether the man they've *already* committed themselves to will ever eventually get around to choosing them.

Marriage, Jane Austen Heroine-Style

Look at two different ways of getting married in Jane Austen novels. First, there's her heroines' way of finding permanent happiness in love. The heroine gets to know a man she finds attractive. He pays her attention. Maybe it will turn out to be the kind of attention you expect from a man who's seriously interested in you. Or maybe it's really just polite interest, gallantry, cousinly affection, or friendship. You do your best to figure out his feelings, and your own. Complications ensue. (Perhaps the man's father prematurely and mysteriously sends you home from your visit to the family's abbey; or the guy turns out to be secretly engaged already; or you angrily refuse his proposal under a series of misconceptions about his character, and only afterwards discover that he's perfect for you. The possibilities are endless.)

But through all the vicissitudes and complications, you follow those real, original rules for finding happiness in love. You keep your distance until getting close is warranted by unmistakable signs that you're the guy's object of pursuit. You don't offer him "unsolicited proofs of tenderness." You weigh his character, and you determine his intentions. You pace the progress of your own falling-in-love as carefully as you can. And having determined 1) that he's seriously interested in you, and 2) that he's worth loving—not just for his fine figure and the beautiful grounds of his Derbyshire estate, but for his character, too, that is, what he's really like as a person—you decide that you love him. Or at least that you could, if he loves you. But you don't blurt it out to him, and you don't start scheming to rush him into a commitment. You wait for him to catch up to you—and you do that very uncomfortable waiting in the full knowledge that he may not. You don't let yourself depend on his love until he gives you the unmistakable evidence that he's stepped out of present-bound views into the kind of love that comes so naturally to you as a woman—love that makes him as eager as you are to offer you a permanent commitment, and secure one from you.

And when he finally tells you he loves you that way, you're blissfully happy. Because what the hero offers the Jane Austen heroine isn't just a big step toward happily ever after, or one part of what she's longing for. It's the whole ball of wax: love, sex, marriage, real mutual respect grounded in knowledge of each other's characters, children, shared financial resources, a family of her own.[24]

"But I Do Not Particularly Like Your Way of Getting Husbands"

But there's also another way of pairing up for life in Jane Austen novels. You could call it marriage on the installment plan, or love by increments. Besides the heroines, we also see Lydia Bennet get married to Wickham; Mrs. Clay in the process of (it sure looks like) persuading Mr. Elliot to make her his wife; and Maria Bertram Rushworth trying but failing to get a permanent commitment from Henry Crawford. These women *don't* follow the original rules.

Lydia and Maria have certainly showered "unsolicited proofs of tenderness" on their lovers. Jane Austen tells us in both cases that it was the strength of the woman's love that drove the elopement; the men more or less willingly went along for the ride. Mrs. Clay, too, finds that her affections overpower her, so that she abandons scheming to marry Sir Walter and goes to live with Mr. Elliot instead.[25] Jane Austen makes it clear that you *can* end up married this way, too, just as you can by following the rules.

It's a bit of an iffy proposition, of course. Maria can't hold Henry; the bitter end of their relationship is one of the ugliest things in all Jane Austen's novels: "She hoped to marry him, and they continued together till she was obliged to be convinced that such hope was vain, and till the disappointment and wretchedness arising from the conviction, rendered her temper so bad, and her feelings for him, so like hatred, as to make them for a while each other's punishment, and then induce a voluntary separation."

And Lydia is very lucky to—just barely—end up married rather than used and dumped. But Mrs. Clay does seem well on her way to snagging Mr. Elliot: "She has abilities, however, as well as affections; and it is now a doubtful point whether his cunning, or hers, may finally carry the day; whether, after preventing her from being the wife of Sir Walter, he may not be wheedled and caressed at last into making her the wife of Sir William."

My money's on Mrs. Clay to succeed at marriage on the installment plan. Sometimes it does work.

The real difference between the two ways of dealing with men isn't that the heroines' rules guarantee you snag the guy. The difference is all about *on what terms* you get him. Remember, you can fail to end up with the man you want if you're living by the original Jane Austen heroine rules, too. In fact, a crucial element of abiding by those rules is keeping it clear in your mind that there's no guarantee you'll get the guy in the end. Being willing to live with that uncertainty is necessary if you're not going to try to rush things, either by "Rules"-style manipulation or by prematurely revealing your feelings for him. The difference between an Elizabeth Bennet and a Mrs. Clay isn't just about: do you end up married, or not? It's about the nature and quality of the relationship, about your dignity, and especially about your freedom to choose.

At first glance, Mrs. Clay's waiting-to-be-made-an-honest-woman plight may seem completely outdated, now that society no longer punishes living together before marriage. But Mrs. Clay's situation actually has a lot of resonance today. Are women in the twenty-first century still wheedling and caressing the men they're living with into marriage? Well, sure. It's happening all around us, all the time. In fact, you can make a strong case that Mrs. Clay's relationship style has actually expanded to take over territory that used to be occupied by the Jane Austen heroine dynamic. Today the wheedling and caressing—and arguing and pressuring and ultimatuming, and the use of every other possible method of persuasion that might get a guy to agree to the things we desperately want, but that he's not inspired to offer us—don't end with marriage any more. Now even *after* we're married, we still have to start a whole *new* campaign to talk the man into being willing to have a baby. And a second child. And to share a life together, pooling financial resources and divvying up responsibilities like a real family.[26]

How come we don't get to be like Elizabeth Bennet, saying Yes to a Mr. Darcy who's eager to offer us everything we want? Or like the heroine of *Mansfield Park*, with an Edmund Bertram "as anxious to marry Fanny, as Fanny herself could desire"? Compare Elizabeth and Darcy's happiness to the "patched-up business" of Lydia's marriage to Wickham, and you can see why Elizabeth tells Lydia that she does "not particularly like your way of getting husbands." Why do we have to be like Mrs. Clay, already attached to a man, but with all the work still ahead of us to talk him into giving us the things we want from him? Why does it seem a bridge too far to hope that he might ever actually want those things himself?

The answer has to do with "attachment."[27] Mrs. Clay, Lydia, and Maria Bertram all end up definitively attached to men who haven't committed to them yet because they've broken the rules meant to protect their freedom to choose. Given the realities of female psychology,[28] the intimacy that all three women share with the men they love is bound to attach them with powerful bonds. They're no longer in a position to evaluate and choose a guy; they've already chosen him, and have yet to persuade him to choose them.

Don't Try Love on
the Installment Plan

Speaking of scientific research, let's look briefly at what our modern studies show about living together, since that's the one big thing in common to all three stories: Maria Bertram's, Lydia's, and Mrs. Clay's. Research tells us that couples who live together before getting married—at least if they're not engaged before they move in together—are less happy when they do get married, and have a higher divorce rate. Which backs up Jane Austen's insight that living together is a far from optimal arrangment. But why? "The cohabitation effect" is one of those stubborn results, replicated in study after study despite the fact that nobody seems to have a definitive explanation for it. There's all kinds of speculation about why this is. Maybe it's self-selection: people who are bad marriage risks in the first place (children of divorced parents, for example[29]) tend to cohabit more often than people who aren't. There's also the "experience of cohabitation" theory, according to which couples who live together are learning habits that will later undermine their marriages, starting with the basic lack of commitment that defines the living-together relationship. And one team of researchers suggests that "people may choose riskier, less compatible partners in the first place, because they think that cohabitation will be easier to break up than marriage."[30] All likely enough to be true.

But think about it Jane Austen's way: don't compare living together with being married; compare it with what you would be doing *before* getting married if you were a Jane Austen heroine. In other words, consider two alternate ways of "getting husbands": living together versus following the real, original rules. Living together may be easier to break up than a marriage, but it's a heck of a lot *harder* to walk away from than the kind of rational evaluation of a guy's character and careful pacing of your attachment that Jane Austen heroines manage. Compared to the Jane Austen heroine method, the Mrs. Clay or modern relationship pattern is going to ensure that a lot of women double down on their initial mistakes.

So Jane Austen wouldn't advise you to move in with your boyfriend? Not exactly late-breaking news. Why make so much of this rather obvious point? Not just because most couples today do live together before the wedding. More crucially, because the Mrs. Clay-type situation that too many twenty-first-century women find themselves in sheds light on a big, important difference between us and Jane Austen's heroines—a difference that affects us and our relationships long before we're making the decision to move in together or not. Exactly *why* and *how* living together constrains your freedom to choose a man matters to us all because today the very same dynamic is at work in relationships even much earlier on.

When women say they'd never marry a man without living with him first—that that's the only way to really get to know a guy well enough to be able to decide whether he's right for them[31]—they're forgetting the power of "attachment." Sure, you know more about a guy once you've shared an apartment with him. But the knowledge you gain by setting up housekeeping with him is not free. As you get to know your man better, you also become more attached to him. For every bit of knowledge that you gain, you lose, in some measure, your objectivity, your ability to evaluate him, and your freedom of judgment. And who doubts that attachment is generally a more powerful game changer for women than for men? That's even assuming that your feelings and his were equally tentative at the beginning—that moving in together in the first place wasn't, instead, the exact same compromise as the one between 1) Mrs. Clay's desire to marry Mr. Elliot and 2) Mr. Elliot's desire to move the relationship along without making a permanent commitment.

If the point of getting to know guys better is for women to *choose for ourselves*, and to choose *well*, then any mating scheme that progressively strips us of our power to evaluate men is seriously defective. Unfortunately, modern dating in general—not just our 60 to 70 percent cohabitation-before-we-marry rate[32]—tends to maneuver us into a position where we've got more data to evaluate the man by, but we're no longer able to see him as clearly as we did at first. At the end of that piece for the *New York Times*, Marguerite Fields knew a lot more about her recent hook-up, including some information that might have been a definite turn-off if she'd been told it about a man she *didn't* know: "During the night he kicked and snored, grabbing greedily at me with his well-moisturized hands like a child snatching at free candy." But she acquired that knowledge only at the cost of having her view of him softened by attachment. When he blows her off, she has to struggle to remind herself she had originally thought him "arrogant."

A friend once told me, after an apparently promising romance fizzled, that she had realized people who are more objective—your family, your friends—can see the guy you're dating more clearly than you can. This is an important point in light of the project Jane Austen was engaged in: helping women do a wise job of picking a man, once they were free to pick for themselves instead of submitting to the choice of their parents and guardians. True, your friends and family don't get as close to the man you're interested in as you do, so there are things they don't know about him. But they're also not intoxicated by the emotions that make it hard for you to see him straight. And an awful lot of the really big things your happiness will depend on are going to be more obvious to them than to you—and clearer to you *before* than *after* you get attached.

Notice that all those arcane rules Jane Austen's happy heroines abide by are set up with the same end in view. They all allow women to spend time with men and get to know them, but in a way that preserves their independence until they've got a definitive commitment from the man. Regency Era social arrangements were all arrangements for maximizing women's interactions with men to the precise extent that is possible while still minimizing the possibility that women will commit themselves to any relationship of a tentative nature. They were about fending off attachment, maintaining women's freedom to pick a man by preserving the scope for her observation and judgment.

Jane Austen could poke fun at decorum when it was pushed to an extreme, with the woman making a great parade of her modesty.[33] And *Persuasion* shows Jane Austen thought that protecting women from anything tentative in their relationships could be taken *too* far—at least when the source of uncertainty was only external circumstances (Captain Wentworth's lack of fortune), not any hesitation to commit on the man's part.[34] And of course after Jane Austen's day, the Victorians took the whole thing to an absurd and stifling extreme, so that concern about "compromising" your all-important reputation eclipsed the really significant issue that Jane Austen saw: compromising your heart and your judgment. Jane Austen would never have followed the Victorians down that dead end. But she was 100 percent on board with the basic idea that women benefited from the rules that warned them against committing themselves before a man commits to them.

Don't "Work on Your Relationship"

Besides keeping her from prematurely belonging to a man who didn't quite belong to her yet, the rules also helped a woman attract and evaluate potential mates by avoiding *another* major distraction that women today are plagued by, above and beyond premature attachment. We call it "working on our relationship." I'm inclined to suspect Jane Austen would have called it "making a good wife." Which she wouldn't have thought made a lot of sense…before you're a wife at all. Once a woman is "in a relationship"—just as soon as there's an understanding that we're together with a guy, whether or not we're living together, or sleeping together, yet[35]—our attention is bound to switch from 1) evaluating him as a potential mate to 2) doing everything we can to make the relationship work.[36]

It has come to seem perfectly normal to us that a couple should be, at one and the same time, "working on their relationship" and also deciding whether that relationship is going to last.[37] In fact, we're so used to a kind of tentative togetherness—where there's already a commitment, but it's a temporary or partial one—that we act like the actual decisions about whether to take the relationship to the next level of commitment, and even whether to stay together at all, are decisions we can make jointly with the man, as part of the relationship. But if you think about it rationally, it doesn't make a lot of sense. The two of you can't really decide together to what extent and even whether you're going to be together. In the end, these are decisions each of you has to make for yourself.

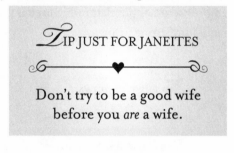

*Z*IP JUST FOR JANEITES

Don't try to be a good wife before you *are* a wife.

A friend of mine (a psychologist in private practice as a therapist, for whatever extra authority that gives his story) was once telling me the story of how he and his wife decided to get married. At the point in their relationship where they were getting really serious, he found himself in the process of a career move—from one academic institution to another—that meant he would also be moving to a different state. He had fallen in love and was thinking he wanted to get married. But the decision was complicated by the move. Telling me the story, he happened to say: "We still had a decision to make. Well, two decisions, actually." By which he meant that he had to decide whether he wanted to marry her, and then she had her own separate decision to make about whether she wanted to marry him. Something about the way he said it clarified in my mind the fact that any permanent romantic commitment really requires two individual decisions—a point that we lose sight of with all our talk about "the talk" and "working on our relationship."

Compared to us, Jane Austen heroines are willing to forego a lot of things to maintain their freedom to choose a man from a position of independence, instead of wheedling and caressing one into choosing them. In the short term they do without sexual pleasure…and the thrill of that moment with a new guy when you first admit to being interested in each other and cross personal boundaries…and the togetherness that you can enjoy in a romantic relationship even if it's tentative or short-lived. They're incredibly strong women.[38]

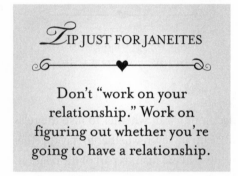

TIP JUST FOR JANEITES

Don't "work on your relationship." Work on figuring out whether you're going to have a relationship.

To live like a Jane Austen heroine, do you have to be bravely lonely? No, you don't.[39] But you *do* have to be strong enough to be willing to postpone some very good and desirable things—the relief and exhilaration of letting him into the secret of your feelings, plus pleasure, romance, and comfortable togetherness with a guy—until it's all justified by a firm commitment on his part. Going for those things prematurely means giving up your freedom to choose a man wisely; it means short-circuiting the delicate kind of courtship in which Jane Austen heroines and their heroes find permanent happiness. That's the purpose of all those rules in Jane Austen—from the arcane ones about how many dances you could dance with one partner, to the perennial principles about pacing the speed of your attachment. They're all for preserving a woman's freedom to choose permanent happiness.[40]

But this is all sounding awfully hard and a bit depressing. Do the real, original rules for women disappointingly boil down to keeping your legs crossed before marriage? Is our only real choice between being a Marguerite Fields—caught in the attachment gap between men and women—and being forty-year-old virgins?[41] Well, no. The conservative Christian no-sex-before-marriage rule is not the complete recipe for Jane Austen heroine status. How do I know? I've lived it.

I grew up an Evangelical Christian in Memphis, Tennessee. I went to an all-girls' school; boys were alien and fascinating creatures to me. Before I'd ever been asked on a date, I heard from the speakers at "Youth Week" at my church the very precise limits we were supposed to abide by once we got started mingling with the opposite sex. After hyping the titillating "How far can we go?" question all week, the charismatic guest speaker announced the definitive answer on the last night. *A kiss good night.* That was it. If you always stopped right there, you'd save yourself from the ugly fate the speaker had been warning us against all week with his stories—which even to my naïve ears sounded strangely 1950s-vintage—about the kind of girl who ended up going "all the way," asked the guy afterwards if he still "respected" her, and ended up the brunt of derisive male laughter when her question was the punchline of the story the guy told his street-corner buddies.

So when I did start dating a guy, that's the standard I tried to live by. But it didn't really work. It was a failure in two different ways, actually. First of all, "a good night kiss" can mean a lot of different things, some of which tend to have a certain momentum beyond anything that can be covered by that description. But that wasn't the only deficiency in the admittedly well-meaning advice I was trying to follow. The other problem was that the stop-at-a-good-night-kiss rule didn't address the main point of the real, original rules that Jane Austen heroines follow. It didn't do anything to keep me from glomming onto the first guy who took a serious interest in me. I spent two years in a relationship that had almost all the exact problems Jane Austen heroines avoid by following the real, original rules.

It kept other guys from asking me out. It kept me busy "working on our relationship"—a miserable combination of 1) trying to improve my character and curb my expectations to accommodate the guy, and 2) badgering him to change himself to accommodate my expectations—instead of asking myself whether he was really the right guy. It gave me the illusion that the two of us were in something together, when really we were just trying each other out. And—surprise!—it turned out that the guy I was working so hard to be together with wasn't as committed to me as I was to him. I spent the whole time feeling way too much like Mrs. Clay, and not nearly enough like Elizabeth Bennet. And high school wasn't the last time I made that mistake.

Some of the attachment was no doubt from the (oxytocin-inducing) good-night kisses. But it wasn't just that. Even more important, I think, was the "dangerous particularity"—the reality that I'd already chosen him, the tentative commitment, the fact that we were a couple. The "relationship" itself was the problem.

In college I converted to Catholicism[42] and progressively lost touch with the Evangelical Christian world. But eventually I read up on "honorable courtship," which is a new solution for the problem addressed by the old good-night-kiss rule I picked up as a teenager. Apparently at one Christian college, students aren't supposed to pay each other any romantic attention before consulting with both their parents and agreeing to undertake a "courtship," in which their stated goal is to figure out whether they want to get married. But notice, a woman who has entered into an "honorable courtship" is now in a tentative quasi-commitment with a man. It's not courtship as Jane Austen understood it—where a man has made his interest clear, but the woman hasn't yet said *yes*.

Quasi-commitment even without sex falls afoul of the real, original rules Jane Austen heroines live by. But so does physical intimacy without even quasi-commitment. As I was finishing this chapter, I came across a blog called "Hooking Up Smart," where Susan Walsh offers women "5 Ways to Get More Control of Your Relationships." Walsh rejects both *Rules*-style and *He's Just Not That Into You*-based approaches and argues for self-control. So far, so good.[43] A lot of Walsh's advice matches up with what you can learn from Jane Austen. But Walsh seems to expect that women can do things like "Make sure that your level of interest is no greater than his," "Think of yourself as 'single' because you are," and "Try not to discuss him constantly with your girlfriends" at the same time that they're sharing a level of physical intimacy with a guy that's more Lydia than Elizabeth Bennet. That's exactly the miserable state of affairs Marguerite Fields describes in her *New York Times* piece. A woman who tries to follow Walsh's advice is going to find herself vainly struggling for that "Zenlike form of nonattachment" that seems to come so easily to men, so hard to women.

One more thing about that guy I dated in high school. Notice how I keep calling him "that guy I dated in high school"? Instead of "my high school boyfriend"? That's because even back then I had a certain reluctance to claim him as my "boyfriend" or admit that I was his "girlfriend." My hesitation came mainly from a source quite different from my Evangelical church, where pairing up was all the rage in the youth group.[44]

That reluctance was picked up from my grandmother who, having been raised by *her* grandmother, was a link to much older ideas about relations between the sexes. She called the boys in our lives "beaux," not "boyfriends," because a "beau" is any man who's interested in you—not necessarily one whose attentions *you* have accepted.[45] Raising her own children in the 1950s and '60s, Grandmother was totally out of touch with the going-steady, pin-ceremony, "be true to your school now Just like you would to your girl or guy"[46] romantic ethic of the fifties.[47] There's a story in our family about the engagement party for my aunt. Grandmother had been so insistent that her daughter keep her options open until she was *officially* engaged that Aunt Mary had been dating different guys in Memphis while the man she had decided to marry was in medical school in Baltimore. So when Aunt Mary called a male friend to ask him to the party, he asked whose engagement it was for—assuming she was asking him to be her date. My grandmother brought a kind of faint memory of those real, original rules into the late twentieth century. She gave me at least a whisper of a feel for what it might be like to live in the system that Jane Austen brought to perfection, when women were freer to find their way to love without premature commitments.

But it's all a long time ago. What if you truly wanted to live like a Jane Austen heroine today? To go beyond learning to be a little wiser about why love, twenty-first-century-style, is making you unhappy? To do more than minimally protect yourself from the hazards that Jane Austen understood better than we do? What if you wanted to get to fall in love the way Elizabeth Bennet does? Is it even still possible? That's the subject of the next and final chapter.

$\mathcal{A}$DOPT AN AUSTEN ATTITUDE:

- Remember that manipulating men is beneath your dignity. Respect men as autonomous human beings, and require the same kind of respect from them.
- Realize that honesty about your feelings is not the silver bullet, either.
- Understand that getting close to a guy makes judging whether he's right for you both easier and harder. Intimacy—physical *or* emotional—does mean you learn more about him. But you also get more attached, and therefore less objective.

$\mathcal{W}$HAT WOULD JANE DO?

- She'd live by the real, original rules for maintaining a woman's freedom to choose a man and to win through to a heroine-class happy ending.
- She'd be willing to postpone some very good things to keep her options for permanent happiness open.
- She'd remember that her job is to choose the right man, not to "work on her relationship."

$\mathcal{I}$F WE *REALLY* WANT TO BRING BACK JANE AUSTEN . . .

- We'll quit running our love lives on the installment plan.
- We won't settle for anything less than real love and commitment.

CHAPTER SIXTEEN

RRANGE YOUR OWN MARRIAGE— IN THE MOST PLEASANT MANNER POSSIBLE

(by Falling in Love the Jane Austen Way)

IS FINDING HAPPY LOVE JANE AUSTEN'S WAY OUT OF reach for us? How on earth are you supposed to signal to a guy that you have any interest in him—let alone keep him interested in you—while you keep your distance? After all, Jane Austen herself never got married. Why? Were her standards just *too* high?

Susan Walsh's advice for "Hooking Up Smart" includes this critique of the *Sex and the City* writer's *He's Just Not That Into You* approach, which we've seen overlaps with Jane Austen's in some surprising ways: "On the other hand, this approach can lead straight to the dating desert. You don't waste time with jerks, but where are the great guys who want to date [you]? Guys know you won't hook up randomly, so you find yourself ignored at a party. You may not be getting dumped, but life sure gets boring when there is no guy intrigue or boy drama."[1]

"Where Are the Great Guys?"

Okay, first of all, if what you're looking for from guys is intrigue and drama instead of love and happiness, please go back and read chapters 1 to 3. Still, "Where are the great guys?" is an entirely valid question.

Jane Austen, like us, was living in an era and in a slice of society when a lot of women didn't have great marriage prospects. And for some of the same reasons as today. Women tend to want to marry "up." We find guys attractive if they're smarter, more successful than we are, and competent at things we don't understand.[2] And no, not because we're all heartless gold-diggers on the prowl for an easy meal ticket. A woman who's going to entrust herself to a man for the long term needs to be able to rely on and respect him. As a matter of fact, the more intelligent and assertive we are ourselves, the more important respect for our man is going to be for our happiness—and yet the harder it's going to be to find a guy who can inspire it. Mr. Bennet tells Elizabeth, Jane Austen's wittiest heroine, "I know your disposition, Lizzy. I know that you could be neither happy nor respectable, unless you truly esteemed your husband; unless you looked up to him as a superior. Your lively talents would place you in the greatest danger in an unequal marriage." So if you're at the absolute top of the heap—as English gentlewomen were in the eighteen-teens and we educated, liberated, successful American women are today[3]—good matches are going to seem thin on the ground.[4]

But besides being in competition for the cream of the crop, we're also suffering from some flaws in modern social arrangements. This is where Jane Austen heroines have a terrific advantage over us. Whatever their difficulties, at least they have the benefit of a social scene deliberately organized to bring women into contact with interested men without putting them under a lot of pressure to get too close too early.

Compare the ways we get to know men to their opportunities. The quintessential social setting at which Jane Austen heroines mingle with potential heroes is the assembly ball, like the one in *Pride and Prejudice* where Elizabeth first sees Mr. Darcy.[5] Jane Austen lived at the height of the period when "assemblies"—monthly public balls typically at a town's inn, drawing families and single men from all over the local area for dancing through each winter—were held in "most places."[6]

Entertainments of this kind were something new, at least if we take the long historical perspective. Jane Austen's own favorite novelist, Samuel Richardson, played the aging curmudgeon on this subject in a 1751 letter to the *Rambler*,[7] complaining about assemblies and other innovations since his own youth, when, he claimed, "the young ladies contented themselves to be found employed in domestick duties; for then routs, drums, balls, assemblies, and such like markets for women, were not known." Richardson explains the good old-fashioned method of courtship that prevailed before assembly balls and other new-fangled social events designed to facilitate actual (gasp!) meetings and conversation between young men and women.

Before the days of assemblies, Richardson claims, men would go to churches, "almost the only places where single women were to be seen by strangers." A young woman in church wouldn't talk to or even look at the men there: "Her eyes were her own, her ears the preacher's. Women are always most observed, when they seem themselves least to observe, or to lay out for observation. The eye of a respectful lover loves rather to receive confidence from the withdrawn eye of the fair-one, than to find itself obliged to retreat."[8]

Taking an interest in a woman he saw at church, a young man would inquire into her "domestick excellence." If he found out she was likely to be a good housekeeper, he'd be "confirmed...in his choice," and he'd get his friends to propose him to her parents, who, if they approved, would tell her he was interested. The news probably wouldn't be a real surprise to her, Richardson explains; she would have noticed him staring at church. If she liked him, she'd dutifully tell her parents that she was ready to meet their approved choice.

As you can see, assembly balls and the other novel social events Richardson was complaining about were part of the move away from marriage arranged by parents and toward women's freedom to make our own choices. Things were moving towards romantic relationships based on a more intimate knowledge of the other person. But there were still special rules for these occasions—a subset of those arcane rules that happy Jane Austen heroines follow and Marianne Dashwood disregards to her peril. You allowed each partner only two dances and the break in between, then separated from him and (hopefully, if someone else asked you) spent the next two dances with a different man. Dancing more than twice in a row—or for more than two pairs of dances in a whole evening—with the same partner was a breach of decorum because it meant you were showing a "dangerous particularity"—favoring one man.

These dances, and the rules that went with them, were the perfect setting for a kind of male-female interaction that's much harder to find today. On the one hand, assembly balls *were*, in a sense, the "markets for women" that Richardson accuses them of being. Everybody involved knew that pretty much everybody else involved was "looking." So you avoided all the awkwardness—and the missed opportunities—that come with meeting guys at work or in your neighborhood, where it's hard to know who's available and what their interest means. (And where it's difficult to make your own interest clear without risking major embarrassment.) On the other hand, no man expected you to go straight home with him from an assembly ball. If a guy liked you, he'd have to follow up by paying you more attention later and getting to know you slowly over time. The rules slowed the progress of the relationship down to a pace at which his feelings would have a chance to catch up to yours, before you committed yourself.

Trial Marriage, Jane Austen-Style

There's even a sense in which the actual entertainment men and women enjoyed at these balls was a kind of trial marriage. But it was almost the exact opposite of our love on the installment plan. The dancing was arranged precisely to bring men and women together to try each other out *without* undermining a woman's independence and freedom of choice. Here's Henry Tilney explaining how dancing is like marriage:

> I consider a country-dance as an emblem of marriage. Fidelity and complaisance are the principal duties of both.... You will allow, that in both the man has the advantage of choice, the woman only the power of refusal; that in both, it is an engagement between man and woman, formed for the advantage of each; and that when once entered into they belong exclusively to each other till the moment of its dissolution; that it is their

duty, each to endeavour to give the other no cause for wishing that he or she had bestowed themselves elsewhere, and their best interest to keep their imaginations from wandering toward the perfections of their neighbors, or fancying that they should have been better off with any one else.

Henry is being facetious. But accepting a man's offer to stand up with you for a couple of dances *was* a sort of marriage in miniature. That's why it was "improper" for brothers and sisters to dance with each other.

Agreeing to dance with a man was "accepting him" on a temporary basis. A woman got to try out being courted, won, enjoyed, and cherished[9] by a particular man—without the risks inherent in our more intimate and unregulated trials and errors in love. The physical nature of the dancing contributed to the trial-marriage aspect of the experience. Who can doubt that Mr. Collins, "awkward and solemn, apologising instead of attending, and often moving wrong without being aware of it," was as utterly ghastly in bed as he was on the dance floor?[10] Luckily Elizabeth's exposure to this unhappiness is limited and temporary; he's able to give her only "all the shame and misery which a disagreeable partner for a couple of dances can give."

Ironically, it was the limitations that allowed the freedom. Here's yet another case of that perfect eighteenth-century balance. The society that invented this kind of social life hit on a happy medium. They made it safe (well, relatively safe—as safe as such an inherently life-altering thing ever can be) for women to fall in love. Partly because the rules allowed women to get just close enough to men, but not too close. And partly because those same rules facilitated some up-front screening of the male population. Men whose character made them really bad romantic risks were made unwelcome—by the heroines themselves. True, there was chaperonage from older married women. But Jane Austen, no Victorian fetishist of decorum, is quite scathing about the women who feed their egos by bustling about presuming to manage other people's love affairs.[11] She expects her heroines to realize it's ultimately their job, not the responsibility of their mothers or married sisters, to police their own love lives. *They're* responsible for avoiding men who are obviously bad bets.

The Mad, the Bad,
and the Dangerous to Know

We modern women have a curious blind spot on this subject. We've got enough historical memory of the Victorian dispensation (or at least of its overthrow at the beginning of the twentieth century) to be vaguely aware of all the fuss about how much leg and neck and breast women could show without being blamed for tempting men. But the opposite precaution—that men were ever expected to curb the way they talk to women—has long since vanished down the memory hole. The danger to women, as Jane Austen and her contemporaries understood very well, is more in what men *say* than in how they look. Our sexuality is auditory where theirs is visual. Men look at porn, we read romance novels or erotica. In Jane Austen's day, responsible members of both sexes avoided exploiting the weak spots of the other sex. A man who went around telling women he loved them without meaning anything in particular by it could find himself excluded from the company of women worth pursuing.[12]

You know the good girl-bad girl divide people talk about prevailing in the 1950s? Once upon a time, there used to be something like it for men, too. In Marilyn Monroe's day, you were a bad girl if you dressed and behaved to tempt men. In Jane Austen's day, you were a bad man if you told a woman you loved her without having the most serious intentions. Really bad. Worse than Willoughby or even Henry Crawford, both of whom carefully avoid ever going that far—they know they'll be crossing a line and exiling themselves from polite company if they do. That's why a "declaration" (of love) always implies a "proposal" (of marriage) in Jane Austen. If a man said "I love you," it was *totally fair* for you to assume that he meant, "And will you marry me?" The rules for what men could say were tailored to avoid prematurely triggering women's susceptibilities—considering how swayable we are by male attention, and how quick we are to imagine love as soon as we see admiration, and marriage as soon as we find love—just as the standards for women's dress were tailored to avoid prematurely pushing men's buttons.[13]

With the really "mad, bad, and dangerous to know"[14] members of the male sex excluded from the field, there was a pretty good chance that a social life built around assembly balls and similar entertainments would give you the opportunity to fall in love at your leisure. And, if you were taking care of the responsibilities of a Jane Austen heroine—looking for happiness, using those skeleton keys to guys' characters, discerning men's intentions, paying attention to the rules, and so forth—you could manage to fall in love with somebody that you would be happy with for the rest of your life.

It was the most pleasant way of arranging marriages ever invented. Not to mention the most dignified. Young women got to choose for themselves; they were no longer at the mercy of parents and guardians. But they didn't simply let themselves be buffeted about on the tide of their emotions, either. You went about the process rationally, as well as feelingly. You got to have all the thrills of falling in love, but without the tragic repercussions. Jane Austen heroines aren't irresponsible Juliets—still children whose parents make all the adult decisions for them. They notice the kinds of things that parents or traditional matchmakers notice about men, as well as the things that girls with crushes think about. As a matter of fact, Jane Austen heroines care most about a whole set of things that immature girls and their jaded, materialistic parents are *both* inclined to overlook—the very most important things about the man when it comes to their future happiness.[15] The virtue of this system was that it allowed women to arrange their own marriages by falling in love—as long as they did their best to let themselves fall in love only when falling in love was likely to lead to "rational happiness."

But what good is any of this to us? *We* can't go to assembly balls. It would be quite a trick to exclude the men who don't follow rules of propriety from our social circle. And if we assume "I love you" means "will you marry me?" we need our heads examined.

How can we expect to have the same opportunities, living as we do in an era where Jane Austen-style courtship has been forgotten? How can we get just close enough to a guy to see if he might be a good mate, without getting too close to see him clearly? Unless we're willing go along with modern love on the installment plan—however unsatisfactory it may be—how can we even let a man know that we might be interested? Do we simply have to settle for being Mrs. Clays, Maria Bertrams, and Lydia Bennets? Is it impossible to be an Elizabeth Bennet in the twenty-first century?

Modern Love—Ideals and Realities

Well, first of all, let's examine our assumptions. *Are* we all living in a hookups-are-the-only-way-to-get-started world? And if we are, do we have to?

You know how Alfred Kinsey's studies paved the way for the sexual revolution in the sixties by busting up the sexually repressive myths of the straitlaced fifties? People read "scientific" evidence that a lot more sex of all kinds was going on than they had thought, and barriers came down. It's since emerged that Kinsey's research was worse than seriously flawed.[16] And that's over and above the inherent methodological problem. Any survey of people's sexual habits is inevitably going to get more data from people who are willing to tell strangers about their sex lives than from people who aren't—which might just possibly tend to skew such studies in the direction of the more sexually experienced and adventurous. But there's no doubt that Kinsey struck a nerve. He and the sexologists who followed him had enormous influence. For one thing, they provided scientific authority for something a lot of people at the time had reason to suspect from their own experience—that the 1950s myths about sex were often quite different from the sexual reality people were living. The ideal wasn't as close to reality as they'd been assuming. Not everybody back then really waited for marriage. Not every married person was faithful. Not everybody was interested only in the opposite sex.

I thought of the impact Kinsey & Co. had when I saw stories about a recent U.S. government study involving a survey of 13,500 people. A headline reporting the research expressed shock that there really are some virgins out there; more than a quarter of the fifteen- to twenty-four-year-olds reported never having had sex. But the even more striking statistic was the numbers of "lifetime partners" for both sexes. It's just five for men and only *three* for women.[17]

If those results are even close to accurate,[18] then either there are a heck of a lot *fewer* Carrie Bradshaws and Samantha Joneses out there than you would think, and love lives like the ones on *Sex and the City* are in a real minority—or else, balancing them out in the statistics, there are a heck of a lot *more* women who sleep with only two, or even only with one guy, in their whole life than you'd ever guess. If a lot of us are like Andie MacDowell's character in *Four Weddings and a Funeral*, able to count thirty-odd sex partners—and many women do "have a high number"—then there must also be more of us with a very "low number" than you'd ever, ever guess. Why is that so surprising? Because it goes against the sexual myths of *our* day, just as Kinsey went against the myths of his. Contemporary "science" on this subject would seem to suggest that sexual experience isn't as widespread as we assume.

I put "science" in quotes because it seems so absurd to expect that you can achieve anything like scientific accuracy by asking people questions about their sexual history.[19] The Heisenberg uncertainty principle already ought to be turned up to eleven when it comes to the social sciences—and maybe to twelve or thirteen when they attempt to study human sexuality. Still, survey results like these are at least some kind of indication[20] that a significant proportion of women today are already further removed from the hookup-or-bust environment than you might think, and closer to Jane Austen's world.

Now a lot of us do meet men in contexts where everyone's expectations are very un-Jane Austen. Those venues—bars, some kinds of singles groups, parties in many social circles—make meeting men easy in one sense. But, interestingly, that's because of an advantage that those contexts *share* with Jane Austen's assembly balls. When you're at a bar, everybody knows that other people there are "looking." It's easy to signal interest without making anyone uncomfortable[21] or damaging other kinds of relationships. You can't so easily embarrass yourself by letting a guy know you're open to a romantic encounter, the way you might with a guy at work. Unfortunately, what the bar-style kind of venue *doesn't* have is the other half of the Jane Austen-era formula. It's not so easy to get just intimate enough with a man to see him close up, without getting so close that you lose your perspective.

Regency-Era Social Life in the Twenty-first Century

But there are other contexts where you can meet guys. Let's take a look at two venues that already exist, either of which is probably a better setting for a Jane Austen heroine today than the bar or party scene: one that's really old-fashioned, and another that's quite new. And let's start with the old first.

The really old venue (older than Jane Austen, in fact) for finding a man is one we've looked at already. You guessed it: church. Okay, don't groan and shut the book quite yet. First of all, church, considered from this angle, has changed a lot since Samuel Richardson's day. Now, if a guy sees you there and likes you, he no longer admires you from a distance and sends his friends to ask your father about meeting you.

But seriously, I might never have considered church-going in quite this light—as a viable alternative to bar-hopping—if I hadn't seen a long comment at one of those "pickup artist" websites, actually comparing the different kinds of dating experiences that bars and churches offer.[22] The rather smarmy fellow who wrote the comment had apparently resorted to church in pursuit of a new and different kind of pickup experience. What he found was that the rules of the game were different in that different context. At the church, he was pursuing women who didn't believe in sex before marriage. Under pressure from him, not all of them seem to have stuck to their resolution.[23] But the speed and quality of the relationships was quite different from the ones with the women he met in bars. At church, he had to get to know them first. The expectations were different, the progress of the physical relationships, and possibly of the woman's attachment, was slower. The relationships weren't Jane Austen-heroine-quality. But they sounded quite a bit closer to it than what he was sharing (if you can call it sharing) with the women he met in bars. And just think how much better those women he met at church might have done if they hadn't had the extraordinary bad luck to meet the guy who happened to be at their church just to see how he could apply "Game" there.

The lessons we can take away from his experience? Even in the most sanctified setting, you will find men of bad character—use Jane Austen's skeleton keys! But also, there are nooks and crannies out there that the hookup culture hasn't pervaded. In one of those contexts, your Jane Austen-heroine-style desire to get close enough to guys, but not too close, might be easier to indulge. But remember, the distance a Jane Austen heroine maintains is not just about sex. Even if you never sleep with the guy—even if you never touch him—you're not being a Jane Austen heroine if you let yourself become emotionally glued to him before he's serious about you.

"Church" doesn't have to mean the regular worship service with the long sermon on Sunday morning, either (though Sunday morning church has changed quite a lot since Richardson's day, too). There are religious groups specifically for young singles in every city that has a bar scene. And in many of them, you're going to have an easier time keeping the kind of distance Jane Austen heroines make such good use of.[24] C. S. Lewis warned that people "who think they can revive the Faith in order to make a good society might just as well think they can use the stairs of Heaven as a short cut to the nearest chemist's shop."[25] Fair enough. On the other hand, my cousin Michael used to tell his friends, when they were all in the new-parents phase of family life, that there are worse reasons to start going back to church than for the sake of your kids. You can say the same thing about going to church to find your Jane Austen hero—there are much worse reasons to be there.

And church may not be the only venue where you can meet guys in an atmosphere shaped by standards that come from beyond our hookup culture. If I were unmarried and looking, I'd definitely try church. But I'd also scope out other pockets of culture where some really old-fashioned ideas are taken seriously—the Jane Austen Society of North America, say, and maybe the Wodehouse and Chesterton societies, too, figuring that men who take old-fashioned and chivalrous ideas seriously at all might be amenable to courtship on other-than-modern terms.

But if I were single and interested in meeting men, I'd also try a really newfangled method. At the opposite end of the spectrum from looking for a mate at church, we have—computer matchmaking. Okay, once again, please hear me out before you roll your eyes and close the book. And right up front, let me tell you that, doing a little informal research over the last few months, I uncovered the fact that *four* of the most attractive and together women I have ever worked with all met their men via internet sites for singles. Honestly, finding out how many impressive women I know have met great guys this way has completely changed how I see computer dating. One of the co-workers mentioned above is engaged, and I've heard that the other is about to be. And two are now married to men they met online. One is a thirty-something mom of a two-year-old who's had great jobs in TV

246 　◆◇◆　The Jane Austen Guide to Happily Ever After

and publicity. The other was a widow in her forties juggling a high-powered publishing career and raising three teenagers; she's now remarried. They both met their husbands on Match.com.

Meeting men via online dating services is a new option, but it's essentially just personal ads transfigured by technology. And personals have been around for quite a while. For so long that *the eighty-four-year-old pope's parents* actually met through a personal ad.[26] (Meeting girls at church wasn't working for him, apparently.) More recently, but still in the Dark Ages compared to today's computer matchmaking, Amy Dacyczyn in the 1990s-era *Tightwad Gazette* wrote the best argument ever for personals.[27] Amy found her husband by answering a singles ad in a Boston paper. She points out several reasons that personal ads are a good option. Rereading her now, I see that finding men via singles ads strangely has a lot in common with Jane Austen-era opportunities for meeting guys.

Dacyczyn addresses the most common objections to this kind of matchmaking—that it's only for "weirdos and losers," that it's dangerous, and that it's "unromantic." She gives the now-standard prudent warning against giving out personal information or getting into a car with anyone before you're sure he's safe. (Notice that those precautions might possibly improve the pacing of any relationship.) And she says she met some losers, but also some "'take-charge' people who refused to wait around for the perfect mate to materialize." (Those guys sound like Jane Austen-hero material to me.) And she's got an answer for "it's unromantic," too: "Some people believe love should be left up to chance…all 'calculating' methods are unromantic. But, whether they know it or not, nearly all unattached adults are looking for a relationship, and so, on some level, are using 'calculating' methods to attract people. It's rarely a true chance meeting." She also talks about how you miss opportunities with casual acquaintances and co-workers because it's not so easy to know who's available.

This is where computer matchmaking or any other way of finding men by advertisement really starts to have a clear advantage, and a lot in common with the methods of Jane Austen's day. Ads "tell people clearly that you're available, rejection is relatively painless, and you can meet a lot of available people in a short time." You can also present yourself, and screen the guys, based on what you really want. Dacyczyn's own requirements were almost

A Jane Austen Heroine in the Twenty-first Century

Lydia W. is the founder and organizer of "Friends in S—," an online-organized but offline-meeting group in a medium-sized city (that doesn't really start with an S) on the eastern seaboard. They plan hikes and cook-outs and other social occasions. You can meet members of the opposite sex through the group—but the whole setup is supposed to be more about friends than hookups. In fact, Lydia started the group because another social network she belonged to was, she thought, too much like the bar-based hookup scene to work well.

"The fact that the word 'Nightlife' was in the group's name was part of the problem," Lydia told me. Members of that original group were gossiping about who was doing what with whom, getting into high-drama conflicts, and then refusing to accept apologies. "It's bad enough when people have to go through that stuff in high school; there's no reason for adults to act like that." Since Lydia was already refereeing disputes between members of the group, she figured she might as well really take charge.

So she started the new group, where she gets to gatekeep the membership. "I've only told two people No," she explained to me. They had helped create the totally unnecessary drama in the other group. Her new role is not unlike that of a Regency Era woman deciding whether or not to accept introductions and when it's necessary to drop an acquaintance. And it's all in aid of creating an atmosphere that will allow people to get to know each other without the counter-productive pressure created by high-speed, high-stakes hookups. Instead, people can get to know each other against a background of genuine friendship and mutual respect for what Jane Austen calls our "fellow creatures."

Regency Era in their clear-sighted realism: "I wanted a man who was at least 6' tall, single (not divorced), between 25 and 35 and had a good-paying job (plumbers, yes; perpetual students, no)." And she got one. The story of how Amy Dacyczyn first selected four potential guys, then got caught up in a massive project to repaint her grandmother's house and had less time for going out with anyone, found her future husband suddenly "much more attractive" when the others were frustrated but he volunteered to help out, and ended up engaged "by the time the house was painted" is very appealing.

There's a lot more room for rationality in a process that begins with some deliberation on your part. But applying rationality to making your own match does *not* have to mean excluding romance (just Romanticism). Computer dating is not unlike letting the master of ceremonies at the Upper Rooms introduce you to a dance partner because you're in Bath with family friends who don't have any acquaintance there. That's how Catherine Morland meets Henry Tilney, and Jane Austen clearly approves. A third party (whether the MC or the computer service) has the job of providing introductions. Both you and the man you meet are free to walk away after a couple of dances (or today, after lunch or a cup of coffee in a public place),[28] or to pursue the acquaintance further. If things develop from there, that's plenty romantic enough for Jane Austen. If the man you meet that way turns out to be a stand-up human being and you start seriously falling for each other, it's going to get plenty exciting.

Okay, so computer matchmaking is not Bath at the turn of the nineteenth century. How come Jane Austen heroines have these glittering occasions on which to meet potential mates, and twenty-first-century women have to subscribe to Match.com? Well, those assembly balls didn't drop out of the sky. Human beings planned them. True, they were drawing on some cultural reserves that have since been exhausted. The social life of the eighteenth and nineteenth centuries—and the real, original rules Regency ladies and gentlemen lived by—developed out of a long cultural process. But that process was driven by the choices of individual men and women. If we think Jane Austen and her predecessors developed a marvelous way of arranging matches, there's absolutely nothing to stop us from taking it as our model.

Social networking sites like Meetup.com make it easy to organize local groups of people around any interest. If I were single and looking—and ambitious enough to try for something more like the opportunities Jane Austen heroines had—I'd try organizing something around dancing. Mr. Darcy says, "Every savage can dance." Sadly, a lot of us highly civilized people have lost touch with this nearly universal human experience, which was a huge part of the social scene in Jane Austen's day.

On the theory that you can never have enough of everything Jane Austen at any stage of your life, my husband and I have actually done some "contra dancing." That's what the folklorists and hobbyists who still practice it now call the "country-dance" that Henry Tilney compares to marriage.[29] "The man leads," said one of our instructors, "but it's not like the waltz, where he does all the work and she just clings on for dear life."[30] I notice that at contra dances, there's a lot more of strangers asking strangers to dance than at other similar public events. The style of dancing itself seems to promote more mixing—but a kind of mixing that's structured by limits. And when I helped organize contra dancing for the kids at my son's school, you could see the same thing. Dancing with more than one partner is part of the nature of each dance anyway, so it models something more like Jane Austen-era social life than modern people often see. Contra dances seem to be most popular with the kids who aren't natural "alpha male" or "queen bee" types. They're a trip back to a time when the mating game was less ruthlessly competitive.

But it wouldn't have to be a contra dance. *By far* the most successful social event for the kids in my son's class has been a parent-organized series of dance lessons followed by parties on consecutive weekends. Not the ghastly cotillion thing where the children get shown the box step once or twice but never really learn how to waltz. Instead, two-hour-solid lessons in swing and Latin dance, followed by dinners and then parties at which the kids actually dance because they *know how*. Part of the reason it works, I think, is that one family that helped organize it is from Latin America. When I showed up to pick up my son one Saturday night, I got to hear all about the kind of social life one mom had growing up in Colombia, where dance parties broke out on every possible occasion, and the girls all made sure their brothers showed up so everybody would have somebody to dance with. She married a friend's brother she had met at that kind of dance— shades of Jane Austen.

Being a Jane Austen Heroine

But if I can't sell you on ambitious plans to reintroduce the assembly ball via online social networking, or even on looking at church or online matchmaking—then how about making one simple choice in your own personal life? Try laying down some Jane Austen-style boundaries, wherever and whenever you happen to find yourself in the company of an interesting guy—even if it's at a bar. After all, in even the hookupiest of hookup scenes, there *are* men who, like a lot of women, are interested in something they can't typically get there.[31]

What happens if you tell the guys you meet, wherever you meet them, that you're playing by different rules? A married friend of mine was actually on the receiving end of something very much like this from her now-husband. He explained on their first date: the fact that he wasn't trying to jump her bones didn't mean he was gay; he found her very attractive, just not worth going to hell for. I think I saw a suggestion for something along these lines—only less jive-cat and more suitable for people whose limits aren't for religious reasons—somewhere on Susan Walsh's "Hooking Up Smart" blog: simply tell a guy that you don't sleep with men you don't know well.

A girl in my class at the University of North Carolina went a step further than that (and closer to Jane Austen). The scuttlebutt our freshman year in Chapel Hill was that she explained to every guy she went out with that she wasn't planning on pairing up; she was interested in going out with people, not having a boyfriend. And you know what? It didn't turn men off at all. They found it intriguing. I think she got more male attention than any woman I knew. And probably had more fun freshman year, too, getting to know different guys in a we're-all-friends-here sort of way, without allowing her life to be swallowed by one intense relationship, or by all the drama that comes with hookups and breakups.

It is possible to be a Jane Austen heroine in a twenty-first-century world. But only if you're sometimes willing to swim against the tide. Even in the novels, Fanny and Anne, Elizabeth and Jane are not just living like everybody else. Their circumstances have some advantages over ours. But they're extraordinary women, willing to pick their way through the "folly" and "vice" around them to value what's really important, maintain their own dignity, treat their fellow creatures with respect and compassion, and never lose sight of the fact that love is for happiness. If you want a love story like Jane Austen's love stories, you're going to have to aim that high.

ADOPT AN AUSTEN ATTITUDE:

- Consider what your methods of meeting men are lacking that Jane Austen-style social life had.
- Ask yourself if there might be a way to introduce any of its features into your life.

WHAT WOULD JANE DO?

- She'd take advantage of social settings that made it more possible to get to know men without committing prematurely.
- She'd steer clear of men in the habit of preying on women's vulnerabilities.

IF WE *REALLY* WANT TO BRING BACK JANE AUSTEN ...

- We'll work to revive social arrangements that give women the opportunity to get to know men without being hurried into premature intimacy.
- We'll arrange our own marriages.

"THE JANE AUSTEN GUIDE TO HAPPILY EVER AFTER"—*REALLY?*

DID JANE AUSTEN REALLY MEAN TO GIVE US ADVICE? Aren't novels just entertainment? And, anyway, isn't the whole relationship advice scene a bit beneath Jane Austen's dignity?

On the one hand, we've got Jane Austen's elegance, the high aspirations of her characters, their impressive self-understanding, and their competence about men. On the other, pep talks about finding the right man, tips for the lovelorn, and dating advice. Isn't she in a whole different league? After all, one of the most cringe-inducing moments in Bridget Jones's career—when the hopeless gap between her life and Elizabeth Bennet's is clear as day—is the conversation with Mark Darcy when she lets slip that her religion is: self-help. Isn't the advice book industry part and parcel of what's substandard about our twenty-first-century lives?

Well, yes and no. Of course Jane Austen's novels are in a completely different class from *Women Who Love Too Much* and *He's Just Not That Into You*. But the issues books like those deal with aren't beneath Jane Austen's dignity. In fact, she was keenly interested in the very same problems. Her solutions are just so much more elevated. Jane Austen absolutely did *not* consider it beneath her to offer women models and advice for their daily lives, for their choices, and especially for their courtships. On occasion, she can even give what-to-wear advice that's vaguely reminiscent of the kind of thing we read in our women's magazines.[1]

Jane Austen is not above any of our concerns, however apparently superficial. Now, the older woman of her acquaintance who called young Jane "the prettiest, silliest, most affected, husband-hunting butterfly"[2] obviously missed something; Jane Austen was always quite a bit more complicated than that. But as a girl she *could* be silly about young men,[3] she *did* want to get married,[4] and she went on to write fiction that's about those very things. Jane Austen was interested in everything that interests us, from clothes to men to advice for recovering from depression to strategies for coping with your older sister the narcissist. And she was far readier than modern "literary" authors to wade right in and give advice about them. She's never the heavy-handed Victorian moralist. But there's no doubt that Jane Austen considered it her job as a novelist to enlighten as well as to entertain. Here's her famous definition of the kind of book she wrote:

> "Oh! It is only a novel!" replies the young lady, while she lays down her book with affected indifference, or momentary shame.
>
> "It is only Cecilia, or Camilla, or Belinda"; or, in short, only some work in which the greatest powers of the mind are displayed, in which the most thorough knowledge of human nature, the happiest delineation of its varieties, the liveliest effusions of wit and humour, are conveyed to the world in the best-chosen language.

Art for the Sake of More than Art

We put Jane Austen and relationship advice in different categories partly because we moderns think of literature as "art." And we assume that "art" has nothing to do with advice. We take it for granted that only the worst kind of literature tells people how to live: moralistic Victorian novels, the dreary productions of Soviet socialist realism, TV dramas that "send a message" about domestic violence or drunk driving.

But in Jane Austen's day, "art for art's sake" wasn't even a gleam in Edgar Allan Poe's eye. Back then it wasn't only the dregs of literature that were "didactic." Even great literary art was meant to teach a lesson. It was intended to improve readers' lives. And not just by opening their minds (whether to "the best which has been thought and said" or to the latest "transgressive" challenge to bourgeois values). But rather by showing them something about how to live.

If you think about it, writers in Jane Austen's day were more realistic about how fiction actually influences readers. The fact is that we can't help learning from our entertainment. We do imitate what we read—or, today, what we see on the screen. Otherwise advertisers wouldn't pay for "product placement." Writers have real power to make us want to be part of the world they show us. Shouldn't they admit they have that power? And since they're inevitably *going* to change us, for better or worse, why not aim for *better*? Jane Austen most certainly did.

Her novels combine different things that we're used to putting in three separate categories: 1) fiction as art or entertainment; 2) practical advice; and 3) the exploration—almost the scientific investigation—of the basis of that advice in what motivates human beings and what will really make them happy. That third category is what she's talking about when she says that novels offer "the most thorough knowledge of human nature."[5]

Life Imitates Art

Art is supposed to be an imitation of nature. But life also imitates art. And Jane Austen was fascinated by that fact. She was very much aware of the power a writer can have in the lives of her readers.[6] One of the things that her "most thorough knowledge of human nature" told her was that we have a powerful urge to imitate the stories we enjoy. Human beings learn by imitation.[7] Jane Austen was fascinated by this phenomenon, and especially by how books make their readers want to be like the people in them.

Her own writing is full of characters who make their way through life copying the characters in the books *they've* read.

As a teenager she wrote hilarious parody fiction about hopeless Romantics who act out their favorite fiction by importing overwrought ideals and totally unnecessary drama into their increasingly chaotic lives. Remember how, in *Love and Friendship*, the hero's father guesses the origin of the problem: "Where Edward in the name of wonder did you pick up this unmeaning Gibberish? You have been studying Novels I suspect"?

Then the main plot of *Northanger Abbey* turns on Catherine's addiction to Gothic fiction. She's such an enthusiastic fan of those early horror stories that she talks herself into believing that the father of the man she's smitten with has murdered his wife. And in *Sense and Sensibility*, Marianne's tragedy is that she acts so much like the heroine of a Romantic tragedy that she can't see what's in front of her in the real world. Now, those are two of Jane Austen's earliest novels, and of course imitation is a natural preoccupation for any young writer. Because she has to learn her craft from earlier masters, she is immersed in imitation herself; if she's self-aware, she's going to take an interest in the subject.

But Jane Austen stayed interested in how people imitate what they read. In her last two novels, she's back on the same subject. In *Persuasion*, the last book she finished, we've seen her heroine warn a younger man against reading too much Romantic poetry; Anne Elliot thinks the heartbroken and depressed Captain Benwick shouldn't immerse himself in "impassioned descriptions of hopeless agony"—because they're only going to make him even more heartbroken and depressed. And in *Sanditon*, the novel Jane Austen had only started writing when she died, she gives us a young man who acts like a complete jackass because he's imitating the books he's read. In this case, her character has quite literally decided to be a villain—just like one in a Samuel Richardson novel. He has learned all the wrong lessons from the books he's been reading:

> The truth was that Sir Edw[ard] whom circumstances had confined very much to one spot had read more sentimental Novels than agreed with him. His fancy had been early caught

by all the impassioned, & most exceptionable parts of Richardson's [novels] ... so far as Man's determined pursuit of Woman
in defiance of every opposition of feeling ... the Spirit, the Sagac-
ity, & the Perseverance, of the Villain of the Story outweighed
all his absurdities & all his Atrocities with Sir Edward. With him,
such Conduct was Genius, Fire & Feeling....

    Sir Edw[ard]'s great object in life was to be seductive.... He
felt that he was formed to be a dangerous Man—quite in the
line of the Lovelaces.... It was Clara whom he meant to seduce.

Lovelace is the villain (or from Sir Edward's peculiar point of view, the
hero) of Samuel Richardson's *Clarissa*. And Richardson was Jane Austen's
favorite novelist, no less than Sir Edward's. Though of course she took
Richardson in a very different way.

The Novel of Manners

    Both Richardson's and Jane Austen's books are called "novels of man-
ners" for good reason. "Manners" meant so much more to Jane Austen's
original readers than they mean to us. They weren't just about which fork
to use, or even how not to hurt people's feelings. Manners were how you
regulated your conduct to meet all life's challenges.[8] They were the rules
and resources that smoothed over all the rough places in the ordinary course
of life—from how to fend off rude questions about the cost of your dress
to how to get through a painful first meeting with the only man you ever
loved (whom you sent away seven years ago and haven't seen since). They
covered the whole range of questions about how to behave, everything
between mere formal etiquette and full-fledged moral issues. And women
in Jane Austen's day read her kind of novel expecting to pick up tips from
them—not just to be entertained, but also to learn how to manage their
lives better.

    The original "novel of manners" actually started as a how-to book. It's
called *Pamela: Or, Virtue Rewarded. In a Series of Familiar Letters from a
Beautiful Young Damsel to Her Parents.* Like many another inventor, Samuel

Richardson stumbled on his great discovery almost by accident. Richardson was a mid-eighteenth-century printer who was hoping to make some money selling a volume of model letters. England in his day was in a great ferment of improvement, education, and refinement. Richardson saw the chance to appeal to a growing demographic: people whose social skills hadn't caught up to their new literacy. The nouveau-literate[9] were sure to find themselves in situations where they were at a loss for how to act, and particularly how to express themselves in writing.[10] Richardson sat down to imagine the situations in which letter-writing skills would be needed, and to write a variety of model letters (which he eventually did publish as *Letters Written to and for Particular Friends, on the Most Important Occasions*). But in the course of writing that frankly instructional book, he also began to imagine a more complex situation that he could tell a story about in a long series of connected letters. For his story, Richardson imagined the difficult and dangerous position of a young female servant whose employer was trying to seduce her.

At the beginning of the book, the sixteen-year-old Pamela goes to work as a servant in the house of the rich and lustful "Mr. B." Mr. B finds her attractive but naturally doesn't see her as marriage material; she's got no money and she's several rungs below him on the social ladder. So he does his best to seduce her and even comes close to rape. Pamela is in an ugly and probably all too realistic dilemma, suffering the indignities that innumerable victims of eighteenth-century-style sexual harassment were no doubt subjected to. But, improbably, Pamela manages not only to fend off Mr. B's dishonorable attentions, but in the end inspires him to fall in love with and marry her.

Richardson had hit on a situation with huge potential to interest readers. The "manners" involved may be very different from ours. But the problem itself is universal: men and women often want different, sometimes wholly incompatible things from each other. But they can—sometimes, somehow, miraculously, they do—negotiate their way to that intoxicating state of affairs in which each does really want exactly what will make the other happy.

Pamela's story is meant to be just as instructive in its own way as the book of model letters Richardson was working on when he thought of it.

Pamela's alternate title, after all, is "*Virtue Rewarded.*" But it's not just Pamela's "virtue" that gets its reward when Mr. B finally falls in love with her and proposes marriage. In addition to real integrity (sexual "virtue" is *not* the only virtue she's got), Pamela needs all her intelligence, too, to manage the tight spot she's in. Mr. B is continually astonished by her command of language and the quality of the reasons she gives to fend him off—she's very clever about answering his indecent proposals effectively without offending against either the social requirements of her day or her job description. It's *reading her letters* that makes Mr. B see Pamela as a real person. He's been thinking of her as just another hot body.

Pamela is a new kind of heroine. Richardson "substituted social embarrassment for tragic conflict, thus developing the first novel of manners."[11] Before Richardson, heroes fought their way through wars and quests, or suffered a catastrophic fall on account of their tragic flaws. After Richardson, heroines fight their way through a new kind of adventure, using their wit and hard-won social skills (their "manners") to manage the more ordinary dangers that women are threatened by in real life—predatory suitors, painful encounters with old flames, back-stabbing friends, clueless parents. Instead of a knight slaying the dragon to rescue the princess, the novel of manners gives us a young lady struggling through awkwardnesses and misunderstandings to happiness with the hero of her dreams.[12]

Pamela's adventures are crude, occasionally bordering on soft porn.[13] In comparison, Jane Austen's novels are marvels of good taste, psychological realism, and subtle insights into relationships. Part of the difference is Jane Austen's natural "delicacy of mind" and original genius. But also, the novel of manners—and the whole great societal refinement and improvement project it was part of—were half a century further along in Jane Austen's day than in Richardson's.

An Era of Refinement and Improvement

In fact, the novel of manners reached its high point with Jane Austen. Her novels are the best of the kind Richardson invented. And they're also the last great English novels in the Richardson strain. That is, the last that take an optimistic—not an angst-ridden—view of society's rules and a realistic—rather than Romantic—view of human nature. During Jane Austen's lifetime, the great literary and societal improvement project that her novels are the fruit and flower of reached its high tide and began to recede. By the time she was writing *Emma* and *Persuasion*, the enthusiasm that was still shaping her own work was no longer the cutting-edge attitude.

Instead of a culture war or a sexual revolution, English society in the eighteenth and early nineteenth centuries had been engaged in a great cultural building project. Or, rather, a great retooling project. The century into which Jane Austen was born was the great age of improvement in modes and manners. Grammar and spelling, dress and hygiene, the behavior of ladies and gentlemen (and of those who aspired to be ladies and gentlemen)—all were in a ferment of refinement. The English novel of manners arose out of this ferment, and one of its functions was to teach proper behavior by example.

What was this great project for improvement and refinement? It was part of the Enlightenment, of course. But not the Enlightenment as we usually think of it. Nothing could be more alien to Jane Austen than the world of the French *philosophes*. But remember, there was an English, or an Anglo-American, Enlightenment too. It wasn't all Voltaire and Rousseau. It was also Edmund Burke and James Madison. The Enlightenment was responsible for the constructive American Revolution, as well as the destructive French one. The great figures of the Enlightenment in England and her American colonies were moved by an impulse of lively and intelligent curiosity to test every pin and spar in the great edifice of their civilization—only to leave every individual part cleaned and polished and the whole machine running more smoothly than before—not "to pull it to bits and put something else in its place."[14]

And one of the things they were reforming and improving was love and marriage. There *were* radicals and revolutionaries on that subject—Shelleys and Godwins and Wollstonecrafts who argued that marriage was slavery, called for the abolition of monogamy, and wanted to reinvent love from scratch on the basis of reason alone—the same way the revolutionaries were starting everything from the year zero in France.[15] But Jane Austen was a reformer, not a revolutionary. She didn't take a slash-and-burn or Voltaire-and-Rousseau approach to human institutions. Instead, she was firmly in the moderate wing of the English Enlightenment. (Think Edward Coke, not Thomas Hobbes; Dr. Johnson, not John Locke.)

Understanding That Culture Is Natural to Human Beings

The Enlightenment reformers weren't radicals, but they weren't hidebound conservatives either, unquestioningly accepting everything their ancestors believed and did, à la Sir Roger de Coverley in the *Spectator*. They *were* busy improving and refining human institutions, but all the time they were taking care not to throw the baby out with the bath water. They approached human traditions in need of reform with care and respect. More care and respect than the French *philosophes* and revolutionaries, of course. But also more than our modern social scientists and public health experts.

You can argue that since the Enlightenment the human race has been acting like a highly evolved flock of geese. A few especially advanced ganders got smart enough to ask, *Why do we have this irrational tradition of flying south every winter?* but not quite bright enough to figure out the reason.

The modern scientific establishment has often been reductionist—too ready either to dismiss human conventions altogether (as "myths" and "old wives' tales"), or else to tell us that scientists have discovered "the" reason for some universal human custom or traditional bit of wisdom and to triumphantly supply a substitute—which experience and additional research eventually reveal isn't completely adequate: "Hygienic" baby bottles and formula for breastfeeding. Scientifically formulated vitamins for consuming actual vegetables. Lowfat foods as a substitute for eating and drinking in moderation. Antibiotics and condoms instead of being selective about your sex partners. In contrast, the moderate Enlightenment tradition that Jane Austen belonged to was not only critical but also respectful of the aggregate wisdom contained in longstanding human habits and conventions.

Jane Austen and her contemporaries took a less root-and-branch attitude toward human culture. In fact, they had a positive value for human civilization as over against mere nature.[16] Jane Austen's heroes and heroines take such an anti-Rousseauian-back-to-nature attitude that they aren't even enthusiastic picnickers![17] They understand that culture is natural to human beings.[18]

Can We Have Love *and* Happiness?

So the great reform of marriage, sex, and family life that Jane Austen contributed to took as its starting point the things that human beings have always wanted and tried to capture in those institutions, with varying degrees of success over the course of history: love and happiness.

Marriage had been in a state of flux and even of reinvention for many years leading up to Jane Austen's lifetime. We forget how close she was to the days of mercenary alliances and old-fashioned arranged marriage. We don't think a lot about how and when marriage for love became the norm. As a matter of fact, it's a long and a complicated story, involving a lot of surprising history, including the power struggles between the Catholic bishops of late antiquity and the great Roman families whose influence survived the collapse of the Empire; the literary fad for courtly love in the High Middle Ages; and the settlement of America. But the long and the short of it is that, by Jane Austen's day, while a good many European, English, and American women were marrying for love, the love marriage was still in some sense a live issue.

As it still is on the world scene today.[19] And as in a theoretical sense it is everywhere, and always will be. Love is a perennial dilemma for the human race. It's not ever easy to manage things so that the volatile energy of erotic love can be channeled into lasting matches and long-term happiness.

Love promises perfect bliss. It can deliver the greatest happiness we're capable of in this life ("all which this world could do for her," as Jane Austen says of Captain Wentworth's love for Anne Elliot, when Anne is in suspense about it). The promise of happily ever after is an essential part of the experience of love. Love itself tells us that love is the guarantor of our happiness: it promises that being with that one person means being happy.

But love often fails of its promise. And it doesn't just fall short of intense bliss. Love can, in fact, cause untold misery. All of us know, at least in our saner moments, that happiness really, and especially in the long run, depends on more than the intensity of our feelings. Ironically, whether we'll be happy in love depends on factors that it's easier for people who aren't in love—our friends, and sometimes even our parents—to see while we're under love's enchantment. For example, whether he has a good temper; whether he treats us with respect; whether he mixes well with our friends and family; whether his goals in life are compatible with ours; whether our principles and beliefs are in conflict.

It's a paradox. Love is necessarily unplanned, even irrational. It's about the choice of the heart, not the head. If it's real love, it's precisely love *no matter what*—casting aside all prudent calculations about compatibility, worthiness, suitability, social status, whether there will be enough money to live on. And yet ignoring all those factors means ignoring red flags that absolutely can wreck the happily-ever-after that love looks forward to. Love promises happiness, but it makes it hard to plan for.

Let's set aside for a minute the splendid arrangement Jane Austen and her contemporaries came up with, and look at two completely different— and opposite—ways of managing the love-and-happiness paradox: first, traditional arranged marriage and second, love as conducted according to modern feminist theory. We're familiar with both schemes for love, but what we may not notice is that they're two different plans for solving the love-happiness paradox. Each one solves the same problem, but they solve it in diametrically opposed ways, by eliminating either love or else lasting happiness from the equation. Neither approach guarantees either love or happily ever after—that's for sure—but each opposite scheme abandons one of those things in pursuit of the other.

The Feminist and the Sheikh

Let's start with traditional arranged marriage. Absurd as this sounds, arranged marriage leaves out love to aim for—happiness. Okay, so in reality arranged marriages cause an enormous amount of *unhappiness*. But still the theory behind them is to try to guarantee life-long happiness in marriage—by ignoring the free choice of the human heart, bypassing the essence of erotic love. Where marriage is arranged, it's thought to be too serious a business to be left to flighty young lovers, who don't know what will make them happy in the long run.

We picture young lovers—Juliet, Maria in *West Side Story*, or some poor girl in Pakistan today who falls in love with a man from the wrong tribe— who desperately want to escape arranged marriages. They want to pursue real love, which promises them an intoxicating happiness beyond the dreams of their stodgy or cynical elders.

But look at it from their parents' point of view. *They're* trying to take into account all those factors that do to some degree determine long-term happiness—from the real character of the other person to whether the young couple will be able to support themselves or not. Now, from *Romeo and Juliet*, as well as from the real-live honor killing stories in the news, we know that parents aren't in fact always promoting their children's happiness by the marriages they arrange.[20] But the *theory* that justifies arranged marriage is that love is too volatile a foundation to build a happy family on. "If marriage was left up to the woman without her guardian's consent," argues Sheikh Muhammad S. al-Munajjid, "you would see most girls marrying those who enchant them of the wolves of men, who are eager to rob them of their chastity and then throw them aside."[21]

Setting aside the question of chastity—on which we're unlikely ever to see eye-to-eye with the sheikh—let's look for the grain of truth that gives power to his perverse understanding of marriage. Is it true, after all, when women are free to choose for themselves, that most Juliets find their Romeos? Do women often find love stronger than death, and lovers who are faithful to the grave? How many young women have lovers of Romeo's caliber? And it's not that they always find "wolves among men" instead— though there certainly are some wolves out there.[22] But even when the men our hearts choose aren't wolves, is following the choice of our hearts any guarantee of lasting happiness? It has to be admitted that succumbing to youthful passion is no guarantee even of a love affair of Romeo-and-Juliet intensity, much less of lifelong happiness together.

So let's turn to the other extreme from Sheikh Muhammad S. al-Munajjid. Our radical feminists, at the opposite end of the spectrum on the love-happiness continuum, urge us to give up on hopes for lasting happiness, in order to be able to enjoy love—or at least really intense sex—in the here and now. They're as unhappy with the Romeo-and-Juliet scenario as the sheikh is, but for the opposite reason. The sheikh is afraid that the intoxicating power of love will make a life-long union impossible. Nona Willis-Aronowitz, writing for the *Nation*, is afraid that a woman's wish for life-long happiness with the man she loves will interfere with the intoxication of the moment.[23] "Why," she asks, "should sex have an everlasting warranty of love attached to it? Sex is the ultimate risk, a risk that makes human relationships complicated, intoxicating and wonderful." In the name of erotic love—the intoxicating and the wonderful—Ms. Willis-Aronowitz wants us to quit aiming for "eternal companionship" altogether. She recommends the pursuit of love with no happily-ever-after promise attached.

Love and Happiness in Balance

So why should we care about these extreme examples? Surely most of us are going to have enough sense to ignore Muslim sheikhs *and* radical feminists when we're arranging our love lives. The problem is, these extremes point up something that's gone horribly wrong even with the middle, where the great majority of relationships are today. Love and living happily ever after aren't so easy for any of us to fit together any more. It isn't just the divorce rate, which, it has to be admitted, climbed most steeply in the very same decades when love became *the* pervasive theme of our pop culture. It's not even the fact that fewer people are risking marriage at all, now that there's no other reason but love to get married—the shotgun wedding being a relic of the past,[24] societal pressure to marry being at an all-time low, and increasing numbers of us having come 'round to the point of view that there's no requirement to wait until marriage for either sex or children. (In 2005, apparently for the first time in world history, more women were living without than with husbands.)[25] It's that we've lost faith in the promise that love itself makes to us—that the excitement of falling in love is an invitation to a lifetime of being happy together.

Jane Austen is the cure for that disillusionment. She figured out how love and happiness could go together. She took the perennial problem that Richardson built that first "novel of manners" around—how men and women can negotiate the minefield created by the different and often conflicting things we want from each other. The love match comes to its absolute perfection in her novels.

Jane Austen gives us heroines who are quite as clever as Sheikh Muhammad S. al-Munajjid at spotting the "wolves among men." The sheikh would be amazed—and likely not all that pleased—at their capacity to protect themselves from heartbreakers, and arrange their own happily-ever-after endings. And yet the relationships of Elizabeth Bennet, Emma Woodhouse, and Anne Elliot are every bit as "complicated, intoxicating and wonderful" as anything we can believe we'd ever find in the kind of love (or sex) that Ms. Willis-Aronowitz is recommending. Even though—we might say *especially because*—in the lives of Jane Austen heroines, sex *does* "have an everlasting warranty of love attached to it."

If we do love the Jane Austen way, we don't have to give up on either love *or* happiness. She shows us exactly how we can have both.

ACKNOWLEDGMENTS

THIS BOOK WAS CROWDSOURCED AMONG MANY
friends, who helped me to new insights about love in the twenty-first century
and into Jane Austen; answered frantic Facebook blegs for the sources of
quotations I couldn't find; read the manuscript and offered valuable
suggestions; and generously contributed other kinds of help too numerous
to mention. I'm also grateful to my colleagues at Regnery who worked on the
book, a number of whom are also friends described above. Many thanks to
the Acevedos, David Alexander, Noorah Al-Meer, Natalie Barg, Adam Bellow,
Joseph Breslin, Matt Bronzi, Tommy Campbell, Amber Colleran, Harry
Crocker, Jeanne Crotty, Dawn Eden, Louise and Brock Fowler, Anne Fisher,
Percy Galbreath, Mary Hills Baker Gill, Jay Glasgow, James Guinivan, Zélie
Guinivan, Charlotte Hays, Karen Hickey, Kathy Hofer, Liz Holmes, Vera
Hough, Mary Jabaley, Nicole and Michael Jabaley, Patricia Jackson, John
Janaro, Liza Jabaley Johnson, Caitlin Jones, both Jeff and Billy Kantor, Pat
Lally, John Lalor, Jack Langer, Amanda Larsen, Anne and Matt Lloyd,
Margaret Harper McCarthy, Rebekah McCarthy, Joseph McPherson,

Frank Moncher, Sean Munns, Alex Novak, Kate Oates, Michelle Oddis, Pat Lally, Melissa Pop-Lazarova, Sam Phillips, Anastasia Pimentel, Gregory Pimentel, Stephen Pimentel, Mark Reed, Marji Ross, Jeff Rubin, Maria Ruhl, Andy Schwarz, Karl Selzer, Cassandra Snyder, Siobhan and Richard Solomon, Leslie Spencer, Matt Stroot, Jason Sunde, Kathleen Sweetapple, Mary-Powel Thomas, Tom Tobin, Gretchen Tombes, Adam Tragone, Kara Verducci, Charmie Vince, Dave Washburn, Deborah Whelan, Lydia Whitney, Susan White, Rachel Wolford, Maggie Wynne, and Lionel Yaceczko. Of course none of these folks is responsible for the advice in this book, and they should not be presumed to agree with it. Special thanks to Mary Beth Baker for her grueling work, and gratitude for the rare combination—really high standards plus a sense of proportion—that makes her such a good editor. This also seems like a good place to thank to Ruel Tyson, in whose graduate seminar I first read *Sense and Sensibility*, and whom I unaccountably forgot to mention in the acknowledgments to my book on English literature. If you helped me with this book and I've unaccountably left you out, please forgive!

NOTES

INTRODUCTION

1. Jennifer Frey, "Jane Austen: A Love Story," *Washington Post*, August 22, 2004, p. D1.
2. Jane Austen didn't just write about the Regency period, she actually lived then.
3. Helen Fielding, *Bridget Jones's Diary* (Viking, 1996).
4. "...in taking so decided a dislike to him, without any reason...one cannot be always laughing at a man without now and then stumbling on something witty." Her sister Jane knows that Elizabeth is really embarrassed, however much she tries to turn it into a joke: "Lizzy, when you first read that letter, I am sure you could not treat the matter as you do now." And Elizabeth admits it. "I was uncomfortable enough. I was very uncomfortable, I may say unhappy. And with no one to speak to, of what I felt, no Jane to comfort me and say that I had not been so very weak and vain and nonsensical as I knew I had!"
5. Hephzibah Anderson, *Chastened: The Unexpected Story of My Year without Sex* (Viking, 2010), p. 15.
6. Helen Fielding, *Bridget Jones: The Edge of Reason* (Viking, 1999).
7. Anderson, op. cit.
8. On a whole different scale from even Emma, whose story was reworked into a movie of that title.
9. "Elizabeth longed to observe that Mr. Bingley had been a most delightful friend; so easily guided that his worth was invaluable; but she checked herself. She remembered that [Mr. Darcy] had yet to learn to be laught at, and it was rather too early to begin."
10. Hephzibah Anderson is just the tip of the iceberg. In the spring of 2010, abstinence was a fad among New York City sophisticates. See Mandy Stadtmiller, "No More Sex in the City: New York Women Are Going Celibate—and They Feel Happier Than Ever," the *New York Post*, May 11, 2010. Dawn Eden was an early adopter; see *The Thrill of the Chaste: Finding Fulfillment by Keeping Your Clothes*

On (Thomas Nelson, 2006). There's also Joan Sewell, *I'd Rather Eat Chocolate: Learning to Love My Low Libido* (Crown Archetype, 2007).

11. Caitlin Flanagan, "Love, Actually: How Girls Reluctantly Endure the Hookup Culture," *Atlantic*, June 2010; Kathleen A. Bogle, *Hooking Up: Sex, Dating, and Relationships on Campus* (NYU Press, 2008); Laura Sessions, *Unhooked: How Young Women Pursue Sex, Delay Love, and Lose at Both* (Riverhead Trade, 2008).

12. See chapter 4 below.

13. Okay, so Jane Austen heroines don't have jobs. But then again, neither do most of the men they marry. Elizabeth Bennet settles down to manage a family and a household. And her husband…manages his estate.

14. *Sanditon* is complete with bathing machines, a gourmandizing hypochondriac hypocrite, an officious do-gooding spinster, a seaside resort town in which sound economic fundamentals are giving way to speculative get-rich-quick schemes, a heroine who's a poor relation and companion to a rich old lady, and a black-hearted Snidely Whiplash-style villain.

15. There's Elizabeth's boy-crazy sister Lydia, who thinks she's being eloped with for love when really she's just being used for sex. There's Mrs. Bennet, whose frenetic desire for her daughters to marry well actually drives men away. ("The business of her life was to get her daughters married…." There's something wrong there. Love is a serious part of our lives, but it shouldn't be anybody's "business" in quite that frantic way.) There's empty-headed Anne Steele, desperate to be teased about her non-existent relationship with "the Doctor." There's Isabella Thorpe, talking archly about "the men" and making calculating use of her feminine wiles to pursue an ambitious marriage.

16. She was "the daughter of Dr. Johnson," as C. S. Lewis argued in "A Note on Jane Austen," *Selected Literacy Essays* (Cambridge University Press, 1969), p. 186. Remember that Jane Austen turned twenty-five in 1800, in an era when people, particularly women, grew up faster than we do today. But the real tip-off is her prose style. Read George Washington's correspondence, or the letters between John and Abigail Adams, and you'd almost think you were in a Jane Austen novel. There's a watershed in style after Jane Austen just like—okay, maybe not *just* like, but it's the same sort of difference as—the one between Frank Sinatra and Elvis. Wordsworth's famous preface to *Lyrical Ballads* offers insights into, and also provided impetus for, this change.

17. Versus Bridget Jones's *Edge of Reason*, where we too often find ourselves instead.

18. Benjamin Roth, *The Great Depression: A Diary* (Public Affairs, 2009), p. 4.

19. As one woman who vainly beat herself against life's limitations like a bird breaking its body against a plate-glass window was able to recognize, "At fifteen [Jane

Austen] had few illusions about other people and none about herself." Virginia Woolf, "Jane Austen," *The Common Reader* (Mariner Books, 2002), p. 136.

20. So that Alexis de Tocqueville, writing a couple decades after Jane Austen, could argue that marriages worked better in America because American women got to choose their own husbands. *Democracy in America.* See especially vol. II, section III, chapter 11, "How Equality of Condition in America Contributes to Good Morals."

CHAPTER ONE

1. "She saw with the creative eye of fancy, the streets of that gay bathing place covered with officers. She saw herself the object of attention, to tens and to scores of them at present unknown."

2. A popular destination for elopements, on account of Scottish marriage law.

3. "'And they are really to be married!' cried Elizabeth, as soon as they were by themselves. 'How strange this is! And for *this* we are to be thankful. That they should marry, small as is their chance of happiness, and wretched as is his character, we are forced to rejoice! Oh Lydia!'"

4. "A conceited, pompous, narrow-minded, silly man."

5. "The stupidity with which he was favored by nature, must guard his courtship from any charm that could make a woman wish for its continuance; and Miss Lucas, who accepted him solely from the pure and disinterested desire of an establishment, cared not how soon that establishment were gained."

6. Elizabeth's thoughts on Lydia's prospects for happiness with Wickham: "neither rational happiness nor worldly prosperity, could be justly expected for her sister"; and "how little of permanent happiness could belong to a couple who were only brought together because their passions were stronger than their virtue, she could easily conjecture." And on Charlotte's future with Mr. Collins: "the distressing conviction that it was impossible for that friend to be tolerably happy in the lot she had chosen."

7. "Without thinking highly of men or matrimony, marriage had always been her object; it was the only honorable provision for well-educated young women of small fortune, and however uncertain of giving happiness, must be their pleasantest preservative from want."

8. She and her sister are "the finest young women" in their neighborhood.

9. And she doesn't have Charlotte's excuse, either; the Bertrams are so well-off that Maria will never have to worry about money, whether she marries or not.

10. "Independence was more needful than ever; the want of it at Mansfield more sensibly felt. She was less and less able to endure the restraint which her father

imposed. The liberty which his absence had given was now become absolutely necessary."

11. Headlines on *Cosmo* covers from May 2007, March 2006, November 2010, and July 2007, respectively.

12. Though it's good to remember that men's attention comes in kinds and degrees. And it's definitely worth asking yourself whether the kind of attention you're attracting is really the kind you want—not to mention, the kind that's likely to last as *long* as you want.

13. For every example Jane Austen's unhappy characters give of approaching men and marriage the wrong way, you can find an example of a Jane Austen heroine who does what seems like almost exactly the same thing, except that she gets it right. Charlotte Lucas wants "nothing more than a comfortable home" and ends up married to an embarrassing fool. But Elinor Dashwood, prudently insisting on a certain degree of financial security before embarking on marriage, wins her way through to the only kind of *really* comfortable home—that is, one she shares with a man she loves and respects. Maria Bertram's pride in Mr. Rushworth's extensive property is a pitiful caricature of Elizabeth Bennet's admiration for Mr. Darcy as a just master and liberal patron of the poor. And every happy Jane Austen heroine in the end finds exquisite delight in one man's intense "admiration."

14. According to the *New York Times* review of *The Washingtonienne: A Novel*—Cutler's fictionalized account of her experiences in D.C.—she and her friends were "concerning themselves only fleetingly with finding long-term mates. Indeed, jaded Jackie compares marriage to suicide. 'Love is not enough,' she declares to April during one of their frequent girls' nights out. 'It just doesn't cut it anymore.'" Alexandra Jacobs, "'The Washingtonienne': D.C. Horizontal," *New York Times*, June 26, 2005, http://www.nytimes.com/2005/06/26/books/review/26JACOBSL.html.

15. Life expectancy is longer. Adolescence is extended; women don't have to grow up so fast. We don't get married in our teens or early twenties. Just think of Anne Elliot: when *Persuasion* begins she's past her bloom and in the autumn of her life, where love is concerned—at age twenty-seven! That's just about the age that one of my high school friends was when she got married, and the women she had worked with in the movie business worried about her: Was she making a big mistake, tying herself down at such an early age?

16. C. S. Lewis discusses all three examples, op. cit., pp. 175–86.

17. "If you, my dear father," she argues, "will not take the trouble of checking her exuberant spirits, and of teaching her that her present pursuits are not to be the business of her life, she will soon be beyond the reach of amendment."

18. "A flirt, too, in the worst and meanest degree of flirtation; without any attraction beyond youth and a tolerable person; and from the ignorance and emptiness of her mind, wholly unable to ward off any portion of that universal contempt which her rage for admiration will excite."

19. Those happy-escape stories were always the unusual ones. (They're part of what makes Jane Austen's heroines rare and delightful.)

20. Anderson, op. cit., pp. 12ff.

21. Stories about, for example, the guy who asked her to lick his face, the one who tried to get her to wear a burka, and the one who carefully explained the security system in his apartment building in advance "in case I should want to flee while he was sleeping."

22. Anderson, op. cit., pp. 5–15.

23. Ibid., pp. 245–46.

24. She makes it clear, for example, that Julia Bertram might have nipped her hopeless crush on Henry Crawford in the bud if she'd had more "knowledge of her own heart": "He went for a fortnight; a fortnight of such dullness to the Miss Bertrams, as ought to have put them both on their guard, and made even Julia admit in her jealousy of her sister, the absolute necessity of distrusting his attentions, and wishing him not to return...."

CHAPTER TWO

1. With setbacks and strategic retreats, but always roaring ahead again in the end.

2. If you had to pinpoint one event that marks the introduction of the Romantic mindset to the world, your best bet might be the publication of Rousseau's popular epistolary novel *Julie* in 1761. That's thirty-five years before we know Jane Austen was working on *Elinor and Marianne*, an early version of the novel that became *Sense and Sensibility* (originally also a novel in letters), in an era when, without the twenty-four-hour news cycle or the internet, and when magazines were quarterlies instead of weeklies, fashions reached saturation point at a much slower pace.

3. "Everything crammed in the box and the Victorians sitting on the lid smiling serenely...." F. Scott Fitzgerald, *This Side of Paradise* (Modern Library, Random House, 2005), p. 146.

4.   The last of the three quotations is from "Me and Bobby McGee," written by Kris Kristofferson and Fred Foster and most memorably sung by Janis Joplin. "Live fast, die young, and have [rather than leave] a good-looking corpse" seems to be originally from William Motley's *Knock on Any Door*, made into a 1949 movie starring Humphrey Bogart (but the actor speaking this particular line was John Derek); see http://www.thisdayinquotes.com/2010/02/real-origin-of-live-fast-die-young-and.html. And "If it feels good, do it" was apparently emitted by the 1960s zeitgeist.

5.   "Victuals and Drink! Replied my Husband in a most nobly contemptuous manner [to his sister, who's so unRomantic as to suggest that marrying Laura with no visible means of support may have been a mistake] and dost thou then imagine that there is no other support for an exalted Mind (such as is my Laura's) than the mean and indelicate employment of Eating and Drinking?"

6.   Not to mention the less grievous matter that his conversation is practically incomprehensible on account of the jargon he's picked up from the literary criticism he reads.

7.   "She had been forced into prudence in her youth, she learned romance as she grew older—the natural sequence of an unnatural beginning."

8.   Respectively, "Love the Way You Lie," written by Eminiem and Skylar Grey and sung by Eminem and Rihanna (2010); "Someone like you," written by Adele and Dan Wilson and performed by Adele (2011); "Lucille," written by Roger Bowling and Hal Bynum and sung by Kenny Rogers (1977); and "Hallelujah," written by Leonard Cohen and sung by k.d. lang (2004). And, yes, I know, Rihanna and Eminem are supposed to be engaging in some sort of public service announcement against domestic violence. Nevertheless, it's the intensity of their suffering that makes the song compelling.

9.   And *Arthur* and *Marty* (the 1955 Oscar winner), are versions of the same story but with the sexes reversed. The odd romance in *Napoleon Dynamite* between Napoleon's brother Kip and his soul mate LaFawnduh is a sendup of the same plot.

10.   As the author of the actual *When Stella Got Her Groove Back* sadly discovered when her much younger Jamaican husband came out of the closet. She divorced and subsequently sued him, claiming that he had married her for a green card and that he and his lawyer had engaged in a plot to humiliate her in the divorce proceedings. As Jane Austen might say, she discovered that the young lover whose attentions had at first seemed so "bewitching" turned out to be "an unprincipled Fortune-hunter."

11.   Anne Elliot is quite capable of feeling "a nervous thrill all over her." But for her, that intensity is not the acid test of love.

12. Of course Elinor isn't simply a mouthpiece for Jane Austen's own views. She and Marianne are fully realized characters, each with her own limitations. Elinor's flaws become crystal clear when her habitual equanimity leads her to underestimate the very real danger of Marianne's near-fatal illness. But Jane Austen's criticism of Romanticism is real, too. And it's worth noting that she, like Elinor, had suffered because a man loved her and yet his family and financial situation made it impossible for him to marry her. Almost *three years* after Jane Austen saw Tom Lefroy for the last time, she was "too proud to make any enquiries" about him to his aunt, visiting the Austens at Steventon. In his old age Tom Lefroy admitted to having loved Jane Austen in his youth, though only with "a boy's love."

13. "You Belong with Me," written by Taylor Swift and Liz Rose and performed by Taylor Swift (2008).

14. "My dear Fanny, you feel these things a great deal too much."

15. Does pursuing happy love instead of Romantic love mean you have to prefer Taylor Swift to Leonard Cohen? No. But one reason happy love can seem trite is that it's even harder to create truly great art from happiness than from misery. How many of the world's greatest literary artists is a comedian? Shakespeare pulled it off. And Dante, Mozart, Jane Austen. There aren't many in that class.

16. She's having difficulty managing her toddler nephew while she tends to his big brother, who has a broken collar bone: "In another moment, however, she found herself in the state of being released from him; some one was taking him from her, though he had bent down her head so much, that his little sturdy hands were unfastened from around her neck, and he was resolutely borne away, before she knew that Captain Wentworth had done it.

    "Her sensations on the discovery made her perfectly speechless. She could not even thank him. She could only hang over little Charles, with most disordered feelings."

17. "A great tendency to lowness."

18. And also "Love don't make things nice—it ruins everything.... We are here to ruin ourselves and to break our hearts and love the wrong people and die." *Moonstruck*, script by John Patrick Shanley.

19. Jane Austen famously called Emma "a heroine whom no-one but myself will much like." And even if you do like Emma, you can see what Jane Austen meant. Emma is one of the most aggravating women in all of fiction. (My husband, in an aggravating moment of his own, once claimed that Emma is the perfect picture of what any woman looks like to a man who loves her—unaccountably

interfering, with infinite inexplicable energy for detail, and always starting trouble of one kind or another, yet somehow enchanting despite or even because of it all. As Mr. Knightley says, "sweetest and best of all creatures, faultless in spite of all her faults.") She's bossy. She's a snob who's indignant about other people's snobbery. She's a thorough menace to her friends and neighbors.

And then—she suddenly sees it all, herself: "With what insufferable vanity had she believed herself in the secret of everybody's feelings; with unpardonable arrogance proposed to arrange everybody's destiny. She was proved to have been universally mistaken; and she had not quite done nothing—for she had done mischief."

Of course, Emma doesn't see any of this until the possibility that Mr. Knightley may be falling for Harriet makes Emma realize "with the speed of an arrow, that Mr. Knightley must marry no one but herself!"—and that with her too-clever schemes she's been unconsciously encouraging a match that will break her own heart. Emma's pain is certainly self-provoked. But it's only after she takes that pain as a jumping-off point for acquiring some real, honest "knowledge of self" that she begins to win our grudging admiration. And when we see her resolve to lead a more rational, self-controlled, and truly generous life—and actually struggle to start doing it—our admiration is not so grudging. We can't help feeling that she may be beginning to deserve her happy ending.

20. And along the way, there were a few folks who made themselves infamous by pushing the Romantic recipe for love—break the rules to pursue intense experiences at all costs—to some particularly ugly (if undoubtedly interesting) ends; think of the Marquis de Sade, Edgar Allan Poe, and Oscar Wilde. Here's Wilde in the last dry desert he got to, following Romantic boredom with happiness to its ultimate conclusion: "In Algiers, Wilde remarked, 'I have a duty to myself to amuse myself most frightfully.' Then he added, 'Not happiness. Above all not happiness. Pleasure! You must always aim at the most tragic.' He bore Gide off to a café, where the young man was captivated by a young Arab boy playing the flute. Outside, Wilde asked him, 'Dear, *vous voulez the petit musicien*,'—do you want the little musician?' Gide, 'in the most choked of voices,' said yes. Wilde burst into what Gide called 'satanic laughter' and made the arrangements." Richard Ellman, *Oscar Wilde* (Vintage, 1988), pp. 429–30.

21. Not a caricature like Laura and Sophia.

CHAPTER THREE

1. Marianne is a genuine heroine, not like the minor characters whose mistakes we looked at in chapter 1. In a literary-critical sense, Lydia Bennet and Charlotte

Lucas and Maria Bertram are just "foils" for our heroines—more modern and sophisticated versions of the clownish characters in a Shakespeare comedy whose rough courtships and mock heroics show off the pure love and noble heroism of the main characters all the more brightly.

2.   Elinor's instinctive tact smoothes over the tensions created by Marianne's too obvious impatience with people who don't meet her high standards. (It's against Marianne's Romantic principles to pretend to be interested in boring people, or to show respect for people she thinks are ridiculous.) And prudent Elinor's advice about money is of real value to their impulsive mother, whose enthusiastic temperament Marianne has inherited.

3.   "But I thought it was right, Elinor," says Marianne, expressing her own Romantic insistence on authenticity, in contrast with Elinor's more conventional ideas, "to be guided wholly by the opinions of other people. I thought our judgments were given us merely to be subservient to those of our neighbours. This has always been your doctrine, I am sure." Elinor's answer: "My doctrine has never aimed at the subjection of the understanding."

4.   Marianne and Elinor love each other dearly, but each sister thinks the other one is very wrongheaded. It's not just Marianne's feelings; "her opinions," too, "are all romantic."

5.   Marianne respects her sister's mind and her taste, if not her good manners.

6.   That's Elinor's opinion, in any case: "A few years however will settle her opinions on the reasonable basis of common sense and observation; and then they may be more easy to define and to justify than they now are, by any body but herself.... There are inconveniences attending such feelings as Marianne's, which all the charms of enthusiasm and ignorance of the world cannot atone for. Her systems have all the unfortunate tendency of setting propriety at nought; and a better acquaintance with the world is what I look forward to as her greatest possible advantage."

7.   Note that Marianne's Romantic intensity is different from gaiety, merriment, delight (not to mention solid happiness): "'Nor do I think [gaiety] a part of Marianne's [character],' said Elinor; 'I should hardly call her a lively girl; she is very earnest, very eager in all she does—sometimes talks a great deal and always with animation—but she is not often really merry.'"

8.   "You know what he thinks of Cowper and Scott; you are certain of his estimating their beauties as he ought, and you have received every assurance of his admiring Pope no more than is proper. But how is your acquaintance to be long supported, under such extraordinary dispatch of every subject for discourse?"

9.   "I have not known him long indeed, but I am much better acquainted with him, than I am with any other creature in the world, except yourself and mama."

(Intensity.) Marianne admits, "I have erred against every common-place notion of decorum." (Liberation.) But really, she's proud of it: "I have been open and sincere where I ought to have been reserved, spiritless, and deceitful." (Authenticity.)

Elinor keeps trying to talk Marianne into being a little more cautious about showing her feelings, a little more conventional in her behavior, but to no avail. At one point Elinor is upset to discover that Marianne has actually agreed to accept the present of a horse from Willoughby. It's the kind of expensive gift that tends to make a woman feel an unhealthy sense of obligation to a man, and to give the man an unhealthy sense of entitlement about her.

But the most egregious breach of propriety occurs when Willoughby is driving Marianne around the countryside in his open carriage. He takes her to the house where he has been staying with a Mrs. Smith, the old lady cousin from whom he depends on inheriting, to show her the rooms and the garden. Elinor is shocked; Marianne hasn't been introduced to Mrs. Smith and can't legitimately visit her. There's something hole-and-corner about going through the house without meeting its owner, particularly with an attractive young man. It's the kind of behavior that young women were taught to avoid because of its potential to put them in a vulnerable position vis-à-vis a predatory male.

10.   "'I never spent a pleasanter morning in my life.'

"'I am afraid,' replied Elinor, 'that the pleasantness of an employment does not always evince its propriety.'

"'On the contrary, nothing can be a stronger proof of it Elinor; for if there had been any real impropriety in what I did, I should have been sensible of it at the time, for we always know when we are acting wrong, and with such a conviction I could have had no pleasure.'"

Nobody in the Regency Period was saying "If it feels good, do it," yet. But the idea was already in the air.

11.   "This was the season of happiness to Marianne. Her heart was devoted to Willoughby."

12.   She runs out of the room in tears; she can't eat. "The slightest mention of anything relative to Willoughby overpower[s] her in an instant" and makes her cry again.

13.   It's easy to see where Marianne gets her temperament, and at least some proportion of her principles.

14. Willoughby's letter is a pack of bald-faced and insulting lies. He's flatly denying everything that happened between them—everything that Marianne, and not *just* Marianne, knows *did*. It's not only Marianne who thought from the way Willoughby behaved toward her that he was in love with her. Her family, friends, and neighbors have all been expecting to hear that she's engaged to him.

15. Apart from anything else, Willoughby's fiancée owed Marianne "no duty, and therefore could have transgressed none," as Jane Austen says in a different context.

16. "Pursuing fresh schemes, always gay, always happy."

17. The passage from *Sense and Sensibility* that perfectly answers Charlotte Brontë's attack on Jane Austen—"I understand you.—You do not suppose that I have ever felt much…."—is Elinor's answer to Marianne's initial reaction when she finds out that Elinor has been living with her own secret heartbreak for all the weeks when she's been comforting Marianne in her distress. Just like Charlotte Brontë, who thought that Jane Austen must not have "even a speaking acquaintance" with the "stormy sisterhood" of the passions, Marianne is sure that Elinor doesn't understand real pain. Why? Because Elinor believes in self-control, and she keeps her eyes on the ultimate prize—to be happy with the man she loves, if she can, and to do her best to be as happy as she can without him, if she has to.

18. Marianne still prides herself on the intensity of her emotions. Her self-image is tied up with the idea of herself as a person who can feel more keenly, judge more authentically, and act more freely than other people.

19. Marianne purposely seeks out situations that will exacerbate her misery: "In such moments of precious, of invaluable misery, she rejoiced in tears of agony."

20. His vanity was flattered by her too-obvious preference for him. And so, he explains, he "endeavoured, by every means in my power, to make myself pleasing to her, without any design of returning her affection."

21. "To re-establish my circumstances by marrying a woman of fortune," as Willoughby puts it. "To attach myself to your sister, therefore, was not a thing to be thought of…."

22. And, what makes it much worse, who *knows* he doesn't love her.

23. And pines for "a comparative poverty, which her affection and her society would have deprived of all its horrors."

24. Elinor to Willoughby: "You have proved your heart less wicked, much less wicked. But I hardly know—the misery that you have inflicted—I hardly know what could have made it worse."

25. See the next chapter for more on the strange phenomenon in which indulging the Romantic sensibility is, paradoxically, likely to make you more vulnerable to

"settling," while a more balanced, Jane Austen-style approach will inoculate you against cynicism.

26. "That Marianne found her own happiness in forming his, was equally the persuasion and delight of each observing friend. Marianne could never love by halves; and her whole heart became, in time, as much devoted to her husband, as it had once been to Willoughby."

27. "His expensiveness is acknowledged even by himself, and his whole conduct declares that self-denial is a word hardly understood by him. His demands and your inexperience together on a small, very small income, must have brought on distresses.... *Your* sense of honour and honesty would have led you, I know, when aware of your situation, to attempt all the economy that would appear to you possible; and perhaps as long as your frugality retrenched only on your own comfort, you might have been suffered to practice it...had you endeavoured, however reasonably, to abridge *his* enjoyments, is it not to be feared, that instead of prevailing on feelings so selfish to consent to it, you would have lessened your own influence on his heart, and made him regret the connection which had involved him in such difficulties?"

28. Assuming that Elinor is right about Marianne's approach to household finances.

29. Especially as long as we keep other pictures out of our minds—of Willoughby's sincere repentance for what he's done; of his powerful charm and "ardour of mind" so perfectly suited to Marianne's own temperament; of his passionate love for Marianne, stronger than ever now that it's entirely hopeless. Even sensible Elinor has to allow some time to pass before she can shake Willoughby's "influence over her mind" and judge the situation on "reason" and "merits."

30. That's Mr. Collins's cut-rate way of dealing with disappointment in love: "I have often observed that resignation is never so perfect as when the blessing denied begins to lose somewhat of its value in our estimation."

31. Especially for the first Mrs. Willoughby—an excellent candidate for the First Wives' Club.

32. It seems to be a type much *more* common today than then.

33. I'd say five years, tops.

34. She's busy establishing that she and Willoughby agree exactly about music and poetry, that they share the same "taste" and "enthusiasm," that he's capable of making her feel the powerful emotions that she's been looking forward to whenever she's imagined being in love.

35. Which Angela, thank heavens, did. *Strong Fathers, Strong Daughters*, Meg Meeker (Regnery, 2006), pp. 106–8.

36. Complete with sleepless nights, running out of rooms in tears, and so forth.

37. This is a special kind of blindness in love. Marianne's not just enchanted with Willoughby despite his faults, or telling herself his flaws don't really matter. She's blind to his actions, intentions, and motivations, and to the whole reality of the situation he's created, because she's enchanted with Romantic love.

38. Please see chapter 13, note 4 below for more on my cluelessness in this instance.

CHAPTER FOUR

1. Elizabeth is talking about Mr. Collins; she's setting off to visit Charlotte Lucas, now Collins, in her married home the next day.

2. He has deserted her to court another young woman, whom he had paid "not the smallest attention" until she inherited ten thousand pounds.

3. By warning her early on that he can't afford to marry Elizabeth, and that she'd better not encourage either him or herself to fall in love.

4. For tips on how to distinguish them, see chapters 11 and 14 below.

5. "I should deserve utter contempt," Anne says, "if I dared to suppose that true attachment and constancy were known only by women."

6. Mary Eberstadt, ed., *Why I Turned Right: Leading Baby Boom Conservatives Chronicle Their Political Journeys* (Threshold, 2007), p. 19.

7. Not coincidentally, Jane Austen brought the same clear-eyed eighteenth-century ambition to the problem of domestic happiness as the American Founders brought to the problem of the public welfare. It's hard to think of a group of men in world history with a less sentimental view of nature. And yet it's also hard to think of a more ambitious project than the founding of the American Republic.

8. Remember how Bridget Jones breaks up with Mark Darcy under the influence of an all-men-are-bastards-go-girl-power state of mind.

9. Mrs. Bennet complains incessantly about Mr. Bennet, and he has zero respect for her: "To his wife he was very little otherwise indebted, than as her ignorance and folly had contributed to his amusement. This is not the sort of happiness which a man would in general wish to owe to his wife; but where other powers of entertainment are wanting, the true philosopher will derive benefit from such as are given."

10. "Something's Gotta Give," by Craig Wiseman and Tony Mullins, recorded by LeAnn Rimes (2005).

11. Lori Gottlieb, single mother by choice, explains how she responds to her married friends' complaints: "'OK, if you're so unhappy, and if I'm so lucky, leave your husband! In fact, send him over here!' Not one person has taken me up on this offer." Lori Gottlieb, "Marry Him! The Case for Settling for Mr. Good Enough,"

Atlantic, March 2008, http://www.theatlantic.com/magazine/archive/2008/03/
marry-him/6651/. But note that Jane Austen is absolutely not about "settling."
That's just a different kind of cynicism (about which, see more later in this
chapter).

12.   As Elizabeth Bennet says, "The misfortune of speaking with bitterness is a most
natural consequence of the prejudices I had been encouraging." And, believe me,
the things Elizabeth is ashamed of having said to Darcy are really quite civilized
compared to what will come out of our mouths if we indulge ourselves in cynicism and resentment.

13.   Somewhat improbably attributed to Plato. The real author of this sentiment
seems to have been a John Watson, writing under the name Ian MacLaren around
the turn of the twentieth century. See "Be Kind; Everyone You Meet Is Fighting
a Hard Battle: Plato? Philo of Alexandria? Ian MacLaren? John Watson?" Quote
Investigator: Dedicated to the Investigation and Tracing of Quotes, http://
quoteinvestigator.com/2010/06/29/be-kind/.

14.   "I was proud, too proud, to ask again," Wentworth finally realizes. "I did not understand you. I shut my eyes, and would not understand you, or do you justice. This
is a recollection which ought to make me forgive every one sooner than myself."

15.   As Colonel Brandon observes, "When the romantic refinements of a young mind
are obliged to give way, how frequently are they succeeded by such opinions as
are but too common and too dangerous!" Romanticism over-promises and
under-delivers. When the inevitable happens, and Romantic illusions are exposed
as illusory, it's easy to overreact in the opposite direction and become too practical—ready to settle. That's why it's the ever-Romantic Mrs. Dashwood, not
the sensible Elinor, who is most eager to rush Marianne into marrying Colonel
Brandon. Mrs. Dashwood goes straight from one extreme—being almost as
bewitched by Willoughby as Marianne is and having too much "romantic delicacy" to ask her seventeen-year-old daughter if she's actually engaged or not—to
the other. Once it becomes clear that Willoughby was deceiving them all, Mrs.
Dashwood is ready to pressure Marianne into marriage with a rich man twice
her age, all the while deceiving herself about her own motivations and her
daughter's heart.

16.   Apu: "But one in twenty-five arranged marriages end in divorce!" "The Two Mrs.
Nahasapeemapetilons" by Richard Appel, *The Simpsons* Season 9 (1997). Noorah
al-Meer, a friend of mine from Oman in Arabia—where they still have arranged
marriage—saw another American friend put up that Simpsons quote on
Facebook and pointed out that from her experience, "Nine of those arranged
marriages stay intact because they're forced to stay in it" by their families.

17. *Married by America*, the 2003 reality show on FOX.

18. Reva Seth, *First Comes Marriage: Modern Relationship Advice from the Wisdom of Arranged Marriages* (Fireside, 2008).

19. Gottlieb, op. cit.

20. Gottlieb, op. cit.: "Back when I was still convinced I'd find my soul mate, I did, although I never articulated this, have certain requirements. I thought that the person I married would have to have a sense of wonderment about the world, would be both spontaneous and grounded, and would acknowledge that life is hard but also be able to navigate its ups and downs with humor. Many of the guys I dated possessed these qualities, but if one of them lacked a certain degree of kindness, another didn't seem emotionally stable enough, and another's values clashed with mine. Others were sweet but so boring that I preferred reading during dinner to sitting through another tedious conversation. I also dated someone who appeared to be highly compatible with me—we had much in common, and strong physical chemistry—but while our sensibilities were similar, they proved to be a half-note off, so we never quite felt in harmony, or never viewed the world through quite the same lens." It all sounds an awful lot like Marianne's "I could not be happy with a man whose taste did not in every point coincide with my own. He must enter into all my feelings.... The more I know of the world, the more am I convinced that I shall never see a man whom I can really love. I require so much!"

21. "Disinterested affection," not "the pure and disinterested desire of an establishment."

22. November 18, 1814, Letter from Jane Austen to Fanny Knight.

23. During a period when she was especially unhappy at home and around the time when she must have "felt her approach to the years of danger" (it was the month of her twenty-seventh birthday, roughly equivalent to a woman's thirty-seventh, today, in terms of romantic prospects), Jane Austen received—and at first accepted—an offer of marriage from Harris Big-Wither, a young man as awkward and unattractive as his name, but a very rich one. But by the next morning Jane Austen had decided she couldn't bring herself to marry him, and called off the engagement.

24. Anne means "a man to whom I am indifferent."

25. And Emma Watson, the heroine of Jane Austen's unfinished novel *The Watsons*, finds the idea of marrying without love shocking and incomprehensible: "To be so bent on Marriage—to pursue a Man merely for the sake of situation—is a sort of thing that shocks me; I cannot understand it."

26.   Megan McArdle, "The Case against Settling," *Atlantic*, June 8, 2010, http://www.theatlantic.com/culture/archive/2010/06/the-case-against-settling/57836/.

27.   As Jane Austen says of a poor girl's feelings about being sent out to India to find a husband because she has no other way of securing "a Maintenance": it is "so opposite to all her ideas of Propriety, so contrary to her Wishes, so repugnant to her feelings, that she would almost have preferred Servitude to it, had Choice been allowed her." And "to a Girl of any Delicacy, the voyage in itself, since the object of it is so universally known, is a punishment that needs no other to make it very severe."

28.   From Jane Austen's next letter to Fanny Knight, on November 30, 1814, warning her niece about the misery of finding yourself in love with a different man from the one you've "settled" for—a very possible outcome if you've made a commitment your heart isn't really in.

CHAPTER FIVE

1.   Mrs. Smith tells Anne Elliot, "When one lives in the world, a man or woman's marrying for money is too common to strike one as it ought."

2.   And us! You don't expect sodomy jokes in a Jane Austen novel: "'Post captains may be a very good sort of man, but they do not belong to *us*. Of various admirals, I could tell you a great deal…. Of *Rears* and *Vices*, I saw enough. Now, do not suspect me of a pun, I entreat.'
       "Edmund again felt grave, and only replied, 'It is a noble profession.'"

3.   "She had felt an early presentiment that she *should* like the eldest best. She knew it was her way."

4.   Later, when Mary's equally worldly brother Henry falls for Fanny, he's similarly incapable of naming—and thus of seeing really clearly—what it is that's so attractive about her: "Henry Crawford had too much sense not to feel the worth of good principles in a wife, though he was too little accustomed to serious reflection to know them by their proper name…."

5.   And to poor Fanny, who's forced to listen to the man she loves talk himself into falling in love with another woman against his better judgment. Edmund blames Mary's mercenary opinions and sometimes crude language on her unfortunate upbringing. He's charmed by her "lively mind" even when it pains him that she "can hardly be serious even on serious subjects."

6.   "The misunderstanding is incurable. She will never know Edmund." Lewis, op. cit., p. 184.

7.   Mary does see that there's no love between Janet Fraser and her husband: "In their house I shall call to mind the conjugal manners of Mansfield Parsonage

with respect. Even Dr. Grant does shew a thorough confidence in my sister, and a certain consideration for her judgment, which makes one feel there is attachment; but of that, I shall see nothing with the Frasers."

But though she sees that the Frasers are "about as unhappy as most other married people," Mary still thinks of the marriage as "a most desirable match for Janet at the time": "We were all delighted. She could not do otherwise than accept him, for he was rich, and she had nothing; but he turns out ill-tempered and *exigeant*; and wants a young woman, a beautiful young woman of five-and-twenty, to be as steady as himself. And my friend does not manage him well; she does not seem to know how to make the best of it. There is a spirit of irritation, which, to say nothing worse, is certainly very ill-bred."

8.   It is sad to see Mary, who in Mansfield seemed to appreciate Edmund's real worth as a human being, now thinking about him in these terms: "My friends here are very much struck with his gentleman-like appearance. Mrs. Fraser (no bad judge), declares she knows but three men in town who have so good a person, height, and air; there were none to compare with him, and we were a party of sixteen. Luckily there is no distinction of dress [to mark Edmund out as a clergyman] now-a-days to tell tales, but—but—but."

9.   Or even just when they issue "a short decisive sentence of praise or condemnation on the face of every woman" they see, like the appalling John Thorpe.

10. Fanny, Jane Austen's most religious heroine, would approve!

11. "I became accustomed to seeing myself as a commodity—a varied collection of looks, wit, intellect, and *je ne sais quoi*. I looked for men whose commodities were worth as much as my own." Eden met "nice guys…but either they seemed boring—as nice guys so often are when you're used to players—or I KO'd the budding relationship by trying to rush things." She writes about being forced by her sex-and-the-city lifestyle to follow "a set of Darwinian rules—dressing and acting a certain way to outperform other women competing for mates." Eden, op. cit., pp. 87, 3, and xi, respectively.

12. Hephzibah Anderson's experience is hardly unique: "Unfortunately, the moment I fell into bed with a man, I'd fall at least a little in love. Was it biological? Or was I responding to the notionally dead double standard—a double standard lively enough for women to continue scaling down their sexual conquests while men fibbed upward? And was it really so unreasonable of me to stubbornly link sex and love?" Anderson, op. cit., p. 18. Dawn Eden doesn't call it falling in love, but she writes about how sex inevitably made her feel attached: "I knew I'd be no more likely to fall in love after sex than I was at the moment. I would, however,

feel more attached to him, even if it wasn't love. Sex does that to me whether I want it to or not; it's part of how I'm wired as a woman." Eden, op. cit., p. 9.

13.   She's got a better sense of self-preservation than even de Merteuil. And in any case, she seems to prefer teasing guys.

14.   Caitlin Flanagan, "Love, Actually: How Girls Reluctantly Endure the Hookup Culture," *Atlantic*, June 2010, http://www.theatlantic.com/magazine/archive/2010/06/love-actually/8094/.

15.   Or just because some accident of circumstances entirely beyond their control gave them that reputation.

16.   And he's pilloried by the other students. "It was the first day of an undergraduate seminar…on the subject of men and women in literary perspective. The students were asked what they thought was the most important decision that they would ever have to make in their lives. Nearly all the students answered in terms related to personal fulfillment: 'Deciding which career to pursue,' 'Figuring out which graduate or professional school to attend,' 'Choosing where I should live.' Only one fellow answered otherwise: 'Deciding who should be the mother of my children.' For his eccentric opinion, and especially for his quaint way of putting it, he was promptly attacked by nearly every member of the class, men and women alike. The men and nearly all the women berated him for wanting to sacrifice his freedom or for foolishly putting such matters ahead of his career; the women and some of the men were offended that he would look upon and judge women for their prospective capacities as prospective mothers, worse yet, as mothers for *his* children…." Amy A. Kass and Leon R. Kass, *Wing to Wing, Oar to Oar* (University of Notre Dame Press, 2000), p. 1.

17.   Mrs. Jennings on Marianne and Willoughby: "Poor thing! she looks very bad. No wonder. Aye, it is but too true. He is to be married very soon—a good-for-nothing fellow! I have no patience with him. Mrs. Taylor told me of it half an hour ago, and she was told it by a particular friend of Miss Grey herself, else I am sure I should not have believed it; and I was almost ready to sink as it was. Well, said I, all I can say is, that if it is true, he has used a young lady of my acquaintance abominably ill."

18.   The married professors who team-taught the class in which that male student got major grief for making his choice of mate his top priority argue from their experience that he was right. "Our reaction was quite different. As a happily married couple, and as parents of children (now grown and married) whose existence and rearing have been central to our happiness, we could—albeit with hindsight—endorse the young man's view. Indeed, we wondered only how he could have acquired such a mature outlook at such a tender age. Far from con-

demning him as a freak, this opinion revealed an admirable seriousness about life…. Why, we wondered, were not more of our young people aware of the importance—to their own flourishing future—of private life, marriage, and family? Why did they not foresee the supreme importance of finding the right person with whom they might make a life?" Kass and Kass, op. cit., p. 1.

19. "She had humoured, or softened, or concealed his failings, and promoted his real respectability for seventeen years; and though not the very happiest being in the world herself, had found enough in her duties, her friends, and her children, to attach her to life, and to make it no matter of indifference to her when she was called on to quit them."

20. Eliza found herself living with a husband who had "no regard for her; his pleasures were not what they ought to have been; and from the first he treated her unkindly." And Eliza had a mind "so young, so lively, so inexperienced" that she couldn't resign herself to managing married unhappiness à la Lady Elliot.

21. Colonel Brandon: "I could not trace her beyond her first seducer, and there was every reason to fear that she had removed from him only to sink deeper in a life of sin. Her legal allowance was not adequate to her fortune, nor sufficient for her comfortable maintenance, and I learnt from my brother that the power of receiving it had been made over some months before to another person. He imagined, and calmly could he imagine it, that her extravagance and consequent distress had obliged her to dispose of it for some immediate relief. At last, however, and after I had been six months in England, I *did* find her. Regard for a former servant of my own, who had since fallen into misfortune, carried me to visit him in a spunging-house, where he was confined for debt; and there, in the same house, under a similar confinement, was my unfortunate sister. So altered—so faded—worn down by acute suffering of every kind! hardly could I believe the melancholy and sickly figure before me, to be the remains of the lovely, blooming, healthful girl, on whom I had once doated."

22. At the moment Emma accepts Mr. Knightley, Jane Austen comments, "Seldom, very seldom, does complete truth belong to any human disclosure; seldom can it happen that something is not a little disguised, or a little mistaken; but where, as in this case, though the conduct is mistaken, the feelings are not, it may not be very material." And later, once Harriet accepts Robert Martin, "High in the rank of her most serious and heartfelt felicities, was the reflection that all necessity of concealment from Mr. Knightley would soon be over."

23. Mr. Knightley: "My Emma, does not every thing serve to prove more and more the beauty of truth and sincerity in all our dealings with each other?"

24.   Emma, when she realizes that her schemes for Mr. Elton to marry Harriet have come to naught: "'Here have I,' said she, 'actually talked poor Harriet into being very much attached to this man. She might never have thought of him but for me; and certainly never would have thought of him with hope, if I had not assured her of his attachment, for she is as modest and humble as I used to think him. Oh! that I had been satisfied with persuading her not to accept young Martin. There I was quite right. That was well done of me; but there I should have stopped, and left the rest to time and chance. I was introducing her into good company, and giving her the opportunity of pleasing some one worth having; I ought not to have attempted more. But now, poor girl, her peace is cut up for some time. I have been but half a friend to her; and if she were *not* to feel this disappointment so very much, I am sure I have not an idea of any body else who would be at all desirable for her;—William Coxe—Oh! no, I could not endure William Coxe—a pert young lawyer.'

"She stopt to blush and laugh at her own relapse."

CHAPTER SIX

1.   To put it in literary-critical terms, she starts out writing cruel Jonsonian comedy of humors, but somehow works her way into writing generous Shakespearean comedy.

2.   "Dear Eloisa (said I) there's no occasion for your crying so much about such a trifle (for I was willing to make light of it in order to comfort her). I beg you would not mind it—,You see it does not vex me in the least; though perhaps *I* may suffer most from it after all; for I shall not only be obliged to eat up all the Victuals I have dressed already, but must if Hervey should recover (which however is not very likely) dress as much for you again; or should he die (as I suppose he will) I shall still have to prepare a Dinner for you whenever you marry some-one else.... Thus I did all in my power to console her, but without any effect."

3.   In these caricatures—and in the imbalances that her heroes and heroines fall into—Jane Austen touches on a phenomenon that philosophers since ancient times have addressed: the tension between "the good" and what's our own. To some extent we all naturally admire whatever's excellent. But we also all give special weight to what belongs to us, reminds us of ourselves, or is associated with our own group. Modern psychologists talk about "identity issues." Teenag-ers will neglect what's obviously and objectively better for them in order to pursue what subjectively makes them feel good about themselves—fitting in, or being able to tell themselves they're a certain kind of person.

And we never entirely grow out of our prejudice toward what belongs to us. Jane Austen was keenly aware of this phenomenon. Susan Lesley in *Lesley Castle* thinks her stepdaughters are "two great, tall, out of the way, over-grown Girls." And one of those girls returns the favor, writing of her stepmother that "there is something so extremely unmajestic in her little diminutive figure, as to render her in comparison with the elegant height of Matilda and Myself, an insignificant dwarf." In *Sanditon*, Jane Austen's last, unfinished novel, she gives us the proto-Victorian spinster Parker sisters, who enjoy the typical Victorian spinster hobbies—hypochondria and do-gooding: "The Sisters were perhaps driven to dissipate [their "Imagination and quick feelings"] in the invention of odd complaints.—The whole of their mental vivacity was evidently not so employed; Part was laid out in a Zeal for being useful.—It should seem that they must either be very busy for the Good of others, or else extremely ill themselves. Some natural delicacy of Constitution in fact, with an unfortunate turn for Medicine, especially quack Medicine, had given them an early tendency at various times, to various Disorders;—the rest of their sufferings was from Fancy, the love of Distinction & the love of the Wonderful.—They had Charitable hearts & many amiable feelings—but a spirit of restless activity, & the glory of doing more than anybody else, had their share in every exertion of Benevolence—and there was Vanity in all they did, as well as in all they endured."

"Vanity," "the glory of doing more than anybody else," "the love of Distinction"—those are the motivators that a modern psychologist would put under the "identity issues" label. Jane Austen thought of that impulse (what we might think of as a need to cater to your own ego) as a drag away from a balanced (what we might call an objective) view of things. She understood that the chief handicap preventing us from seeing the real value of something—or, when it comes to love, the true excellence of some*one*— is some distorting influence proceeding from our own issues, those absurd extremes her minor characters fall into. Being in the right balance means standing in the center, where you can see things straight and clear, not from any distorting angle.

4. Sir John Middleton, whose ruling humor is "the dread of being alone," is delighted to hear that Elinor and Marianne are coming to London because to him even "the acquisition of two, to the number of inhabitants in London, was something." Charlotte Palmer, "thoroughly good-natured," and "determined to be happy," laughs at absolutely everything, from her husband's rudeness to "the

loss of her favourite plants, unwarily exposed, and nipped by the lingering frost."
John Dashwood is the epitome of transparent selfishness, just guilty enough
about doing nothing for his sisters that he's "exceedingly anxious that everybody
else should do a good deal; and an offer from Colonel Brandon, or a legacy from
Mrs. Jennings, was the easiest means of atoning for his own neglect."

5.   Lady Middleton's insipid elegance, Lucy Steele's clever scheming.

6.   "The violence of [Eliza's] passions" and "the weakness of her understanding."

7.   He tells Louisa, "It is the worst evil of too yielding and indecisive a character, that
no influence over it can be depended on.—You are never sure of a good impression being durable. Every body may sway it; let those who would be happy be
firm."

8.   That's the theme of the conversation between him and Louisa, when Anne
overhears him comparing Louisa to "a beautiful glossy nut, which, blessed with
its original strength, has outlived all the storms of autumn."

9.   "Now armed with the idea of merit in maintaining her own way."

10.   Anne was "exalt[ed] in his estimation" once he "understood the perfect excellence
of the mind with which Louisa's could so ill bear a comparison."

11.   Lydia's empty-headed "rage for admiration" and Wickham's weaknesses for
women and gambling are absurdities that pull them off center and make them
more like the caricatures in Jane Austen's early works than like her happy lovers.

12.   She thinks that everyone who knows the two of them must be coupling their
names. ("She could not but suppose it to be a match that every body who knew
them must think of.") She pictures him declaring his love. She thinks about how
she'll answer him.

13.   "She looked back; she compared the two—compared them, as they had always
stood in her estimation, from the time of [Frank's] becoming known to her—and
as they must at any time have been compared by her, had it—oh! Had it, by any
blessed felicity, occurred to her, to institute the comparison.—She saw that there
never had been a time when she did not consider Mr. Knightley as infinitely
superior, or when his regard for her had not been infinitely the most dear."

14.   Including her uncle "who lived by trade, and within view of his own ware-
houses"—one thing Darcy was referring to when he wrote of the "objectionable"
"situation of your mother's family."

15.   When that same uncle fortuitously brings her to Pemberley. "[Elizabeth] could
hardly suppress a smile, at his being now seeking the acquaintance of those very
people, against whom his pride had revolted, in his offer to herself."

16.   "He had followed [Wickham and Lydia] purposely to town, he had taken on
himself all the trouble and mortification attendant on such a research; in which

supplication had been necessary to a woman [the former companion who had attempted to betray his sister into marriage with the fortune- and revenge-hunting Wickham] whom he must abominate and despise, and where he was reduced to meet, frequently meet, reason with, persuade, and finally bribe, the man whom he always most wished to avoid, and whose very name it was punishment for him to pronounce."

17.   Any woman who ever gave way to the foolish urge to wash the horrifying pile of dishes in some guy's apartment sink (yes, I once stupidly did this in a fit of premature domesticity aimed at a man who, I knew but didn't want to admit to myself, had already moved on) will feel the psychological realism of Jane Austen heroines' finding that love is a powerful impulse for noble self-sacrifice. Think, for example, of the fact that Anne Elliot "would have attended on Louisa with a zeal above the common claims of regard, for his sake" and, later, of her "musings of high-wrought love and eternal constancy...almost enough to spread purification and perfume all the way." Or of how Elinor makes the arrangements between Colonel Brandon and Edward over the living that's going to make it possible for him to marry Lucy. The way love impels us to goodness—even of this extreme, self-denying, and possibly counter-productive kind, but also of the sort that makes Elizabeth so happy with Darcy—has something to do with courting displays, wanting to look good to a potential mate. But it's more than that; human beings are more than peacocks. As Jane Austen knew, love and goodness are real.

18.   Way too much of our modern love lives is just playacting—because we've long since given up any hope of getting what we want in reality. Rihanna doesn't even aspire to be the "the only girl"—just to feel like she is, for one night. "Only Girl (in the World)," written and recorded by Rihanna.

19.   Going by my totally unscientific guestimate that at least ninety-nine percent of people can understand why sex shops stock handcuffs for every one percent who can see the point of a shoe fetish.

20.   So that Elizabeth can ask him why "you chose to tell me that you liked me against your will, against your reason, and even against your character?"

CHAPTER SEVEN

1.   See R. W. Chapman, "The Manners of the Age," appended to *Emma* (vol. IV) of Chapman's edition of *The Novels of Jane Austen: The Text based on Collation of the Early Editions, With Notes Indexes and Illustrations from Contemporary Sources in Five Volumes*, 3rd ed. (Oxford University Press, 1933, reprinted 1988), pp. 506–7.

2.   Jane shared a room with her sister Cassandra all her life. And besides long visits to friends and family, Jane Austen lived outside her parents' home only as a baby at the wet nurse's and then for two periods of schooling as a little girl, one *en famille* with a connection of her mother's, and both together with Cassandra. On her visits to friends as a grown woman, she would expect the kind of sleepover-style intimacy that most of us today leave behind in our teens. Here's Jane Austen describing a visit—when she was twenty-three years old—with her friend Martha Lloyd: "Martha kindly made room for me in her bed, which was the shut-up one in the new nursery. Nurse and the child slept upon the floor, and there we all were in some confusion and great comfort. The bed did exceedingly well for us, both to lie awake in and talk till two o'clock, and to sleep in the rest of the night" (January 8, 1799 letter to Cassandra). Martha Lloyd eventually joined the Austen household—Jane and Cassandra and their mother—and kept house with them at Chawton. Jane Austen lived in a world so full of brothers and sisters, cousins and friends living cheek by jowl that she could find a young woman's "great want of a companion at home" a remarkable circumstance that "may well make any tolerable acquaintance important to her" and give "her a claim on my attention" (April 21, 1805, letter to Cassandra).

    Jane Austen's parents not only raised seven children (an eighth, a son with disabilities, was permanently lodged elsewhere; two of the five other boys did leave home early to be Royal Navy midshipmen; and a third was eventually adopted by wealthy relatives) in a country rectory but also maintained a substantial number of servants and took in paying pupils. The house was so crowded that Jane Austen's father warned a niece that the only time of year there was room for visitors was during his pupils' summer and Christmas vacations. But with barely "a place to hide your head" at the Austens' house even during vacation time, extended family still did come to visit and put on amateur theatricals at the holidays. William Austen-Leigh and Richard Arthur Austen-Leigh, *Jane Austen: Her Life and Letters: A Family Record* (Russell & Russell, 1965), pp. 39–40, 65.

    On the size of the Steventon rectory, see Linda Walker Robinson, "Why Was Jane Austen Sent Away to School at Seven? An Empirical Look at a Vexing Question," Persuasions On-Line (a publication of the Jane Austen Society of North America) 26, no. 1 (winter 2005), http://www.jasna.org/persuasions/on-line/vol26no1/walker.htm. The article is marred by high dudgeon against Jane Austen's parents, justified only by Robinson's apparent assumption that late twentieth- and twenty-first-century childrearing norms—in the wake of what John Zmirak has called "the collapse of the extended family into its unstable 'nuclear' core" (John Zmirak and Denise Matychowiak, *The Bad Catholic's Guide to Wine, Whiskey, & Song: A Spirited Look at Catholic Life and Lore from the Apocalypse to Zinfandel* (Crossroad, 2007), p. 108.)—are the standard by which all parental choices should be judged. But Robinson has dug up many fascinating facts and spins some interesting speculation about the Austens' living arrangements. (Assuming, that is, that her historical judgment is more to be trusted than her logic. Robinson: "By logic alone, we know that Jane Austen had an unhappy childhood. If her home life was happy, then she was exiled from it for three years; if her home life wasn't happy, then it's doubtful her childhood was either.")

3. See Chapman, op. cit., "Indoor games, on the other hand, were a much larger part of domestic life than they are today."

4. From Jane Austen's unfinished novel *The Watsons*: "The Edwards were people of fortune who lived in town and kept their coach; the Watsons inhabited a village about three miles distant, were poor, & had no close carriage; & ever since there had been Balls in the place, the former were accustomed to invite the Latter to dress, dine, & sleep at their House, on every monthly return throughout the winter." For a dramatization of the humiliation that accepting this kind of favor could involve, see "Letter the third: From a young Lady in distress'd Circumstances to her friend" from *Volume the Second* of Jane Austen's juvenilia.

5. See Emma and Mr. Knightley's discussion—on the subject of which, more in the next chapter—of whether Frank Churchill should come pay his respects to his new stepmother even if it might offend the rich aunt and uncle on whom he's financially dependent: "It might not be so easy to burst forth at once into perfect independence, and set all their claims on his gratitude and regard at nought."

6. Thank you, Lionel Yaceczko, for this important insight, not to mention for teaching Billy all that Latin.

7. Partly because we *do* have to be so buttoned up at the office.

8. A husband wouldn't expect to have a say about the flower garden, or manage the household servants; a wife wouldn't expect to help get the hay in, or decide on the family investments. See Chapman, op. cit., especially pp. 509–10, but more, Jane Austen's novels themselves.

9. Interestingly, it's of Mary Crawford that Jane Austen says "her attention was all for men and women." But it's true about Jane Austen herself, too: "Mary and I, after disposing of her father and mother, went to the Liverpool Museum and the British Gallery, and I had some amusement at each, though my preference for men and women always inclines me to attend more to the company than to the sight." April 18, 2011, letter to Cassandra.

10. "She had no separate study to retire to, and most of the work must have been done in the general sitting-room, subject to all kinds of casual interruptions. She was careful that her occupation should not be suspected by servants, or visitors, or any persons beyond her own family party. She wrote upon small sheets of paper which could easily be put away, or covered with a piece of blotting paper. There was, between the front door and the offices, a swing door which creaked when it was opened; but she objected to having this little inconvenience remedied, because it gave her notice when anyone was coming.... I have no doubt that I and my sisters and cousins, in our visits to Chawton, frequently disturbed this mystic process, without having any idea of the mischief that we were doing; certainly we never should have guessed it by any signs of impatience or irritability in the writer." James Edward Austen-Leigh's *Memoir* of his aunt.

11. Jane Austen herself said of being the author of *Pride and Prejudice*: "What a trifle it is, in all its bearings, to the really important points of one's existence, even in this world."

12. Okay, I plead guilty.

13. She was quite sharp, for example, about how little her own comfort and convenience were considered in the move with her parents to Bath from the Steventon rectory where she had grown up. (Her father was retiring in order to make way for his eldest son James at Steventon.) "You are very kind in planning presents for me to make, & my Mother has shewn me exactly the same attention, but as I do not chuse to have Generosity dictated to me, I shall not resolve on giving my cabinet to Anna till the first thought of it has been my own." The miserable bustle of Anne Elliot's unwelcome move from Kellynch to Bath has something of the flavor of Jane Austen's life at this time: "My father's old Ministers are already deserting him to pay their court to his Son; the brown Mare, which as well as the black was to devolve on James at our removal, has not had patience to wait for that, & has settled herself even now at Deane.... & everything else I suppose will be seized by degrees in the same manner. Martha & I work at the books every day."

14. "In short, if I live to be an old Woman, I must expect to wish I had died now; blessed in the tenderness of such a Family, & before I had survived either them or their affection," she wrote in her final illness. May 22, 1817, letter to Anne Sharpe.

CHAPTER EIGHT

1. She was only Emma's governess and the Woodhouses' live-in companion. "Had she been a person of consequence herself, he would have come I dare say; and it

would not have signified whether he did or no. Can you think your friend behind-hand in these sort of considerations? Do you suppose she does not often say all this to herself?" Mr. Knightley argues to Emma.

2. "No, Emma, your amiable young man can be amiable only in French, not in English. He may be very 'aimable,' have very good manners, and be very agreeable; but he can have no English delicacy towards the feelings of other people: nothing really amiable about him."

3. When people in Jane Austen's day said *nature*, they sometimes meant "rocks and mountains," trees and animals, and so forth. But sometimes they were thinking more along the lines of "human nature." Newton had discovered natural laws that governed the physical universe, and people tended to think in a similar way about the principles that human beings should live by. They thought of rules for "right conduct" as part of another kind of natural law, which could also be discovered by applying reason to our observations from nature. Except that the nature to be observed in this case was the behavior of human beings, not of falling objects. And the laws you could derive from those observations were the principles by which men and women ought to conduct their lives, not the laws of gravity or inertia.

    The sense of a law of nature in human affairs as something like the laws of physics—a set of principles that underlies and explains human behavior the way Newton's law of gravitation explains how objects fall—was connected with an older idea of "natural law" based on the realization that there are some moral axioms that every human being knows without being taught them, just the same way we *have* to think 2+2=4, not 2+2=5.

4. Thomas Jefferson, Second Inaugural Address, 1805.

5. *Not* that they believed in some kind of "prosperity gospel," where if you get into God's good graces all your problems will melt away and you'll be made instantly rich and happy. (Or that everything was "all for the best in the best of all possible worlds," the philosophy formulated by Gottfried Leibniz and embodied in the character of Dr. Pangloss in Voltaire's *Candide*.) They didn't see the connection between right conduct and happiness as a crude *quid pro quo*—you do what God wants and He rewards you with success—so much as an expression of a natural relationship between doing the right thing and being right with God, other people, and the world in general.

6. A modern natural law philosopher, J. Budziszewski, does a good job of explaining what it means for certain moral principles to be axiomatic. There are some things, he points out, that you "can't not know." Just the same way that you *can't not know* that 2+2=4, you *can't not know* that injustice is wrong, or that courage

is good. We can argue about what counts as injustice, or about whether or not someone was really being brave or foolish in a particular case. But no one can actually look down on another person for having courage (only for showing off, or being stupid, or for something else other than the actual bravery). And we can't really approve of unfairness, either, or admire cheating for its own sake. (We only make excuses for it, or do it because we think the end justifies the means, or admire a cheater's cleverness.) Unfairness always needs justifying by something, while fairness is self-justifying. J. Budziszewski, *What We Can't Not Know: A Guide* (Ignatius Press revised and expanded edition, 2011).

This is exactly what Mr. Knightley is talking about when he argues that Frank Churchill's aunt and uncle won't be able to help respecting him if he does the right thing—even though they're actually trying to keep him from doing it for their own selfish reasons.

7. The "natural light" of her mind, in the absence of good example or good principles from her parents.

8. One more example: Mrs. Bennet sends Jane to Netherfield on horseback on a rainy day, hoping she'll catch a cold and have to stay for a few days, so that propinquity will bring the rich Mr. Bingley to an early proposal of marriage. And Mr. Bennet doesn't step in to put a stop to her scheming. Instead, when Jane really does get sick, he indulges his wit at his wife's expense, as usual: "Well, my dear…if your daughter should have a dangerous fit of illness, if she should die, it would be a comfort to know that it was all in pursuit of Mr. Bingley, and under your orders." When Jane recovers faster than her mother hopes and Mrs. Bennet, "who had calculated on her daughters remaining at Netherfield till the following Tuesday, which would exactly finish Jane's week," won't send the carriage to pick them up, Jane asks Mr. Bingley to lend her his and goes home as soon as she's well, rather than taking every advantage of the opportunity to ply Mr. Bingley with her charms. Jane Austen's commentary on Jane's resistance to her mother's manipulations: "Jane was firm where she felt herself to be right."

The equally principled Mr. Darcy sees that Jane and Elizabeth live by a high standard that they haven't learned from their parents. It's one of the reasons he can't help loving Elizabeth: Considering the "total want of propriety so frequently, so almost uniformly betrayed by…[Mrs. Bennet], by your three younger sisters, and occasionally even by your father," Mr. Darcy thinks it should console Elizabeth to know that, "to have conducted yourselves so as to avoid any share of the like censure, is praise no less generally bestowed on you and your eldest sister, than it is honourable to the sense and disposition of both."

9. For example, "While politics and Mr. Elton were talked over, Emma could fairly surrender all her attention to the pleasantness of her neighbour" and, in *Northanger Abbey*, "Henry suffered the subject to decline…he shortly found himself arrived at politics; and from politics, it was an easy step to silence."

10. Though her heroes and heroines do think it's part of their duty to be both fair and charitable to people in need.

11. When Captain Tilney wrecks her brother's engagement, Catherine is willing to see the whole situation fairly, instead of judging everything by "family partiality, or a desire for revenge."

12. Fanny hesitates to tell Edmund her real opinion of his pursuit of Mary Crawford even when he asks her to, partly because she's afraid that as an "interested" party—being in love with Edmund herself—she can't be an impartial advisor. That's her scrupulous sense of justice. She thinks it wouldn't be right to pose as a disinterested friend while giving advice that can't help but be tainted by her interest in Edmund.

13. As Edmund says, "Family squabbling is the greatest evil of all, and we had better do any thing than be altogether by the ears."

14. À la Uriah Heep in Dickens's *David Copperfield*, to drag in Victorian unpleasantness one last time.

CHAPTER NINE

1. Catherine is "My dearest creature" to Isabella "after an acquaintance of eight or nine days." "I quite doated on you the first moment I saw you," she tells her.

2. "There is nothing I would not do for those who are really my friends, I have no notion of loving people by halves; it is not in my nature."

3. "Nothing, she declared, should induce her to join the set before her dear Catherine could join it too: 'I assure you,' said she, 'I would not stand up without your dear sister for all the world; for if I did we should certainly be separated the whole evening.' Catherine accepted this kindness with gratitude, and they continued as they were for three minutes longer, when Isabella, who had been talking to James on the other side of her, turned to his sister and whispered, 'My dear creature, I am afraid I must leave you, your brother is so amazingly impatient to begin; I know you will not mind my going away.'"

4. Isabella is shamelessly using Catherine in pursuit of Catherine's brother James, under a misapprehension that he's rich. In pursuit of her own plan for a drive to Clifton (during which she's hoping James will propose to her), Isabella uses everything—argument, peer pressure, "expos[ing Catherine's] feelings to the notice of others" (in front of both their brothers she accuses Catherine of putting

interest in Henry Tilney and his sister ahead of friendship with herself), cold resentment, and even turning Catherine's brother against her—to persuade Catherine to break her second engagement for a walk with the Tilneys on a false excuse. What Isabella is trying to talk Catherine into doing would be an act of rudeness so appalling on Catherine's part that her acquaintance with the Tilneys could never recover from it. And Isabella knows how much Catherine likes Henry. She just doesn't care.

5.   For who she is: "Open, candid, artless, guileless, with affections strong but simple, forming no pretensions, knowing no disguise."

6.   They can't talk about Mr. Collins—Charlotte knows exactly what Elizabeth thinks about him, and about her for marrying him. And they can't talk about Elizabeth's life either. If they did, everything Elizabeth said about men or her own marriage prospects would be a tacit criticism of Charlotte; Elizabeth would be reminding her friend that her own standards are so much higher. The last completely honest thing Elizabeth says to Charlotte is when Charlotte first announces her engagement and Elizabeth can't help "crying out, 'Engaged to Mr. Collins! my dear Charlotte,—impossible!'"

7.   Elizabeth: "My dear Jane, Mr. Collins is a conceited, pompous, narrow-minded, silly man; you know he is, as well as I do; and you must feel, as well as I do, that the woman who married him cannot have a proper way of thinking. You shall not defend her, though it is Charlotte Lucas. You shall not, for the sake of one individual, change the meaning of principle and integrity."

8.   "Mrs. Weston was the object of a regard, which had its basis in gratitude and esteem. Harriet would be loved as one to whom she could be useful. For Mrs. Weston there was nothing to be done; for Harriet every thing."

9.   For a high-quality example, see F. Scott Fitzgerald's "Bernice Bobs Her Hair."

10.   Apart from everything else squirm-worthy about Emma's behavior, don't miss that she glosses Harriet's highly ambivalent statement of her intentions as "now that you are so completely decided."

11.   Or, in this case, as a farmer's wife. "And as for Harriet, I will venture to say that she cannot gain by the acquaintance. Hartfield will only put her out of conceit with all the other places she belongs to. She will grow just refined enough to be uncomfortable with those among whom birth and circumstances have placed her home."

12.   At least, it's obvious to Mr. Knightley.

13.   Distinctions based on wealth and "rank" were more important in her day than now. Or at least their importance was more openly acknowledged back then. We're not like Sir Walter and Miss Elliot, with noble cousins like Lady Dalrymple

and Miss Carterert to suck up to, on one hand, and a Mrs. Clay—a lowly employee's widowed daughter who's willing to make it her full-time job to suck up to us—on the other.

14. "[Reginald] is less polished, less insinuating than Manwaring, and is comparatively deficient in the power of saying those delightful things which put one in good humour with oneself and all the world." Lady Susan doesn't want *ever* to deal with other people as equals. She busily manipulates everyone, and then she relaxes by enjoying other people's flattery.

15. That's even in trivial things, like her height. Harriet's not as smart as Emma is. She's got only a very basic education, and she's very unsophisticated.

16. "Every body had supposed they must be so fond of each other."

17. As Emma tells Harriet: "We are always forced to be acquainted whenever she comes to Highbury."

18. But a friendship between Emma and Jane Fairfax wouldn't be unequal in the opposite direction. It's not that Emma could do nothing for Jane. As a matter of fact, she could benefit her in ways that no one else in Highbury can. Emma is Jane's only chance at really "equal society" when she's staying with her relatives—someone she could talk to on her own intellectual level. Jane spends what must be monotonous days with her *very* talkative aunt, good-natured but not very bright, and her old grandmother who's "almost past every thing but tea and quadrille." And, more and more as the novel goes on, Jane is forced to spend time with the awful Mrs. Elton, a vain, stupid woman who patronizes Jane and presumes to arrange her future. *That* relationship is a much uglier version of what Emma is up to with Harriet. Mrs. Elton is incapable of recognizing Jane Fairfax's real superiority, not to mention any limits that good manners might suggest to what extent she should plan Jane's life out for her. Mrs. Elton thinks she is doing Jane Fairfax as much a favor by finding her a job that Jane has explicitly and repeatedly said she doesn't want, as by giving her a ride in her carriage.

On this subject Emma, Mr. Knightley, and Mrs. Weston have yet another one of the discussions among Jane Austen's ladies and gentlemen about their neighbors' conduct. But in *this* disagreement with Mr. Knightley (though Mr. Knightley articulates some true and very interesting principles), I think Emma has the more accurate diagnosis of what's really going on between Mrs. Elton and Jane Fairfax.

Mr. Knightley: "Mrs. Elton does not talk *to* Miss Fairfax as she speaks *of* her. We all know the difference between the the pronouns he and she and thou, the plainest-spoken among us; we all feel the influence of something beyond common civility in our personal intercourse with each other—a something more early implanted. We cannot give any body the disagreeable hints that we may have been very full of the hour before. We feel things differently. And besides the operation of this, as a general principle, you may be sure that Miss Fairfax awes Mrs. Elton by her superiority both of mind and manner; and that face to face Mrs. Elton treats her with all the respect which she has a claim to. Such a woman as Jane Fairfax probably never fell in Mrs. Elton's way before—and no degree of vanity can prevent her acknowledging her own comparative littleness in action, if not in consciousness."

Emma: "I have no faith in Mrs. Elton's acknowledging herself the inferior in thought, word, or deed; or in her being under any restraint beyond her own scanty rule of good-breeding. I cannot imagine that she will not continually be insulting her visitor with praise, encouragement, and offers of service; that she will not be continually detailing her magnificent intentions, from the procuring her a permanent situation to the including her in those delightful exploring parties which are to take place in the barouche-landau."

19. With absolutely no basis in fact; it's all straight out of Emma's over-active imagination.

CHAPTER TEN

1. Cheryl Wetzstein, "Hopeless Romantics Yearn for Soul Mates: Study Finds Their Bliss Won't Last," *Washington Times,* September 6, 2010, http://www.washington times.com/news/2010/sep/6/hopeless-romantics-yearn-for-soul-mates/print/, reporting on W. Bradford Wilcox and Jeffrey Dew, "Is Love a Flimsy Foundation? Soul-mate versus Institutional Models of Marriage," *Social Science,* vol. 39, issue 5, September 2010, pp. 687–99.

2. Harriet Smith, "a good-tempered, soft-hearted girl, not likely to be very, very determined against any young man who told her he loved her," is not Jane Austen's ideal woman. Nor is Lydia Bennet, who "had wanted only encouragement to attach herself to any body."

3. Or possibly for two types, what C. S. Lewis calls "a terrestrial and an infernal Venus." C. S. Lewis, *The Screwtape Letters with Screwtape Proposes a Toast* (HarperCollins, 2001), p. 108.

4. Thus Anne defends Captain Benwick against the imputation that his "soft sort of manner" betrays a lack of "spirit," but she doesn't mean "to represent Captain Benwick's manners as the very best that could possibly be."

5. Even his commentary on the weather makes "her feel that the commonest, dullest, most threadbare topic might be rendered interesting by the skill of the speaker," something that's true about her own conversation, too—as when, for

example, Elizabeth explains how her sisters were educated, or parries Lady
Catherine's rude question about how old she is.

6. "Had he married a more amiable woman, he might have been made still more
    respectable than he was:—he might even have been made amiable himself....
    But Mrs. John Dashwood was a strong caricature of himself;—more narrow-
    minded and selfish."

7. John agrees with Fanny that the three thousand pounds that might make
    all the difference to his sisters' marriage prospects is better not separated
    from the enormous fortune their son will inherit: "The time may come when
    Harry will regret that such a sum was parted with. If he should have a
    numerous family, for instance, it would be a very convenient addition."
    Interestingly, in light of the "Friendship, the School of Love" principle,
    Fanny Dashwood picks her friends on exactly the same impulse as she seems
    to have picked her husband: "As for Lady Middleton, [Fanny Dashwood]
    found her one of the most charming women in the world! Lady Middleton
    was equally pleased with Mrs. Dashwood. There was a kind of cold-hearted
    selfishness on both sides, which mutually attracted them; and they sym-
    pathised with each other in an insipid propriety of demeanour, and a gen-
    eral want of understanding."

8. Even before he met his bride, Mr. Elton thought quite a lot of himself. But she
    inspires him to hitherto-unseen outbursts of touchy wounded pride and rude
    put-downs of other people, including his cruel public snubbing of Harriet Smith
    at the ball at the Crown—which the Eltons celebrate with "smiles of high glee"
    at each other.

9. That's how Robert ends up with both his brother's inheritance and his brother's
    fiancée—and how Lucy (that fiancée) ultimately does find herself in possession
    of the fortune that was her aim in engaging herself to Robert's brother Edward
    in the first place.

10. "It was impossible for any one to be more thoroughly good-natured or more
    determined to be happy than Mrs. Palmer. The studied indifference, insolence,
    and discontent of her husband gave her no pain: and when he scolded or abused
    [verbally insulted, that is; Jane Austen doesn't mean physically abused] her, she
    was highly diverted. 'Mr. Palmer is so droll!' said she, in a whisper to Elinor. 'He
    is always out of humour.'"

11. "He was not an ill-tempered man, not so often unreasonably cross as to deserve
    such a reproach; but his temper was not his great perfection."

12. When John Knightley rides to the Westons' house for a dinner engagement in
    the carriage with Emma, instead of his wife, Emma is "not...equal to give the

pleased assent, which no doubt he was in the habit of receiving, to emulate the 'Very true, my love,' which must have been usually administered by his traveling companion" in response to his intemperate expressions of righteous indignation against Mr. Weston—for having a dinner party that requires John Knightley to go out in bad weather and miss seeing his children after dinner.

13.   "She was a woman who spent her days in sitting, nicely dressed, on a sofa, doing some long piece of needlework, of little use and no beauty, thinking more of her pug than her children, but very indulgent to the latter when it did not put herself to inconvenience, guided in everything important by Sir Thomas, and in smaller concerns by her sister." Jane Austen's description of Lady Bertram's accomplishments during her husband's extended absence in the West Indies pretty much sums up her life's work: "She had done a great deal of carpet-work and made many yards of fringe."

14.   Partly because he had "formed her mind" as well as "engaged her affections."

15.   "I am perfectly persuaded that the tempers had better be unlike; I mean unlike in the flow of the spirits, in the manners, in the inclination for much or little company, in the propensity to talk or be silent, to be grave or to be gay. Some opposition here is, I am thoroughly convinced, friendly to matrimonial happiness," says Edmund in the throes of love for Mary Crawford.

16.   Fanny thinks, of Mary Crawford, "She might love, but she did not deserve Edmund by any other sentiment. Fanny believed there was scarcely a second feeling in common between them; and she may be forgiven by older sages for looking on the chance of Miss Crawford's future improvement as nearly desperate, for thinking that if Edmund's influence in this season of love had already done so little in clearing her judgment, and regulating her notions, his worth would be finally wasted on her even in years of matrimony."

But Jane Austen opines, "Experience might have hoped more for any young people so circumstanced, and impartiality would not have denied to Miss Crawford's nature that participation of the general nature of women which would lead her to adopt the opinions of the man she loved and respected as her own."

Take note that despite the obiter dictum about our "general nature," it's not just women in Jane Austen who rise—or fall—to the level of the person they marry. Besides John Dashwood, there's Charles Musgrove, who "was civil and agreeable; in sense and temper he was undoubtedly superior to his wife, but not of powers, or conversation, or grace, to make the past, as [he and Anne] were connected together, at all a dangerous contemplation; though, at the same time, Anne could believe, with Lady Russell, that a more equal match might have greatly improved him; and that a woman of real understanding might have given more consequence to his character, and more usefulness, rationality, and elegance to his habits and pursuits." And there's also Frank Churchill whose "character will improve" under the influence of Jane Fairfax. See chapter 11, n. 33 below.

And while Anne Elliot believes that being persuadable is "no bad part of a woman's portion," notice that she's maintaining that opinion in opposition to the position of Captain Wentworth, her future husband—who eventually comes around to her opinion on this point, rather than the other way around!

17. "Could [Henry Crawford] have been satisfied with the conquest of one amiable woman's affections, could he have found sufficient exultation in overcoming the reluctance, in working himself into the esteem and tenderness of Fanny Price, there would have been every probability of success and felicity for him. His affection had already done something. Her influence over him had already given him some influence over her. Would he have deserved more, there can be no doubt that more would have been obtained, especially when that marriage had taken place, which would have given him the assistance of her conscience in subduing her first inclination, and brought them very often together. Would he have persevered, and uprightly, Fanny must have been his reward, and a reward very voluntarily bestowed, within a reasonable period from Edmund's marrying Mary."

18. "It is not by equality of merit that you can be won. That is out of the question. It is he who sees and worships your merit the strongest, who loves you most devotedly, that has a best right to a return. There I build my confidence. By that right I do and will deserve you."

19. Henry really *sees* and notices Fanny in a way that Edmund may never get around to doing. Listen to Henry describing her to his sister: "Attending with such ineffable sweetness and patience to all the demands of her aunt's stupidity, working with her, and for her, her colour beautifully heightened as she leant over the work, then returning to her seat to finish a note which she was previously engaged in writing for that stupid woman's service, and all this with such unpretending gentleness, so much as if it were a matter of course that she was not to have a moment at her own command, her hair arranged as neatly as it always is, and one little curl falling forward as she wrote, which she now and then shook back, and in the midst of all this, still speaking at intervals to *me*, or listening, and as if she liked to listen, to what I said."

20. "Yes, Mary, my Fanny will feel a difference indeed: a daily, hourly difference, in the behaviour of every being who approaches her; and it will be the completion

of my happiness to know that I am the doer of it, that I am the person to give the consequence so justly her due. Now she is dependent, helpless, friendless, neglected, forgotten."

21. Their niece Louisa Knight remembered overhearing the sisters discussing this point.

22. If Jane Austen had been writing sentimental melodrama, a rake like Henry Crawford might actually have had a better chance of getting the girl. His wicked past could be redeemed by his love for a pure woman. Jane Austen was more realistic. Her clear-eyed understanding of human nature told her that a man of Henry Crawford's habits with women is, in fact and reality, very unlikely to pull off a happy ending with one woman—even if he has truly fallen in love with her. Henry Crawford's punishment doesn't come from some deus ex machina arranged by the novelist. Henry just simply and naturally falls right back into the old ruts that his past choices have worn into his personality, and loses Fanny as a result. If he'd been a little less used to grabbing at "immediate pleasure" in general (and more accustomed to occasionally doing without something he wanted), or if he'd been less addicted to the heady ego trips he reguarly gets from breaking down women's resistance and making them fall in love with him against their better judgment, then things with Fanny might have worked out for him: "But he was pressed to stay for Mrs. Fraser's party; his staying was made of flattering consequence, and he was to meet Mrs. Rushworth there. Curiosity and vanity were both engaged, and the temptation of immediate pleasure was too strong for a mind unused to make any sacrifice to right; he resolved to defer his Norfolk journey, resolved that writing should answer the purpose of it, or that its purpose was unimportant—and staid. He saw Mrs. Rushworth.... He was mortified, he could not bear to be thrown off by a woman whose smiles had been so wholly at his command."

23. On "true merit" on both sides, in fact, as well as on "true love."

24. Think how, at the end of *Persuasion*, Anne Elliot's love for Captain Wentworth is heightened by the possibility of a naval war: "She gloried in being a sailor's wife, but she must pay the tax of quick alarm for belonging to a profession which is, if possible, more distinguished in its domestic virtues than its national importance." Anne's tender heart has to stretch to bear the risks that make Wentworth the truly admirable man she loves.

25. Almost all of us having had more love affairs than any Jane Austen heroine. And if we haven't, we've at least seen more up close.

26. In the worst cases (where what Jane Austen would call a man's "character" is really bad) he'll deliberately refine whatever works with one woman—what feels at the

time like something arising naturally from the unique chemistry of their relationship—into a technique that he uses deliberately on a succession of women, like the double headphones Rob Lowe used to get Demi Moore into bed in *About Last Night*.

27. What Jane Austen calls "infatuation" or being "bewitched."

28. And obviously Jane Austen's heroines *do* feel the chemistry; they experience real love as intense, intoxicating, bewitching.

29. "She respected, she esteemed, she was grateful to him, she felt a real interest in his welfare; and she only wanted to know how far she wished that welfare to depend upon herself, and how far it would be for the happiness of both that she should employ the power, which her fancy told her she still possessed, of bringing on the renewal of his addresses." After Jane's letters about Lydia arrive, Elizabeth's heart tells her the answer: "It [Elizabeth's fear that Darcy won't want to marry her now, because of Lydia] was, on the contrary, exactly calculated to make her understand her own wishes; and never had she so honestly felt that she could have loved him, as now, when all love must be vain."

CHAPTER ELEVEN

1. Which, incidentally, was Jane Austen's earlier title for *Pride and Prejudice*.

2. "At present, I know him so well, that I think him really handsome; or, at least, almost so." In fact, Jane Austen tells us Edward is "not handsome." Elinor may be wearing rose-colored glasses, but at least she has enough self-knowledge to realize she's got them on.

Likewise, Mr. Knightley's jaundiced view of Frank Churchill tips him off to his feelings for Emma: "He had been in love with Emma, and jealous of Frank Churchill, from about the same period, one sentiment having probably enlightened him as to the other."

The dramatic reversals of feeling that Mr. Knightley undergoes toward Frank Churchill in the course of discovering that Frank hasn't really broken Emma's heart, and that Emma really loves him (Mr. Knightley) demonstrate Jane Austen's keen awareness of how the judgments of even the wisest of us are subject to the vicissitudes of our personal desires: "[Mr. Knightley] had found [Emma] agitated and low.—Frank Churchill was a villain. [Mr. Knightley] heard her declare that she had never loved [Frank]. Frank Churchill's character was not desperate.—She was his own Emma, by hand and word, when they returned to the house; and if he could have thought of Frank Churchill then he might have deemed him a very good sort of fellow."

Our postmodernists notice exactly the same thing about human nature. But Jane Austen is so much more ambitious than they are. While their idea is that we have to resign ourselves to float helplessly on the tide of our unaccountable preferences and irrational desires—"the heart wants what it wants," in Woody Allen's famous excuse for himself—Jane Austen expects us to rise above the distorting effects on our vision, to use our self-knowledge to correct our skewed judgment, and to strive for and actually attain balance and a measure of objectivity.

3.   Fanny exclaims scornfully, about Mary Crawford: "The woman who could speak of [Edmund], and speak only of his appearance!" But there's all the difference in the world between keeping looks in proportion to more important qualities—Jane Austen thoroughly approved of that—and not being able to see them clearly. It's the clear-sighted Fanny who "still continued to think Mr. Crawford very plain, in spite of her two cousins having repeatedly proved the contrary," while the deluded Maria and Julia are undergoing this transformation in their perceptions: "[Henry Crawford] was not handsome: no, when they first saw him he was absolutely plain . . . but still he was the gentleman, with a pleasing address. The second meeting proved him not so very plain: he was plain, to be sure, but then he had so much countenance, and his teeth were so good, and he was so well made, that one soon forgot he was plain; and after a third interview, after dining in company with him at the Parsonage, he was no longer allowed to be called so by anybody."

4.   Notice what Fanny Price thinks when her uncle is trying to pressure her into marrying Henry Crawford. Her uncle asks her, "'Have you any reason, child, to think ill of Mr. Crawford's temper?' 'No, sir.' She longed to add, 'but of his principles I have.'" Fanny takes it for granted that everyone (including the overbearing Sir Thomas Bertram) knows it's a terrible idea to marry a man whose principles you can't trust. Besides this dialogue between Sir Thomas and Fanny, think of Anne and Captain Wentworth canvassing the match between Benwick and Louisa Musgrove: "But it appears—I should hope it would be a very good match. There are on both sides good principles and good temper."

5.   "Break Your Heart," written by Taio Cruz and Fraser T. Smith and performed by Taio Cruz (2009).

6.   Perhaps not quite as clearly as Henry's sister, who has actually heard him brag about it, but clearly enough.

7.   It's no accident that Jane Austen uses the word "character" to mean two things that we think of today as very different, but that she knew often coincide. "Character" in Jane Austen's day could mean the actual reality of what you're like as a

person, as when Elizabeth says, about Wickham, "When *my* eyes were opened to his real character...." But it could also mean just your reputation, as when Mr. Gardiner hopes, about Lydia and Wickham's future, that "among different people, where they may each have a character to preserve, they will both be more prudent." In reality, there's more overlap between people's reputations—especially if those reputations are grounded in knowledge of their past behavior—and their real characters than we recovering Romantics like to think.

8.   "Henry Crawford had too much sense not to feel the worth of good principles in a wife, though he was too little accustomed to serious reflection to know them by their proper name; but when he talked of her having such a steadiness and regularity of conduct, such a high notion of honour, and such an observance of decorum as might warrant any man in the fullest dependence on her faith and integrity, he expressed what was inspired by the knowledge of her being well principled...."

9.   Which is one reason that it's very foolish to ignore any information about how a man talks and acts when you aren't around, as Emma does when Mr. Knightley tells her that Mr. Elton "does not mean to throw himself away. I have heard him speak with great animation of a large family of young ladies that his sisters are intimate with, who have all twenty thousand pounds apiece."

10.   "Though they had now been acquainted a month, she could not be satisfied that she really knew his character. That he was a sensible man, an agreeable man,— that he talked well, professed good opinions, seemed to judge properly and as a man of principle,—this was all clear enough. He certainly knew what was right, nor could she fix on any one article of moral duty evidently transgressed; but yet she would have been afraid to answer for his conduct. She distrusted the past, if not the present. The names which occasionally dropt of former associates, the allusions to former practices and pursuits, suggested suspicions not favorable of what he had been. She saw that there had been bad habits...and, though he might now think very differently, who could answer for the true sentiments of a clever, cautious man, grown old enough to appreciate a fair character?"

    Given the contradiction that she has detected between his past actions and the standards he claims now, Mr. Elliot's smooth manners and his ability to please everyone equally are not in his favor: Anne "felt that she could so much more depend upon the sincerity of those who sometimes looked or said a careless or a hasty thing, than of those whose presence of mind never varied, whose tongue never slipped."

11.   "The manoeuvres of selfishness and duplicity must ever be revolting, but I have heard nothing that really surprises me."

12. See, for example, Nicholas Carr, *The Shallows: What the Internet Is Doing to Our Brains* (W.W. Norton and Company, 2010); William Powers, *Hamlet's Blackberry: A Practical Philosophy for Building a Good Life in the Digital Age* (HarperCollins, 2010); and Sherry Turkle, *Alone Together: Why We Expect More from Technology and Less from Each Other* (Basic Books, 2011).

13. If you don't believe me, check out those rare early color photos from the Great Depression. Everyone in the 1930s and '40s, and I mean *everyone*—frighteningly skinny people in the Dust Bowl, sharecroppers actually chopping cotton— dressed with more formality than we do now. "Captured: America in Color from 1939–1943 [sic]," *Denver Post* online July 26, 2010, http://blogs.denverpost.com/ captured/2010/07/26/captured-america-in-color-from-1939-1943/2363/.

14. Hitting a watershed with the 1970s jogging craze, when suddenly it was the done thing to be seen in public in your sweats, and yet every middle-aged woman still had that one last hat from the Jackie O. era gathering dust on a shelf in her closet, and one last pair of white gloves in a drawer somewhere.

15. Miss Manners permitted an e-thank you note only as a prelude to an ink-and-paper letter. Sticklers for grammar and punctuation fretted that email would be the death of formal correspondence, possibly even killing off standard English.

16. Jane Fairfax would be able to sympathize with William Powers's concerns (op. cit.) about the harried lives we live today because of continual demands on our attention via electronic media, and with Sherry Turkle's worry (op. cit.) that teenagers are stressed by the need to be constantly "on" to respond in a timely manner to every text from their friends: "'Oh, Miss Woodhouse, the comfort of being sometimes alone!' seemed to burst from an over-charged heart...."

17. "She had never heard of him before his entrance into the —shire Militia.... Of his former way of life, nothing had been known in Hertfordshire but what he told himself." That's one reason soldiers and marines are typically very risky suitors in Jane Austen novels: Wickham, Fanny Price's father, and Captain Hunter in *The Watsons*. (Jane Fairfax's father is the exception that proves the rule.) They were the one class of strangers who *could* typically get themselves introduced to girls without anybody really knowing their past—just on the strength of their military rank and the short-term relationships they'd formed with the other officers. (Jane Austen's family connection with and enthusiastic boostership for the British Navy probably comes into play here, as well. There's absolutely no doubt which side Jane Austen would cheer for in the Army-Navy game.)

18. An introduction was no longer a guarantee that a trustworthy social network had enough collective knowledge about a guy to give him a recommendation.

People had more freedom to reinvent themselves, to start again with a clean slate; guys were judged mostly on what they did and said in the present.

19. Today if you meet a new guy, it's harder for him to confine what you learn about him to what he tells you about himself. You can always google him, and he knows it.

20. You don't have to hire a private investigator or demand that potential suitors agree to a credit check to be able to do some vetting of your prospects.

21. The "misery" that makes Anne "shudder" to realize she might have been persuaded to marry Mr. Elliot and then been horrified to find out the truth about her husband when "time had disclosed all, too late."

22. "They wanted him to make a fine figure in the world in some manner or other. His mother wished to interest him in political concerns, to get him into parliament, or to see him connected with some of the great men of the day. Mrs. John Dashwood wished it likewise; but in the mean while, till one of these superior blessings could be attained, it would have quieted her ambition to see him driving a barouche. But Edward had no turn for great men or barouches. All his wishes centered in domestic comfort and the quiet of private life."

23. Even where there's no romantic interest involved, she's going to gravitate toward that kind of person, as Elinor does to Colonel Brandon, in whom "alone, of all her new acquaintance did Elinor find a person who could, in any degree, claim the respect of abilities, excite the interest of friendship, or give pleasure as a companion." If you're a principled woman yourself, spending time with a principled man like Brandon means being able to relax from the meaningless bustle—the essential nothingness of dealing with people who grab and manipulate and care only about superficials—into something genuine. It's a kind of "cut through the crap" experience—if you can use that expression when you're talking about Elinor Dashwood.

24. Jane Austen put a lot of distance between her faulty-tempered men and the kind of physically dangerous man who doesn't belong in a Jane Austen novel at all. That's the difference between General Tilney as he really is—a bad-tempered man who makes life in his family really unpleasant by insisting that everyone cater to his whims—and General Tilney as he appears to Catherine's Gothic novel-addled mind—capable of murdering his wife. The kinds of things Catherine imagines about the general aren't material for a Jane Austen novel; in the regions her heroines inhabit, crimes of that magnitude don't go undetected and unpunished. Murders and false imprisonment are fodder for peace-keeping authorities and the justice system, not material for novels of manners in which

women thread their way through social minefields with no weapons but their good principles, their wits, and their social skills. "Charming as were all Mrs. Radcliffe's works, and charming even as were the works of all her imitators, it was not in them perhaps that human nature, at least in the Midland counties of England, was to be looked for. Of the Alps and Pyrenees, with their pine forests and their vices, they might give a faithful delineation; and Italy, Switzerland, and the south of France might be as fruitful in horrors as they were there represented. Catherine dared not doubt beyond her own country, and even of that, if hard pressed, would have yielded the northern and western extremities. But in the central part of England there was surely some security for the existence even of a wife not beloved, in the laws of the land, and the manners of the age. Murder was not tolerated, servants were not slaves, and neither poison nor sleeping potions to be procured, like rhubarb, from every druggist."

　　And the faults in Dr. Grant's and John Knightley's tempers are so mild, compared to those of a violently bad-tempered man, that Jane Austen and her characters hesitate even to say their tempers are actually *bad*. We've seen that John Knightley was "not so often unreasonably cross as to deserve" to be called "an ill-tempered man," but that "his temper was not his great perfection." And Fanny bites her tongue rather than call Dr. Grant's temper bad: "Whatever profession Dr. Grant had chosen, he would have taken a— not a good temper into it."

　　And yet Jane Austen is quite clear that even these men's mildly uncertain tempers can cause quite enough misery. Henry Tilney on the subject of his parents' marriage: "He loved her, I am persuaded, as well as it was possible for him to—we have not all, you know, the same tenderness of disposition—and I will not pretend to say that while she lived, she might not often have had much to bear, but though his temper injured her, his judgment never did. His value of her was sincere; and, if not permanently, he was truly afflicted by her death."

25.　From a bedtime prayer Jane Austen wrote: "Bring to our knowledge every fault of temper and every evil habit in which we have indulged to the discomfort of our fellow-creatures."

26.　Jane Austen can criticize characters even for not saying anything at all, as she does the aunt in "Catherine, or the Bower" who "continued silent & Gloomy and was a restraint upon the vivacity of her companions."

27.　Fanny sees Mary very differently from how Edmund does: "so partial and so angry, and so little scrupulous of what she said" and "I knew she would be very angry with me."

28. That would include me, I'm sorry to say—though I'm not quite as bad as I used to be.

29. Like "character." See note 7 above.

30. As in Mr. Weston's "friendly and social disposition," Elizabeth Watson's similarly "hospitable, social temper" or Susan Price's "disposition so totally different from [Fanny's] own": Susan has got an "open" and energetic temperament (Susan "tried to be useful, where *she* [Fanny] could only have gone away and cried") in contrast to Fanny's "more supine and yielding temper." Or consider the contrast between Bingley and Darcy: "Bingley was endeared to Darcy by the easiness, openness, ductility of his temper, though no disposition could offer a greater contrast to his own, and though with his own he never appeared dissatisfied." Note that Henry Crawford's "temper" in these two distinct senses comes under discussion in different contexts. Fanny has no objection at all to Henry's temper in the first sense; she agrees with Sir Thomas that she has no reason "to think ill of Mr. Crawford's temper." But talking to Edmund, she prefaces her objection to Henry's principles with an objection to his temper in the other sense, that of temperament: "It is not merely in *temper* that I consider him as totally unsuited to myself; though, in *that* respect, I think the difference between us too great, infinitely too great: his spirits often oppress me."

31. They also compare minds that are firm and persevering to those that are yielding, "supine," and persuadable.

32. He talks about her "superiority of mind and manner," refers to "such a woman as Jane Fairfax," and so forth.

33. That's how he puts it at first, but it's really Mr. Knightley in particular—who says of himself "I love an open temper"—and *not* every man in general, who wants that particular disposition in a wife. When it comes out that Jane Fairfax is secretly engaged to Frank Churchill, it never occurs to anyone, Mr. Knightley included, to think that Jane's reserve will be a handicap to their happiness, or that Frank Churchill will ever regret choosing her. (Just the opposite, in fact. Here's Mr. Knightley on Frank Churchill's prospects: "As he is, beyond a doubt, really attached to Miss Fairfax, and will soon, it may be hoped, have the advantage of being constantly with her, I am very ready to believe his character will improve, and acquire from her's [sic] the steadiness and delicacy of principle that it wants.") Mr. Knightley's value for an open temper in a woman doesn't really apply to all men.

And it may not necessarily even be the absolute truth about Mr. Knightley himself. It's not that he's being dishonest; it's just that certain circumstances may obscure his clear vision of his own mind and heart. It seems that whenever Jane Austen characters are thinking that they could never love some particular person because of a temperamental dissimilarity between them, it inevitably turns out that they're not *really* considering the question in the abstract at all. They're already in love with a person who happens to have one sort of "temper," so that of course the opposite temperament—the kind that the person they're in love with *doesn't* have—looks deficient in comparison.

Notice that by the time he's explaining that he could never love Jane Fairfax on account of her reserve and his love for an open temper, Mr. Knightley is already realizing that he's in love with Emma.

Notice, too, that Anne Elliot's preference for an open temper was formed by her "early impressions"—in other words, by having fallen in love with Frederick Wentworth before she ever met Mr. Elliot. "Her early impressions were incurable. She prized the frank, the open-hearted, the eager character beyond all others. Warmth and enthusiasm did captivate her still." And take note that Fanny Price states her opposite temperamental preference—she feels oppressed by Henry Crawford's high spirits—only when she, too, is already in love with someone of the opposite "temper" from the man whose personality type she's rejecting.

It's quite possible that in other circumstances Mr. Knightley could have fallen for a woman of the very temperament that he thinks (because he's actually in love with Emma) would never suit him. And the same thing is true about Anne Elliot as well. And of course about Fanny; Jane Austen herself makes that case.

34. Wouldn't this rule apply to principles, too, then? How can Jane Austen treat them as absolutes—and an absolute requirement for the kind of man a Jane Austen heroine ought to pick—if all mental qualities ought to have "proportions and limits"? The answer is that Jane Austen didn't think of principles as qualities of the mind, so much as truths ("self-evident" ones, in Jefferson's phrase) about nature: human nature and the nature of the universe.

35. That's the question about Edward that Marianne answers in his favor when Jane Austen tells us that she "knew his heart to be warm and his temper affectionate." Marianne is recognizing Edward's real "worth"—particularly in contrast to the shallow selfishness of their mutual relations. That's why she considers him qualified to pay his addresses to her sister.

36. Sir Thomas thinks his daugher Maria is one of those to whom it's less important; "her feelings, probably, were not acute," he tells himself, when he's blindly push-ing along her disastrous marriage to Mr. Rushworth, only to discover too late

that his daughter's "real disposition"—particularly Maria's "high spirit and strong passions"—was totally "unknown to him."

37. Henry doesn't know it, but *we* know that mousy little Fanny is capable of passion because we've seen how she's passionately in love with Edmund, crazy enough about him to treasure his "handwriting itself" with an "enthusiasm…beyond the biographer's"—that "of a woman's love."

38. But Emma's prejudice against him isn't about a lack of intelligence. In fact, she has to disregard Mr. Martin's "good sense" (not to mention his "warm attachment, liberality, propriety, even delicacy of feeling") to be able to persuade herself that he's not good enough for Harriet. Emma does her best to make it seem like Robert Martin is not up to Harriet's intellectual level—but she's really reaching.

Emma tries to convince Harriet that Mr. Martin is a man of little knowledge or curiosity outside the business of farming. She makes a lot of the fact that he hasn't yet gotten around to reading a book Harriet recommended—trying to make him look so engrossed in his earthy job that he doesn't have time or mental energy for the higher things, like someone who is eventually sure to end up as "a completely gross, vulgar farmer, totally inattentive to appearances, and thinking of nothing but profit and loss." The truth is, as Mr. Knightley points out, that Robert Martin is "as much [Harriet's] superior in sense as in situation."

39. "'Will Mr. Frank Churchill pass through Bath as well as Oxford?' was a question however, which did not augur much."

40. "It was there our acquaintance begun, for my sister and me was often staying with my uncle."

41. Men who, like Sir John Middleton, suffer from such "total want of talent and taste" that they can't think of anything to do when they're not in a big social group are not much fun to be alone with. Lady Middleton shares her husband's limitations, "which confined their employments, unconnected with such as society produced, within a very narrow compass."

42. "The youthful infatuation of nineteen would naturally blind him to everything but her beauty and good nature; but the four succeeding years—years which, if rationally spent, give such improvement to the understanding—must have opened his eyes to her defects of education, while the same period of time, spent on her side in inferior society and more frivolous pursuits, had perhaps robbed her of that simplicity which might once have given an interesting character to her beauty."

43. "Lucy was naturally clever; her remarks were often just and amusing; and as a companion for half an hour Elinor frequently found her agreeable; but her powers

had received no aid from education: she was ignorant and illiterate; and her deficiency of all mental improvement, her want of information in the most common particulars, could not be concealed from Miss Dashwood, in spite of her constant endeavour to appear to advantage."

44.   The ultimate result is what Jane Austen calls an "illiberal" mind—like Mrs. Bennet's, characterized by "little information" and a "mean understanding."

45.   "Men of sense do not want silly wives," says Mr. Knightley.

46.   For some reason I can hear Annette Funicello singing, "The perfect boy / Doesn't have to be Euripides." "*Ripides*," the backup singers chime in. In one of several beach scenes from a movie entitled, no kidding, *How to Stuff a Wild Bikini*. A far cry from Anne Elliot and Captain Wentworth at Lyme.

47.   As with all the qualities Jane Austen characters look for in other people, it's much better to think about how important "sense," "understanding," "education," "talent," and "taste" are to you *before* you've gotten too deeply involved with a man who may be lacking them.

48.   "Address" can be more particular and deliberate than just general manners. It names both the tact that enables a woman to go about getting her way without ruffling other people's feathers and a man's style of paying attention to women. So in a rough and ready sort of way, you might say your "address" is your "manners" when you're in pursuit of something you want.

49.   Darcy, before Elizabeth inspires him to try harder, doesn't think of it as his responsibility to entertain other people or to put them at their ease. When Elizabeth suggests he'd get along with new people better if he practiced his social skills, she is quite right. Edward and Edmund are both on the shy side, too. Edward's "quietness of manner," Jane Austen tells us, "militated against all [Marianne's] established ideas of what a young man's address ought to be." But of course Elinor is on the quiet side herself, and not really looking for a man who takes up a lot of social space. Her Edward, like Edmund and Mr. Darcy (at least by the end of his story), is clearly within the range of "manners" that a Jane Austen heroine can live with.

50.   Edward's brother Robert Ferrars is affected, with all his attention given over to trivial matters that feed his vanity—particularly in the unforgettable scene when we first meet him, engrossed in "examining and debating" at elaborate length his order for a custom-made ivory, gold, and pearl toothpick-case. In contrast to Edward's "simple taste" and "diffident feelings," Robert's mental outlook is the essence of impertinent "puppyism." He has "no leisure to bestow any other attention on the two ladies, than what was comprised in two or three very broad stares." With a final look at the Dashwoods that seems "rather to demand than

to express admiration," he walks out of the shop "with an happy air of real conceit and affected indifference." John Thorpe in *Northanger Abbey* is "a rattle," whose non-stop mile-a-minute conversation is a farrago of "idle assertions and impudent falsehoods."

51.   Though, take note, there are cases where the social classification we use to group people in is a reliable marker for their principles. And I'm not thinking only of self-styled "pickup artists" who pride themselves on being members of "the Seduction Community" and see "female insecurity" as "the gift that keeps on giving." (You can check out, for example, Neil Strauss, *The Game: Penetrating the Secret Society of Pickup Artists* (It Books, 2005) or http://www.tuckermax.com/—but it's advisable only if you've got a really strong stomach.) I'm also thinking of, for example, the campus radicals who used to hang around the Marxist book store in Chapel Hill, North Carolina, when I was an undergraduate at U.N.C. When I became friends with "Caroline the Communist" (she didn't like people to know her last name, as she was nervous about the police, being a fan and possibly—friends suspected—an actual member of the Maoist Revolutionary Communist Party then sponsoring the Shining Path's guerilla war in Peru), I learned that the group shared an anti-monogamy principle that was causing serious unhappiness among its female members.

52.   Turning over Jane Austen's skeleton keys, I can see that for me, intelligence has always been the great aphrodisiac, to the point where in my twenties I was virtually indifferent to all sorts of other valuable qualities, right down to a man's looks and even hygiene. Note that that's not something a Jane Austen heroine would be specially proud of. But being a young Romantic at the time, with nearly the intensity of a Marianne Dashwood, I was quite pleased with myself on that score. The passage of time, which tends to teach us all the value of qualities we didn't appreciate early or easily (think of Captain Wentworth's late appreciation for the persuadable temper of Anne's mind) has made me see ending up with a handsome husband—out of the various brilliant men I was smitten with at one time or another—as a gratuitous perk that I certainly didn't deserve.

53.   We've seen that when fathers, mothers, and uncles weigh in on a young woman's marriage arrangements, it's too often on the side of crass self-interest or at best world-weary cynicism.

CHAPTER TWELVE

1.   General Tilney is the closest thing we meet with, in any of the novels, to the oppressive father who doesn't hesitate to interfere in the love lives of his children. Still, he's much less oppressive than Catherine suspects him of being! And

Northanger Abbey is the novel that includes an apology for the fact that it was already old-fashioned when it was published. ("The public are entreated to bear in mind that thirteen years have passed since it was finished, many more since it was begun, and that during that period, places, manners, books, and opinions have undergone considerable changes.") Even in that novel, General Tilney and his overbearing methods are balanced by the more modern paternal style of Catherine's father, who was "not in the least addicted to locking up his daughters." The most oppressive patriarch we get a glimpse of in Jane Austen's novels is literally from an earlier generation. Colonel Brandon tells Elinor the story of his poor cousin Eliza, who loved him but was forced into a marriage against her will by his father: "She was married—married against her inclination to my brother. Her fortune was large, and our family estate much encumbered. And this, I fear, is all that can be said for the conduct of one, who was at once her uncle and guardian." But the older Mr. Brandon's methods—"I was banished to the house of a relation far distant, and she was allowed no liberty, no society, no amusement till my father's point was gained"—are clearly from another era.

2.   Catherine Morland is at a distance from her parents, visiting Bath with family friends. (And the same thing is true about the heroine in Jane Austen's last, unfinished novel, though in that case she's at "Sanditon" instead of Bath). Elinor and Marianne's father has died—and their mother's "romantic delicacy" forbids her from stepping up to ask the uncomfortable questions her husband might have insisted on.

Mr. Bennet is so detached that he treats his daughters' affairs—like virtually everything else that goes wrong in his family—as a joke: "'So, Lizzy,' said he one day, 'your sister is crossed in love I find. I congratulate her. Next to being married, a girl likes to be crossed in love a little now and then. It is something to think of, and gives her a sort of distinction among her companions. When is your turn to come?'" At the time of Wickham's dishonorable elopement with Lydia, Elizabeth guesses that Wickham "might imagine, from my father's behaviour, from his indolence and the little attention he has ever seemed to give to what was going forward in his family, that *he* would do as little, and think as little about it, as any father could do, in such a matter."

Jane Austen sends Sir Thomas Bertram off to the West Indies, "leaving his daughters to the direction of others at their present most interesting time of life." Emma's father is on the spot but incapable of even noticing, much less interfering in, her love life. Partly from not being the sharpest tack in the box ("his talents could not have recommended him at any time") and partly from "habits of gentle selfishness, and of being never able to suppose that other people could feel differently from himself," he's oblivious: "Though always objecting to every marriage that was arranged, he never suffered beforehand from the apprehension of any.... She blessed the favouring blindness." Emma's long-ago-dead mother, Jane Austen tells us, was "the only person able to cope with her. She inherits her mother's talents, and must have been under subjection to her."

Anne Elliot lost her mother early, too, and her father's cold disapproval is a factor in her broken engagement, but he doesn't really arrange or forbid— he's distantly disgusted. Her only real adviser is Lady Russell, the family friend who doesn't understand Anne or Captain Wentworth.

3. Mme. d'Arblay, the novelist that John Thorpe knew wouldn't be worth reading once he heard she was "married to an emigrant" from Revolutionary France.

4. Richardson goes to even more extreme lengths than Jane Austen to arrange for his heroines to be alone and exposed to all the dangers inherent in arranging their own affairs without parental advice and consent: He sends his Pamela into domestic service in the house of a man who threatens seduction and even rape— in a case of *extreme* hostile work environment, eighteenth-century style. And he arranges for his Clarissa to be actually kidnapped and lodged in a house of ill repute by the villain of her novel.

5. Mrs. Dashwood's "romantic delicacy" doesn't turn out so well for her daughter. Mr. and Mrs. Musgrove look a bit irresponsible, seeming "either from seeing little, or from an entire confidence in the discretion of both their daughters, and of all the young men who came near them…to leave everything to take its chance." And Mrs. Norris is guilty of serious dereliction of duty: "Mrs. Norris was too busy in contriving and directing the general little matters of the company, superintending their various dresses with economical expedient, for which no one thanked her, and saving, with delighted integrity, half-a-crown here and there to the absent Sir Thomas, to have leisure for watching the behaviour, or guarding the happiness of his daughters." And "No one would have supposed, from [Mrs. Norris's] confident triumph [in Maria's marriage to Mr. Rushworth], that she had ever heard of conjugal infelicity in her life, or could have the smallest insight into the disposition of the niece who had been brought up under her eye."

6. Jane Austen tells us of Henry that, though he did eventually become "sincerely attached to [Catherine]…felt and delighted in all the excellencies of her character and truly loved her society, I must confess that his affection originated in nothing better than gratitude, or, in other words, that a persuasion of her partiality for him had been the only cause of giving her a serious thought."

7.   And doubly flattered to be singled out by him when "every girl in or near Meryton was out of her senses about him."

8.   "His lengthened absence from Mansfield, without anything but pleasure in view,
and his own will to consult, made it perfectly clear that he did not care about her."

9.   "Wishin' and Hopin,'" by Hal David and Burt Bacharach, sung by Dusty Springfield
(1964).

10.   "It is all very strange," Elinor remarks to her mother about Willoughby's abrupt
departure—when Marianne is simply wrapped up in her role of brokenhearted
Romantic. "So suddenly to be gone! It seems but the work of a moment. And last
night he was with us so happy, so cheerful, so affectionate? And now after only
ten minutes notice—Gone too without intending to return!—Something more
than what he owned to us must have happened. He did not speak, he did not
behave like himself. *You* must have seen the difference as well as I. What can it be?"

11.   Marianne rebuffs "with energy" not just Elinor's advice but her eventual attempt
to force Marianne's confidence: "We have neither of us any thing to tell; you,
because you communicate, and I, because I conceal nothing." Elinor also tries to
persuade their mother to interfere, to no effect.

12.   She tries, even, to keep her Romantic sister Marianne from jumping to the conclusion that Edward loves her, but that's a hopeless cause.

13.   "Disappointed, however, and vexed as she was, and sometimes displeased with
his uncertain behaviour to herself, she was very well disposed on the whole to
regard [Edward's] actions with all the candid allowances and generous qualifications, which had been rather more painfully extorted from her, for Willoughby's
service, by her mother." But still Elinor thinks "of Edward, and of Edward's
behaviour," with "censure, and doubt" as well as with "tenderness."

14.   "He must be either indifferent or unwilling. Had he ever wished to see her again,
he need not have waited till this time; he would have done what she could not
but believe that in his place she should have done long ago, when events had been
early giving him the independence which alone had been wanting."

15.   Or, if he's an actual pickup artist, cooperating in his deliberate deception of you.

16.   As Elinor does in evaluating Willoughby: "Suspicion of something unpleasant
is the inevitable consequence of such an alteration as we have just witnessed in
him.... Willoughby may undoubtedly have very sufficient reasons for his conduct, and I will hope that he has. But it would have been more like Willoughby
to acknowledge them at once."

17.   Thus at Darcy's first proposal, Elizabeth's "intentions did not vary for an
instant," though "she was at first sorry for the pain he was to receive." And Mary
Crawford "*had* begun to think of [Edmund]; she felt that she had, with great

regard, with almost decided intentions; but she would now meet him with his own cool feelings."

18. Most especially Edmund Bertram, who spends weeks on tenterhooks, in a variety of different situations, on the lookout for "confirmation of Miss Crawford's attachment."

19. In fact, rather more so, as Frank Churchill happens to be in a situation—as a man who expects to inherit a very large fortune, marrying a woman with virtually none—in which men are often deceived about a woman's true feelings. So that it's all the more valuable that Jane Fairfax's sterling character testifies to her "disinterested" attachment.

CHAPTER THIRTEEN

1. Don't forget that in Jane Austen, insofar as protecting women from relationship-induced pain is at issue at all, it's *self*-protection we're talking about. She's relying on us to be strong enough to look out for ourselves, and she's teaching us how to do it better. She's not suggesting that any special female weakness authorizes those side-whiskered Victorian older brothers to manage our love lives for us. Also, as we'll see in the next chapter, Jane Austen actually expects men to pay quite a lot of attention to their relationships (certainly more than we're used to expecting of them). But still, Jane Austen noticed things about women that are bound to raise our eyebrows—her observations are so out of step with our assumptions.

2. Even women who aren't models of constancy themselves still grossly underestimate men's capacity for not being committed. Isabella Thorpe fails as a heartless gold-digger because she's not callous *enough*; she lets Captain Tilney definitively detach her from her engagement to Catherine's brother without making sure of Tilney first. The giddy Lydia Bennet, with "continually fluctuating" affections— "sometimes one officer, sometimes another had been her favourite"—consents to live with Wickham without benefit of clergy, not seeing that he's less attached than she is.

And you don't even have to be blinded by love to make the false assumption that you're a man's sole object. Emma's not in love with Frank Churchill. And still she's so convinced that he's falling in love with her that she blithely dismisses Mr. Knightley's observations of a secret understanding between Frank and Jane Fairfax.

A woman can even know perfectly well that a man has quit loving her—as Anne Elliot knows about Captain Wentworth—and still keep hoping against hope that when he sees her again, he'll after all feel for her what she still feels for him. (When they meet after more than seven years apart, she can't help hoping, if just for a moment, "Now, how were his sentiments to be read. Was this like wishing to avoid her? And the next moment she was hating herself for the folly which asked the question.")

3. From the "Opinions of *Mansfield Park*" collected by Jane Austen: "Henry C.s going off with Mrs. R.—at such a time, when so much in love with Fanny, thought unnatural by Edward." James Edward Austen also "Objected to Mrs. Rushworth's elopement as unnatural."

4. Here's Fanny confronting the possibility that Henry may put off going to Norfolk to make sure his tenants are treated justly—a project inspired by his love for Fanny—so that he can stay for a party at which he'll see Maria for the first time since her marriage: "Whether Mr. Crawford went into Norfolk before or after the 14th, was certainly no concern of hers, though, every thing considered, she thought he *would* go without delay." And of course Fanny's shock at Henry's adulterous elopement with Maria when he's "a man professing himself devoted, even *engaged* to" Fanny herself is even greater.

    I still have a vivid memory of my own astonishment on my first such discovery. I've explained (see chapter 3 above) how I foolishly decided to continue my relationship on the same terms—which were now really wholly different terms—with the guy I dated in high school practically as soon as I found out that he'd been seeing someone else. He was a sophomore in college a few hours away from our home town, and I had been to the campus to visit him several times that year. When he told me about the other girl, I suddenly understood what had really been happening on my last visit. He'd been obviously stressed about my being there, told me he was under a lot of pressure with upcoming tests, and left me on my own quite a bit while he went "to the library to study." When I found out the reality behind that excuse, I was really hurt, of course. And embarrassed—to think that his friends must have known the whole time that he was parking me somewhere while he "studied" (really, went out with her). But my *complete astonishment* nearly swallowed up my pain and humiliation. The signs seem obvious in retrospect. But I'd been so focused on him and our relationship, that it never entered my brain (any more than it entered Marianne's) that he might be otherwise occupied.

5. "I only want her to look kindly on me, to give me smiles as well as blushes, to keep a chair for me by herself wherever we are, and be all animation when I take it and talk to her, to think as I think, be interested in all my possessions and

pleasures, try to keep me longer at Mansfield, and feel when I go away that she shall never be happy again."

6. "I have no inclination...to think that with so much tenderness of disposition, and so much taste as belonged to her, she could have escaped heart-whole from the courtship (though the courtship of only a fortnight) of such a man as Crawford, in spite of there being some previous ill-opinion of him to overcome, had not her affection been engaged elsewhere."

7. These "unconquerable ladies of eighteen" are obvious figments of the imaginations of authors whose grasp of female psychology is less firm than Jane Austen's.

8. Now clearly, there are some men—less attractive than Henry Crawford—whose attention is not intoxicating. The more we see of *them*, the more we want to run screaming. As Jane Austen says in *Northanger Abbey*, "Every young lady may feel for my heroine in this critical moment, for every young lady has at some time or other known the same agitation. All have been, or at least all have believed themselves to be, in danger from the pursuit of some one whom they wished to avoid; and all have been anxious for the attentions of some one whom they wished to please." And of course women break men's hearts, too. But by and large men don't seem to fall prey to the pattern we see repeated over and over again in women's lives—both in Jane Austen novels and in our own experience—in which a guy's attention fixes our heart on him prematurely, so that we're ready to belong to him before he's ready to belong to us.

9. "To think as I think."

10. As Jane Austen would say.

11. "Revealed: The Mufti Uncut," *Australian*, October 28, 2006, http://www.theaustralian.com.au/news/features/revealed-the-mufti-uncut/story-e6frg6z6-1111112429963.

12. Michael S. Kimmel, *Guyland: The Perilous World Where Boys Become Men* (Harper, 2008), especially pp. 172–77.

13. Men can be as ashamed and frustrated about their characteristic weakness as we are about ours. Though it's easier for them to see in *other* men—especially when those other men take an interest in their own female relatives. In worst-case scenarios involving men who think along the lines of the Australian mufti, the whole thing can end in "honor killings" and other horrors. But it's something that even much more civilized men know about their own sex. There's a story in my family about my grandparents and a date that my sixteen-year-old Aunt Mary went on, circa 1954. She stayed out really late, and my grandfather was pacing the floor restlessly in the wee hours of the morning waiting for her to get home.

My grandmother reassured him: "Don't worry, Billy, he's a nice boy." In response to which, my grandfather exploded, "*I* was a nice boy! There's no such *thing* as a nice boy!"

14. As Darcy suggests Elizabeth and Caroline Bingley are doing when Elizabeth accepts Caroline's invitation to "take a turn about" the drawing room at Netherfield—"because you are conscious that your figures appear to the greatest advantage in walking."

15. Marguerite Fields, "Want to Be My Boyfriend? Please Define," *New York Times*, May 4, 2008, http://www.nytimes.com/2008/05/04/fashion/04love.html.

16. Pretty much the same way that Fanny Price, if Henry's scheme against her had turned out just the way he planned, might have tried reminding herself that she'd always known Henry was an unprincipled man, unworthy of her good opinion.

17. Shades of Elizabeth Bennet's "permanent happiness."

18. By David Chelsea.

19. And for us, who've been living inside Elizabeth's head for most of the novel.

20. The one time in the novels when Jane Austen directly challenges the infamous "double standard," according to which society shames women more than men for sexual transgressions, her complaint isn't that women suffer too much, but that men get off too lightly! In other words, if she could have changed the double standard, she might actually have changed it in the direction of *more* societal disapproval for male adulterers and other men who make selfish and destructive choices where sex is concerned, not *less* for women.

   She takes up the issue at the end of *Mansfield Park*, when she's wrapping up all the characters' individual stories with their fictional rewards and punishments. Jane Austen explains that while Maria Bertram ended up exiled from Mansfield, living in a "remote and private" location with Mrs. Norris ("where, shut up together, with little society, on one side no affection, on the other, no judgment, it may be reasonably supposed that their tempers became their mutual punishment"), Henry Crawford—Maria's partner in adultery, who began the affair without even the excuse Maria had, of being hopelessly in love like her—apparently got off scot free: "In this world, the penalty is less equal than could be wished; but without presuming, to look forward to a more equal penalty hereafter, we may fairly consider a man of sense like Henry Crawford, to be providing for himself no small portion of vexation and regret—vexation that must rise sometimes to self-reproach, and regret to wretchedness—in having so requited hospitality, so injured family peace, so forfeited his best, most estimable and endeared acquaintance, and so lost the woman whom he had rationally, as well as passionately loved."

21. This friendly debate between Anne and Captain Harville is the conversation that Captain Wentworth overhears, so that he guesses Anne still loves him, and is emboldened to approach her again.

22. Whose "disposition," according to Captain Wentworth, is "of the sort which must suffer heavily, uniting strong feelings with quiet, serious, and retiring manners"— in other words, he's a steady, decent guy, no Willoughby or Henry Crawford.

23. "If the change be not from outward circumstances, it must be from within; it must be nature, man's nature, which has done the business for Captain Benwick."

24. It has also outlived the deconstruction of a lot of other "social constructs" that used to prop it up, and even some very significant fooling with Mother Nature. Our astonishment at male inconstancy has survived the invention of the Pill and the legalization of abortion—both of which have gone some distance to equalize the consequences of sex to men and to women. If those things haven't made sex less risky for women, they have at least changed what women's risks are. They've certainly made the negative consequences less publicly humiliating for women than they were in Jane Austen's day (think about where sex with Willoughby took Eliza), so that women today are less keenly aware of sexual vulnerabilities. The difference between men and women when it comes to sexual constancy has also outlasted Second Wave feminism, the erosion of "the virginity fetish"—i.e., the sexual double standard raised to the nth degree, according to which a single sexual experience "ruined" a woman—and the complete reversal of how we're educated about sex: the point of the current system being to give young women greater acquaintance with and fewer inhibitions on the subject, rather than the other way around. (In the eighteenth century, Samuel Johnson tried to defend the sexual double standard on a kind of "cultural construct" basis, by arguing from the fact that the main point of girls' education at that time was sexual restraint. Messing up there, he claimed, was justly punished by society because it meant failing at the one thing women had been taught to get right. It's interesting that Jane Austen, just two or three generations after Dr. Johnson, and with a considerably subtler understanding of female psychology, leans instead toward the "nature" understanding of the question.) Despite huge changes in both biological and social repercussions, the differences between men and women's sexual behavior, assumptions, and desires—a gap so wide that men are continually astonishing us with their comparative detachment—persists. As Horace warned two thousand years ago, "Naturam expellas furca, tamen usque recurret": "You can drive nature out with a pitchfork, and still it will come back."

25. The chemical that floods our brains during childbirth and breastfeeding. But we manufacture oxytocin in response to interactions with men, too. Almost any

kind of physical contact with a guy—not just having sex with him, though that can certainly do it, but even just a twenty-second hug—can result in the release of oxytocin, and a spike in our trust and "attachment." In fact, once we've begun to get attached, even just seeing the man we're interested in can boost our oxytocin levels. See Louann Brizendine, *The Female Brain* (Morgan Road Books, 2006), pp. 37, 65–74.

26.　Attributed to William James, who is supposed to have scribbled it while high on nitrous oxide and under the impression that he was recording the great secret of the universe. See "Hogamous, Higamous," Tony Percy's investigation of the attribution, http://coldspur.com/HogamousHigamous%28V2%29.htm.

27.　The time she has to spend pregnant, breastfeeding, and rearing even one child to ensure that it can reach adulthood and reproduce.

28.　Review of Judith Stacey, *Unhitched: Love, Marriage, and Family Values from West Hollywood to Western China* (New York University Press, 2011), in *Publishers Weekly*, January 31, 2011, p. 37. Apparently Stacey reached this tentative conclusion after spending more than ten years studying family structures on three continents.

29.　Dorothy Parker:

> Love is woman's moon and sun;
> Man has other forms of fun.
> Woman lives but in her lord;
> Count to ten, and man is bored.

("The General Review of the Sexual Situation," *Enough Rope*, quoted in Tony Percy, op. cit.)

　　And at the other end of the spectrum, J. R. R. Tolkien (yes, the creator of Aragorn, who has to be the most monogamous male character in all of modern literature—he falls in love with Arwen when he's twenty years old; waits, works, and wins a kingdom for her; along the way handles another beautiful woman's falling for him with such perfect chivalry that her own brother can say, "I hold you blameless in this matter" (*The Return of the King: Being the Third Part of the Lord of the Rings* [Houghton Mufflin, 1983], p. 848); finally marries Arwen sixty-eight years after he first fell in love with her; and enjoys 122 years of happy, faithful marriage) wrote to his son, "No good pretending. Men just ain't, not by their animal nature. Monogamy (although it has long been fundamental to our inherited ideas) is for us men a piece o'revealed ethic, according to faith and not the flesh. Each of us could healthily beget, in our 30 odd years of full manhood, a few hundred children, and enjoy the process." Letter to Michael Tolkien, March 6–8, 1941, in *The*

Letters of J.R.R. Tolkien, selected and edited by Humphrey Carpenter with the assistance of Christopher Tolkien (Houghton Mifflin Company, 1981), no. 43, p. 51.

30. Not general superiority—Jane Austen is not fighting the battle of the sexes here—but superiority in this one aspect of our lives.

31. There's nothing unprincipled or predatory about Reginald; he's the innocent victim of Lady Susan Vernon's deliberate scheme to revenge herself on his sister.

32. Or, if he's of bad character, like Henry Crawford, when he's away from the girl he loves for even a few days. In Henry Crawford's story, we actually get to see Anne's "so long as you have an object" principle at work in the case of a man who is *not* among "those who resemble" Captain Harville. Mary Crawford is probably right that if Fanny had accepted Henry "they might now have been on the point of marriage, and Henry would have been too happy and too busy to want any other object"—i.e., to get entangled with Maria again. (Mary's likely also right that his thing with Maria would have wound down to "a regular standing flirtation, in yearly meetings at Southerton and Everingham"—a prospect that Fanny regards with a horror Mary Crawford can't possibly understand.) Henry leaves Portsmouth full of the woman he loves and preoccupied with the serious responsibilities for his tenants that she's inspired him to pay new attention to. But when he ceases, only for a few days, to "have an object" in the form of Fanny actually in his presence daily to court and admire, love and pursue, then he's subject again to impressions as they come along, living in the present, letting momentary impulses—to help his sister make a social splash…to subdue Maria's pride by making her want him again—put Fanny, love, and responsibility out of his head, just long enough to wreck everything.

33. "To His Coy Mistress."

34. Or having theirs catered to, for that matter. See Davy Rothbart, "He's Just Not That Into Anyone: Even, and Perhaps Especially, When His Girlfriend Is Acting like the Women He Can't Stop Watching Online," *New York* [magazine], January 30, 2011, http://nymag.com/news/features/70976/.

35. As I happened to do one morning when my son was about two years old. Having grown up in a very female environment—my sister and I (no brothers) were raised by our divorced mother, and she sent us to a girls' school, where she also taught—I was just beginning to get that up-close-and-personal understanding of raw male psychology that you can't get any other way than by raising a little boy.

36. Brizendine, op. cit., pp. 14–19. The original research was conducted by Simon Baron-Cohen, professor of developmental psychopathology at Cambridge, who also points out that "the higher the baby's level of fetal testosterone, the less eye

contact the child makes at 12 months old. And also the slower they are to develop language at 18 months old." And "The MacArthur infant vocabulary scales report different norms for boys and girls at age 12 months precisely because girls['] vocabularies are bigger than boys['] from that age, and remain bigger over the next 24 months. Many independent studies show that girls on average also make more eye contact, and play with different kinds of toys to boys, from as early as 12 months old." "The Assortative Mating Theory: A Talk with Simon Baron-Cohen," Edge.org, April 6, 2005, http://www.edge.org/3rd_culture/baron-cohen05/baron-cohen05_index.html.

37.   A fictional but telling example: "'Don't you understand how Cho's feeling at the moment?' [Hermione] asked.

"'No,' said Harry and Ron together.

"'Well, obviously, she's feeling very sad, because of Cedric dying. Then I expect she's feeling confused because she liked Cedric and now she likes Harry, and she can't work out who she likes best. Then she'll be feeling guilty, thinking it's an insult to Cedric's memory to be kissing Harry at all, and she'll be worrying about what everyone else might say about her if she starts going out with Harry. And she probably can't work out what her feelings toward Harry are anyway, because he was the one with Cedric when Cedric died, so that's all very mixed up and painful. Oh, and she's afraid she's going to be thrown off the Ravenclaw Quidditch team because she's been flying so badly.'

"A slightly stunned silence greeted the end of this speech, then Ron said, 'One person can't feel all that at once, they'd explode.'" J. K. Rowling, *Harry Potter and the Order of the Phoenix* (Scholastic, 2003), p. 459.

38.   "Fanny was the only one of the party who found anything to dislike, but since the day at Sotherton, she could never see Mr. Crawford with either sister without observation, and seldom without wonder or censure; and had her confidence in her own judgment been equal to her exercise of it in every other respect, had she been sure that she was seeing clearly, and judging candidly, she would probably have made some important communications to her usual confidant [Edmund, that is]. As it was, however, she only hazarded a hint, and the hint was lost." Lost because Edmund is clueless about what Henry Crawford's up to.

39.   "'I rather wonder Julia is not in love with Henry,' was [Mrs. Grant's] observation to Mary.

"'I dare say she is,' replied Mary coldly. 'I imagine both sisters are.'"

40.   Which is especially noble of her, considering that she's still in love with Wentworth herself!

41.   Besides personal experience and the testimony of world literature, see Linda J. Waite and Maggie Gallagher, *The Case for Marriage: Why Married People Are Happier, Healthier, and Better Off Financially* (Doubleday, 2000), especially chapter 6, "With My Body I Thee Worship: The Sexual Advantages of Marriage." Even if all that men really wanted from women was just sex, marriage would still be in their interests, considering the frequency of sex and men's higher levels of physical satisfaction in marriage. I was recently talking to a friend at the office (a divorced guy) about the high level of hostility between men and women today. I'm more intimately familiar with the bitterness women feel toward men, but men are angry too. Angrier than they used to be, I think. If I put something up on Facebook about the difficulties men and women have connecting—or, worse, look at "pickup artist" blogs— I see a cascade of hostile comments from resentful, mostly divorced men, excoriating modern women as, essentially, frigid gold-digging layabouts. So I was asking my friend (who is not this kind of woman-bashing jackass) to theorize about the reasons for the increased bitterness. His insight was based on his observation that men tend to want sex from women more than we want it from them. It's true that a man has a better chance of getting a woman into bed today than a few decades ago. But the same modern dispensation essentially extends the negotiations on this issue over a much longer period of time. The bargaining between men and women—to eventually reach some kind of stable arrangement in which he is assured of getting at least some definite portion of what he wants from her, and she gets some fixed percentage of what she wants from him—goes on for longer. For decades altogether, as negotiations break down in break-ups and divorces, and both partners move on to try again with somebody else.

42.   See Leonard Sax, *Boys Adrift: The Five Factors Driving the Growing Epidemic of Unmotivated Boys and Underachieving Young Men* (Basic Books, 2007), especially chapter 6, "End Result: Failure to Launch."

43.   See Kimmel, op. cit., especially chapter 2, "'What's the Rush?': Guyland as a New Stage of Development."

44.   See "When Marriage Disappears: The New Middle America (The State of Our Unions: Marriage in America 2010)," the National Marriage Project at the University of Virginia, http://www.virginia.edu/marriageproject/pdfs/Union_11_12_10.pdf.

45.   See Mark J. Perry, "'Man-cession' Worsens; Male (10%)-Female (7.6%) Jobless Rate Gap of 2.4% Is Highest in History," *Carpe Diem: Professor Mark J. Perry's Blog for Economics and Finance*, May 8, 2009, http://mjperry.blogspot.com/2009/05/man-cession-worsens-male-10-female-76.html.

46.   See Brizendine, op. cit., pp. 14, 36.

47. As the relationship experts, we're responsible for taking both our own special vulnerabilities and their particular blind spots into account in the course of maneuvering our way to a happy ending.

48. "It was the highest satisfaction to her, to believe Captain Wentworth not in the least aware of the pain he was occasioning."

49. Emma, who is confident way beyond the bounds of her real expertise, and who exaggerates feminine intuition and female prerogatives in this area, being the obvious exception that proves the rule.

50. She has been grounded and resilient while he was stubborn and brittle, doing the take-my-ball-and-go-home thing.

51. As Jane Austen says of Fanny and Edmund.

52. All of which suggests a question: If women are the relationship experts, if that's what we bring to the table, then what unique contribution does the man make to a happy match? Well, there's a certain restless, inventive masculine energy that Jane Austen captures in her portrayal of the navy men in *Persuasion*, with their life of "exertion" "continual occupation and change." That hasn't really altered with women's advance into the realm of "profession, pursuits," and "business" that were men's province alone in Jane Austen's day. There's definitely something to Camille Paglia's argument that if the human race were 100 percent female, "we'd still be living in grass huts." See *Sexual Personae: Art and Decadence from Nefertiti to Emily Dickinson* (Yale University Press, 1990), p. 38. And doing beautifully coordinated cooperative subsistence farming, no doubt, but still subsistence farming.

But there's also something valuable in men's obsession with sex—itself a special case of that restless male energy—which is just as strong as our passion for relationships. When it comes to happy love, you can argue that for men, just as for women, the aspect of their character that looks most like a weakness in the worst of circumstances (wherever men and women are preying on each other's vulnerabilities, using and discarding each other, and failing to give each other what makes them both happy) is in the best of circumstances a great strength and resource for truly mutual happy endings. My grandmother used to say that she knew she wanted to marry my grandfather (in 1936!) because he was the first man she wanted to sleep with—as presumably he knew he wanted to marry her because she was the first woman he wanted to commit to.

The conventional wisdom today is that it was a disaster when, up through the repressed 1950s, people got married "just so they could have sex." That's why Caitlin Flanagan reports, in that article for the *Atlantic* (see chapter 5 above) that one of the tidbits of wisdom her mother suddenly sprang on her—in her well-meaning but ham-fisted 1970s feminist-era attempt to reverse the repressed sexual socialization of an earlier era and free the teenaged Caitlin to have a woman's sex life without having to take on irreversible adult commitments—was "Never marry a man because you want to have sex with him. Just have sex with him." You can see the horror story her mother was proactively trying to rescue her from; she didn't want her daughter trapped in marriage in her teens or early twenties to a guy she'd realize she didn't love or even like all that much, once she woke up from being hypnotized by the sexual magnetism of the first guy who appealed to her in that particular way.

But that's not what was going on with my grandmother. It wasn't a question of sex appeal overwhelming her good judgment about whether a man was really the person she wanted to spend the rest of her life with. It was something much healthier than that (and ultimately very successful, leading to one of the longest and happiest marriages I've known). It was about a guy being so right for her altogether that she could love him with a passion that transcended anything she'd felt for any man before. I've read my grandmother's diary from long before she met my grandfather. It's obvious that it came quite naturally to her to have crushes on guys and fantasize about the future. She went through her adolescence in a way that seems quite familiar. Like women in general—like us—she was a natural at relationships. But something about her relationship with the man she would marry pushed her into territory that didn't come so naturally to her. As bizarre as it seems, maybe there's some sense in which men come to sex more naturally than women, just as we find it easier to fall in love than they do.

But what does this Depression-era story really have to do with us? It would be a rare woman today, to put it mildly, who had never wanted to have sex with a man until she met her husband. My grandparents' lives are ancient history at this point. But you can still see vestiges of the same dynamic in more recent times. Remember how, near the beginning of *When Harry Met Sally*, Billy Crystal infuriates Meg Ryan by claiming that she hasn't ever had really great sex? He can tell because she prefers Victor Laszlo to Humphrey Bogart in *Casablanca*. Then, when Harry and Sally meet again later, she prefers Humphrey Bogart and can't even remember that she ever thought any different. What has happened in the interval, apparently, is that she *has* had great sex. Only it didn't turn out as well for Sally as it did for my grandmother. The guy who showed Sally how great sex could be—who inspired her to enjoy something she had to stretch to learn—wasn't inspired by *her* to jump the bounds of what came naturally to *him*, and want love and commitment and permanence. He went on for a few years, content to have his views still bounded by the present, enjoying living with and making love to her, without freighting it all with future significance. Meanwhile, long-term love was becoming increasingly important to Sally—eventually an urgent need that ruined her enjoyment of their present pleasures: she realized that being able to have sex on the kitchen floor without the kids walking in wasn't all it was cracked up to be. After living together for years, Sally wanted marriage and a family, and he didn't. They broke up, and in short order he found a different woman who *did*, somehow or other, inspire him to want the very things that Sally wanted but couldn't get him to want with her: lasting love, long-term commitment, marriage.

CHAPTER FOURTEEN

1.   Julia Bertram makes no "endeavour at rational tranquillity for herself" after she realizes that Henry Crawford doesn't love her. But Fanny is suspicious of Henry, supposing "that he wanted … to cheat her of her tranquillity, as he had cheated [her cousins]." And Elinor hopes in time, if Edmund marries Lucy, to get over her broken heart and "regain tranquillity."

2.   "For a day or two after the affront was given, Henry Crawford had endeavoured to do [Julia's resentment at his preference for her sister] away by the usual attack of gallantry and compliment, but he had not cared enough about it to persevere against a few repulses; and becoming soon too busy with his play to have time for more than one flirtation, he grew indifferent to the quarrel, or rather thought it a lucky occurrence, as quietly putting an end to what might ere long have raised expectations.…"

3.   "There was a return of [Mr. Rushworth's] jealousy, which Maria, from increasing hopes of Crawford, was at little pains to remove."

4.   There's a P. J. O'Rourke story about a girl he was in love with in his misspent youth. The way he tells the tale, everything was perfect: "She was the most beautiful girl I have ever seen.… We slept in a hug, arms and legs tangled together. I've never been able to sleep that way with anyone else. It's claustrophobic now, or an arm goes to sleep."

He was in love with her. But he couldn't bring himself to commit: "She wanted to get married. But I was a poor kid who could see the future. Me with a teacher's salary and her at home with the kids—a sea of small debts, rented homes, and used cars stretched out before us, a life like my parents' or hers.… I was too cowardly to go through with it.… I'd never made love to anyone but Juanita. I wanted to fuck all the women in the world. So I did not do the decent thing and make her breasts and belly swell and buy a pair of matching goldlike rings. I didn't even treat her very well." "Ghosts of Responsibility," *Age and Guile Beat Youth, Innocence and a Bad Haircut* (The Atlantic Monthly Press, 1995), pp. 78–80.

I don't think this is at all an uncommon attitude among men, and particularly among men who feel that they haven't got their own lives together yet—which is, unfortunately, a large and increasing proportion of the men out there these days. When they feel their enthusiasm for you pulling them to get beyond living in the moment and make a commitment, they dig in their heels and commit in the other direction—to their own freedom, to have the option to enjoy themselves with multiple women in the future. Some guys just aren't ready to commit to any woman. As O'Rourke has said more recently, it's a good thing he and his wife were grownups when they fell in love, so they knew what to do about it. He's now happily married with three children.

5.   Like Captain Wentworth: "It was now his object to marry. He was rich, and being turned on shore, fully intended to settle as soon as he could be properly tempted; actually looking round, ready to fall in love with all the speed which a clear head and quick taste could allow." He tells his sister, "'Yes, here I am, Sophia, quite ready to make a foolish match. Anybody between fifteen and thirty may have me for asking. A little beauty, and a few smiles, and a few compliments to the Navy, and I am a lost man.'"

6.   "Some Enchanted Evening," *South Pacific*, lyrics by Oscar Hammerstein, music by Richard Rodgers.

7.   As a matter of fact, the high tide of Frank's belief that Emma guesses his secret love for Jane is also the high point of Emma's belief that he's in love with her-self—his farewell call to Hartfield to say good-bye to Emma at the end of his first visit to Highbury. For a while Emma *was* interested in Frank Churchill, and it's not his fault that his attention doesn't end in a lot of pain for her. Later, Emma tells Mr. Knightley, "I will farther tell you, that there was a period in the early part of our acquaintance, when I did like him, when I was very much disposed to be attached to him—nay, was attached—and how it came to cease, is perhaps the wonder." And Mr. Knightley justly remarks to her that Frank was "playing a most dangerous game. Too much indebted to the event for his acquittal.—No judge of his own manners by you.—Always deceived in fact by his own wishes, and regardless of little besides his own convenience." As we've seen, even though Emma isn't really in love with him, she can't help making the characteristic

female errors about Frank: she thinks his attention to her means more than it does, and she's astonished to discover that he's really in love with another woman. And even though he is in love with somebody else, Frank can't help making the characteristic male errors about Emma: he pays her the kind of attention that's bound to seem more serious to her than to him, and he underestimates the power that attention has on her.

8. Though this is a judgment that Elizabeth has to back down from to some extent after she reads Darcy's letter. Bingley's lack of "resolution" in courting Jane against the advice of Darcy and his sisters wasn't really blamable if he had no reason to believe she was in love with him. And, Jane, Elizabeth eventually realizes, is particularly hard to read; there's an unusual disconnect between her "fervent" feelings and the "constant complacency" of her manner.

9. It's not likely to be his social-climbing sisters and overbearing friend deciding that your family's inferior connections, ignorance, and lack of propriety make you unworthy of him—and besides, they hope he'll marry the overbearing friend's younger sister.

10. "All In," by Lifehouse (2010).

11. Ross Jeffries, "How to Manage Her Commitment Expectations," February 15, 2011, Ross Jeffries Uncensored: Gets You the Women You Want, Predictably and Reliably, without Guesswork or Games, Guaranteed, http://www.seduction.com/blog/commitment-expectations/?utm_source=feedburner&utm_medium=feed&utm_campaign=Feed%3A+RossJeffriesUncensored+%28Ross+Jeffries+Uncensored%29&utm_content=Google+International.

12. Here Jeffries is referring to his branded "four doorways into any woman's mind and emotions."

13. The last hour of the concert is "an hour of agitation" to her. "She could not quit that room in peace without seeing Captain Wentworth once more, without the interchange of one friendly look."

14. "He would save himself from witnessing again such permitted, encouraged attentions.—He had gone to learn to be indifferent."

15. That's why she feels she has "acquitted herself well" when she manages to say in Wentworth's presence that she "might not attend" to what Mr. Elliot had said about where and when he was leaving Bath; every bit of evidence of her indifference to Mr. Elliot that Anne can make clear is so much encouragement to Captain Wentworth.

16. Which she does so beautifully in her discussion with Captain Harville about men and women in love.

CHAPTER FIFTEEN

1. Ellen Fein and Sherrie Schneider, *The Rules: Time-Tested Secrets for Capturing the Heart of Mr. Right* (Warner Books, 1997), p. 82.

2. Wentworth to Anne: "Tell me if, when I returned to England in the year eight, with a few thousand pounds, and was posted into the Laconia, if I had written to you, would you have answered my letter? Would you, in short, have renewed the engagement then?"

3. Except Marianne, until it's too late.

4. Remember Elizabeth Bennet's conversion from the Romantic "method" of falling in love, "arising on a first interview with its object, and even before two words have been exchanged," to the genuine Jane Austen "esteem"-based "mode of attachment."

5. As Fanny says about Henry Crawford, incidentally pointing up the absurdity of Richardson's tongue-in-cheek rule according to which a woman would wait to fall in love until the man had actually proposed: "I had not an idea that his behaviour before had any meaning; and surely I was not to be teaching myself to like him only because he was taking, what seemed, very idle notice of me…. How then was I to be—to be in love with him the moment he said he was with me? How was I to have an attachment at his service, as soon as it was asked for?"

    If Fanny had fallen in love with Henry when he started taking notice of her, that would have been too soon. Almost certainly he'd have been happy just to mess with her head, satisfied with the success of his "wicked project on her peace." Henry would have amused himself by winning her heart and then moved on, exactly as he did with Maria and Julia. But now that Fanny has been indifferent to him long enough to spark his real interest, she's too slow for him. He's already passionately in love with her, and she hasn't even begun to care for him.

6. "When the Night Comes Falling from the Sky," by Bob Dylan (1985).

7. When Mr. Collins deludes himself that she's refusing his proposal for that reason, she answers that she has "no pretension whatever to that kind of elegance which consists in tormenting a respectable man."

8. As she explains to Darcy when, long after the fact, she can see how it all happened.

9. In Emma's language.

10. Notice that only some of the men in Jane Austen fall in love or are hurried along that path because they're unsure of the woman, because she seems immune to their charms, or because they're jealous: Henry Crawford with Fanny, of course (and note that Edmund is entirely unaware of how Fanny loves him until he's

already decided he wants to marry her); Darcy with Elizabeth; Mr. Knightley with Emma. Others begin to love or take encouragement only because the woman loves them first: Henry Tilney with Catherine, Willoughby with Marianne.

11. How Lucy captivated Robert Ferrars, while engaged to his brother: "Instead of talking of Edward, they came gradually to talk only of Robert,—a subject on which he had always more to say than on any other, and in which she soon betrayed an interest even equal to his own."

12. Whose "wheedl[ing]" and "caress[ing]" of Sir Walter may eventually succeed in persuading him to marry her.

13. In answer to Elizabeth's scruples, Charlotte falls back on the cynical idea that "Happiness in marriage is entirely a matter of chance," so there's no need for Jane to take any more time to study Bingley's character.

14. Consider the description of Charlotte's "scheme" to catch Mr. Collins: "Miss Lucas perceived him from an upper window as he walked towards the house, and instantly set out to meet him accidentally in the lane. But little had she dared to hope that so much love and eloquence awaited her there."

15. They laugh at themselves, or else they're "secretly forming a desperate resolution" if they take even such innocuous measures as when Anne manages to sit at the end of a row at a concert so that Wentworth can approach her more easily, or as when Elizabeth gets up her courage to thank Darcy for helping arrange Lydia's marriage, hoping the subject will make an opening for him to propose again.

16. Though Jane Austen heroines are quite alive to the sad fact that our suffering does entertain other people, and quite eager to avoid, where possible, being fodder for that kind of amusement. After Louisa's accident: "By this time the report of the accident had spread among the workmen and boatmen about the Cobb, and many were collected near them, to be useful if wanted; at any rate, to enjoy the sight of a dead young lady, nay, two dead young ladies, for it proved twice as fine as the first report." And Mr. Bennet: "For what do we live, but to make sport for our neighbours, and laugh at them in our turn?"

17. "She could not enter the house again, could not be in the same room to which she had with such vain artifice retreated three months ago, to lace up her boot, without *recollecting*. A thousand vexatious thoughts would recur."

18. "Catching" husbands is "not an employment to which" Jane Austen heroines "have been brought up," though the Romantic Mrs. Dashwood does say so. They're not susceptible to John Dashwood's cynical advice: "But some of those little attentions and encouragements which ladies can so easily give, will fix him, in spite of himself."

19. According to Mr. Allen's advice in *Northanger Abbey*.

20. *Sense and Sensibility*.

21. Though her preparation isn't perfect, of course. When Lucy tricks the Dashwoods' servant into reporting that she has married Edward, Elinor "found the difference between the expectation of an unpleasant event, however certain the mind may be told to consider it, and certainty itself.… She condemned her heart for the lurking flattery, which so much heightened the pain of the intelligence."

22. "To think of him as Miss Crawford might be justified in thinking, would in her be insanity. To her he could be nothing under any circumstances; nothing dearer than a friend. Why did such an idea occur to her even enough to be reprobated and forbidden? It ought not to have touched on the confines of her imagination. She would endeavour to be rational, and to deserve the right of judging of Miss Crawford's character, and the privilege of true solicitude for him by a sound intellect and an honest heart." We've seen that, if Edmund had married Mary Crawford, Fanny's self control would have prepared her for what Jane Austen calls elsewhere "the only thoroughly natural, happy and sufficient cure" for lost love—falling in love with another man.

23. "How she might have felt [about Mr. Elliot] had there been no Captain Wentworth in the case, was not worth enquiry; for there was a Captain Wentworth; and be the conclusion of the present suspense good or bad, her affection would be his for ever. Their union, she believed, could not divide her more from other men than their final separation."

24. Not to mention a guarantee that he can't blindside her after ten apparently happy years by announcing that he no longer loves her, he wants a divorce, and their family home will be sold out from under her and the proceeds applied to two new separate, unwelcome futures.

25. "Mrs. Clay's affections had overpowered her interest, and she had sacrificed, for the young man's sake, the possibility of scheming longer for Sir Walter."

26. Love by increments is not quite so exciting, nor so deeply satisfying, as love the Jane Austen heroine way. Unfortunately, it's more like what most of us find ourselves living with. Take a look at a couple of testimonies to the realities of marriage today, from the comments to Megan McArdle's blog at the *Atlantic*.

From a woman's point of view: "I married my husband when he was still on the fence about having children, then used relationship blackmail ('I intend to have children, starting by the time I'm 30. If not with you, then we'll split up and I'll find someone else.') to push him over the line. I'm not proud of it and today I can't believe my amoral chutzpah—but I did tell him that BEFORE we were married, at least, so he could have taken his out right there. As it was, each of us gambled on [the] other's changing his or her mind—and I won, and he's an AWESOME father of our three." Comment by Jamie McArdle at http://www.theatlantic.com/national/archive/2011/02/abortion-would-we-change-our-minds-if-we-only-knew/71331/.

And as a man sees it, "She and I kept our pre-marriage money in separate accounts, and the post-marriage money are [sic] comingled in joint accounts. I brought our house into the marriage, but for years I paid for the mortgage and maintenance out of my personal money, so the house stayed out of the community. I quietly started using community money to pay for the mortgage about 5 years into the marriage."

And the same man, following up in response to another commenter who was disturbed that he had "some sort of secret relationship test that you didn't want to let her in on": "When I got married, of course I hoped the marriage would last. But our whole exercise of separating the comingled from the uncomingled is to prepare for when it doesn't. It's a wise precaution, when so many marriages don't last. After the 5-ish years, I just felt secure enough in the marriage and in our maturity that I thought it was no longer necessary to prepare against the possibility of a divorce. Was it a test? I guess you can call it that, but it was nothing so discrete. Balancing my check book one night, I suddenly realized it was silly to keep unmingled my premarriage assets, so I stopped. The test, if you want to call it that, happened in increments and subconsciously over 5 years. Now, a banker friend did have an explicit concept of vesting. He had a pretty concrete schedule of moving assets into the community, and he stuck to it. They're still happily married, as far as I can tell." Comments by "garysixpack" and "yet_another_dave," http://www.theatlantic.com/business/archive/2011/02/money-talks-yours-mine-and-ours/70664/#.

27.   That concept so crucial to Jane Austen's understanding of love—which is finally, after having been neglected for decades between her time and ours, a subject of scientific research into human physiology today. Brizendine, op. cit., pp. 68ff.

28.   And their physiological basis in oxytocin, which Jane Austen didn't know about.

29.   Being one of these myself, I don't like to hear that I start out with this disadvantage, but that's the fact.

30.   "Practice Makes Problems," *Penn State Online Research* 24, no. 1, (May 24, 2004), http://www.rps.psu.edu/0405/practice.html, summarizing the results published by C. M. Camp Dush, C. L. Cohan, and P. R. Amato in "The Relationship between Cohabitation and Marriage Quality and Stability: Change across Cohorts?" in the August 23 *Journal of Marriage and the Family,* vol. 65, no. 3, pp. 539–49.

31.   "I would never commit to spending my life with a man without living with him first. You get to know a person's private face this way, rather than the public face that he presents to the world." Lucy4980, setting up a July 2002 iVillage "Debate of the Month," quoted in "3 Reasons Why Researchers Say Living Together before Marriage Is Risky," *iVillage Health*, July 29, 2002, http://www.ivillage.com/3-reasons-why-researchers-say-living-together-marriage-risky/4-a-284085.

32.   See Ellen McCarthy, "Force of Cohabit: Making or Breaking a Marriage," *Washington Post*, August 16, 2009, http://www.washingtonpost.com/wp-dyn/content/article/2009/08/13/AR2009081304118.html, reporting results from a five-year study of the National Institute of Child Health and Human Development by University of Denver psychologist Scott Stanley, et al.

33.   In which case, as Edmund Bertram points out, she is "acting upon motives of vanity."

34.   See the dialogue on long engagements between Mrs. Musgrove and Mrs. Croft that sets up Anne's conversation with Captain Harville on men and women in love.

35.   Or even before that, as we'll see below.

36.   As with attachment, "working on your relationship" is a greater hazard for women than for men. It calls on all our natural relationship expertise and sometimes carries us to absurd lengths. Remember the scene in *Fried Green Tomatoes* when Kathy Bates's husband comes home to find her knocking down an interior wall of their house with a sledgehammer? She astonishes him by revealing the motivation behind her frenetic activities. She's been "TRYING TO SAVE OUR MARRIAGE!"—a marriage he is astonished to learn needs saving.

37.   But consider how the two projects are in conflict. If you are deciding whether to commit to someone, his character and yours are the givens. You're solving an equation using those givens to determine the variable, which is whether the relationship should continue. "Working on your relationship" means exactly the reverse—the relationship is the given, and the man and woman are the variables that are going to be changed by it—the relationship is the standard by which the individuals are measured and to which they must increasingly conform themselves. Taking on this project makes sense after marriage; at least, it makes sense if marriage is for life. But deciding whether to marry a person requires the opposite attitude—starting from your own character and desires as the standard, and evaluating the man to judge whether a permanent relationship with him is a good thing. But once the relationship (rather than the individuals and their characters, hopes, and freedom to choose) is the given, "working on our relationship" can become a full-time project for the woman. She becomes occupied with

changing the man—and, even more, with changing herself—for the sake of what they have together.

Any two people trying to get along encounter frictions that have to be worked through; any reasonable people know that the fault is never all on one side. Even in relationships with clear and very narrow limits (between coworkers, for example), people learn that they have to curb their own tempers and expectations to get along.

And a woman in a romantic relationship with a man feels an infinitely greater need to learn accommodation. Not so much because men are particularly unaccommodating, as because women are caught between two overpowering desires. On the one hand, women have a compelling need to have everything just so. We want our houses decorated according to our own taste and our kitchen utensils arranged by our own organizational principles; we want our weddings to be just like we've imagined since we were eight years old; we want our husbands to guess what we want for our birthdays; we want Valentine's Day to unfold just the way we've secretly been hoping it would. A woman wants a man to meet a thousand expectations she has about what her man will be like. On the other hand, the ordinary woman has a real talent for generous, self-critical, even self-sacrificing, love. (Joseph McPherson, a friend who became the headmaster of a girls' school after a long career educating boys, told me the thing that has surprised him most: girls are so eager to please—they care so much about and work so hard to meet the teachers' expectations.) Any woman seeing a man as a potential mate is at some point going to become frustrated that he doesn't exactly meet her expectations. She's going to want to ask him to change. But any woman of sense is going to realize very soon that some of her wishes are unreasonable. She's going to begin struggling against the worse angels of her nature, to learn to love more generously. This struggle, essential to happiness if you've got a long-term commitment you can count on, can be a fatal distraction from the task of figuring out how to pick the right person in the first place.

Which is one reason Jane Austen's heroines don't "work on their relationships" until they've got permanent relationships. During courtship, they expect men to be the ones working hard to please. (As Henry Tilney explains when he's comparing dancing to marriage, men's and women's "duties are exactly exchanged; the agreeableness, the compliance are expected from him" in dancing; from her, in marriage.)

38.   Think how alone Jane Austen heroines are. They exhibit almost superhuman control in keeping their secrets—and not just from men. Elinor can't tell anyone

about Edmund's secret engagement; she suffers in silence. Elizabeth doesn't let even Jane know that she's coming to love Darcy, after all. Fanny keeps her feelings for Edmund a deep, dark secret from everyone for years, until he finally comes to want to love her as much as her heart desires. Emma suffers the pangs of hopeless love for Mr. Knightley for only two days, but they're forty-eight hours she spends under torture, believing that every future year of her life is going to be miserably inferior to her happy past. And Anne doesn't tell even her one real friend that she regrets giving up Captain Wentworth, much less that she now cares for him as much as ever.

39.   Her heroines do have confidantes, and some of this secret-keeping is a result of special circumstances that make her plots run better—Lucy's telling Elinor about the engagement in confidence, and so forth.

40.   Stop right there, some indignant women's studies professor is bound to be think-ing—you've got it exactly backwards. The old rules weren't about women's freedom and happiness at all. Just the opposite! Those rules were really for virgin-ity preservation, which is by no stretch of the imagination about female liberty. It's all about controlling women by catering to men's patriarchal desire to treat us as property. Men get off on having a piece of sexual property that belongs only to themselves. And their brittle egos can't hold up under the comparisons women will make if we're sexually experienced. So a patriarchal society arranges for girls to be locked up by their fathers until they can be handed over to their husbands. That way, a husband will never have to compete with other men for his wife's esteem, and he can get pretty much the same kind of kick out of deflowering her that little boys get from making impressions in virgin snow. All the rules Jane Austen heroines live by are just vestiges of the patriarchal system for controlling women—internalized chastity belts, as it were, constraining women's freedom and happiness, not promoting them.

Well, the angry women's studies professor would have just one thing right. Jane Austen was—don't faint from shock, now—no fan of sex outside marriage. But if you think Jane Austen was, either consciously or unconsciously, in league with the patriarchy to keep women inexperienced for the benefit of possessive men, please tell me what you're smoking. And if you think the rules Elizabeth Bennet and Anne Elliot live by put them at the mercy of men's greed and selfishness— in comparison with modern women like Marguerite Fields, say—please explain where you've been for the past few decades of the mating scene on Planet Earth.

41.   After all, Jane Austen was one of those when she started writing *Persuasion*!

42.   Partly because of the residual influence of that very guy I dated in high school. For which—and for a lot of other things—I don't mean to sound ungrateful! I

first read Kierkegaard and Tolstoy because of him. Our friendship was a good thing in many ways, despite the "working on our relationship" trap. Now that I'm so much older than we both were then, I find myself taking a kind of maternal interest in his welfare, hoping that he eventually managed to unlearn the lessons of our relationship and find a woman he could love with his whole heart.

43. And so much evidence that modern women are ready to try what Jane Austen has to offer.

44. Though one youth minister (Craig Strickland, now the pastor of Hope Presbyterian Church in Cordova, Tennessee) did make an argument that you should never say "I love you" until you also meant "and I want to marry you." (I now very much wonder from what source or process of reasoning he derived this idea, which was taken for granted in Jane Austen's day.) I tried to follow this advice, too; the guy I dated in high school had a heck of a time prying the first "I love you" out of me. But there wasn't enough of a context for that one rule to make any real difference in the progress of the relationship. By the time we were wrangling over whether I should answer his "I love you's," we were already well into a quasi-commitment of the very sort the real, original rules were designed to keep me clear of.

45. Though "beau" is old-fashioned and quaint to us, notice that to Jane Austen it was new and rather vulgar: "'And had you a great many smart beaux [in the neighborhood of Norland]?'" asks Lucy's Steele's appalling older sister. "'I suppose you have not so many in this part of the world; for my part, I think they are a vast addition always.'

"'But why should you think,' said Lucy, looking ashamed of her sister, 'that there are not as many genteel young men in Devonshire as in Sussex?'...

"'I suppose your brother was quite a beau, Miss Dashwood, before he married, as he is so rich?'

"'Upon my word,' replied Elinor, 'I cannot tell you, for I do not perfectly comprehend the meaning of the word. But this I can say, that if he ever was a beau before he married, he is one still, for there is not the smallest alteration in him.'"

46. "Be True to Your School," by The Beach Boys (1963).

47. Not to mention the Sexual Revolution that came next.

CHAPTER SIXTEEN

1. Susan Walsh, "5 Ways to Get More Control of Your Relationships," June 29, 2009, *Hooking Up Smart*, http://www.hookingupsmart.com/2009/06/29/hookingup realities/how-to-get-hand-in-your-relationships/.

2. And if they're taller, as the 6'2" Megan McArdle explains in "The Long and Short of Dating" at her blog on the *Atlantic*'s website, April 20, 2011, http://www.theatlantic.com/personal/archive/2011/04/the-long-and-short-of-dating/237600/. It's interesting to note that while McArdle casts aspersions on men's hankering for "someone they can look down on. (Physically, not necessarily spiritually)" and on women's "fantasy about being tiny and delicate," and she's clearly happy to have married a man "who labored mightily when he carried me over the threshold"—still, she *did* let him carry her over the threshold.

3. Yes, we really are, in world-historical terms, however inferior we may feel to the glamorous but mostly imaginary people we see in the media and the movies.

4. Which is one more reason to remember that your hero doesn't need to be superior in *every* way. Especially not in ways that aren't ultimately important—the flashy stuff that impresses the world, but that Jane Austen heroines see right through. If you care about integrity and can admire a man for keeping his priorities straight, you can be deliriously happy with an Edmund Bertram or an Edward Ferrars, despite their moderate incomes and the fact that they don't cut much of a figure in the world. Your perfect match needs to be superior only in the things that matter to you.

5. And conceives her "prejudice" against him, when she happens to overhear him describe her as "tolerable, but not handsome enough to tempt *me*; and I am in no humour at present to give consequence to young ladies slighted by other men."

6. So Charles Dickens tells us, near the middle of the nineteenth century, looking back on the Regency Era: "There used to be Assembly Balls at most places then." Chapter 38 of *Great Expectations*, published in the 1860s, but set in the eighteen-teens.

7. No. 97, February 19, 1751. As it happens, we know that Jane Austen certainly had read this number of the *Rambler* because she refers to Richardson's letter in *Northanger Abbey* (in the passage where she considers whether it's improper of a woman to fall in love with a man—or to dream about him—before he tells her his love or dreams about her), which she wrote at roughly the halfway point between Richardson's letter looking back to the days before assembly balls and Dickens's remark looking back on the balls themselves.

8. As, interestingly, Darcy's eye is forced to do at the Meryton assembly ball where "turning round, he looked for a moment at Elizabeth, till catching her eye, he withdrew his own and coldly said" those cutting things about her merely "tolerable" looks.

9. Apart from "fidelity" and "complaisance" in the actual dancing, he was also supposed to make sure you got refreshments, sit with you, and converse with you and your friends in the break between dances.

10. Being driven in a horse-drawn carriage by a man was another way of seeing whether you liked his physical style—whether you enjoyed being in his hands, as it were: "Henry [Tilney] drove so well—so quietly—without making any disturbance, without parading to her, or swearing at them: so different from the only gentleman-coachman whom it was in [Catherine's] power to compare him with!...To be driven by him, next to being dancing with him, was certainly the greatest happiness in the world."

11. Besides Lydia Bennet's offer to find her sisters husbands, scorned by Elizabeth, there's the completely absurd Mary in "The Three Sisters," who is egged into marrying the "extremely disagreeable" Mr. Watts by her more human younger sister Georgiana when their mother insists on his being accepted by one of her daughters. Georgiana excuses herself for manipulating Mary into accepting him thus: "Mary will have real pleasure in being a married Woman, & able to chaperone us, which she certainly shall do, for I think myself bound to contribute as much as possible to her happiness in a State I have made her choose. They will probably have a new Carriage, which will be paradise to her, & if we can prevail on Mr. W. to set up his Phaeton she will be too happy. These things however would be no consolation to Sophy or me for domestic misery."

12. And how did they separate the sheep from the goats? We're not talking about picking a hero here, only about identifying the kind of jerks who ought to be altogether excluded from the pool of possibles before you start picking. The ones to kick out were the men who were known to prey on women's vulnerabilities. You could refuse an introduction to a man, and you would if he had that kind of reputation. That's why Mrs. Edwards "testif[ies] by the coldness of her manner" that she introduces Tom Musgrave to Emma Watson only "very reluctantly." Tom has managed to circumvent Emma's right to refuse the introduction, and Mrs. Edwards's right to refuse to make it, by impertinently asking to be introduced in front of Emma. Thus Mrs. Edwards can't say no without creating some social awkwardness. Which she would likely be willing to do if Tom were just a little bit more dangerous; he's a borderline case. Besides refusing introductions, if you found out that a man you already knew had started behaving like that you could "drop his acquaintance immediately." Willoughby doesn't care how bad he looks to Marianne's friends because he knows that in any case that he'll be "shut out forever from their society" once the essentials of how he treated her are known.

13. But isn't it psychologically unhealthy for one person to consider himself responsible for the emotions of another? I don't think so, in this sense. Was it any less reasonable for a man to take into account the overpowering effect that the

honest expression of his interest is likely to have on the woman than it was for her to take into account the overpowering effect the display of her body is likely to have on him? Male attention is as distracting, befuddling, and intoxicating to the average human female as a woman's body is to the average human male. A woman used to dress to avoid exposing her body, and a man used to talk so as not to honestly expose his interest and his current (passing, present-bound) feelings for a woman, unless and until he was sure that interest was serious. If women are more level-headed about physical desire, it makes some sense for us to notice the effect our bodies are having on men. If men are less susceptible to emotional seduction, it makes sense for us to require *them* to notice the effect their words can have on women.

14. As Lady Caroline Lamb said of Byron.

15. The quality of analysis that Jane Austen heroines put into considering their prospects is really impressive. Any woman falling in love is going to be thinking how fabulous the man is. But how often do we appreciate the kinds of things Elizabeth appreciates about Darcy: what his responsible management means for the large number of people who work for and depend on him, and the fact that with very good reasons to be proud, he's actually learning to master himself. Any woman regretting a man she has lost is going to be sighing about what her future with him could have been. But very few heartbroken women are going to have as truly mature and realistic a grasp of what they've lost as Anne Elliot: "There was so much attachment to Captain Wentworth in all this, and such a bewitching charm in a degree of hospitality so uncommon, so unlike the usual style of give-and-take invitations, and dinners of formality and display, that Anne felt her spirits not likely to be benefited by an increasing acquaintance among his brother-officers. 'These would have been all my friends,' was her thought; and she had to struggle against a great tendency to lowness."

16. See Judith A. Reisman, *Kinsey: Crimes and Consequences* (Institute for Media Education, 1998).

17. Cheryl Wetzstein, "Government Survey: Virgins at 40 Do Exist: New Report Also Takes Note of Same-Sex Activity," *Washington Times*, March 3, 2011, http://www.washingtontimes.com/news/2011/mar/3/government-survey-virgins-at-40-do-exist/, reporting on a survey by the National Center for Health Statistics.

18. And this study is subject to some, though certainly not all, of the same criticisms you can make of Kinsey. Setting aside the possibility of a really significant amount of homosexual activity (and much more of it among men than among women), the only explanation for the gap between men's and women's lifetime sexual experience is inaccuracy in self-reporting—which seems far more likely than

that the study is accurate. Almost certainly men are exaggerating and women are underestimating their numbers of partners.

19. The testimony of the human race, from the Psalmist to Bill Clinton's apologists, is unanimous. Every man is a liar. And that's "man" in the generic sense, including "woman."

20. Perhaps the most solid bit of data—remembering that men's and women's average numbers have to be roughly equal in reality (minus only the difference between the amount of male-with-male and female-with-female sexual activity) was that on average men didn't feel it either necessary or plausible to exaggerate their number of lifetime partners beyond five.

21. Note that to be ideal, a venue should be a place where it's easy to signal interest, but also where you can preserve some plausible deniability, as women were able to do in Jane Austen's day. Otherwise women's "rapid" imaginations—our ability to envision the endgame long before the guy does—will scare some men off. A married friend of mine has a story about a group of women she knew in her single days. They were housemates, and all serious Christians. They were all also very serious about getting married; they had become persuaded that it was wrong to go out with a guy at all if you didn't consider him a possible future husband. They let their friends know what they thought—with the result that none of them ever had any dates. Guys who are just getting interested in you do not want to sign up for immediate vetting as possible future husbands. There's an ambiguity, a playfulness, that's desirable at the early stages of any romantic affair.

22. I'm working from an imperfect memory here, as unfortunately I can't find this account again online. But for other "pickup artists'" ideas on "gaming church girls," see http://www.pick-up-artist-forum.com/gaming-church-girls-vt8161.html.

23. We can only hope, "without presuming to look forward to a juster appointment hereafter" that this jerk will eventually come to feel the "vexation and regret" that he ought to for "having so requited" the "hospitality" of the people who welcomed him into their church.

24. Though Dawn Eden (op. cit., p. 138) warns, you also may not: "The wrong kind is one of those that my pastor aptly describes as 'young adult groups that are neither young nor adult.' It focuses its activities around drinking.... The free-flowing booze invites them to treat one another just as they would in a singles bar—as objects." So you may want to steer clear of church activities along the lines of the "Extreme Charity Pub Crawl" Eden mentions.

25. C. S. Lewis, *The Screwtape Letters with Screwtape Proposes a Toast* (HarperSan-Francisco, 2000), p. 127.

26. "Middle-ranking civil servant, single, Catholic, 43, immaculate past, from the country, is looking for a good Catholic, pure girl who can cook well, tackle all household chores, with a talent for sewing and homemaking with a view to marriage as soon as possible. Fortune desirable but not a precondition." He ended up married to a girl without a fortune, http://www.catholicvote.org/discuss/index.php?p=5158.

27. Amy Dacyczyn, "Cut-Rate Soulmate," *Tightwad Gazette* 40, September 1993, p. 4.

28. In a "contract of mutual agreeableness" in which "all [your] agreeableness belongs solely to each other for that time," but that time is no longer than "for the space of an evening," as Henry Tilney explains.

29. Apparently the name was garbled by the French before arriving in America.

30. That certainly sheds light on the difference between Jane Austen and the Victorians, doesn't it?

31. Take the commenter on another one of those "pickup artist" posts who has "nothing against casual sex—I'd be happy to have more of it in my life" but who also sees the limitations of the "Game" that is played for only that prize. He points out, "if your objective is a woman who won't go from bar to bed in an hour no matter what you say, then trying to get her there is an exercise in futility." "Alsadius" commenting on "A Natural Contemplates Game," March 3, 2011, on *Armed and Dangerous: Sex, software, politics, and firearms. Life's simple pleasures...*, http://esr.ibiblio.org/?p=3000.

APPENDIX

1. "It would be mortifying to the feelings of many ladies, could they be made to understand how little the heart of man is affected by what is costly or new in their attire; how little it is biased by the texture of their muslin, and how unsusceptible of peculiar tenderness towards the spotted, the sprigged, the mull, or the jackonet."

2. The Mrs. Mitford quoted in James Edward Austen-Leigh's *Memoir* (and to great effect in Virginia Woolf's essay on Jane Austen in *The Common Reader*).

3. From her January 9, 1796 letter to her sister Cassandra about Tom Lefroy: "You scold me so much in the nice long letter which I have this moment received from you, that I am almost afraid to tell you how my Irish friend and I behaved. Imagine to yourself everything most profligate and shocking in the way of dancing and sitting down together. I *can* expose myself however, only *once more*, because he leaves the country soon after next Friday, on which day we *are* to have a dance at Ashe after all."

4.   As a little girl, Jane Austen registered an imaginary marriage for herself in the official book her father kept for the parish to "Henry Fredrich Howard Fitzwilliam"—presumably a cousin to Mr. Darcy.

5.   Today novelists, and educated people in general, have ceded all that interesting territory to the expert social scientists. Now we have scientific experts breathlessly announcing such astonishing discoveries as "Study: Women Drawn to Men with Muscles." (No kidding, "Study: Men Drawn to Women with Muscles," *Life Two*, July 11, 2007, reporting on research published by U.C.L.A. graduate student David A. Frederick in the *Personality and Social Psychology Bulletin*, http://lifetwo. com/production/node/20070711-study-women-drawn-to-men-with-muscles. Other groundbreaking research I've seen reported reveals: Boys and girls actually *are* different; children tend to do better with married parents; toddlers who exhibit superior self-control grow up to succeed as adults; and parents can actually affect whether their children try illegal drugs or not—they're less likely to if you tell them not to!) Or, even more annoying, the experts tell us that beauty boils down to an epiphenomenon of the evolutionary imperative: men find younger women more attractive only because of their superior reproductive potential. The pain we feel when our partner is unfaithful is just our selfish genes talking: we care only because the affair could distract him from contributing to the support of a child of ours and so make it less likely that that child will reach sexual maturity and transmit our genes to future generations. Right.

6.   She could joke about the morals of her stories, as at the end of *Northanger Abbey* when she "leave[s] it to be settled by whomsoever it may concern, whether the tendency of this work be altogether to recommend parental tyranny, or reward filial disobedience." And she made fun of crude, proto-Victorian attempts at moralizing literature, as in her sarcastic "Plan of a Novel, according to hints from various quarters": The heroine of that imaginary crowd-sourced work was to be "a faultless character herself—, perfectly good, with much tenderness and sentiment, & not the least Wit." Jane Austen aimed higher, at stories that displayed "the most thorough knowledge of human nature" in all its "varieties," "wit," and "humour." But she still expected women to learn from her novels, and to want to be like her heroines.

7.   We're unique in the animal kingdom in the extraordinarily long time it takes members of our species to mature. Ducks and horses learn to walk the day they're born. Frogs know how to be frogs without seeing their parents' example. But human beings take years to become competent adults, and all the time we learn by copying other human beings. And even when we've reached maturity, we can't

stop learning by imitation. Just look at our fashions, in everything from clothes to music to kitchen counters.

8. As Edmund Bertram says, "The manners I speak of might rather be called conduct, perhaps, the result of good principles."

9. Still far from rich, but more prosperous than their parents and grandparents.

10. A skill in some ways even more important then than today because travel was ruinously expensive and all communication at a distance was written communication.

11. "Samuel Richardson," *Gale Contextual Encyclopedia of World Literature*, January 1, 2009, www.highbeam.com/doc/1G2-2507200387.html. The claim is about Richardson's later novel *Sir Charles Grandist*, but I would argue that it applies to *Pamela*.

12. Of the six Jane Austen novels, *Pride and Prejudice* has a story the most like Richardson's original plot. Elizabeth Bennet marries a man enormously richer and more important than herself, and she succeeds with him because of the same qualities that Mr. B was surprised to find in Pamela: sound principles, intelligence, and self-command (all in a degree most unexpected in a girl from her background—remember how Darcy says of Elizabeth and Jane that they have conducted themselves "so as to avoid any share of the like censure" as their mother, younger sisters, and sometimes even their father deserve for their "total want of propriety"), in combination with a kind of teasing sauciness that a man in his position is unused to from any woman. But instead of needing all her self-command, intelligence, and skill with the English language to fight off her lover's physical attacks, Elizabeth needs these same qualities to win through to her happy ending despite the appalling rudeness and vulgarity of relatives (both hers and Darcy's) and to come to terms with her own conscience.

Even though the drama is more psychological and less physical, the basic pattern Richardson invented is there—and in all the novels, not just *Pride and Prejudice*. The scene in *Sense and Sensibility* when the scheming Lucy Steele tells Elinor Dashwood all about her own secret engagement to the man she knows Elinor loves is very much like a scene from *Pamela*. Jane Austen's novels are all about a woman making her way through the minefields of courtship, with all the attendant misunderstandings between the sexes, unaccountable interference by third parties, and mixed motives on the woman's own part. Whatever the crises they face, Jane Austen's heroines manage them with the same weapons that recommended Pamela to Mr. B, and that Richardson thought would recommend her story to a public interested in self-improvement: self-control in difficult circumstances, remarkable verbal skills, intelligence and integrity applied to social difficulties—though on an exponentially more sophisticated level than in *Pamela*.

13. Richardson was accused of prurience; there's a famous parody of *Pamela* by the author of *Tom Jones*, making explicit all the nastiest implications you can read into Richardson's book.

14. C. S. Lewis, *That Hideous Strength* (Scribner, 1996), p. 69.

15. The French Enlightenment viewed convention, tradition, and every kind of authority handed down from the past with hostility. Voltaire's motto was "*écrasez l'infâme*"—crush the infamous thing! By which he meant the whole weight of the absolute French monarchy and the established Catholic Church (all "superstition" to Voltaire). In other words, he wanted to eradicate every vestige of traditional authority that stood in the way of re-making the world according to the dictates of reason. Mankind would never be free, Voltaire insisted, until the last king was strangled with the entrails of the last priest. And of course when the French Revolutionaries got the chance to build a new world from scratch, they really did try to throw out every vestige of received wisdom from the past—down to the names of months and the days of the week. They invented entirely new ones, from nature and reason alone. Their lasting legacy to us: the metric system. (Which was actually standardized by a committee appointed by Louis XVI—previous versions had been mooted by scientists as early as the seventeenth century—but adopted by the French Republic along with the new Revolutionary calendar in 1793, the year of the Terror. The metric system's origin in the pre-Revolutionary Enlightenment period in France is something it shares with much of the Revolution's intellectual content.)

16. Enlightenment-Era Englishmen thought quite a lot about civilized versus primitive human existence. They pondered which elements of their culture were natural, and which were unique to their civilization. By Jane Austen's day, Europeans had had three centuries since the discovery of America to compare themselves with the Homeric culture of the peoples they found living there. The discovery set them thinking about their own culture in a more critical way. (For some early examples of this line of inquiry, see Michel de Montaigne's "Of Cannibals," 1580; Sir Walter Raleigh's *The Discovery of Guiana*, 1596; and William Shakespeare's *The Tempest*, 1610–1611.) But in Jane Austen's youth it was a minority view, and not a typically English one, to prefer the primitive to the civilized—though the influence of Jean-Jacques Rousseau, the great champion of the pro-primitive, pro-natural, anti-civilization point of view, was certainly growing.

Edmund Burke (Jane Austen was not a fan—she took the side of Warren Hastings, a family friend, in the impeachment trial that Burke masterminded against Hastings—but here Burke is expressing moderate Anglo-American Enlightenment views that she shared) in his *Reflections on the Revolution in France* defended civilization and tradition against the Rousseauian back-to-nature impulses of the French revolutionaries: "All the decent drapery of life is to be rudely torn off. All the superadded ideas, furnished from the wardrobe of a moral imagination, which the heart owns, and the understanding ratifies, as necessary to cover the defects of our naked, shivering nature, and to raise it to dignity in our own estimation, are to be exploded as a ridiculous, absurd, and antiquated fashion.

"On this scheme of things, a king is but a man, a queen is but a woman; a woman is but an animal, and an animal not of the highest order."

Jane Austen's characters share Burke's preference for the civilized over the merely natural. Consider Mr. Darcy's put-down of Sir William Lucas on the subject of dancing. Everyone in the neighborhood knows Darcy scorns to dance with mere acquaintances, preferring to pass an evening in intelligent conversation with his intimate friends. Sir William attempts to persuade him to think otherwise: "What a charming amusement for young people this is, Mr. Darcy!" he exclaims. "There is nothing like dancing after all. I consider it as one of the first [first in importance, he means, not earliest] refinements of polished societies." To which Darcy replies, "Certainly, sir; and it has the advantage also of being in vogue amongst the less polished societies of the world. Every savage can dance."

17. Mrs. Elton suggests a picnic, and Mr. Knightley declines to take her up on the offer:

Mrs. Elton: "There is to be no form or parade—a sort of gipsy party.—We are to walk about your gardens, and gather the strawberries ourselves, and sit under trees;—and whatever else you may like to provide, it is to be all out of doors—a table spread in the shade, you know. Everything must be as natural and simple as possible. Is not that your idea?"

Mr. Knightley: "Not quite. My idea of the simple and the natural will be to have the table spread in the dining-room. The nature and the simplicity of gentlemen and ladies, with their servants and furniture, I think is best observed by meals indoors."

18. It's funny. Modern scientists who work with *other* species don't take the same dismissive attitude toward *their* cultures. They're busy encouraging adolescent whooping cranes to learn all about migration from experienced sandhill cranes,

or dressing up in adult condor puppet suits so they can help baby condors learn how to be condors the traditional way. (See James C. Lewis, "Whooping Crane, Grus Americana," in *Birds of North America Online*, http://bna.birds.cornell.edu/bna/species/153/articles/conservation, and Matt Kaplan, "Puppet Parents Raise Troubled Condors," *Nature*, August 7, 2007, http://www.nature.com/news/2007/070806/full/news070806-3.html.) Scientists know that without condor or crane culture, condors and whooping cranes won't survive as free and healthy species—only as freakish individuals, zoo exhibits, cut off from nature and dependent on the scientists for their whole existence. How different from their cavalier attitude toward human culture.

19. We've all seen the horrifying "honour killings" stories out of Pakistan and even from some Muslim enclaves in Europe and America. On a lighter and happier note, see Wilbur Sargunaraj, "Love Marriage," http://www.youtube.com/watch?v=TojTlYNNm9w.

20. Sometimes they're being selfish about money or alliances—sadly true about some parents even in less traditional societies: Mrs. Bennet cares more that her daughters marry "greatly" than that they marry happily.

21. "Western human rights organizations and the ruling on referring to them for judgement," Islam QA, Question No. 97827, http:/islam-aq.com/index.php?ref+97827&In=eng#, quoted in Robert Spencer, *Religion of Peace? Why Chrstianity Is and Islam Isn't* (Regnery, 2007), pp. 205–6.

22. But we've got things arranged so that the wolves can do us less obvious and material harm here than in the sheikh's Saudi Arabia—even less harm than wolves of their sort could do our great-grandmothers. Unfaithful men can still break our hearts, but at least they don't shame us and our families, or starve us.

23. Nona Willis-Aronowitz ,"The Virginity Mystique," *Nation*, July 19, 2007, http://www.thenation.com/article/virginity-mystique.

24. I think I last saw one on *The Andy Griffith Show*.

25. Sam Roberts, "51% of Women Are Now Living without Spouse," *New York Times*, January 16, 2007, http://www.nytimes.com/2007/01/16/us/16census.html.

INDEX

heartbreak, xvi, 21, 28, 32, 42, 45–46,
49–50, 54–56, 66, 69–70, 73, 76, 167,
177, 186, 192, 205, 219–20, 222, 266
Hertfordshire, 54, 128, 143
High Middle Ages, 262
Highbury, 122
Hobbes, Thomas, 261
Hollywood, 39, 86
Holmes, Sherlock, 142
honesty
in character, xv, 20
in relationships, 204–7, 217–18, 220,
234
honor killing, 264
"Hooking Up Smart," 232, 235, 250
hookup culture, xv, 175, 242–45, 247
How Stella Got Her Groove Back, 22
human nature, xviii, 106, 121, 140, 254–
55, 260
"humour," 82, 130, 154, 158, 254

I
imitation, 255–56
inconstancy, 74, 172
independence, 6, 24, 31, 93–96, 228, 230,
238
financial independence, 95
India, 74
infidelity, 172
information, 42, 127–28, 139, 142, 150,
152–53, 158, 192, 227, 246
installment plan, 223–25, 234, 238, 241
intentions, 51
bad intentions, 43
discerning of, 171, 192, 222, 241
honesty about, 205, 218
no intentions, 159–70, 174, 193, 210

internet, 8, 100, 143–45, 245
internet dating. *See* computer dating,
online matchmaking
intimacy, 117, 137, 198, 202–3, 225
emotional, 39
physical, 178, 232, 234
premature, 51, 79, 220, 251

J
Jack and Alice, 80
Jane Austen Book Club, The, ix
"Jane Austen: A Love Story," x
Jane Austen Society of North America,
245
Jane Eyre, 25
jealousy, 163, 193, 207–8, 210
Jefferson, Thomas, 106
Jeffries, Ross, 204–6
Jeffs, Warren, 60
Johnson, Dr., 261
Jones, Bridget, ix–x, xiii–xv, 8, 253
Jones, Samantha, 242
judgment, 21, 38, 67, 92, 140, 150, 152,
227–28
Juliet, 241, 264–65
"just my type," 130, 133–34, 137
justice, 110, 113–14, 115

K
Kimmel, Michael, 175
King, Tom, 209
Kinsey, Alfred, 242–43
Knightley, George, 11, 18, 35, 77, 84,
100, 103–8, 113, 117, 120–21, 123,
131, 149, 152, 154, 169, 207–9, 210,
217, 220

Your Guide to Happily Ever After Isn't Over Just Yet...

WE'RE CONTINUING THE CONVERSATION ONLINE!
Join *The Jane Austen Guide to Happily Ever After* community on Facebook and Twitter, where you can:

- Connect with fellow Janeites
- Learn the latest news about the book and author
- Take quizzes such as, "What Jane Austen character are you?"
- Get extra tips and advice from the author that you can only find online
- Share your own happily ever after story
- And much more!

So what are you waiting for?

Join *The Jane Austen Guide to Happily Ever After* on Facebook:
Facebook.com/JaneAustenGuide

Follow Elizabeth Kantor on Twitter:
Twitter.com/ElizabethKantor

Since 1947
REGNERY PUBLISHING, INC.
An Eagle Publishing Company • Washington, DC
www.Regnery.com